Managing
Organizational Change

1807
WILEY
2007

BICENTENNIAL
BICENTENNIAL
BICENTENNIAL
BICENTENNIAL

THE WILEY BICENTENNIAL—KNOWLEDGE FOR GENERATIONS

$\mathcal{E}$ach generation has its unique needs and aspirations. When Charles Wiley first opened his small printing shop in lower Manhattan in 1807, it was a generation of boundless potential searching for an identity. And we were there, helping to define a new American literary tradition. Over half a century later, in the midst of the Second Industrial Revolution, it was a generation focused on building the future. Once again, we were there, supplying the critical scientific, technical, and engineering knowledge that helped frame the world. Throughout the 20th Century, and into the new millennium, nations began to reach out beyond their own borders and a new international community was born. Wiley was there, expanding its operations around the world to enable a global exchange of ideas, opinions, and know-how.

For 200 years, Wiley has been an integral part of each generation's journey, enabling the flow of information and understanding necessary to meet their needs and fulfill their aspirations. Today, bold new technologies are changing the way we live and learn. Wiley will be there, providing you the must-have knowledge you need to imagine new worlds, new possibilities, and new opportunities.

Generations come and go, but you can always count on Wiley to provide you the knowledge you need, when and where you need it!

WILLIAM J. PESCE
PRESIDENT AND CHIEF EXECUTIVE OFFICER

PETER BOOTH WILEY
CHAIRMAN OF THE BOARD

Managing Organizational Change

Second Edition

Bill Leban
DeVry University

Romuald Stone
DeVry University

BICENTENNIAL
1807
WILEY
2007
BICENTENNIAL

John Wiley & Sons.

ACQUISITIONS EDITOR	Jay Beck
PROJECT EDITOR	Sharon Prendergast
PUBLISHER	Rick Leyh
ASSOCIATE DIRECTOR, MARKETING	Jennifer Powers
PRODUCTION MANAGER	Dorothy Sinclair
COVER ART	Designed and developed by Jennifer Miller and Todd William Leban
PROJECT MANAGER	Thomson Digital

This book was set in 10/12 pt Century Old Style by Thomson Digital.

This book is printed on acid free paper. ∞

To order books or for customer service please, call 1-800-CALL WILEY (225-5945).

ISBN-13 978-0470-89716-4

Printed in the United States of America

10 9 8 7 6 5 4 3

ORGANIZATIONAL CHANGE...
Work to develop and understand it!
Provide input and feedback to it!
Adapt to it!
Learn from it!
And
Embrace and recognize it as a better tomorrow!

-Bill Leban

Foreword

What is the better way to ensure competence in change management in your organization—building a "center of excellence" comprised of highly trained and experienced experts who provide organization change and development services to the leaders and managers of the organization? Or is it better to forget about a core of experts who are internal to the organization and instead train all managers and leaders in change management concepts and skills? Lest you think I am proposing a phony dichotomy, and it should be both, some organizations have clearly made a choice. Capital One, for example, concentrates on training all managers in change management skills. So do GE and BP. Pfizer, on the other hand, continues with the opposite approach, a center of internal experts who provide change consultation to management.

Actually there is a third model (and perhaps a fourth or fifth approach that I am unaware of). The third approach with which I am familiar is the one at the EMC Corporation, that is, to train all HR people as change management or OD experts, in addition to their regular HR roles and responsibilities.

What is the ultimate point I am attempting to make, you may ask? It is this: More and more organizational leaders are waking up to the facts that (a) change has now joined death and taxes and (b) they had better do something about it. Regardless of which model or approach that organizational leaders may choose, a highly beneficial step that they can take that would greatly support any of these choices is to use this book by Leban and Stone. Clearly the knowledge and expertise to be gained from this book will significantly increase the probability of success when planning and implementing organization change and development in any organization.

W. Warner Burke, Ph.D.
Edward Lee Thorndike
Professor of Psychology and Education

Chair, Department of Organization and Leadership
Teachers College, Columbia University

Preface

❏ BOOK DESCRIPTION

Organizations must evolve to keep up with today's dynamic and competitive environment. This 2nd edition textbook, with updated readings, explores a set of concepts, theories, and techniques that address the successful planning and implementation of strategic change across an organization. It focuses on why a company needs to change, what can be changed and how to appropriately plan and implement that change. The authors address both the rational and emotional aspects of change and also explain how individuals, groups, and the organization can improve their ability to move through the change process. Readings and cases enable faculty to apply the concepts and theory covered in each chapter. Self-assessments are also used to help the reader better understand their change management competencies. Finally, the text was written to help the reader be more comfortable with the uncertainties of change.

❏ ADDITIONS TO THE 2ND EDITION

In this 2nd edition, we have added change initiative examples, recent trends driving change, manager style and scale of change, distinct categories of projects, success rates for different types of organizational change, more detail on Kotter's 8 Stage Model for Change, why organizations need to be more organic and less mechanistic, risks inherent to managing change, how to incorporate external trends into internal strategies, a generic change initiative project plan, linkages between change and project management, learnings from previous change projects, characteristics of traditional versus strategic change projects, and a strategic change project profile tool in *Chapters 1 through 3*. In *Chapters 4 through 7*, we have added empowering employees to help lead change, nine key motivators of employees, using emotional intelligence to build good working relationships, a matrix of leader emotional intelligence and change management competencies, employee engagement in the change process, the 10 Cs of employee engagement, gauging the success of a strategic change initiative using the DICE framework, effective vision characteristics, an example of vision, mission, strategy, and action plans, strategic fit and flexibility, best practices in change management, future trends in managing change, greatest change management obstacles, and what to do differently on

your next change project. Finally, we have *updated Chapter 6 and 7 readings* and *added a case study in Appendix C* that reflects how effective project management can be used to achieve business success.

❏ CHAPTER FORMAT

The beginning of each chapter provides highlights of the chapter (*Chapter at a Glance*), a real-world perspective (*Vignette*) on the subject areas addressed, and a brief summary of what will be covered in the chapter (*Chapter Perspective*). The main text of each chapter covers concepts, theory, and techniques that apply to the subject areas covered and include brief real-world examples that relate to that content. At the end of each chapter, there is a reading and case (*Reading and Case*) that allows for discussion of the application of the concepts, theory, and techniques covered. For each reading and case, the authors have provided content support (*Focus, Questions, and Linkage to Chapter*). This format enables the reader to focus on key topic areas and then to apply them to real-world situations. This combination of content and application enables the reader to draw upon their own experiences and therefore results in optimal learning.

❏ CHAPTER AND APPENDIX CONTENT

Chapter 1

The pace of economic, global, and technological developments coupled with hyper competition in today's world makes *confronting the realities of change* an inevitable feature of organizational life. Today's managers do not have sufficient change management competencies.

Chapter 2

If we really want to *understand how organizations should view change,* we need to use change models that can guide managers in planning and implementing change. Today, more companies are faced with strategic change that cuts across their organization.

Chapter 3

Organizations should use the four *dimensions of change management* (strategy, resources, systems, and culture) to plan and implement a desired and feasible future state. By *using a project management approach*, organizations can increase the probability of successfully implementing a strategic change initiative.

Chapter 4

Leadership is critical to the success of any change initiative. By understanding differences between management and leadership, attributes of transactional and transformational leadership styles, and key factors in *leading change*, you can better understand what needs to be done to successfully lead change by *empowering employees*. Emotional intelligence can also be used to help establish good working relationships to get things done.

Chapter 5

Managing the evolution of change means that you will need to understand the rational reasons for change and the behavioral states that one goes through, how different levels of the organization move through change, and how *employee engagement* enables employees and management to work together in support of the change. Organizations can also gauge the success of a strategic change initiative by using the DICE framework.

Chapter 6

Change initiatives often flounder because not enough attention is given to *developing and communicating*

a shared vision. Developing a shared vision enables employees to commit to the change. Communicating that vision to all stakeholders helps everyone understand what is most important to the organization.

Chapter 7

In this chapter, you will explore *aligning strategy and culture* and how important it is for the beliefs, guiding values, and behavior norms of the organization to support the goals and objectives of the strategic change initiative. Change management *best practices and future trends* are also addressed, further supporting the content of the text!

Appendix A

Historical Seeds of Change Management provide an overview of the evolution of organizational change from the late 1940s to present.

Appendix B

The Managing Change Questionnaire (Subset MCQ) Answer Key with Comments.

Appendix C

Effective Project Management To Help Achieve Business Success.

About the Authors

Bill Leban received his Ph.D. in Organization Development from Benedictine University in 2003. He is a senior faculty and course architect at Keller Graduate School of Management of DeVry University. Bill is also the Director of Business (undergraduate) and Management (graduate) Programs. His presentations include the 21st Organization Development World Congress in Vienna, Austria, the Midwest Academy of Management, the Western Academy of Management, the Southwest Academy of Management, the Project Management Institute (PMI), and the Portland International Conference on Management, among others. His work has been published in the PM Network Magazine and The Leadership & Organization Development Journal. Dr. Leban has over 25 years of experience in the field of management (manufacturing, operations, engineering, compliance, new product development, organizational effectiveness, strategic planning, and competitive analysis). Bill is a Certified Project Management Professional (PMP) and a Registered Organization Development Professional (RODP). In addition, he is a Member of the Project Management Journal (PMJ) Editorial Advisory Board for the Project Management Institute and an instructor for the DeVry Leadership Academy.

Romuald Stone received his doctorate in business administration from Nova Southeastern University in 1990. He is a senior faculty of organizational behavior at Keller Graduate School of Management, DeVry University. He is also the Program Director for the Masters in Human Resources program. Dr. Stone has held previous professional appointments at James Madison University and George Mason University. His research and writings include numerous strategy case studies, practitioner-oriented articles, and a chapter contribution related to managing an HRIS implementation and change. His work has appeared in the Academy of Management Executive, Psychological Reports, the Journal of Management Education, Computers in Human Behavior, Educational and Psychological Measurement, Business Horizons, Employment Relations Today, SAM Advanced Management Journal, and the Journal of Applied Management and Entrepreneurship. As a practitioner, Dr. Stone has over 25 years of experience as a trainer and consultant in the areas of organizational management and leadership.

Table of Contents

Confronting the Realities of Change

❏ CHAPTER AT A GLANCE

Highlights of this chapter include the following:

1. In this era of rapid business and technological change, effective management of change represents a critical core competence all organizations and leaders must master.

2. In these turbulent times, forces for change guarantee that change will remain a constant in organizational life. Organizations must be deeply conscious of what's changing and perpetually wiling to consider how those changes are likely to affect its current success.

3. Change management is a process whereby an organization responds to and adapts to the forces in its micro- and macroenvironment in order to increase its effectiveness and ensure its survival. Moreover, to ignore the behavioral aspects of change amplifies the probability of failure.

4. Organizations face two kinds of changes: the traditional type that is internally driven and managed and the externally driven changes that are not easily controlled. Forces of change include human capital, technological forces, political–legal forces, competitive forces, economic forces, and globalization.

5. Many change initiatives fail to deliver their promised value. To mitigate the potential for failure, three key factors important to success include top management support and involvement, the needs of the employees, and effective project management.

6. People cannot change their behaviors overnight, get smarter over the weekend, or "grow" skills they do not have. Both groups and individuals resist change.

7. There are two fundamental goals that drive change initiatives: "Theory E" and "Theory O." Both approaches are based on differing assumptions about how change should be managed. Theory E is considered the "hard side" of change and is focused on creating economic value by increasing shareholder value. Theory O is characterized as a softer approach to change. The focus is on building organizational capability by capitalizing on its human capital, building employee commitment, and creating a

learning culture that can respond, adapt, and change in the face of the driving forces in its environment.

8. In order to make change work, organizations need to follow a process to enhance the probability of success versus just "winging it." The model of change introduced in the chapter provides a useful way to think about creating and implementing organization-wide change.

The changes facing health care organizations in the following vignette are not uncommon. Managing change is a critical competency all organizations must master. Increased competition, globalization, changing market dynamics, and pressures from stakeholders move business leaders to consider new strategies and how to improve performance. Key to this process is a deep understanding the forces influencing change in one's industry and how to plan and design an effective change program. Effective change management allows an organization "to evolve and grow over time and respond appropriately to external market forces that have a significant impact on organizations."[1]

❏ VIGNETTE[2]

Health care is a vital service that daily touches the lives of millions of Americans at significant and vulnerable times: birth, illness, and death. In recent decades, technology, pharmaceuticals, and know-how have substantially improved how care is delivered and the prospects for recovery. American markets for innovation in pharmaceuticals and medical devices are second to none. The miracles of modern medicine have become almost commonplace. Health care spending in the United States far exceeds that of other countries. Americans spend an average of $6280 per capita on health care every year, more than two times the rest of the industrialized world.[3] Approximately 16% of gross domestic product, or $1.9 trillion in 2004, is spent on health care services in the United States.[4] This level of spending is expected to grow to $4 trillion by 2015, or 20% of GDP.

Powerful driving forces, ranging from technological advancements to economic and social pressures have dramatically impacted how we deliver heath care today. Competition especially has affected health care markets substantially over the past several decades. As such, we are witnessing a change in the way health care is delivered. New forms of organization have developed in response to pressures for lower costs, and new strategies for lowering costs and enhancing quality have emerged. A study by the National Committee for Quality Assurance found that the quality of health care delivered to Americans who are enrolled in health plans improved markedly in 2004, but the health care system remains plagued by enormous "quality gaps," and the majority of Americans still receive less than optimal care.[5]

In the mix of health care providers in the United States, we have 4800 general hospitals who face competition from a variety of sources, including the approximately 4100 Ambulatory Surgical Centers (ASCs), 2400 Imaging Centers, and 100 Specialty Hospitals. ASCs perform surgical procedures on patients who do not require an overnight stay in the hospital. Technological advances in surgery and anesthetic agents have made it possible for ASCs to perform a wide range of surgical procedures. Medicare reimbursement has had a profound effect on the number of ASCs and the amount and types of surgery performed in them.

Specialty hospitals provide care for a specific specialty (e.g., cardiac) or type of patient (e.g., children). Newer single-specialty hospitals (SSHs) tend to specialize in cardiac or orthopedic surgery, and participating physicians often have an ownership interest in the facility. Some contend that SSHs have achieved better outcomes through increased volume, better disease management, and better clinical standards.

Moreover, the competitive dynamics for SSHs is affected by general hospitals who have successfully lobbied medicare to not reimburse these physician-owned specialty hospitals as they feel they are an unfair advantage. Specialty hospitals do not have all of the infrastructure and services that general hospitals do such as an emergency room, and so on, which are usually huge drains on revenues. Specialty hospitals provide care to cardiac patients, which are usually reimbursed at a higher dollar rate without many of the other associated experiences that general hospitals incur. Recently, medicare said that after almost 3 years of suspended payments, they will not renew that suspension but will begin reimbursement under tightly regulated guidelines.

As a result, we can expect competition to intensify.

According to a 2006 GAO study, general hospitals in particular have had to make operational and clinical service changes in order to remain competitive. Competition from other general hospitals has increased as well as competition from limited service facilities (ASCs, imaging centers, urgent care centers, and gastroenterology centers). The GAO study reported that general hospitals reported making an average of 22 operational changes, such as introducing a formal process for evaluating efforts to improve quality and reduce costs, and 8 clinical changes, such as adding or expanding cardiology services, from 2000 to 2005.

It should also be noted that major performance improvement and other quality management initiatives are vital in the health care industry today. One of the biggest things going on in health care is an attempt to reduce the number of medical errors and make the provision of care in health care organizations safer for patients. As a result, there are huge initiatives driven by regulatory agencies as well as market competition for error reduction and process/systems improvement, and thus enhancing the services of a particular facility. Reimbursement is also putting some traction to this effort as they are beginning to reimburse at higher rates for some services provided for organizations with higher performance scores. This is expected to continue and increase.

As is evident from the foregoing discussion, change is a given in today's health care environment. General hospitals have a choice. They can either respond to the forces that drive change and build a competitive advantage in the process, or they can continue to embrace the status quo and slip into mediocrity. To survive and navigate this sea of change smoothly, general hospitals must effectively manage the change process in ways that sustains a high level of morale, satisfaction, and commitment with its human capital. As Bob Dylan reminded us in a 1963 song,[6] there is danger in the waters of change; if we do not learn to swim with them, we risk sinking like a stone.

> *You better start swimin'*
> *Or you'll sink like a stone*
> *For the times are a-changin'*

Swimming through the waters of change depends on "understanding how to maximize people's efforts, align human resources, create a vision and choose a direction, and gain and maintain customer loyalty."[7] This chapter begins to lay the groundwork for learning the change management strategies and processes for effectively managing change.

❑ CHAPTER PERSPECTIVE

The pace of economic, global, and technological developments coupled with hypercompetition in today's world makes change an inevitable feature of organizational life. In fact, this may be the only thing that does not change in today's business climate. The success of any business today depends on its ability to sense and adapt to rapid change from within and outside the organization. What worked in the past is no guarantee of success today. In fact, it may be a prescription for failure. Therefore, its essential organizations develop a high level of competency and expertise in managing change.

Chapter 1 addresses the importance of developing competencies in, and understanding what is, managing change; of understanding the drivers of change; of appreciating the characteristics of effective change programs; as well as appreciating some of the barriers to change. The chapter concludes by introducing a useful framework for thinking about creating and implementing change programs.

❑ THE REALITIES OF CHANGE

For hospitals or any other company, to excel in this era of rapid business and technological change, effective management of change represents a critical core competence all organizations and leaders must master. In an *Across the Board* article, Moshe Rubinstein offered a trenchant metaphor that captures the central role change management must play in organizations today:

A metaphor for the organizations of the future is taxis cruising the roads of major cities, looking to pick up passengers. Taxis cruise in a somewhat random manner, without fixed stations, and without fixed times of arrival and departure. Uncertainty, surprise, and the unexpected are the rule. Whereas the railroads have no traffic jams (in fact, traffic is stopped to let trains go through, to ensure that the plan is not disrupted), for the taxi, traffic jams are a possibility. Yet the taxi can adapt and use alternate surface roads, making just-in-time decisions as events unfold on the road.

The taxi has some rules of conduct–fixed pickup locations in airports and hotels, traffic lights and laws that must be obeyed, and a taxi may have arrangements with some customers for fixed and regular pickup times. Even while cruising the city streets, the route taken by a taxi is not entirely random, because it follows a path that tries to match the randomness in time and place of potential passengers. Thus, some streets will have more taxis cruising, others fewer. As demand changes because of new office buildings and hotels, or the demolition of such buildings, the number and frequency of taxis cruising the streets changes.

Although the system has a communication center, scheduled maintenance, and other planned activities, it is a self-organizing system to a degree. It embraces uncertainty, chaos, and the unexpected by adapting a flexible, random plan with a repertoire of responses that attempts to match the uncertainty and chaos of the world within which it operates. The organizations of the future will embrace the metaphor of the taxi, in which uncertainty is a reality, and the need to perpetually adapt to new emerging realities is a way of life.[8]

As the taxi metaphor suggests, the twenty-first century world is markedly different from past decades. Gary Hammel echoed this point in his book, *Leading the Revolution*, that the world of change has changed. "No longer is it additive. No longer does it move in a straight line (linear). In the twenty-first century, change is discontinuous, abrupt, [and] seditious."[9] As a result, the pressure for change on organizations is occurring so rapidly that many are unable to respond quickly and/or reinvent their business models and strategies as circumstances change.[10] How quickly organizations respond to a changing environment will largely determine if they continue to enjoy a future state of enhanced vitality or if it they face disappointing results or even extinction. Despite all the excellent research and frameworks promulgated in the change management field, there are no silver bullets or easy answers.

Moreover, it's not unrealistic to suggest that every individual, work group, department, company, industry, and even nations face periods of transition and accelerating change. In fact, most mangers face change management issues every day; managing change is now a permanent part of every manager's job. What we see happening in organizations today is that expectations are shifting

from viewing change as an extraordinary event to seeing it as a permanent feature of organizational life.[11] And with this shift in expectation we're also seeing change management become more institutionalized in companies in several ways:[12]

- Designing a change management function in the organization
- Developing tools and techniques for planning and implementation
- Establishing communication methods for facilitating change, and
- Reorienting corporate culture toward flexibility and agility

We should keep in mind that no matter how hard managers try to create a stable and healthy organization, forces for change guarantee we will experience dramatic changes — some within our control and many far beyond our control. For example, the U.S. airline industry has faced a brutal environment in recent years with high labor costs, soaring oil prices further exacerbated by hurricane Katrina in 2005, strife in the middle east, and fierce competition. The financial picture for the major U.S. air carriers seems parlous. The airlines have performed worse financially and are more prone to failure than most other industries. Almost 30 years after deregulation, major airlines' costs exceed revenues, and they can neither cut costs nor raise fares enough to turn a profit.[13] The U.S. airline industry lost 135,000 jobs and $33 billion since 2000—more than double what it had earned since the start of commercial aviation.[14]

Today, the major carriers continue to struggle for their long-term survival. If they don't remake themselves in face of an industry undergoing transformation, many carriers face the strong possibility of bankruptcy and even liquidation.[15] In fact, by the fall of 2005, four of the nation's seven biggest carriers operated under Chapter 11 protection (since 1978, there have been 162 airline bankruptcies). A headline in the Wall Street Journal captured the reality of the situation: "How airlines resisted change for 25 years, and finally lost."[16]

It's important, therefore, that we confront the realities of change by understanding how organizations and managers should view and properly lead change. As Hamel and Valikangas aptly observed, the challenge for any organization is that "It must be deeply conscious of what's changing and perpetually wiling to consider how those changes are likely to affect its current success."[17]

Equally important is the challenge of ensuring senior management, managers, supervisors, and other employees understand how to effectively lead and manage change. This important competency is reinforced in a 2004 Accenture High Performance Workplace Study. Two hundred and forty-four executive respondents were asked to identify the challenges companies face in building a high-performance workplace. Based on the survey results and from Accenture's years of research and consulting in this field, they identified nine key organizational capabilities. Of the nine core capabilities, four focus specifically on managing change:[18]

- Sensing shifts in the business and economic environment before competitors
- Generating insights into how these shifts are affecting or could affect the business
- Managing large-scale change, and
- Creating an organization and culture that adapt effectively to change

The difference between the financial fortunes (based on shareholder value) of companies that manage business changes well and those that do not is significant. A Watson Wyatt study[19] found that the total shareholder returns to companies that manage change well are seven times higher than those that do not. In short, incomplete understanding or ineffective management of the change process can have devastating consequences on overall performance and the employees involved.

So by better understanding the field of knowledge and competencies related to managing change, we can better manage change in our organizations and reap the rewards that accrue to successful change initiatives. The benefits are huge. However, as the research suggests, the track record of most change initiatives — be they restructuring, introduction of new technology, mergers, process improvement, or reengineering — is poor. One expert in the field noted that at best only one third of these kinds of initiatives achieve any success at all.[20] Clearly, learning to effectively manage change is an important managerial competency and competitive advantage.

Not withstanding the fact that the discipline of organizational change is one of the most important skills, leaders need to include in their repertoire; it

Dimension	Score
Entire survey	71
Individual Response to Change	61
General nature of change	68
Planning change	74
Managing people side of change	69
Managing organization side of change	79
Evaluating change	74

Figure 1.1   *What Do Managers Know About Change*

remains one of the least understood subjects. "Many managers and executives are limited in their understanding of the complexities and timing invxolved in driving large-scale change."[21] For example, using a questionnaire that contained 25 questions to measure knowledge of 25 key issues on how to manage organizational change, a survey of over 700 executives in more than seven industries resulted in an average score of only 71 out of a possible 100.[22] The survey results do not indicate how much of the 71% of the essential knowledge is actually used, however. Figure 1.1 depicts managers' scores on the managing change knowledge survey.*

Only with a solid understanding of the change management process, can executives and managers effectively lead the change process and face their periods of swiftly changing environments with confidence. According to experts in the field,

Any company that can make sense of its environment, generate strategic options, and realign its resources faster than its rivals will enjoy a decisive advantage... and it will prove to be the ultimate competitive advantage in the age of turbulence — when companies are being challenged to change more profoundly, and more rapidly, than ever before.[23]

And Gregory Smith's metaphor of managing change as a ship in a stormy sea provides a vivid example of the importance of learning to manage change effectively.

---

*A subset of this self-assessment questionnaire is addressed in Chapter 3.

Change in the 21st century is like sailing a ship during a storm. Waves coming at you from every direction. Hidden rocks threatening to tear your ship apart. The water never stops churning and there is no time to rest. Falling overboard is a scary possibility and if you fail to work together to chart a course, disaster could very well be your companion.

There is this same sense of urgency in today's economy, even in the best companies, with no guarantees that tomorrow will bring the same success as today. How can we survive in this type of environment? By becoming leaders and agents of change successful people will learn to read the ocean, prepare for the storm, avoid the rocks, work as a team, and feel the excitement of becoming a different, better organization.[24]

Unless organizations can learn and act at a faster rate than the competition, sustainable success will become more elusive. Let's now turn our attention to defining what we mean by change management and the forces that drive change.

❏ WHAT IS CHANGE MANAGEMENT?

Change management is a systematic process whereby an organization responds to and adapts to the forces in its micro- and macroenvironment in order to increase its effectiveness and ensure its survival. In short, managing change is all about moving an organization from its current state to some future desired state. And because what happens in an organization is driven by the attitudes and behavior of the individuals in that organization, change management must also consider altering the behavior patterns of the people within that organization. If the change is planned, the process typically involves the use of a systematic approach to ensure the change activities are on course and on target with respect to cost, time, and expected results.

There is a discipline to managing change. As such, we know that managing change can be applied to any change initiative with reasonable expectation for success. We discuss a general model of change later in the chapter.

Change initiatives can take many forms. Figure 1.2 summarizes some common examples.

What is the common thread that runs through all these change initiative examples? Change is more than just changing the way we do business or how we operate. Change involves managing the transition from where we are now to where we want to be at some future state. At the core of managing

- Mergers and acquisitions
- Downsizing
- Restructuring
- Work process improvement
- Culture change
- New information systems (i.e., systems integration)
- Customer relationship management
- Supply chain management and sales force automation
- Technology obsolescence and replacement
- New strategy
- New structure
- Relocation
- Improve quality of products and services
- Cost reduction initiatives
- New procedures

Figure 1.2   *Change Initiative Examples*

this transition is the human element and how we deal with human resistance to change.

In order to be successful in any change initiative, we need to pay attention to changing how people behave. To ignore the behavioral aspects of change amplifies the probability of failure. If we can understand why people resist change and the strategies available to overcome this resistance, the change may go much faster and smoother. For example, the research clearly shows that most mergers fail to produce intended business results. One contributing factor is because the new management fails to consider the impact of the merger (and change) on the employees and people issues. What often happens in a merger or acquisition is that people are asked to stop doing things the old way and to get onboard with the "new way" of doing things. Getting people to buy-in and support the change is the key challenge. We need to learn how to manage the psychological process people go through when faced with change.[25] Ultimately, change is all about people — if they do not change, nothing significant changes.[26]

Consider this example. When catalog retailer Lillian Veron undertook a major transformation of their IT infrastructure, the initial results proved dismal. What happened was that the change management team — that included the president and CIO — failed to take change management seriously. In particular, they overlooked the importance of assessing and managing readiness for change. "Employees resisted mightily, avoiding training and blaming new applications for their frustration....The employees had already made up their minds that the system was not going to work, and they didn't want any part of it."[27] The net result was that the company fell short of its ambitious timeline for implementation and missed an opportunity to leverage the new information system to improve overall performance. The lesson here is that implementing change goes beyond just installing the physical equipment and system. What Lillian failed to do was help the employees understand how the new IT system will be any better than the current system (we address change communication in Chapter 6). Successful change requires a "critical mass of people who are committed, are willing to change and will sustain their new behavior to align with the needs of the change."[28]

In his book, *The Age of Unreason*, Charles Handy, tells a story about Peruvian Indians who, when they spotted the sails of the Spanish invaders on the horizon, wrote it off as a mirage or weather-based illusion and went about their daily business. The Peruvian Indian had no cognitive concept of sailing ships in their limited experience. Because the sailing ships did not fit into their preexisting mental maps of the world, they screened out what did not fit and let disaster in.[29]

Likewise, we see organizations today that achieve less than optimal results or even fail because they did not respond to the radical way the world around them is changing. And as we know, the pace of change is getting faster every day. We need to ask the question then: Will today's organizations suffer the same fate as the Peruvian Indians? Or will they have the foresight and will change before they are forced to do so?[30] If they do, then it's critical they anticipate and respond to the forces in their micro- and macroenvironment. Organizations cannot thrive in today's competitive climate if they are insensitive to the drivers of change.

❑ DRIVERS OF CHANGE

Change does not just happen out of the blue. Change is typically driven by some causal factor. In 2003, the American Society for Training and Development commissioned a study to identify the key existing and emerging trends driving change in the workplace. These trends are summarized in Figure 1.3.[31]

The drivers of change come from one of two sources: either from outside or from inside the

---

1. **Drastic Times, Drastic Measures:** Uncertain economic conditions in the past several years are causing organizations to rethink how to grow and be profitable.

2. **Small World and Shrinking:** Global communication technology is changing the way people connect.

3. **Blurred Lines—Life or Work?** New organizational structures are altering the nature of work for employees and learning professionals.

4. **New Faces, New Expectations:** Diversity in the workplace is on the rise.

5. **Work Be Nimble, Work Be Quick:** The accelerated pace of change requires more adaptable workers and nimbler organizations.

6. **Security Alert!** Concerns about security and the effectiveness of governments to provide protection have increased people's anxiety worldwide.

7. **Life and Work in the E-Lane:** Technology, especially the Internet, is transforming the way people work and live.

8. **A Higher Ethical Bar:** Ethical lapses at the highest levels in large, high-profile organizations have shaken employees' loyalty, trust, and sense of security.

Figure 1.3   Recent Trends Driving Change

organization.[32] The externally driven changes are not easily controlled.[33] The external environmental factors have the biggest change-shaping impact on influencing organizations to change. What happens is that these environmental shifts influence a firm's business model by creating new requirements for success. This in turn requires firms to rethink their strategies, which in turn may require changes in the organization's structure, administrative support systems, staffing, culture, and processes.

There are numerous forces that affect why organizations change and their ability to remain competitive—for example, demographic shifts, new rivals, new technologies, new regulations, and other environmental changes that sometimes seem to come out of left field.[34] As Jick reminds us, however,

It would be unrealistic to suggest there is universal agreement on the magnitude, the time frame, and the implications of these forces. One part of an organization might perceive reasons for change, while another may not; different parts of the organization might find different forces driving change as well.[35]

Executives may make suboptimal strategic choices if they fail to understand how the different driving forces are changing and how they can exploit the changes as they occur. This is especially acute in complex, rapidly changing environments. Understanding the nature of the driving forces can better prepare management to determine what changes in strategy, structure, human resources, and processes are needed to optimize efficiency.

The more important of these forces include human capital, economic/political, global, technological, and market/competitive forces. Managers at all levels must remain alert and sensitive to these forces as many are interrelated and fuel the constant change that organizations face today and will face in the future. What direction a change initiative takes will depend on whether the driving forces are perceived as an obstacle, challenge, threat, or opportunity. In sum, Mourier and Smith remind us that "understanding the drivers will determine the urgency of the change, the resources needed, and the stakeholders who should be supporting the change effort."[36]

Figure 1.4, Forces for change, depicts some of the more common forces along with examples of each. We discuss a few important forces that drive change in organizations.

Human Capital

Forces impacting the workforce include changing demographics, pockets of labor shortages, skill shortages, increasing turnover, and increased diversity. In some areas of the United States, employers face a crisis with a surfeit of jobs but not enough people to fill the positions. For example, some companies are even turning away business for lack of skilled workers. Accu-Swiss, Inc., who makes specialized metal parts for medical and defense industries, had to turn down between 10% and 20% of potential business because of a lack of skilled machinists.[37] The Bureau of Labor statistics reports that the United States will have 10 million more jobs than people in the year 2010.[38]

Diversity in the workforce is projected to increase across all minority groups in the United States. For example, by 2025 the Hispanic population is expected to become the largest minority group, while the number of Caucasians will decrease by about 19%. The growing diversity in the workforce "means accommodating new attitudes, lifestyles, values, and motivations."[39]

A 2006 Society for Human Resource Management (SHRM) research report on key workplace issues identified 10 key demographic trends believed to impact the workplace (see Figure 1.5). This research suggests the importance of monitoring these trends and to consider the implication they may have on the workplace and the changes management may have to consider to deal with these trends.

Technological Forces

Advances in technology drive change throughout organizations. We can broadly define technology as the set of processes the organization uses to transform inputs into outputs—that is goods and services. Innovation and advances in technology continually affect organizations and how they do business and compete. The speed of innovation is reshaping the way we work, learn, play, and communicate. If we look at the phone industry, for example, the advances in cable, Internet, and wireless technology is seriously impacting the traditional Bell phone companies. The Wall Street Journal reported in August 2004:

In just over a year, one out of every eight households in the Portland, Maine, region has signed up for Internet phone service…for many, the phone jack in the

EXAMPLES	
Human Capital	• Changing demographics
	• Diversity
	• Competency deficit
	• Labor crisis—too many jobs, too few people
	• Employment disputes
	• New CEO, boss or leader
	• Telework and telecommuting
	• Switching to better HR practices
Economic and Global	• Change in interest rates
	• Economic downturn
	• Industry meltdown (e.g., tech sector, dot-coms)
	• Free flow of information
	• Plentiful, cheap, and mobile capital
	• Reduction in trade barriers
	• Increased geopolitical instability
	• Significant shortages of/steep increase in price for raw materials
Technological	• Introduce new automation
	• New Information technology
	• Implementing new enterprise software
Political-Legal	• Major regulatory changes
	• Deregulation
Competitive Dynamics	• Mergers and acquisitions
	• Turnaround
	• Downsizing
	• Bankruptcy
	• Competitive moves of rivals
	• Cost trends/inefficiencies
	• Improve work processes
	• Quality improvement efforts
	• Achieve world class standards
	• Escalating customer expectations
	• Change in ownership
	• Innovation in products, services, and business models
Environmental	• Natural disasters
	• Increased security threats
	• Pandemics

Figure 1.4   *Forces for Change*

1. Aging population driving an increase in health care costs.

2. Aging of workforce.

3. Demographic shifts leading to a shortage of skilled workers.

4. Retirement of large number of baby boomers (born 1945–64) at around the same time.

5. Growth in number of employees who have both eldercare and childcare responsibilities at the same time.

6. Increase in the age individuals choose to retire.

7. Generational issues.

8. Growth in the number of employees with eldercare responsibilities.

9. Implications of the Latino/Hispanic population as the nation's largest minority group.

10. Growth in number of employees for whom English is not first language.

Source: SHRM 2006–2007 Workplace Forecast[40]

Figure 1.5   Key Demographic Trends

wall than connects to the phone company's network is now just a useless hole…across the nation, the business models that have worked for decades for Verizon and other phone giants are showing signs of unraveling….The Bells have lost some 28 million local phone lines since the end of 2000.[41]

A new form of Internet phone service, for example, portends to bring further changes to the phone industry and corporate America. Skype, introduced in August 2003 and later sold to eBay in late 2006 for $2.6 billion, is what is considered a "softphone"—a software-based telephone that uses a computer, cell phone, PDA, or any other equipment connected to the Web to deliver voice with simultaneous file transfer and instant messages over the Internet. Unlike the growing number of "voice over Internet protocol" (VOIP) networks offered by phone and cable companies, Skype is a peer-to-peer system. This means that it creates ad hoc computer-to-computer links over the Internet whenever Skype users want to reach one another. With this approach, no central networks mediate or manage the connection. Because Skype eliminates the middleman, calls between its users are free, although new functions are becoming available that require a fee.[42] At the end of April 2006, the company announced it surpassed 100 million registered users worldwide.

The magnitude of the changes impacting the telcom industry was succinctly articulated by Duane Ackerman, the chairman and CEO of Bell-South Corp when he observed, "Our industry and our business is going to change more in the next 5 years than it has during the last 20 combined".[43]

The pressures for change are enormous; adapt or die is more real than ever before. For Skype, as competitors such as AOL, Yahoo, and Google enter the Web-calling market, the company will be forced to adapt and keep pace or watch its customer base shrink.

There is also no shortage of historical examples where advances in technology threaten the old way of doing business. Following the boom years of World War II, the railroads worried about the proliferation of cars and airplanes that provided people with new opportunities for mobility and travel. Just as Gutenberg's printing press in the fifteenth century opened the door to an information revolution that continues today, the growth of Internet technologies is transforming the way we do business in the twenty-first century.

As another example, the advance in Internet technology is impacting the major tax-software firms as more of the estimated 130 million Americans file their individual tax returns online. More Americans are turning to the Internet to file their taxes, using sites that crunch their numbers and zap returns to the Internal Revenue Service at lower cost.[44] This change has forced the companies that produce TurboTax (Intuit) and TaxCut (H&R Block) to adjust to the growing use of web-based software. Intuit in particular has faced serious pressure from several not so large tax preparation Web sites it long ignored (estimated at over 100). And unless it acts quickly, Intuit may be in "danger of being overtaken by events." Clearly, the tax software providers need to respond to these changes and respond quickly in order to transform their organizations and business models to compete in this ever-changing industry.

We should recognize too that technology does not only center on the Internet or information systems. Technological changes in biotechnology, nanotechnology, hybrid automobiles, solar energy, and so on are equally impactful.

So how should organizations respond to the pressures of technological change? Consider this perspective by Richard Notebaert, CEO of Quest: "If you don't embrace new technologies as an opportunity, then you could find yourself like the riverboat. You can either grab it or be a victim."[45]

Political-Legal Forces

Political-legal forces include the outcomes of elections, legislation, and court judgments, as well as the decisions rendered by various commissions and agencies at every level of government.[46] As one example of these forces, the Investigative Report of the crash of the space shuttle Columbia was released on August 25, 2003.[47] The report was a strong indictment of NASA and the way it failed to prevent this disaster. The independent investigating board suggested in its final reports the changes that needed to take place at NASA:

*"NASA's organizational **culture** had as much to do with this accident as foam did," the investigators wrote, adding that the chain of events [decision making] that led up to the crash showed that NASA had failed to learn or forgotten the lessons of the 1986 Challenger disaster, which also killed seven astronauts.*

The report said the space agency will have to make profound changes to its way of doing business if it is to avoid future calamities. "The scene is set for another accident," it wrote.

NASA does not have "effective checks and balances, does not have an independent safety program and has not demonstrated the characteristics of a learning organization," it added.

*The panel, headed by retired Adm. Harold W. Gehman Jr., said it expected that its recommendations will go unheeded unless the NASA **culture** can be remade. In all, the panel issued 29 recommendations, some necessary before shuttle flights resume and others that should be adopted to make the shuttle safer over the long term.*

*"The changes we recommend will be difficult to accomplish–and will be **internally resisted**," the investigators wrote."[48]*

Following public dissemination of the report, NASA Administrator Sean O'Keefe vowed that he will bring about the fundamental changes demanded by a blistering investigative report that pointed to pervasive management, communication, and "culture" failures as the root cause of the loss of the space shuttle Columbia.

As another example, consider the Sarbanes-Oxley Act passed by Congress in 2002.[49] This act is considered by some the most far-reaching corporate reform legislation in 60 years. The act greatly increased the accountability of auditors, boards, executives, and corporate lawyers, and greatly expanded the role of directors who sit on corporate audit committees. The law also created a five-member accounting oversight board "with the power to examine audit firms and discipline wrongdoing. Under Section 404 of the law, corporate mangers must create tight controls over financial reporting, assess them regularly, and have independent, outside auditors attest to their effectiveness."[50] Stephen Cooper, interim Chief Executive Officer and Chief Restructuring Officer of ENRON Corporation had this to say about the Act:

Sarbanes-Oxley is a "very helpful" blueprint for reform. Requiring corporate managers to certify the firm's financial results, ensure it has appropriate internal controls and be answerable to independent directors "is a framework to create higher responsibility and accountability."[51]

Paul Volcker commented in an op-ed piece in the Wall Street Journal regarding the change this legislation has imposed on many public companies.

... the changes in required practices for many companies have required difficult adjustments in thinking and practice, time and money." Clearly, this legislation has had a profound impact on many organizations throughout the United States and how they conduct their internal affairs. ... We are under no illusion that complying with Sarbanes-Oxley and other new regulations come for free; financial and managerial effort as well as money is required. But we believe that those costs are justified in light of the benefits—the price necessary to pay for more reliability in accounting, clear accountability to shareholders, and more robust and trusted markets.[52]

With Sarbanes–Oxley, many organizations have had to document and test their key IT systems, risks and controls — particularly those that affect financial reporting. Consequently, these firms face a new challenge: dealing with ongoing change. The act requires companies to identify and remediate any deficiencies in IT operations that could impact the financial statements.[53]

With a constant stream of new requirements and increased scrutiny across many jurisdictions, compliance has become a critical issue throughout today's business environment. Firms must be prepared to cope with the constant changes in the regulatory environment.

Competitive Forces

Growing competition forces companies to respond by revising their strategies and how they operate. The pressure for change has been unrelenting and only accelerating. The net result has been companies "pouring executive energy into the search for ever higher levels of quality, service, and overall business agility. Those organizations that fail to reinvent themselves may fail. The treadmill moves faster, companies work harder, results improve slowly or not at all."[54]

Consider the automobile industry, for example. In the United States, there is not a "Big Three" anymore. The industry is now dominated by both foreign-owned manufactures and U.S. firms. Since 1979, the traditional Big Three automakers — GM, Ford, and DaimlerChrysler — have shed some 600,000 jobs. And about a quarter of the U.S. auto-industry workers are employed by foreign-owned manufactures. The entire industry is undergoing a dramatic restructuring. Some observers suggest that nothing short of radical change is necessary if these companies are to reform the way they do business. Ford is a case in point.

In January 2006, Ford announced sweeping restructuring of its unprofitable, North American auto operations. This restructuring will result in huge changes for Ford that include closing at least 10 plants, trimming some 30,000 jobs, a reduction of approximately 25% of its annual capacity, and significant cost reduction strategies across the company's entire value chain. Ford's leader in this turnaround stated that his goal is to "put workers 'in a crisis mode, but not a panic.' "[55] The mantra at Ford is change or die. Will this strategy work? Much will depend on how effectively Ford manages this transformation and the people issues central to executing its strategy for change.

Another example of how competitors force companies to adapt and change is Google's effort to build its own Internet-payment service, going head-to-head with eBay's cash cow PayPal. In early 2006, PayPal was the king of the mountain for the United States Internet online-payment services with a com-

manding 24% market share and generating almost one-quarter of eBay's total revenue. But that could change as PayPal is forced to pay attention to what Google is doing in this area. With Google's ability to quickly create new consumer products and services, to sit back and ignore Google's inroads in this area would be competitive suicide.

Likewise, AT&T's planned $67 billion acquisition of BellSouth Corporation — a deal that could create the world's biggest phone company — changes the telecommunications landscape such that other firms in this industry will be forced to adjust their strategies to complete with AT&T's growth. With competition for phone, TV, and Internet heating up, the cable companies are particularly vulnerable as the phone companies move to selling packages that include all three services. Key to the cable operators' longevity will be their ability to compete and adapt to a changing competitive environment.[56]

Economic Forces

Economic forces impact an organization's ability to meet its goals and objectives. These factors include the general economic health of the country and region where an organization operates, unemployment rates, interest rates, inflation, availability of supplies, and labor. All of which can lead to increased business caution or optimism. In recent years, virtually every company has been forced to alter its direction in order to boost competitiveness as a result of the constantly changing economic environment. For example, in September 2004, US Airways filed for filed for bankruptcy protection for the second time in 2 years. The rising cost of fuel was a factor the airline could not control and so helped push them into bankruptcy. There is no doubt that energy will be one of the defining issues in this century. Over the coming decades, we can expect the global energy system to be characterized by change.

Another economic factor impacting big and small companies alike is the struggle with rising health-care costs. As a consequence many firms — and in particular small businesses — have had to adjust to raising premium hikes.

In July 2005, we witnessed the breakup of the AFL-CIO, the giant union consortium formed in 1955 by George Meany and Walter Reuther, largely because the U.S. economy, has changed.[57] The service sector is growing while the manufacturing sector continues to experience decline. The labor movement failed to adjust with these changes.

Globalization

The world economy and issues of globalization directly or indirectly impact every business, regardless of size. Globalization means the world economy is becoming a single interdependent economic system—whether it is increased trade, increased flows of information and capital, increased foreign investment, and increased mobility of labor and the means of production. Related to and indeed accelerating these trends have been enormous advancements that have occurred in information technology, including the use of the Internet. These advancements allow information to be accessed and transferred throughout the world instantaneously. This has brought about significant changes in the ways that companies do business, creating new opportunities for the global expansion of economic activity. Advances in information and communications technology have made it much easier for companies in all sectors of the economy to "go global," to create multinational workforces, to set up operations and facilities in remote areas of the world, and to market their products and services worldwide.[58]

Several forces combined to spark and sustain globalization:

- Governments and businesses became more aware of the benefits of globalization to their countries and shareholders

- New technologies make international travel, communication, and commerce increasingly easier, faster, and cheaper than ever before

- Travelers can easily fly between most major cities in the United States and the World in 24 h or less

- Competitive pressures — entering foreign markets to keep up with competitors.[59]

The challenges posed by doing business in the international arena run the gamut from dealing with global capital flows to coping with many different cultures, from developing new strategies to marketing in a region with different norms, to outsourcing and strategic partnering in managing the firm's value chain. In many cases, organizations have had to change the way they do business.

"More and more organizations will be pushed to reduce costs, improve the quality of products and services, locate new opportunities for growth, and increase productivity."[60]

One area we see efforts to increase opportunities for growth are in the United States, Europe, and Asia where there have been significant increases in foreign investment in these markets. For example, the Commerce Department reported that in 2003, outlays by foreign direct investors to acquire or establish U.S. businesses were $60.3 billion, up 11% from 2002, when outlays were $54.5 billon.[61] By 2002, foreign firms, excluding banks, employed 5.4 million employees, representing 4.8% of total U.S. employment.

Consider the impact of China and India in the global marketplace. Both have emerged as two economic powerhouses. China is the fourth largest economy in the world. Some economists speculate that China could become the world's largest exporter within the next few years and the world's largest economy within a few decades. In 2005, China shipped goods to the rest of the world worth about $762 billion.[62] Given the relentless competitive pressures, manufacturers from all over the world are forced to figure out how to reduce costs at home or outsource with suppliers who can provide cheaper inputs. In some cases, manufactures have moved some of their operations overseas. This strategy begets huge change in the way the company does business, how it manages its work force, and how it adapts to the hypercompetitive environment.

In 2003, India exported $54 billion in goods and $24 billion in services.[63] Just as China emerged as a powerful force in manufacturing, India is positioned to emerge as an equally formidable supplier of information technology services that portends to impact many IT service firms who will need to respond and change their strategies to deal with the increasing competitive pressures.

The forces affecting organizations today are very real and will only accelerate the rate of change. Collectively, "they (driving forces) have turned a once predictable landscape into a place where constant instability is the only 'certainty.'"[64] And whether organizations become victims or beneficiaries of the rapid change occurring in the world today will depend on how effectively leaders can detect and respond to the driving forces in their environment. In short, we can count on two things for sure: (1) the pace of change will not diminish but instead continue to accelerate. In fact, some observers suggest that the rate of change is doubling every 10 years.[65]; and (2) the complexity of change will increase and require organizations to be more agile and resilient. Consequently, "we can presume that in the future, even more than today, how organizations respond to change will largely determine their effectiveness and survival."[66]

Now that we have an understanding of the forces driving change, let us now consider some of the key factors that can impact an organization's ability to manage change effectively.

❑ CHARACTERISTICS OF EFFECTIVE CHANGE PROGRAMS

Without question, change management is an ongoing challenge for management and organizations. Unfortunately, too many change initiatives fail to deliver their promised value. Kotter looked at over 100 large-scale change initiatives and found that "people did not handle large-scale change well, that they made predictable mistakes, and that they made these mistakes mostly because they had little exposure to highly successful transformations."[67] Likewise a review of the research literature on change suggests that a large percentage of change efforts end in discouraging results. Experts suggest that the figure may be as high as 70%.[68] If only 30% of change efforts are successful, consider then the cost in

terms of economic and human resources: "in too many situations the improvements have been disappointing and the carnage has been appalling, with wasted resources and burned-out, scared, or frustrated employees.[69]

In a world where the only constant is change, this poor track record is disappointing to say the least and suggests there is lot of room for improvement in successfully managing change. Given the high potential for failure, we next review the key factors that distinguish the more successful change efforts as well as the factors that contribute to failed change initiatives.

In their research, Mourier and Smith identified 13 positive factors important to the success of a change initiative. These factors are listed with the most significant to the least significant in Figure 1.6.[70]

From this research, we can pinpoint three key areas important to success: top management support and involvement, the needs of the employees, and effective project management.

Top Management Support and Involvement

Major change is almost impossible without top leadership support. "Leadership must set the direction, pace, and tone and provide a clear consistent rationale that brings everyone together behind a single mission."[71] Any successful major change initiative must also be driven by a strong and stable project management team. It would take a superhuman

---

1. There was visible support from the sponsor throughout the change project
2. People understood what they had to do in order to make the change work
3. The effort was adequately staffed and funded
4. The project team was dedicated and capable
5. There was a strong project manager
6. Other organizational priorities did not get in the way
7. Progress toward the goals was tracked and publicized
8. The change was explained to everyone
9. There was continued support from the sponsor throughout the project
10. The change was kept small and manageable
11. Employees were treated fairly
12. The sponsor had the support of other key executives
13. There was a detailed plan

Figure 1.6   Positive Factors Associated with Change Success

individual to lead a successful change initiative by him or herself. What is needed for successful change is a team of individuals that includes a mix of key executives, department heads, managers, and front-line employees who are committed to the change and who can work together as a team.

Kotter suggests four key characteristics should define the composition of the change project team. These characteristics include[72]

1. *Position power:* Does the team include enough key players to champion the change so that other managers in the organization cannot block or frustrate the change?

2. *Expertise:* Does the make up of the team include individuals with all the technical, cognitive, and interpersonal skills needed to plan and execute the change initiative?

3. *Credibility:* Does the team composition include enough individuals who are respected and who can use their referent power to help persuade others of the need for the change?

4. *Leadership:* Does the team consist of enough individuals with proven leadership talent, change management skills, integrity, courage, and commitment to carry the change project to a successful conclusion? Without competent leadership, with a capital "L," the change project can flounder, fail, or at best produce disappointing results.

Needs of Employees

In order for any change initiative to be successful, management must cultivate the soil (culture) and provide the nourishment (motivation) needed for the change to grow and develop to fruition. One expert suggests that 20% of employees buy-in and tend to support and drive a change from the beginning, another 50% are fence-sitters and don't commit and the remaining 30% tend to take a hard-core stand and oppose the change.[73] One approach to improving the odds of convincing people that the change is necessary is to help them understand that the vision for the change is headed in the right direction. (We explore this important point in depth in Chapter 6.)

For example, peoples' response to change depends on if they understand the basic purpose of the change; why is it necessary? What is the big *picture* of how the end result will look and feel; people need to visualize the change project before they can commit to it in their hearts. What is the step-by-step *plan* for carrying out the change? And what *part* do the employees play in the change; what must they do to support the change.[74] It's important that people understand both emotionally and intellectually why they need to change. The emotional component is what Kotter calls "Creating a Sense of Urgency," where without it "people won't give that extra effort that is often essential. They won't make needed sacrifices. Instead they cling to the status quo and resist initiatives from above."[75]

Along with the needs of employees, we also need to mobilize the support of key players — both inside and outside — the organization who will be impacted by the change. To figure out who these key individuals are, Tushman and O'Reilly offer this advice:

To determine who these key individuals are and what their responses to change might be, ask: Who has the power to make or break the change? Who controls critical resources or expertise? Then think through how the change will likely affect each of these individuals and how each is likely to react toward the change. Who will gain or lose something? What are the relationships among those affected? Are there blocs of individuals likely to mobilize against or in support of the change effort...Managers must actively think in terms of coalitions to shape change.[76]

Effective Project Management

Project management involves the planning, control, and coordination of all aspects of a change program. This includes a focus on the values, attitudes, and behavior of all those involved in order to ensure a successful outcome. It's always good idea to have a skilled project manager in place early in the process. This is especially critical with large-scale change programs.

Unsuccessful change programs consistently failed to pay attention to the characteristics of effective change programs. Mauer and Associates conducted an extensive change survey and noted, "There is a big gap between what leaders know and what they actually do."[77] While managers and leaders of change may know what it takes to lead change successfully, it's almost like they drank from the River Lethe, which according to Greek myth flowed through the Underworld and induced a state of forgetfulness in anyone who drank its water. Maybe change leaders take shortcuts in trying to accelerate the change process or they think they know a better way; unfortunately, shunting steps in the process and failing to pay attention to the key success factors only invites disappointment.

Eric Abahamson offers an excellent suggestion to help mitigate any forgetfulness or perpetuating failures from past change initiatives. He says we should not ignore the memory of employees who have been involved in change programs in the past. To this end, we can learn about "whether a proposed change was attempted previously and what its outcome was and why."[78]

Margaret Wheatley offers equally compelling insight when considering whether a change effort is successful. She suggests change leaders need to ask the following questions:[79]

1. Are people in the organization more committed to being here now than at the beginning of this effort?

2. Do people feel more prepared for the next wave of change?

3. Did we develop capacity (for change) or just stage an event?

4. Do people feel that their creativity and expertise contributed to the changes?

When we pay attention to these kind of questions as indicators, Wheatley argues that "we can create organizations (cultures) that know how to respond continuously" to the driving forces in their operating environment. Why? Because we tap what she calls "the intelligence that lives everywhere" in organizations, and in the process, we succeed in engaging people and their capacity to deal with change.[80]

In following section, we focus specifically on barriers to change.

❑ BARRIERS TO ORGANIZATIONAL CHANGE

At a basic level, when we ask employees to totally change the way they have been working, it's like asking a basketball team to now switch to playing golf. People are not like Playdough, where we can twist and mold them into any shape we want. Unlike Playdough people cannot change their behaviors overnight, "get smarter over the weekend, or 'grow' skills they do not have."[81]

Lou Gerstner, former CEO of IBM, aptly noted why organization change can be so difficult: "Nobody likes change. Whether you are a senior executive or an entry-level employee, change represents uncertainly and, potentially, pain."[82] It's natural for individuals to resist change because they are comfortable with the status quo. Gerstner's observation suggests that it's much easier to hang onto what made you great than to change which can be costly. For example, Kodak was slow in adapting its dependence on its film-based business model to digital technology. As a result, Kodak is now trying to play catch up in a field dominated by others. The fact that the digital business offers much lower margins than film necessitates significant changes on the horizon for Kodak. To help Kodak make the transformation that eluded A&T, Polaroid, and other icons that sank as new technology undercut their businesses, they installed a new CEO in June 2005 to lead them into the digital age.[83]

Both groups and individuals resist change. As Mark Twain said, "Habit is habit, and not to be flung out of the window by any man, but coaxed downstairs a step at a time."[84] Indeed, people's habits are hard to change. Michael Beer captured the essence of why people resist changing old habits:

Changes usually mean losses of power as responsibility and accountability are shifted; losses in relationships as new patters of interaction are demanded by new approaches to management; losses in rewards, particularly status, money, and perquisites as power shifts; and losses in identity as the meaning people make of their work lives is threatened by changes in the firm's strategy and allocation of responsibility.[85]

In the end, what people resist is the loss of control over their lives that they fought so long and hard to create. This sense of loss of control often leads to a lot of uncertainty about the future. One way to help people regain control of their work lives is effective two-way communication—a subject we'll explore more deeply in Chapter 6. People need to understand what is happening, that change is essential. It is through change we learn and grow, although not always without pain.[86]

Another barrier to organizational change related to maintaining the status quo is the tendency for many organizations to develop a comfort level based on their current performance. John D. Rockefeller III described the conservatism of large organizations:

An organization is a system, with a logic of its own, and all the weight of tradition and inertia. The deck is stacked in favor of the tried and proven way of doing things and against the taking of risks and striking out in new directions.[87]

What happens is that management becomes over-confident, complacent, and even a bit arrogant about their success. They develop a myopic view of their company as the center of the competitive universe. They rationalize: Why should we rock the boat or change the formula that has led to our success? And in the process of making better widgets, they fail to notice the competitive land-scape and customer preferences are changing. "That very reluctance to change ultimately turns success into failure."[88]

In addition, Kotter suggests that change initiatives can encounter challenges because of "inwardly focused cultures, a paralyzing bureau-cracy, parochial politics, low levels of trust, lack of teamwork, arrogant attitudes, lack of leadership in middle management, and the general fear of the unknown."[89] To effectively manage change, change agents and managers must learn to address these barriers to change and do it well.

We also know that if an organization accumu-lates a series of failed change initiatives, big or small, expensive or relatively inexpensive, employ-ees can become burned out and cynical. When this happens, its hard to create a feeling of enthusiasm and zeal for the next change. People no longer are motivated nor do they exhibit the level of commit-ment and buy-in necessary for any change program to be a success.

The same outcome can result with what Eric Abrahamson calls "repetitive-change syndrome" whose symptoms include initiative overload, change-related chaos, and employee anxiety, cyni-cism, and burnout.[90] Initiative overload is like huge waves rolling in off the ocean—people are hit with one change initiative after another. Before one change program can be brought to fruition and institutionalized, here comes another wave. Soon people become so overwhelmed that they lose track of which change initiative they are working on and why. To cope with this dilemma, Abraham-son suggests that leaders nurture an organization culture that capable of ongoing adaption. This may require what Abrahamson calls "pacing": "alternat-ing periods of change...with periods of stability during which a business can recover."[91]

If we go beyond the inertia to change or to preserve the status quo, there are indeed powerful lessons to be taken from understanding why change programs fail. Unfortunately, not many organizations bother to assess why change pro-grams don't succeed. Instead they try some other change initiative.

By recognizing the mistakes to avoid in mana-ging change, we can better focus on the key suc-cess factors necessary to increase the probability of success while trying to avoid some of the key pitfalls. Figure 1.7 lists 15 key reasons that Ken Blanchard identified as contributors to failed change projects.[92]

The barriers and pitfalls to change not with standing, change leaders need to anticipate and take on these challenges and manage them accord-ingly. It's important to remain sensitive to the fact that all individuals may have concerns that can lead him or her to act in a way that undermines the change effort.[93]

❏ TWO BASIC APPROACHES TO CHANGE

Based on over 40 years of study and research in the change field, Michael Beer and NItin Nobria sug-gest there are two fundamental goals that drive change initiatives.[94] They call the two basic goals to change "Theory E" and "Theory O." Both appro-aches are based on differing assumptions about how change should be managed.

Theory E is considered the "hard side" of change and is focused on creating economic value by increasing shareholder value (e.g., cash flow and stock price). This approach to change is often related to addressing a financial crisis of some kind. Strategies to improved shareholder value may in-volve use of performance incentives and bonuses, layoffs, downsizing, and restructuring. "Jack Welch's 25% headcount reduction at GE, and his subsequent 'be #1 or #2 in your market or be sold' strategy are prime examples of actions stemming from a Theory E change process."[95] Theory E change is driven from the top.

Corporate departments, operating units, and employ-ees involved in this approach are like pieces on man-agement's strategic chessboard; they are arranged or combined, and occasionally cashed out. Outside con-sultants provide advice to members of the inner circle: strategy consultants help management identify and

1. People leading the change think that announcing the change is the same as implementing it.
2. People's concerns with change are not surfaced or addressed.
3. Those being asked to change are not involved in planning the change.
4. There is no urgent or compelling reason to change. The business case is not communicated.
5. A compelling vision that excites people about the future has not been developed or communicated.
6. The change leadership team doesn't include early adopters, resisters, or informal leaders.
7. The change isn't piloted, so the organization doesn't learn what's needed to support the change.
8. Organizational systems and other initiatives aren't aligned with the change.
9. Leaders lose focus or fail to prioritize, causing "death by 1000 initiatives."
10. People are not enabled or encouraged to build new skills.
11. Those leading the change aren't credible—they undercommunicate, give mixed messages, and do not model the behaviors the change requires.
12. Progress is not measured, and no one recognizes the changes that people have worked hard to make.
13. People are not held accountable for implementing the change.
14. People leading the change fail to respect the power of the culture to kill the change.
15. Possibilities and options are not explored before a specific change is chosen.

Figure 1.7   Reasons Why Change Efforts Typically Fail

weigh its options; valuation specialists and investment bankers arrange for asset sales and/or acquisitions; and HR consultants help with thorny layoffs.[96]

Where short-term performance results tend to be paramount among U.S. companies, the Theory E approach to change is used more than Theory O. Theory O is characterized as a softer approach to change. The focus here is on building organizational capability by capitalizing on its human capital, building employee commitment, and creating a learning culture that can respond, adapt, and change in the face of the driving forces in its environment. With this approach to change, we see companies that embrace high performance human resource practices: high levels of employee involvement, a more organic and flatter structure, and a strong constructive culture. The members in organizations with constructive norms are encouraged to interact with people and approach tasks in ways that will help them to meet their higher order satisfaction needs. We see this profile evident in organizations that truly consider people as their most important asset. Constructive cultures are "consistent with (and supportive of) the objectives behind empower-ment, total quality management, transformational leadership, continuous improvement and change, reengineering, and learning organizations."[97]

Leaders of the Theory O approach to change recognize that they can't manage change by themselves or by issuing an edict from the top. Leaders rely on bringing out the hidden talent in their workforce by involving them in the process and reinforcing behaviors and attitudes that will help ensure success. Most experts agree that the key reason why many change initiatives fail is because of failure to address the people-related challenges.

Figure 1.8 compares and contrasts the two theories on six change dimensions: goals, leadership, focus, process, reward system, and use of consultants.[98]

Beer and Nobria found that most organizations they studied rarely embraced just one theory. Instead they tend to use a combination of the two:

But all too often, managers try to apply theories E and O in tandem without resolving the inherent tensions between them. This impulse to combine the strategies is directionally correct, but theories E and O are so different that it's hard to manage them simultaneously.... Our research suggests, however,

DIMENSIONS OF CHANGE	THEORY E	THEORY O	THEORIES E AND O COMBINED
Goals	Maximize shareholder value	Develop organizational capabilities	Explicitly embrace the paradox between economic value and organizational capability
Leadership	Manage change from the top down	Encourage participation from the bottom up	Set direction from the top and engage the people below
Focus	Emphasize structure and systems	Build up corporate culture; employees' behavior and attitudes	Focus simultaneously on the hard (structures and systems) and the soft corporate culture
Process	Plan and establish programs	Experiment and evolve	Plan for spontaneity
Reward System	Motivate through financial incentives	Motivate through commitment	Use incentives to reinforce change but not to drive it
Use of Consultants	Consultants analyze problems and shape solutions	Consultants support management in shaping their own solutions	Consultants are expert resources who empower employees

Figure 1.8 Comparing Theory E and O

that there is a way to resolve this tension so that businesses can satisfy their shareholders while building viable institutions. Companies that effectively combine hard and soft approaches to change can reap big payoffs in profitability and productivity. Those companies are more likely to achieve sustainable competitive advantage.[99]

One option in using E and O is to sequence them. However, Beer and Nobria suggest it's best to begin with a focus on Theory E first. Why? Because "it is highly unlikely that E would successfully follow O because of the sense of betrayal that would involve. It is hard to imagine how a draconian program of layoffs and downsizing can leave intact the psychological contract and culture a company has so patiently built up over the years."[100] Moreover, the sequencing approach can take many years to implement. A more fruitful approach to combining E and O than sequencing is to consider deploying both simultaneously. However, this approach requires extraordinary skill and wisdom precisely because it is more complex and difficult to execute effectively.

❏ MODEL FOR CHANGE

Managing change is a complex process. Change does not occur in one great swoop. Few organizations manage the process as well as they would like.[101] In order to make change work, organizations need to follow a process to enhance the probability of success versus just "winging it." The model of change shown in Figure 1.9 provides a useful way to think about creating and implementing organization-wide change.

Driving Forces. The model begins with identifying the driving forces impacting one's organization as previously discussed. The driving forces serve as antecedents or catalysts to change. From our previous discussion, we learned there are many forces both in the micro- and macroenvironment that drive the need for change. Understanding these forces is important to designing and implementing an effective change strategy.

Change Assessment. The next phase in the model is change assessment. One of management's important roles is keeping its "ear to the rail" and to assess what impact if any these forces may portend

for the organization. If management is slow to respond to the human capital, competitive, economic, global, and other forces, the organization will most likely fall behind rival firms and possibly impair overall organizational performance. An effective change strategy is unlikely if divorced from the realities of the present situation.[102] Sound analysis of the firm's driving forces is therefore a prerequisite to good change strategy.

Change/Project Leader. One of the key success factors in any change initiative is ensuring you have effective leadership at all levels. It helps to have the best people assigned to work on the project. No longer is the management of change compartmentalized or externalized. Change leaders at all levels across the organization are needed to play an active role in the change process.

A strong project leader or champion who can take ownership and can muster the necessary resources and provide the expertise and operational know-how is necessary to guide the change to success. It helps to have a transformational leader who can communicate the project's vision and rationale, who is passionate about the change, and who can advance the project by removing obstacles and leading the way.

The project leadership should come from the units undergoing change and not some support staff function. By extension, the project leadership should also include key managers and employees whom others trust and respect, who have the technical and interpersonal skills needed to influence others and lead the change. Informal leaders can also be powerful allies in the process.

Planning Change. Effective change is unlikely without a plan. Planning change serves two key purposes: the first is the cognitive aspect of thinking through the issues and their implications. This then leads to the second practical aspect of figuring out the resources needed to effectuate the plan.[103] As the old military maxim states: Plans sometimes may be useless, but the planning process is always indispensable. Planning change has a number of positive outcomes (see Figure 1.10).[104]

Planning change relates to all the activities that must be covered and in alignment before a change is actually implemented. This process includes establishing clear performance goals for the project that align with the overall strategy of the firm.

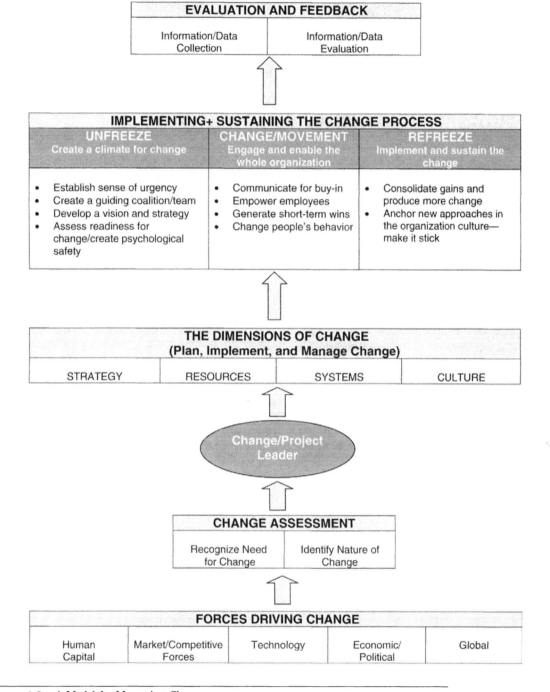

Figure 1.9 *A Model for Managing Change*

Dimensions of Change. The success rate for any major change is enhanced when four key factors in the overall organization system are in alignment. These factors or dimensions represent the key features of any organization: strategy/vision, resources, systems, and organizational culture. The glue that holds this all together is the organizational culture. All four dimensions are interdependent. This is an important point to understand because this shows that effectively managing change requires a good alignment or fit beginning with a good strategy and then appropriately aligning the

- Induce a change of attitudes
- Discriminate between the merits of alternatives
- Foster openness and debate
- Augment opinions with more facts
- Liberate people from previously unchallenged assumptions
- Refine the objectives of change
- Destroy unfounded optimisms
- Converge support the chosen plan
- Indicate needs for new resources and capabilities
- Draw attention to major impediments and contradictions
- Encourage factions to work together as a team
- Indicate time lines, cost, and value proposition
- Create a mindset of preparedness for change
- Show how the change will be managed
- Reduce the stress of enforced change
- Anticipate the consequences before the event
- Prepare the key people for rapid, united action when required

Figure 1.10   *Change Positive Outcomes*

remaining elements to support that strategy. We next define each of the dimensions.

Strategy/vision is the managerial game plan for knocking the socks off the competition. As part of the strategy formation process, organizations determine the kind of performance that is needed, the types of capabilities and competencies necessary to achieve sustainable competitive advantage, and how it intends to respond to the driving forces in its environment.[105] Once the strategy and vision is in place, the other remaining elements need to be addressed.

Resources represent the assets an organization has at its disposal. Assets include things like the human capital, plant and equipment, information technology, raw materials, and financial resources. For example, the people component represents an organization's human resources. The ability to successfully implement any change or strategy initiative depends on the organization's ability to attract and retain good people and, more important, to use their knowledge, wisdom, and insights.[106] In an interview in the Wall Street Journal, Herb Kelleher the former CEO of Southwest Airlines was asked what is the secret to his success:

You have to recognize that people are still most important. How you treat them determines how they treat people on the outside. We have people going around the company all the time doing other people's jobs, but not for cross-utilization. We just want everybody to understand what everybody else's problems are.[107]

Collin Powell aptly captured importance of people in managing change:

The most important assets you have in all of [your organizations] is people, and if you don't put people at the center of the process, you'll fail. Not profit motives, not size of the organization's headquarters, but people.... What differentiates successful companies from unsuccessful companies is rarely the brilliant, secret, take-the-market-by-storm grand plan.... The key to success... lies in exceptional, innovative, fast execution. Execution lies, in turn, in the capacity of people to quickly capitalize on fleeting opportunities in the marketplace; develop imaginative ideas and creative responses; generate fast, constantly changing action plans; mobilize teams and resources; get the job done swiftly and effectively—and then continue that process with relentless commitment.... That's what this "people" thing is all about, because it's people that make all that happen.[108]

The *systems* variable refers to the administrative support systems that the organization puts into place to help facilitate the execution of any new strategy or change initiative. These support systems include information technology systems, financial planning and reporting systems, project management systems, decision support systems, rewards, and communication systems. If any of these systems are lacking or nonexistent, such as effective *project planning and communication systems, then the execution of the change or strategy* initiative may be in jeopardy.

The *systems* variable **is** an important consideration in planning change. It obviously is helpful if all the stakeholders involved are enthusiastically committed and fully support the change or new strategy. This requires management to understand the basic principles of motivation theory and recognition as a tool for motivating employees and rewarding the desired behavior and performance.

Finally, the organizational *culture* variable represents the set of shared values, beliefs, norms, assumptions, symbols, and narratives that collectively influence people's attitudes and behavior. In effect what forms is a set of behavioral norms that everyone in the organization learns to live by if they expect to "fit in" and "survive." The behavioral norms guide the way in which people work and interact with one another.[109] The organization's culture is a key component in the organization system because it is truly the glue that holds the organization together.

Executive sponsors and change agents now recognize there is more to achieving success in a change initiative than just establishing a plan to accomplish its objectives. The best change plan in the world is useless if it can't be implemented effectively. Implementation depends on people. Thus, the people management practices and culture of an organization play a vital role in this process. Consider the following insight from the former CEO of IBM, Lou Gerstner. In a talk to MBA students at Harvard Business School in 2002, Louis V. Gerstner related his efforts to transform IBM when he took over as the new chairman and CEO in 1993. In a nutshell, what Gerstner discovered was that transforming IBM by focusing on strategy was not enough. Strategy is important, but strategy alone would not give IBM a unique competitive advantage. It was a change in IBMs 40-year culture that made the difference. As Gerstner commented,

I always viewed culture as one of those things you talked about, like marketing or advertising. It was one of the tools that a manager had at his disposal when you think about an enterprise....The thing I have learned is that culture is everything."[110]

As another example, Charles O. Prince III, chief executive of Citigroup, faced a ton of negative publicity in 2004 stemming from investigations in the United States, Europe, and Asia related to questionable trades, legal violations, lax governance, conflicts of interest, and failure to supervise analysts and investment bankers. As CEO Prince strives to instill change and create a "sense of universal integrity" at the bank, he's finding that his biggest challenge is changing the culture to align with his vision of probity and integrity in all its dealings. In fact, some critics suggest that the existing cultural flaws may cause irreversible damage to Citigroup's image with customers and governments.[111]

We devote considerable attention to the linkage between strategy and culture in Chapter 7 and how this important organizational system factor is crucial in managing change.

Implementing/Sustaining Change. Implementing change is the most challenging aspect of any change effort. As Machiavelli reminded us nearly 500 years ago:

There is nothing more difficult to take in hand, more perilous to conduct, or more uncertain in its success, than to take the lead in the introduction of a new order of things. Because the innovator has for enemies all those who have done well under the old conditions and lukewarm defenders in those who may do well under the new.[112]

A useful framework for managing any change implementation effort is Lewin's classic three-stage sequence of unfreezing-change/movement-refreezing. We take Lewin's approach and combine it with Kotter's eight-step process for leading change.[113] In short, the unfreezing stage focuses on creating the motivation for change (e.g., changing the status quo) and dealing with resistance to change. The change/movement stage is just that—introducing the new way of doing things. Finally, the refreezing stage involves institutionalizing the new way of doing things into the organization's culture; the new ways of working and improved processes become the norm. Rushing, skipping, or shunting any steps in the process is a recipe for disaster (see Sidebar[114]). Just as it's important to lay a good foundation when building a house, the unfreezing stage is a critical foundation for the entire change program; otherwise, the house of change may come falling down.

Sustaining or anchoring the change is a widespread problem for many organizations. Research suggests that the gains from change often evaporate when the new practices or processes are not sustained.[115] However, while sustained change may clearly demonstrate benefits over short-lived change, we should also consider the downside of sustained change. For example, the new way of working may be rendered obsolete by destabilizing external factors (i.e., changes in technology, new

SIDEBAR

BUDDHIST TEMPLE ANALOGY

In Kyoto, Japan the *Kiyomizu-dera* or "pure water" Buddhist Shrine is located on the slopes of Mount Higashiyama, overlooking a small cliff and Kyoto. The largest building is the Höndö or main hall. At the foot of the hall is a small spring which flows out in three streams. Called *Otowa no taki,* the water is drinkable and, according to local beliefs has curative properties. To drink from the right waterfall makes people intelligent, to drink from the middle waterfall makes people handsome, and to drink water from the left ensures longevity. Some believers say that to drink from all three invites personal misfortune.

Managing change presents a similar dilemma. We want the change to happen now. We also want the change effort to be a huge success. And finally we want the employees involved committed and to exhibit little resistance. But given the poor track record of change initiatives, is it possible to achieve all three?

The answer is yes, but not simultaneously. To achieve all our goals, we must follow the 3-phase change process articulated by Lewin: unfreezing, changing, and refreezing. Unlike the believers of the pure water Buddhist Shrine, to manage change effectively we must embrace all three streams or elements of the Lewin model. We do so by sipping from each stream at a different moment in the change process through careful monitoring of the effects of each drink on the target direction and pace of change. Otherwise, like the believers at the Buddhist temple, we will surely invite misfortune.

regulations, etc.). In addition, organizations can become so locked into current practices that it may blind leaders to other more promising developments and opportunities. The desire to maintain the status quo may also limit opportunities to grow and change. So in some cases, it may "be advantageous to allow some initiatives to decay."[116]

In a classic article in Harvard Business Review, John Kotter identified reasons why change efforts can fail and why they may not be sustained.[117] Steps 7 and 8 in his model center on implementing and sustaining change. Steps 7 involves not letting up. This step is key to ensure that change management teams are "persisting, monitoring, and measuring progress, and not declaring victory too soon."[118] Step 8 involves making the change stick. This final step requires organizational leadership to "recognize, reward, and model the new behavior in order to embed it in the fabric of the organization and make the change 'the way we do business here.'"[119] We will cover more on the Kotter model in Chapter 2.

Evaluation and Feedback. This dimension of the change process focuses on determining what progress is being made with the change effort. However, change plans don't always turn out the way they are intended. As such, consideration must be made for revising plans or altering the process. Just as Helmut von Moltke's often quoted military aphorism notes, "No battle plan survives contact with the enemy," no change management plan survives contact with the real world of implementation.[120]

Kotter and Schlesinger succinctly illuminate the challenges in this phase of managing change:

No matter how good a job one does of initially selecting a change strategy and tactics, something unexpected will eventually occur during implementation. Only by carefully monitoring the process can one identify the unexpected in a timely fashion and react to it intelligently.[121]

What are some of the unexpected factors that trigger adjustments to the plan? According to a Conference Board study, the most common factor leading to plan revision is a change in organizational priorities. As the report noted, when you consider the fact that "lead time for change management planning is often considerable, and market conditions, completive pressures, or organizational restructurings can easily intervene before the change is completed, requiring an alteration of scope or duration."[122] Other factors cited include changes in alignment and commitment, availability of resources, time pressures, and budget considerations. Even the results or magnitude of the change may necessitate adjustments:

Change implementation clearly should be a dynamic process, undergoing frequent revision to accommodate the practical lessons learned. It may turn out that the scope of the project is overly ambitious or doesn't extend far enough.[123]

In sum, the increasing pace of change coupled with growing uncertainty and ambiguity define the world today.[124] Managing change is here to stay; it will never go away. Managers who can learn to apply the basic change management process and principles presented in this text and who can chart an appropriate course to execute and implement the change project plan, possess a powerful competitive advantage. In fact, those who manage and lead change adroitly will not only survive but also thrive, during these turbulent times. It's a never-ending journey.

❏ READING AND CASE

The following Reading and Case reinforce the concepts and theories discussed in the chapter as well as provide an opportunity to apply the learning to real-world situations.

Reading

1-1 "Managing change in a world of excessive change: counterbalancing creative destruction and creative recombination by eric abrahamson," *Ivery Business Journal* (Reprint #9B04TA04), Jan/Feb 2004.

Focus   (from reading, p. 1): Over the years, change management, or sweeping out the old and bringing in the new has…what else? Changed. But rather than initiate something drastic like creative destruction, leaders should consider a much more modest — and perhaps more effective approach — creative recombination. As this author suggests, this can produce a lot of gain with much less pain.

Questions

1. Compare and contrast what is meant by revolutionary (creative destruction) versus evolutionary change.

2. Is continuous creative destruction a good strategy? Evaluate the author's evidence.

3. Consider the bromide, "No pain, no change," in the context of the author's thesis.

4. What does the author mean by the term "sustainable change"?

5. What is the difference between creative destruction and creative recombination?

6. Evaluate the author's statement, "…it is dangerous and downright irresponsible to prescribe change-management practices without addressing two types of questions."

7. The reading describes the vignette of Jennifer at America Online, Inc. to illustrate the "repetitive-change syndrome." Discuss some of the causes and what makes it pervasive and harmful. In your experience, how common is this in your organization? Provide an example.

8. Defend the author's statement, "Evolutionary creative destruction has its advantages. Yet, the more frequently firms change, the greater the likelihood of failing."

9. In discussing the risks associated with creative destruction, the author uses the example of creative destruction by downsizing. Refer to the table in the article that outlines 20 problems associated with downsizing and reflecting on your own experience with downsizing, share how the downsizings you may have experienced impacted your organization on each of the problem areas.

10. The author suggests that one alternative to organizations suffering from repetitive change syndrome, or are at risk of doing so, should not be creative destruction, but rather something less destructive like creative recombination. What is the creative recombination formula? Can you think of another metaphor in addition to the software or Lego example in the article?

11. Describe the essence of the three recombination techniques discussed in the article: cloning, customizing, and translating, and how each works in manifesting change.

12. What is the most important lesson from the reading that practicing managers should take away?

Linkage to Chapter

1. What is change management?
2. Driving forces for change.
3. Barriers to change
4. Elements of the model for change.

Case

1-1 Victoria Hospital Redesign Initiative. Ivey Business Case # 9A96C017, Copyright 1996, Version: (A) 2002-02-27.

Focus: The president and chief executive officer of a hospital is anticipating resistance to his newly formed vision for the hospital. The exact source and reasons for the resistance are not totally clear to him. Notwithstanding the difficulty of the change he would propose, he recognizes that the conventional hospital is no longer able to respond effectively to its demands with the resource constraints caused by government funding cutbacks. With varying degrees of support from the administration, doctors, nurses, and other professionals, he has to take action to get the proposed restructuring plan on track.

Questions

1. Assess the forces driving change at Victoria Hospital. Internal forces? External?
2. Evaluate the position of the various stakeholders involved in this change initiative.
3. Consider Dr. Frelick's vision for change and implementation plan. What did Dr. Frelick do that was good? Not so good?
4. What additional things could Dr. Frelick have done?
5. What are the reasons for resistance to implementation at the Board level of the new structure?
6. What can Dr. Felick do now to mitigate the resistance by the Board and key stakeholders?
7. What development needs might the executive team and managers require in order to shift their behavior and thinking from the traditional way of managing the hospital to embrace the new management and operating structure?
8. What incentives (financial and/or nonfinancial) might be used to get this restructuring initiative back on track?

Linkage to Chapter

1. Understanding the impact of change in organizations.
2. Assessment and identification of driving forces.
3. Understanding some of the key barriers to change.
4. Characteristics of effective change programs.
5. Theory E and O of change.
6. Applying the model for change.
7. Incorporate insights from readings.

❑ ENDNOTES

1. *Change and Lead: A Recipe for Success.* (2004). Retrieved February 13, 2007, from http://www.accenture.com/Global/Services/By_Subject/Change _Mgmt/R_and_I/ChangeSuccess.htm.
2. Extracted in part from U.S. Government Accountability Office. (2006, April). *General Hospitals: Operational and Clinical Changes Largely Unaffected by Presence of Competing Specialty Hospitals.* (Publication No. GAO-06-520). Retrieved May 12, 2006, from GAO Web site: http://www.gao.gov/new.items/d06520.pdf and Federal Trade Commission. (2004, July). *Improving Healthcare: A Dose of Competition.* Retrieved May 12, 2006, from FTC Web site: http://www.usdoj.gov/atr/public/health_care/204694.pdf.
3. Gladwell, M. (2005, August). *The Moral-Hazard Myth.* The New Yorker. Retrieved June 3, 2006, from http://www.newyorker.com/fact/content/articles/050829fa_fact.
4. National Coalition on Health Care. (2004). Health Insurance Cost. Retrieved Feburary 13, 2007, from http://nchc.org/facts/cost.shtml.
5. National Committee for Quality Assurance. (2005). The State of HealthCare Quality: 2005. Washington, DC: Author. Retrived June 3, 2006, from http://www.ncqa.org/Docs/SOHCQ_2005.pdf.
6. Taken from Bob Dylan, *"The Times They Are A-Changin."* Retrieved May 20, 2006, from http://www.bobdylan.com/songs/times.html.
7. Extracted from The Ken Blanchard Companies Web site, Retrieved 20 May 2006, from http://www.kenblanchard.com/solutions/organizational/.
8. Rubinstein, M. F., & Firstenberg, I. R. (2000, March). Cruise control. *Across the Board,* p. 9.
9. Hammel, G. (2000). *Leading The Revolution.* Boston: Harvard Business School Press, p. 4.
10. Hamel, G., & Valikangas, L. (2003, September). The quest for resilience. *Harvard Business Review,* Vol. 81, No. 52, pp. 52–65.
11. Guy, G. R., & Beaman, K. V. (2005). Effecting change in business enterprises. *The Conference Board Research Report.* Retrieved January 21, 2006 from http://www.accenture.com/Global/Services/By_Subject/Change_Mgmt/R_and_I/Effecting Management.htm.
12. Guy, G. R., & Beaman, K. V. (2005), op. cit., p. 8.
13. Wessel, D., & Carey, S. (2005, September 19). For U.S. airlines, a shakeout runs into heavy turbulence. *Wall Street Journal,* p. A1.
14. Arndt, M., & Woellert, L. (2001, September 24). How much heavier can the bagger get? *Business Week,* p. 52.
15. Trottman, M. (2004, August 23). Southwest feels squeeze. *Wall Street Journal,* p. B3.

16. Carey, S., & McCartney, S. (2004, October 5). How airlines resisted change for 25 years, and finally lost. *Wall Street Journal*, p. A1.

17. Hamel, op. cit. (2003).

18. Accenture. (2004). Research report: the high-performance workforce study 2004. Retrieved May 2, 2005, from http://www.accenture.com/xdoc/en/services/hp/research/hp_study_2004_full.pdf, p. 12.

19. WorkUSA® 2002—Weathering the storm: a study of employee attitudes and opinions. Retrieved October 14, 2004, from http://www.watsonwyatt.com/research/printable.asp?id=W-557.

20. Beer, M., & Nohria, N. (2000). Resolving the tension between theories E and O of change. In M., Beer, & N. Nohria, (eds.), *Breaking the Code of Change* (p. 2). Boston: Harvard Business School Press.

21. Church, A. H. (2004, August). Executive commentary. *The Academy of Management Executive*, Vol. 18, No. 3, p. 20.

22. Burke, W. W., et al. (1991, May). Managers get a "c" in managing change. *Training and Development*, pp. 87–92. A copy of the instrument is included in Chapter 3 of this text.

23. Hamel, op. cit. (2003), p. 63.

24. Smith, G. P. (2002). Fighting the storm in sea of change. *The CEO Refresher*. Retrieved October 18, 2004, from http://www.refresher.com/!storm.html.

25. Bridges, W. (1991). *Managing Tranistions*. Addison-Wesley Publishing.

26. Miller, D. (2004). Building sustainable change capability. *Industrial and Commercial Training*, Vol. 36, No. 1, p. 11.

27. Paul, L. G. (2004, December 1). Time to change. *CIO Magazine*. Retrieved December 16, 2004, from http://www.cio.com/archive/120104/change.html.

28. Miller, D. (2004). Building sustainable change capability. *Industrial and Commercial Training*, Vol. 36, No. 1, p. 10.

29. Handy, C. (1989). *The Age of Unreason.* Harvard Business School Press. Boston, p. 9.

30. Penna (2003). 2020 *Vision: The Future of Work.* London. Retrieved 19 July 2006, from http://www.penna.com/newsopinion/research/2020_Vision.pdf, p. 4.

31. Davis, P., Naughton, J., & Rothwell, W. (2004, April). *New Roles and New Competencies for the Profession.* T + D, p. 28.

32. Potts, R., & LaMarsh, J. (2004). *Master Change, Maximize Success.* San Francisco: Chronicle Books, p. 14.

33. Wheatlye, M. (2003). When change is out of control. In M. Effron et al (Eds.), *Human Resources in the 21st Century* (p. 187). New Jersey: John Wiley and Sons.

34. Day, G. S., & Schoemaker, P. J. H. (2005, November). *Scanning the Periphery. Harvard Business Review*, p. 1.

35. Jick, T. D. (1993). *Managing change.* Burr Ridge, IL: McGraw-Hill Irwin, p. 1.

36. Mourier, P., & Smith, M. (2001). *Conquering Organizational Change.* CEP Press, p. 21.

37. Aeppel, T. (2004, August 17). In tepid job scene, certain workers are in hot demand. *The Wall Street Journal*, p. A1, A4.

38. Cadrain, D. (2004, August 13). SHRM Home: Labor crisis isn't far off, futurist tells Illinois SHRM conference. Retrieved August 16, 2004, from http://www.shrm.org/hrnews_published/CMS_009468.asp.

39. Colteryahan, K., & Davis, P. (2004, January). *8 Trends You Need to Know Now.* T + D, p. 31.

40. Schramm, J. (2006, June). SHRM workplace forecast. *Society for Human Resourcs Management*, p. 12. Retrieved December 15, 2006, from http://www.shrm.org/trends/061606WorkplaceForecast.pdf.

41. Brown, K., & Latour, A. (2004, August 25). Phone industry faces upheaval as ways of calling change fast. *Wall Street Journal*, p. A1.

42. Cook, G. (2005, June 29). Skype's challenge. *Business & Strategy enews*. Retrieved June 30, 2005, from http://www.strategy-business.com/enewsarticle/enews062905.

43. Ibid, p. A1.

44. Vara, V. (2006, April 15–16). As users go online, tax-software firms retool strategies. *Wall Street Journal*, pp. A-1, A5.

45. Ibid, p. A8.

46. Wright, P., Pringle, C. D., & Kroll, M. J. (1994). *Strategic Management.* Allyn and Bacon. p. 22.

47. The Columbia Accident Investigation Board released Volume I of its final report on Aug. 26, 2003. The report can be found at the following URL: http://www.nasa.gov/columbia/home/CAIB_Vol. 1.html.

48. Bruzelius, N. (2003, August 26). *Report Cites Flawed NASA Culture: Columbia Investigation Board Faults Space Agency's Relaxation of Safety Vigilance.* Washington Post, A1.

49. Sarbanes-Oxley Act of 2002: http://news.findlaw.com/hdocs/docs/gwbush/Sarbanesoxley072302.pdf.

50. Burns, J. (2004, June 21). Corporate governance (a special report); is sarbanes-oxley working? *Wall Street Journal, p. R8.*

51. Ibid.

52. Vocker, P., & Levitt Jr., A. (2004, June 14). In defense of Sarbanes-Oxley. *Wall Street Journal*, p. A16.

53. O'Donnell, C. (2005). Technology change management and Sarbanes-Oxley: adding value to the process. Retrieved September 24, 2005, from http://www.protiviti.com/portal/site/pro-us/index.jsp?epi-content=GENERIC&folderPath=%252FPRO%25

2Fpro-us%252FFeature_Articles%252F&docName=
FeatureArticle_20050401.html&beanID=3454414
27&viewID=content&showGray=yes.

54. Pascale, R., & Milemann, M. (1997, Dec). Changing the way we change. *Harvard Business Review*, p. 127.

55. McCracken, J. (2006, January 21). Ford will slash capacity by 25%; In a crisis mode. *Wall Street Journal*, p. A3.

56. Grant, P., & Schatz, A. (2006, March 7). For cable giants, AT&T deal is one more reason to worry. *Wall Street Journal*, pp. A-1, A-10.

57. Very old labor. (2005, July 26). *The Wall Street Journal*, p. A24.

58. Extracted from the remarks of Under Secretary of Commerce for Export Administration, December 6, 2001. Retrieved from http://www.bis.doc.gov/News/Archive2001/GlobalizationNScarsdaleNY.htm.

59. Griffin, R. W., & Ebert, R. J. (2004). *Business*. Prentice Hall, p. 96.

60. Kotter, J. P. (1996). *Leading Change*. HBS Press, p. 3.

61. Bureau of Economic Analysis (2004, June1). News release: foreign direct investors' outlays to acquire or establish U.S. businesses rose modestly in 2003. Retrieved August 5, 2005, from http://www.bea.gov/bea/newsrel/fdinewsrelease.htm.

62. Morrison, W. M. (2006, July 12). China's economic conditions. *CRS Report for Congress*. Retrieved December 15, 2006, from http://www.fas.org/sgp/crs/row/RL33534.pdf.

63. Ibid, p. R3.

64. Gorman, C. K. (2004, May). Forces of change. *Information Outlook*, Vol. 8, No. 5, p. 37.

65. Colteryahan, K., & Davis, P. (2004, January). *8 Trends You Need to Know Now*. T + D, p. 32.

66. Passmore, W. A. 1994). *Creating Strategic Change*. John Wiley & Sons, Inc., p. 38.

67. Kotter, J. P., & Cohen, D. S. (2002). *The Heart of Change*. HBS Press, p. ix.

68. Mourier, P., & Smith, M. (op. cit.), p. 17. See Pascale, R., & Milemann, M. (1997, Dec). Changing the way we change. *Harvard Business Review*, p. 139.

69. Kotter (1996), op.cit., p. 4.

70. Mourier and Smith, op cit., p. 23.

71. U.S. Government Accountability Office. (2003, July). Results-oriented cultures: implementation steps to assist mergers and organizational transformations. (Publication No. GAO-03-669). Retrieved January 16, 2007, from GAO Web site http://www.gao.gov/new.items/d03669.pdf, p. 2.

72. Kotter (1996), op. cit, p. 57.

73. Chemical and Engineering News (1997, November 3). In times of change, managers should forget noisemakers and focus on fence-sitters. Retrieved October 30, 2004, from http://pubs.acs.org/hotartcl/cenear/971103/change.html.

74. Bridges, W. (op.cit.), p. 52.

75. Kotter (1996), op. cit, p. 5.

76. Tushman, M. L., & O'Reilly C. A. (1997). *Winning through Innovation*. Harvard Business School Press, p. 190.

77. Maurer, R. (2004). Results of effective change survey. Maurer & Associates. Retrieved October 20, 2004, from http://www.beyondresistance.com/htm/2article/survey.html.

78. Abrahamson, E. (2004, February). The road to better recombination. *Harvard Management Update*, p. 3.

79. Wheatley, M. (1997, Summer). Goodbye, command and control. *Leader to Leader*. Retrieved February 2, 2007, from http://www.pfdf.org/knowledgecenter/L2L/summer97/wheatley.html.

80. Wheatley (1997), op. cit., p. 28.

81. Williams, W. (2003). Why almost all organizational change efforts fail. *The CEO Refresher*. Retrieved October 19, 2004, from http://www.refresher.com/!wwfail.html.

82. Gerstner, L. V. (2002). Who says elephants can't dance? *Inside IBM's Historic Turnaround*. New York: Harper Collins, p. 77.

83. Symonds, W. C. (2005, May 12). A digital warrior for Kodak. *Business Week*. Retrieved May 13, 2005, from http://www.businessweek.com/print/technology/content/may2005/tc20050512_8477_tc024.htm?chan=tc&.

84. Directory of Mark Twain's maxims, quotations, and various opinions. Retrieved September 6, 2004, from http://www.twainquotes.com/Habit.html.

85. Beer, M. (1987, February). Revitalizing organizations: Change process and emergent model. *The Academy of Management Executive*, p. 52.

86. Handy, C. (1989). *The Age of Unreason*. Boston: Harvard Business School Press, p. 28.

87. Rockefeller, op. cit. p. 72.

88. Handy, C. (2002, Spring). Elephants and fleas: is your organization prepared for change. *Leader to Leader*. Retrieved November 9, 2004, from http://www.drucker.org/leaderbooks/l2l/spring2002/handy.html.

89. Kotter (1996), op. cit. p. 20.

90. Abrahamson, E. (2004). *Change Without Pain*. Harvard Business School Press, pp. 2–3.

91. Abrahamson, E. (2004, February). *The Road to Better Recombination*. Harvard Management Update, p. 4.

92. Blanchard, K., et al. (2007). *Leading at a Higher Level*. Upper Saddle River: NJ. Prentice-Hall, pp. 203–4.

93. Baum, D. (2000). *Lighting in a Bottle*. Chicago: Dearborn Publishing, p. 13.

94. Beer, M., & Nohria, N. (2000, May–Jun). *Cracking the Code of Change*. Harvard Business Review.

95. Luecke, R. (2003). *Managing Change and Transition*. (Harvard Business Essentials). Harvard Business School Press, p. 10.

96. Ibid.
97. Organization Culture Inventory™. ©1998 by Human Synergistics, Inc, p. 13.
98. Beer, M., & Nohria, N. (2000, May–Jun). *Cracking the Code of Change*. Harvard Business Review, p. 137.
99. Ibid, p. 134.
100. Ibid, p. 138.
101. Beer, M., & Nohria, N. Op. cit., p. 133.
102. Jenster, P., & Jussey, D. (2001). *Company Analysis*. John Wiley & Sons., p. 14.
103. Eccles, T. (1994). *Succeeding with Change*. London: McGraw-Hill Book Company, p. 48.
104. Eccles, T. (1994). *Succeeding with Change*. London: McGraw-Hill Book Company, p. 49.
105. Lawler, E. E. III (1996). *From the Ground Up*. Jossey-Bass, pp. 46–47.
106. O'Reilly, C. A., & Pfeffer, J. (2000). *Hidden Vallue*. HBS Press, p. 15.
107. Lancaster, H. (1999, August 31). *Herb Kelleher Has One Main Strategy: Treat Employees Well*.
108. Harari, O. (2002). *The Leadership Secrets of Colin Powerll*. McGraw-Hill, p. 128.
109. Organizational Culture Inventory Interpretation and Development Guide (2003). Human Synergistics, Inc.
110. M. Lagace (2002, December 9). Lou Gerstner discusses changing the culture at IBM. *HBS Working Knowledge*. Retrieved September 27, 2004 from http://hbswk.hbs.edu/pubitem.jhtml?id=3209&-sid=0&pid=0&t=organizations.
111. Hovanesian, Mara Der (2004, October 4). Can chuck prince clean up citi? *BusinessWeek*, pp. 32–35.
112. Machiavelli, *The Prince*, 1513.
113. Kotter (1996), op. cit.
114. Source: Information on the Kiyomizu Shrine can be found at http://www.tracyanddale.50megs.com/Japan/html%20files/kiyomizu.html.
115. Buchanan, et al. (2005). No going back: a review of the literature on sustaining organizational change. *International Journal of Management Reviews*, Vol. 7 No. 3, pp. 189–205.
116. Buchanan, et al. (2005), op. cit., p. 191.
117. Kotter, J. P. (1995). Leading change: why transformation efforts fail. *Harvard Business Review*, Vol. 73, pp. 59–67.
118. Cohen, D. S. (2005). *The Heart of Change Field Guide*. Harvard Business School Press, p. 4.
119. Ibid, p. 5.
120. Guy, G. R., & Beaman, K. V. (2005), op. cit., p. 13.
121. Kotter, J. P., & Schlesinger, L. A. (1979, Mar–Apr). *Choosing Strategies for Change*. Harvard Business Review, p. 113.
122. Guy, G. R., & Beaman, K. V. (2005), op. cit., p. 13.
123. Guy, G. R., & Beaman, K. V. (2005), op. cit., p. 13.
124. Hughes, R. L., & Beatty, K. C. (2005). *Becoming a Strategic Leader*. San Francisco: Jossey-Bass, p. 18.

Reading 1-1

Managing Change in a World of Excessive Change: Counterbalancing Creative Destruction and Creative Recombination

BY ERIC ABRAHAMSON

Over the years, change management, or sweeping out the old and bringing in the new has..., what else?... changed. But rather than initiate something drastic like creative destruction, leaders should consider a much more modest — and perhaps more effective approach — creative recombination. As this author suggest, this can produce a lot of gain with much less pain.

ALMOST ANY BOOK, article, course, or consulting advice about how to manage organizational change today will tell you that change is good and that more change is better. Advocates of revolutionary change prescribe change that *destroys*, in one short burst, all the past structures of an organization. The stated goal is to *create* organizations afresh, freed from the cold grip of the past. This approach was described in a recent book that is aptly entitled *Creative Destruction*. Advocates of evolutionary change prefer a kinder, gentlier form of creative destruction, a slower, more gradual, series of smaller changes that incrementally destroy existing practices and replace them, progressively, with newly created ones. Still other students of change recommend both evolution and revolution, in alternation, in which paradigm-busting bursts of revolutionary creative destruction are followed by periods of evolutionary adjustments, which way to another revolutionary outburst.

Despite its diversity, this change-management advice has three features in common. *Creative destruction* is its motto, *change or perish* is its justification, and, *no pain no change* its rationale for overcoming a purportedly innately human "resistance to change" in order to win the race to inventing a spanking new future ahead of their competitors.

❏ NO PAIN, NO GAIN? OR, PAINLESS CHANGE

We all know this change story so well by now, it has become so much of a cliché, that Spencer and Johnson could tell it, fairy-tale style, in their runaway best seller, *Who Moved My Cheese*. Two mice and two mini-humans face change that has destroyed the existing order. Someone (who?) moved their cheese from the place in the maze where they had become used to finding it. Only one of the little humans works through seven change-management steps to counter his "resistance to change", "reach closure", and "move on."

Eric Abrahamson is Professor of Management at the Columbia University Business School, and the author of *Change Without Pain: How Managers Can Overcome Initiative Overload, Organizational Chaos, and Employee Burnout* (Boston: Harvard Business School Press 2004).

One time permission to reproduce granted by Ivey Management Services on 5/27/05.

He lives happily ever after in his freshly created world, ready if not eager to adapt to any and all changes in his food supply.

Wouldn't it be wonderful if each disruptive episode of creative destruction had such a cheesy, fairy-tale ending? What fairy-tale treatments of change management miss, however, is that many global firms started on the path to change by continuous creative destruction, over 20 years ago, when growing global competition caught them off guard. Many of these firms have creatively destroyed themselves, repeatedly, over the last two decades — sometimes quite literally. What fairy tales do not tell you is that we are now in a position to look back and start evaluating the results of the call to continuous creative destruction. A study of one hundred large-scale creative destruction episodes, including TQM, BPR, right sizing, restructuring, cultural change, and turn-arounds, found that more than half did not survive their initial phase, with the vast majority of the remaining half failing partially or completely. Two independent studies report that two thirds of the hundreds of more evolutionary TQM programs studied failed and were abandoned. Another study of the more revolutionary BPR programs, by one of its originators, reports a 70 percent failure rate. What fairy tales do not mention is that we now know that many organizations make big revolutionary changes *and* perish, or worse, they change *and therefore* perish. What they overlook is that continuous evolutionary change has its advantages, but that it can create such intense change-related pain that it erodes organizations' very capacity to change successfully, adapt, and survive.

Many of the CEOs and executives I work with agree wholeheartedly that the pain of continuous disruptive change has become a serious problem in their firm. But, they ask, "Is such pain avoidable?" After all, did not the prominent behavioral scientist, Kurt Lewin, once write "There can be no change without pain"? Or, to put it more succinctly, "No pain, no change." What gives strength to their questions is, to put it bluntly — that Lewin was right. Or, at least, he was right *then*. In the current environment of change created by 20 years of creative destruction, it is important not to accept the change-without-pain wisdom indiscriminately. It is important, rather to build upon it. Yes, often no pain means no change. But, as Al Dunlap of Sunbeam fame showed us so clearly, *excessive levels* of change-related pain can render change slower,

more expensive, and much more likely to fail entirely. In other words: "More pain, less change." We must challenge ourselves, therefore, with the very real possibility that in a world of recurrent highly disruptive change, less pain may enable both more, and more effective, change.

In an earlier article, I took up this challenge, proposing the notion of dynamic stability — alternating periods of stability and change in order to exploit the benefits of each and to counter the disadvantages of both in isolation. This article takes up this challenge in a different way. It outlines a much less painful approach to change—whether it is evolutionary or revolutionary. It is an approach that makes it possible to manage change in a less disruptive fashion in order to achieve "sustainable change" — a series of changes that leaders can execute without the excessive disruption and pain that erodes employees' and organizations' capacities to make still more changes, at equal or lower cost, and with equal or greater success. It is also an approach that does not take the "no pain, no change" cliché as a given, or worse, as a cynical excuse to justify all forms of badly managed change. And it is an approach, rather, that takes "change without pain" as an ideal that, even if unattainable, should be the standard against which we measure change in our current world of already excessive change. I should mention that the interested reader can find this approach developed in much greater detail in my recent book *Change Without Pain,* along with accompanying change management maps, examples, techniques and programs, downloadable at ChangeWithoutPain.com. I call this approach Creative Recombination.

❏ CREATIVE RECOMBINATION

To clarify what recombination is, consider what it is not: Recombination is not *Creative Destruction* — obliterating the past in order to make way for some notion of a brand-new future. This approach is exemplified by divorcing to remarry, gutting your house to rehabilitate it, downsizing your work force in order to rehire, and destroying the current organizational structure in order to restructure, exemplify this approach. Creative destruction is precisely the kind of highly destabilizing and painful change-management process that books about managing change have over-prescribed for several decades.

Creative recombination, by contrast, recognizes that organizations frequently have, in-house, all the existing people, processes, structures, cultures, and social networks they need to bring about change. The creative recombination approach relies on discovering and pulling out these existing organizational assets, redeploying them, and recombining them to bring about change. This approach minimizes disruptive and painful destruction by using the assets organizations already have and recombining them creatively in a new and successful fashion.

It would be natural, at this point, to prescribe actions, as many pragmatic executives might expect. However, as is the case with medical practices, it is dangerous and downright irresponsible to prescribe change-management practices without addressing two types of questions. First, what problem does the practice address, what are its causes, and how does the prescription remedy these causes? Second, and more pragmatically, how does an executive detect the symptoms of the problem in order to know if and how extensively they should use the practice, or whether they should use it at all? The failure to preface management techniques without answers to such questions is probably the main cause of countless management fads. Therefore, before discussing how leaders can use creative recombination to both avoid and alleviate the cause of excessive change, I explore first its symptoms, and then its causes and its consequences.

❏ WHAT ARE THE SYMPTOMS OF EXCESSIVE CHANGE?

To begin answering this question, consider the case of an employee whom I will call Jennifer. In her three years at America Online, Inc., one of the companies under the AOL Time Warner umbrella, she has witnessed one mega merger, followed by a succession of three CEOs. Each one tried to put his own imprimatur on the firm — their mission, their vision, their 100-day plan. Jennifer calls these their "text-book message," messages which, according to her, "all sound the same because every leader today has read the same change management books."

The point that I am making is that the verdict on continuous revolution is now in and, sad but true, creative destruction by revolution *tends to be, on average, extremely risky for companies.*

During her three years at AOL Time Warner, Jennifer's boss has been changed four times; she is about to move on to her fifth boss. Not surprisingly, in Jennifer's words, "the only thing [she] knows is that everything will change every six months." As she puts it "One day this top team in is favor, another day that one is. One day this is the strategy, another day that is. One day this is how we implement, another day that is how." Strategic execution, in particular, swings back and forth, pendulum style, between one approach and another. Indeed, everything changes repeatedly in Jennifer's world, not only her leaders, managers, strategies, and priorities, but also AOL Time Warner companies' culture, structure, evaluation processes, and reward systems.

How does Jennifer react to this constant change turmoil and chaos? She wishes her firm "would give initiatives a chance to take off, yet with each new regime comes another set of execution priorities. . . . No leader or employee is given enough time to follow through a plan." At a personal level, Jennifer lives in a world of perpetual start and stops on projects, of pervasive uncertainty. With constantly shifting bosses and evaluation criteria, Jennifer is very unsure about what she should work hard to achieve. She is even more uncertain about her career prospects. As a result, Jennifer has developed what she calls her "defense mechanisms." Her current boss does not much care for her approach. Yet she does not obsess over this. She does what she hopes will prove itself to be right. Besides, she is about to move to her fifth boss, someone she expects will most likely stress different priorities and have different evaluation criteria.

Don't get the wrong impression. Jennifer is not a complainer or a slacker. She cares about her job and her firm's success. She is ever hopeful that the next CEO will launch AOL Time Warner on the right track, and she embodies, I believe, the resilience of this company. She is ready to throw her all into moving in the right direction, if only that direction would stop changing continuously. Jennifer, in short is not "resistant to change"— how could she be? She is rather resistant to excessive change —"resistant from change" to coin a term.

Jennifer has only been at AOL Time Warner a few years. However, she is already beginning to display many of the symptoms of what I call "repetitive-change syndrome": change weariness, initiative overload, and a corrosive cynicism that builds with each new wave of change, making each succeeding wave all the more difficult to manage. By initiative overload I mean the tendency of organizations to launch more change initiatives than anyone could ever reasonably handle. By change-related chaos I mean the continuous state of upheaval that results when so many waves of initiatives have washed through the organization that hardly anyone knows which change they're implementing or why. By cynicism I mean, in the unforgettable words of H.L Mencken, a person whom "when he smells flowers, looks around for a coffin."

For firms like AOL Time Warner, and for an employees like Jennifer, the best approach to change may not be another wave of painful, destabilizing creative destruction. Before turning to creative recombination as an alternative, I have to discuss what causes repetitive change syndrome and what makes it so pervasive and harmful.

❑ REPETITIVE CHANGE SYNDROME

The cause of repetitive change syndrome can be traced to the change manifestos written in the 1980s, a time when it became clear that global competitors, destroyed during World War II, were making a brutal comeback. These manifestos advocated the use of creative destruction in order to obliterate maladaptive practices that had become institutionalized throughout U.S. businesses during the 1950s, 60s and 70s. They were designed to shock U.S. companies into making the painful changes necessary to compete with the resurgent German, Japanese, or Korean global competitors, to name a few. By the 1990s, however, this creative destruction approach had become too extreme and too over prescribed.

"Don't automate, obliterate" Michael Hammer told us in his book, *Reengineering the Corporation*. Remember now, that following the publication of Michael Hammer's 1993 book, *Business Process Reengineering*, (BPR) spread to companies large and small like wildfire. A Bain & Company survey of management tools indicates that close to 80 percent of major firms in the U. S. and abroad had adopted BPR by 1995. By then, however, the management fad had peaked and had started its brutal collapse. The same survey indicates that from 1995 onward, firms abandoned BPR in droves, and the number of articles eulogizing this technique dropped from close to 300 a year to below 100 articles, most of which attacked and debunked BPR.

Hammer could not stem the tide, even with his 1997 book, *Beyond Reengineering*.

So, let's take a more sober look at the consequences of overselling creative destruction. Begin by looking at creative destruction manifestos like *Reengineering the Corporation*. But, do so quickly, because the bold creative destroyers held up as models for all organizations to emulate frequently end in disaster, only a few months after the manifesto's publication. Even Hammer's consulting firm could not reengineer itself successful when the BPR fad tanked. Another book advocating creative destruction held up Dow Corning and Enron as two successful revolutionaries that should be emulated. A few months after this book was published, it became clear that the market for broadband was not going to materialize as quickly as was once thought and Corning as well as other revolutionary compadres like Marconi were swimming in an ocean of red ink. Then Enron blew up, embarrassing not these authors, but other authors who had propped up Enron as the fashion supermodel of the creative destruction approach.

Clearly, it is dangerous to dwell only on these examples. The risk is to make the overblown point that all creative destruction is bad. There are, after all, the IBM's of the world that revolutionize themselves very successfully. The point that I am making is that the verdict on continuous revolution is now in and, sad but true, creative destruction by revolution *tends to be, on average, extremely risky for companies*. Consider these facts: in 60 percent of industries studied, revolutionary creative destruction decreases — rather than increases — corporate survival rates. Revolutionary creative destruction has been found to hinder rather than help the survival rate of newspapers, hospitals, airlines, wineries, savings and loans, automobile manufacturers, semiconductor manufactures, bicycle manufactures, Japanese banks, and even post-perestroika communist newspapers. Evolutionary creative destruction has its advantages. Yet, the more frequently firms change, the greater the likelihood of failing.

If you need still more evidence highlighting the risks associated with creative destruction, then consider the results of the wave of creative destruction by Downsizing that occurred when BPR rendered so many old employees redundant. While BPR was on the rise, more than 90 percent of firms across Canada, France, Germany, Great Britain, and the United States downsized, and in excess of

Destruction of employee and customer trust and loyalty

Loss of personal relationships between employees and customers

Disruption of smooth, predictable routines in the firm

Increase in and formalization of rules, standardization, and rigidity

Decrease in creativity

Loss of interpersonal interactions over time, leading to decreased cross-unit and cross-level knowledge Less documentation and therefore less sharing of information about changes

Loss of employee productivity

Loss of a common organizational culture

Loss of innovativeness

Increased resistance to change

Decreasing employee morale, commitment, and loyalty

Escalation of politicized special-interest groups and political infighting

Risk aversion and conservatism in decision making

Increased costs and redundancies

Increasing interpersonal conflict

Negative effects on the personal health of employees (e. g. increases in headaches, stomach problems, and elevated blood pressure, as well as reports of increased drinking and smoking)

Increases in negative psychological symptoms (e. g. anxiety, depression, insomnia, feelings of helplessness, cognitive difficulties)

Loss of self esteem, loss of self mastery, dissatisfaction with self, pessimism, powerlessness, and rigidity

Decreases in family cohesion, increases in conflict, decline in spouses' psychological well being, increases in domestic arguments, deteriorating family climate, and a sevenfold increase in divorce and separation

Source: K. S. Cameron 1998. "Strategic organizational downsizing: An extreme case," Research in Organizational Behavior, 20:185–229.

Figure 1.11

two-thirds of these downsizers planned to do it again. This despite a clear pattern of empirical evidence indicating both that fewer than half of the firms that downsized in the 1980s improved profit or productivity, and that their stock price lagged industry averages at the end of the decade. In one study of 281 acute care hospitals, for instance, mortality and morbidity rates were between 200 and 400 percent higher in those that downsized! Moreover, costs savings associated with downsizing disappeared in a period ranging from a year to a year and a half. Moreover, at least two studies, and often many more, report one of the 20 problems associated with downsizing which are listed in Figure 1.11.

❑ CREATIVE DESTRUCTION AND CREATIVE RECOMBINATION

The creative destruction advice is not so much wrong as it has been over generalized. Yes, creative destruction can be necessary. Yes, it can even be less disruptive and costly in certain situations. However, in organizations, like America Online, Inc., suffering from repetitive change syndrome, creative destruction is the change modality most likely to exacerbate repetitive change syndrome, raise the cost of change, and lower its benefits, causing future changes to become even more costly and even less likely to succeed. In short, the default option in the rapidly growing number organizations that are suffering from repetitive change syndrome or are at risk of doing so should not be creative destruction, but rather something much less disruptive like creative recombination.

Creative recombination starts with the assumptions that organizations frequently have, in-house, all the existing people, processes, structures, cultures, and social networks they need to bring about change. Creative recombination relies on discovering and pulling out these existing organizational assets, redeploying them, and recombining them to reach new ends.

As an illustration, consider the creative recombination of business enterprise software. Software designers have known for a long time that, when older or "legacy" software requires updating, it can be expensive and very risky to destroy it and replace it with newly created, state-of-the-art software. Ask any business enterprise software consultant, and he or she can point you to many cases of companies that drove themselves into near or complete bankruptcy by creatively destroying their business enterprise systems. So, why not use a software interface to recombine legacy software with new software objects using what software professionals call "reuse" (reusing software) and "wrapping" (wrapping new software objects around legacy software)?

Take the example of Pacific Bell. Like many companies that did not centralize the development of their IT infrastructure, it found itself in the late 90s with close to a dozen incompatible IT systems handling billing, problem reporting, customer service, and so on—a problem for a company hell bent on presenting a unified IT face to its varied customers. Pacific Bell, however, did not go through the costly, disruptive, and painful exercise of ripping out all its legacy systems and replace them with one massive integrated IT system. Rather, they used a software wrap to recombine 11 new and old systems at a fraction of the cost. Hewlett Packard and Ericsson, to name pioneers of software recombination, provide other good examples of the successful use of this approach.

The creative recombination of software, in particular, and creative recombination, more generally, tends to have at least four major advantages. **First,** it can make change much less costly. The cost of new software, for instance, correlates directly with the amount of software code written. So reusing legacy software code can mean saving thousands upon thousands costly lines of code. **Second,** recombining existing organizational assets capitalizes on existing knowledge and experience developed around these assets. This can eliminate the need to learn entirely new processes. **Third,** recombining existing organizational assets tends to engender much less transition chaos than does creatively destroying them. The later requires stopping the system, obliterating the old processes, redesigning the new one, putting it in place, debugging it, and habituating employees to its entirely new features. **Finally,** the Not-Invented-Here syndrome, the tendency of employees to reject brand new processes when they did not create them, becomes much less of an issue. Again, the method is not a foolproof fad that wprks everywhere and does everything with fantastic results. Software designers have made efforts to specify when creative recombination or destruction are preferable.

The metaphor used most often by those who creatively recombine is that of Lego. To change

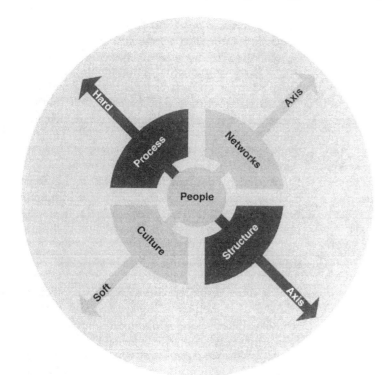

Source: E. Abrahamson, "Change Without Pain: How Managers Can Overcome Initiative Overload, Organizational Chaos, and Employee Burnout." (Boston, Harvard Business School Press, 2004)

Figure 1.12   *The Recombinant Framework*

from one Lego structure to another, it is not necessary to creatively destroy the first structure, throw out the Lego, buy a new set, and rebuild the new structure. This capacity to recombine entities created around a common standard has itself been the basis of Lego's strategy of recombining different Lego elements to sell children products ranging from buckets of loose Legos, to pre-assembled cars, boats, houses or spacecrafts, and more recently — robots. Moreover, children playing with Lego parts, Lego motors, and Lego computer programs are creating all forms of fascinating Lego recombinations — one developed a card-shuffling robot, another one a pneumatic hand capable of picking up spherical objects, and still another a robot that makes coffee.

Other than business enterprise software, what are the organizational equivalents of Legos that could be recombined to bring about change? On the hard axis, the grey Legos are the firms' processes and structures. On the white axis are its people, networks, culture.

A firm uses creative recombination very time it reuses, redeploys, and recombines some aspect of its people, culture, social networks, organizational structure or business processes.

❏ RECOMBINING PROCESSES AND STRUCTURES

In certain ways, as the Nobel Laureate Herbert Simon pointed out, organizations are analogous to computer programs. Just like computers, organizations have to carry out certain processes — business processes we call them — sales, for example. The organization's structure (the sales department, sales reporting lines, sales measures and incentives, for instance) like a computer program, guarantees that business processes are carried out recurrently, reliably, and successfully.

Executives cannot take every organizational asset, clone it, and recombine it, as if they were copying one piece of software onto another computer. Rather, three recombination techniques are worth noting. I call them cloning, customizing and translating.

Consider cloning first. Increasingly, companies have discovered that they can accomplish highly effective process and structural changes simply by cloning and recombining the business process and structures that they already have in-house. Intel,

for example, was dismayed to find wide variations in productivity and quality across its plants throughout the globe. This pushed it to adopt a new production approach it calls it calls "Copy Exactly." In 2002, Intel implemented this approach when it cloned one of its successful factories into an equally successful factory at Rio Rancho, New Mexico. Such cloning, when it is possible, is relatively easy. All that is required is carefully mapping out the clone, cloning it, and turning the on switch.

Creative recombination can involve more than cloning existing processes and structures. It can require rendering compatible processes and structures originating in different locations, in order to recombine them. Consider the example of Ford. The development cycle for a Ford car was slower than that of competitors. It was one full year longer than Toyota's, the industry leader, and more costly as well. Not surprisingly, Ford's performance has been problematic and it is under strong pressures to change.

Ford executives took a closer look at what they already had in house. In particular, they turned their attention to Mazda, a company they had partly owned, and which they had acquired because of its collapsing auto sales. Ford's solution was to recombine Mazda's two-year long development processes with Ford's superior sales and marketing processes and structure. Mazda's development process, itself, exploits the power of creative recombination. The key, in the words of Phil Martens, a Ford executive who learned from his Mazda experience, was "Just copy it if it's better, cheaper, faster and proven . . . Just take it." Recombine body frames, suspension, brakes, engines and transmissions — anything that exist in current models — in order to change to a new model.

Marten's recombination of Mazda's "copy-that" approach was not straightforward cloning however. Ford differed from Mazda in many respects. Ford had lost its long-standing culture which valued reuse and recombination over green field invention. Development at Ford occurred in five big silos organized by vehicle types. For example, there was the "Tough Trucks" silo, such as pickups. Each silo created its own unique auto-components. Each repeatedly reinvented the wheel — sometimes quite literally. So Martens had to customize the approach in order to recombine with Ford's existing processes and silo structure. The net result, without going into detail, has been that 10 cars and car-SUV hybrids were recombined over the last year from existing Mazda-6 auto components.

The Ford example illustrates how recombining business processes and structures often mandates that they be customized, not only in order to fit with other existing business processes and structure, but also to meld with a different set of people, social networks, or cultural norms and values. Customization occurs when change agents have to modify certain means to recombine them in a new context in order to achieve certain ends.

Mere customization may not be enough, however. Consider another example, Northrop, the aerospace manufacturing firm, and how, with the help of a popular maker of pound cake and other food products, it translated a production process used in the sports industry into one useful in the aerospace industry. In making certain fuselages, wings, noses and tail sections, Northrop had begun substituting production processes using aluminum as an input, for production processes using much cheaper, lighter and more durable carbon-composite materials. This meant borrowing and recombining a production processes from tennis racket and ski manufacturing industries. However, as carbon materials have to be kept at low temperatures prior to handling, recombining carbon materials with aircraft production techniques required cooling processes that could keep large sections of aircrafts at low temperatures. The production process for these materials, therefore, had to be translated for their use in the aerospace industry.

Rather than being a slow ponderous process, the reviving of latent cultural values and their recombination with current priorities made culture change a much less painful process, occurring in matter of months rather than years.

In order to design such cooling processes, Northrop engineers turned to engineers at Sara Lee bakery products — experts in the process of refrigerating large facilities. What resulted saved the company time, money, and pain-though it required translating processes used for food, tennis rackets, and ski production to fit the aerospace production context

Involved in this recombination was much more than cloning — using the same means for the same ends. Much more even than customizing — using modified means for the same ends. Some of the means had to be reinvented, following the outlines of existing processes, in order to achieve the desired ends. This third recombination process I call "translating." The French soft drink brand Pshit, for instance, will never work in an Anglo-Saxon context without a bit of inspired translation.

Business processes and structures constitute the hard axis of the recombinant map. People, culture, and social networks form its soft axis. Let's turn to the latter first.

❏ RECOMBINING PEOPLE AND SOCIAL NETWORKS

Compare a social and a computer network. Computer networks are powerful communication tools, but they are hard to design, relatively inflexible, and costly to install, learn, and update. Consider another approach. Rather than creating or updating expensive computer networks, start by exploiting existing social networks within your firm. This is what Ford did in the previous example. Rather than creating a complex B2B supplier network to support its "copy-that" strategy, it leveraged the extensive, well established, and extremely flexible supplier networks Mazda possesses in Hiroshima.

Consider now a more complex example that required more customizing and translating in order to recombine existing social networks. The pressure to separate accounting firms' auditing and tax functions from their consulting functions gave birth to Deloitte Consulting. The type of largely IT consulting the firm does is increasingly specialized. John Smith is a Deloitte Consulting partner whose background was in auditing. John, interestingly, has a network of 500 social contacts that put him, as he puts it "only two phone calls away from every major CEO, CFO or political figure in the U.S." Not surprisingly, John brought in over $50 million of business last year.

The world has changed dramatically for John over the last ten years. As he puts it "Today, no customer would ever engage one of our consultants to take a look around for an opportunity to make something better. Our customers come to us with a very well-defined problem and a very clear idea of what highly specialized solution to the problem they want implemented." As a result, Deloitte consultants have had to become increasingly specialized — "they know more and more about less and less" as John puts it. Not surprisingly, these consultants, who are perpetually on the road to deliver on their specialized engagements, find it hard to develop the type of high-yield social network that John developed in a different practice based more on auditing.

One solution would be to put in place highly sophisticated computerized customer tracking and referral systems, like those that log every referral, customer maintenance active, and customer engagement Deloitte Consulting, however, has gown well beyond such a mechanical solution. It focused instead its existing assets. A little research helped it discover its fifty best-networked junior partners. Following the model established by John, their responsibility is no longer to deliver on specialized engagements, but rather to build their networks and deliver business to the firm.

❏ RECOMBINING CULTURE

There are many examples of cultural recombination. Let's reconsider the Ford-Mazda example. Is Ford's shift towards reusing and recombining existing really a new value for Ford? Or is it rather a dormant value. One that already lies dormant in the firm's culture, waiting to be revived, reused, and recombined? The answer is, unambiguously, the latter. Historians of technology agree; almost every aspect of Ford's mass production system was not invented at Ford. It borrowed from industries as far flung as meat-packing, and customized or translated what it found for auto mass production. At its very core, Ford was a company that was built on inspired copying, reuse, and recombination.

The genius of Ford's leadership is that they understand that the only way to bring about rapid and successful cultural change is not to destroy the old culture in order to create a brand new one. They realize that they can achieve rapid and successful cultural change by reviving existing, if latent, elements of Ford culture. They have learned the experience of Werner Niefer, who brought about swift painless cultural change at Mercedes in the late 1980s by reviving its dormant appreciation for high-performance sporty cars. They have learned the lesson of Charlotte Beers, at Ogilvy and Mathers, who turned around that company by stressing values of brand marketing, developed the year before by its founder, Charles Ogilvy. They have learned of the experience of Steve Jobs at Apple, who revived the firm's latent values for "creating something insanely great" in order to launch the Imac. In each instance, rather than being a slow ponderous process, the reviving of latent cultural values and their recombination with current priorities made culture change a much less painful process, occurring in matter of months rather than years.

❏ THE NEXT CHANGE-MANAGEMENT FAD?

Creative recombination has widespread applicability to many types of changes — process, structure, people, network or cultural changes. Moreover, it should be clear from the Ford example that creative recombination need not be employed with only one type of recombinant at a time. The Ford case, for instance, involved Mazda's development processes, people, and supplier networks, recombined with Ford's marketing processes, latent cultural values, and market clout. The Ford case also signifies that creative recombination need not occur on a small scale. There have been many highly successful large-scale recombinations, some of which are described in my book Change Without Pain, along with the techniques used to implement them successfully.

The versatility of creative recombination, however, makes it necessary to sound one unambiguous warning. Creative recombination is not a change management cure-all. No approach can live up to such a claim, and any approach that successfully disseminates this claim will become the next change management fad. I intend Creative Recombination, rather, to work as an alternative or a counterbalance to creative destruction.

Let's be very clear: Creative destruction may be necessary, and even preferable, in certain situations. In certain cases, it may even provide the best approach to achieve change with the least amount of pain. Creative destruction is not, however, the only option. Like creative recombination, leaders and managers must use it judiciously, at the right time, and in the right balance. Tools that help make this decision are discussed in Change Without Pain and at ChangeWithoutPain.com. In the final analysis, however, senior executives will have to strike this optimal balance between when and how much creative destruction and creative recombination they employ, given the idiosyncrasies of their situation and how much pain their firm can tolerate. It will be a hard and even delicate task, but, without intending to be flippant, it has to be said that that is why executives make the big bucks.

Case 1-1

Victoria Hospital Redesign Initiative

Karen Fryday-Field prepared this case under the supervision of Professor Al Mikalachki solely to provide material for class discussion. The authors do not intend to illustrate either effective or ineffective handling of a managerial situation. The authors may have disguised certain names and other identifying information to protect confidentiality.

Ivey Management Services prohibits any form of reproduction, storage or transmittal without its written permission. This material is not covered under authorization from CanCopy or any reproduction rights organization. To order copies or request permission to reproduce materials, contact Ivey Publishing, Ivey Management Services, c/o Richard Ivey School of Business, The University of Western Ontario, London, Ontario, Canada, N6A 3K7; phone (519) 661-3208; fax (519) 661-3882; e-mail cases @ivey.uwo.ca.

DR LINDEN FRELICK, PRESIDENT and chief executive officer of Victoria Hospital, knew that the organization would have to make major changes if it were to continue its role in providing health care to the community. Recognizing that conventional hospitals were no longer able to respond effectively to the problem of reduced resources, he estimated that there was approximately an 18 month window to make major gains in efficiency before the government imposed even more significant economic constraints. In January 1995, he had presented a restructuring vision which he had determined would lower costs, improve patient care, and utilize employees' full potential. His plan required a far-reaching reorganization of the hospital's services: to replace the traditional hierarchical structure of function-specific groups or "silos" with a flat structure of streamlined interdisciplinary and self-managed clinical teams. Several months later, with no clear consensus among the board of directors and with varying degrees of support from the administration, doctors, nurses, and other professionals, Dr. Frelick had to take action to get his proposed redesign plan back on track.

❏ VICTORIA HOSPITAL

The Public Hospitals Act of Ontario regulated the hospital, which was owned and operated by the Victoria Hospital Corporation, comprising approximately 130 corporate members. In 1995, the hospital had 650 in-patient beds designated for acute care and rehabilitation. In addition, it operated a network of ambulatory services including clinics, day surgery and one-day medical stays. The hospital's areas of specialty included: women's and children's care, cardiac services, cancer care, and life support/trauma services.

The mission of Victoria Hospital was "to provide excellent, compassionate health care for its community; to provide comprehensive health education; and to seek answers through health sciences research." Victoria Hospital, which employed about 4,000 people and delivered the bulk of general care to London and area residents, was indispensable to the people of southwestern Ontario. Staff treated nearly half a million patients from across the region and the province each year. Commitment to education was strong, with training provided annually for more than 1,100 students from over 20 health related disciplines. The spirit of inquiry was alive through the Victoria Hospital Research Institute which administered over $7 million in research grants on an annual basis.

❏ ENVIRONMENTAL FACTORS DRIVING CHANGE

Economic Pressures on Hospitals

After many years of expanding their services before 1990, hospitals were facing funding declines which resulted in many years of cost cutting strategies. The health care system would continue to undergo further profound change and budget cuts over the next two years.

Ontario hospitals were currently funded through the provincial Ministry of Health. Faced with a provincial deficit exceeding $10 billion, a down-graded provincial credit rating and reduced federal transfer payments to health care, the ministry had significantly cut hospital budgets. Because funding would be reallocated amongst existing hospitals based on factors such as efficiency and utilization patterns, as reflected by case costs, hospitals were feeling pressure to demonstrate their cost effectiveness. Teaching hospitals, which traditionally received higher levels of funding than community hospitals, would lose this benefit and receive a standard fee based on the type of service provided. The government was also setting policies designed to drive down the number and length of hospital stays by promoting the provision of more services on an outpatient basis. In addition, the ministry's "delisting" of several health services would result in patients paying the fees for these services that previously had represented a potential revenue source for the hospital.

Operational costs for hospitals continued to be influenced by inflation. Significant cost increases resulted from legislative requirements relating to pensions, pay equity and employee benefits. Seventy per cent of hospital budgets represented salaries and wages. There was pressure for salary increases in 1996 when the Social Contract legislation was due to expire. Hospitals also faced escalating expenses resulting from clinical and technological advancements that required ongoing capital expenditures.

External Forces Affecting Victoria Hospital

Because the city of London had three acute care, teaching hospitals all within a short distance of each other, many services were duplicated. Therefore, the Ministry of Health and the District Health Council indicated that rationalization of the London system must occur. Efforts for joint planning had not yet been successful at creating significant change in city wide co-ordination of health services. However, in September 1995, a committee proposal for a city-wide rationalization of clinical services recommended a relocation of cardiac surgery and neurosurgery from Victoria Hospital to University Hospital.

Another factor was the changing role of health care patients. In the past, doctors and experts analysed, diagnosed and prescribed treatments with little involvement or input from the patient. However, patients were increasing their demands with respect to health care delivery. They and their families wanted more detailed information about the status of their health and the treatment options available, and insisted on participating in the decision making process.

In the face of changing patient expectations and improved technologies and medical practices, the health care system was attempting to reduce the need for overnight hospital stays and to deliver care in an ambulatory mode. As a result, hospitals were shifting many diagnostic tests and therapeutic procedures to services that they could provide on an outpatient basis. In addition, procedures and therapies historically done in hospital were being done in physicians' offices and walk in clinics. The perception was that ambulatory care was beneficial for the patients, who generally could sleep at home, as well as for the hospitals, which saved money on a cost per patient basis. Hospitals continued to develop ways to reach into the community to promote health and to deliver health services.

Victoria Hospital's Competitive Position

Conducting Victoria Hospital's operations on two separate sites created a significant operating cost disadvantage. The Hospital was working toward a long standing objective to consolidate on the Westminster campus in order to reduce operating costs, enhance co-ordination of service delivery, and improve the morale of the care practitioners. Estimations were that consolidation would cost about $100 million and yield annual operating savings of $2 million to $4 million.

Professional Services	Medical Services	Physical Plant/ Hospital Services
Audiology	Anaesthesia	Finance
Nursing	Internal Medicine	Housekeeping/Building
Physiotherapy	Nuclear Medicine	Services
Occupational Therapy	Dentistry	Physical Plant
Social Work	Critical Care	Planning
Psychology	Surgery	Nutrition and Food Services
Speech Pathology	Rheumatology	Transportation
Pastoral Care	Neurosciences	Portering
	Orthopaedics	Sterile Processing
	Nephrology	
	Emergency	

Figure 1.13   Functional Departments (Partial Lists—Examples Only)

Victoria Hospital's 1995 annual budget was roughly $250 million. During the previous five years, government funding of hospitals had been gradually declining and Victoria Hospital had responded by implementing incremental cost cutting strategies each year. In fact, the hospital had achieved a balanced budget for the past 13 years. However, it expected that the Ministry of Health would remove 15 percent to 20 percent of the current operating funding over the next three to five years. Because Victoria Hospital had the highest case costs in the province, further drawbacks in funding would be inevitable if the ministry implemented the plan to reimburse hospitals based on a standard case cost. Therefore, Victoria had developed an economic model that produced the projections shown in Figure 1.14: Given a set of status quo operating assumptions, the overall financial shortfall would total $64 million by the year 2001.

❏ INTERNAL FACTORS DRIVING CHANGE

Functional Organizational Structure

For decades the hospital had been organized along traditional hierarchical lines with various professional groups linked through functional departments. The chart in Figure 1.15 illustrates the administration's organizational structure during the past three years. The numerous medical functional departments received support from 60 other service departments, such as pharmacy, nursing, physical therapy, social work, finance, human re-

sources and building services (see Figure 1.13). The functional departments conducted department specific training and development, selection criteria and performance evaluation of their department members.

These function-specific groupings tended to operate in silos and focus on the needs of the silos. However, in the current rapidly changing health care field, Victoria Hospital's clinical services had to be more flexible, and adaptable to evolving patient needs and reduced resources. In certain ways, these silos inhibited the capacity of Victoria Hospital's clinical services to respond to the environmental changes of the decade.

Under this system, groups of health professionals delivered care to patients with similar needs within designated areas of the hospital called clinical units. For example, patients with heart problems would receive medical care in the cardiology unit. Each health professional belonged to a particular functional department, such as nursing, internal medicine, or surgery, which generally hired, fired, set targets, assessed performance, determined procedures, and controlled the resources which affected the clinical units. A weakness in this system occurred in some clinical units when the health professionals worked side by side to deliver patient care but did not function as a team. In this situation, the overall goals for the clinical area and even for specific patients were often unclear, and inefficiencies existed where tasks were duplicated by staff. A failure in communication could also cause health professionals to feel torn between

	1995/96	1996/97	1997/98	1998/99	1999/00	2000/01	TOTAL
Operating Results	11.7	(5.0)	(19.8)	(34.3)	(48.5)	(52.3)	(148.2)
Regular Capital Expenditures[1]	(6.7)	(7.2)	(7.2)	(7.2)	(7.2)	(7.2)	(42.7)
Commitments[2]		(2.5)	(1.0)				(3.5)
Cash Shortfall	5.0	(14.7)	(28.0)	(41.5)	(55.7)	(59.5)	(194.4)
Redesign Savings	3.5	29.5	31.5	31.5	31.5	31.5	159.0
Redesign Costs	(3.5)	(12.3)					(15.8)
Information Technology[3]	(1.0)	(2.5)	(5.2)	(2.5)	(1.0)	(1.0)	(13.2)
Remaining Shortfall[4]	4.0	(0.0)	(1.7)	(12.5)	(25.2)	(29.0)	(64.4)
Regional Savings, etc.[5]	0.0	0.0	0.0	0.0	0.0	0.0	0.0
Net Results	4.0	(0.0)	(1.7)	(12.5)	(25.2)	(29.0)	(64.4)

Source: Victoria Hospital (CEO's office)
[1]Regular capital expenditures were reduced in 1995/1996 as part of the budget balancing strategies.
[2]In 1996/1997, Victoria Hospital was committed to building a veterans' park ($0.5) and purchasing a magnetic resonance imaging (M.R.I) ($3.0).
[3]Information Technology cost estimates are based on the original I S. Strategic Plan Document which is currently being reviewed.
[4]The $4.0 cash surplus in 1995/1996 represents the achievement of the Board Mandated Savings Plan.
[5]Pending outcome of LACTHRC and merger feasibility.

Figure 1.14 *Five Year Financial Projection for Victoria Hospital Operations ($ millions)*

the goals of their functional department and the perceived goals of their clinical unit.

Often, the successful acquisition of the hospital's limited resources was based on the historical power base of the functional groupings rather than through justifiable requirements based on patients' needs or good business planning. Work processes which flowed horizontally across the functional groups were often disjointed and did not evolve effectively because of the vertical barriers built by the functional departments. Technology and better understanding of the horizontal nature of clinical processes afforded opportunities to re-engineer these procedures.

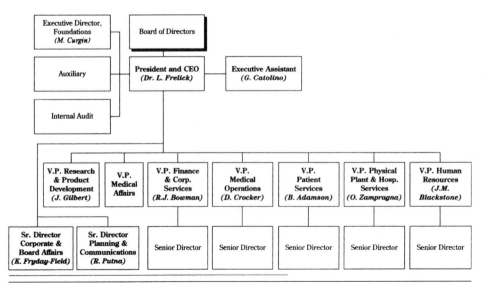

Figure 1.15 *Organizational Structure*

The degree of success afforded by this system varied. Sometimes a silo was inflexible, and resisted changes that it perceived would affect it negatively even if the overall effect for the hospital might be positive. For example, a silo could stall or prevent the implementation of a decision to move resources from one area to another, based on patient need. On the other hand, in some clinical units, groups of health professionals worked to develop methods and processes that allowed them to work as interdisciplinary teams. However, the success of these teams in achieving efficient and effective care delivery processes varied significantly.

Changing Care Delivery Models

One change in the delivery of health service was the movement toward following Patient Care Guidelines and Pathways, a series of research-based recommendations for the delivery of care to patients diagnosed with similar medical conditions. The guidelines were often supported by a plan of care that generally standardized the essential elements of care for approximately 90 per cent of patients in any one diagnostic category.

The development of a standard plan of care caused the clinicians, as a group, to examine every step of the care process and identify the value-added components. As a result, staff could dramatically reduce unnecessary variations in ordinary diagnostic tests and therapies.

Information Technologies

The use of on-line clinical information could result in reaching informed clinical decisions both for groups of patients and for individual patients. Victoria Hospital information technology had historically focused on administrative systems such as finance and payroll, rather than on clinical information such as providing lab information at the bedside or tracking patient statistics. However, the health care industry was rapidly moving to the provision of on-line co-ordination of clinical information.

Physicians

In the past, two main health professions existed to deliver the care—medicine and nursing. Physicians were highly trained in the necessary skills for performing diagnostics and prescribing treatment. Nurses had been developing increasing skills and a body of knowledge on delivering care to patients in a holistic sense. Historically, physicians were the gatekeepers to the system and were the overall planners and co-ordinators who determined the treatment and then designated the actual delivery of care to nurses or other professionals. Physicians traditionally had not been required to function as team players.

Six hundred physicians, who were essentially independent contractors in the health system, worked at Victoria. Physicians were usually affiliated with a hospital by contract and were governed by a medical advisory committee to the board of directors.

As Victoria was a teaching hospital, the affiliation of many of the physicians was through a formal contract with the University of Western Ontario, where they usually had teaching responsibilities. As well, they had the duty residents completing their practical experience. In addition, the university evaluated them for promotion through the system, placing a high weighting on their research publications. Hence, these physicians had dual loyalties to the university and the hospital.

Dr. Mike Lewen, past president of the medical staff, recently provided insight into the physician relationships. He indicated that:

In general, academic physicians are compelled to progress through the professional advancement system of the university. This requires peer reviewed research and publication. Academic physicians' allegiance is often greater to the university than to an individual hospital, including Victoria.

Most physicians do not hold any particular interest in the administrative activities and initiatives of the hospital. The announcement from the hospital that it is planning to redesign patient care delivery systems will be met with indifference or scepticism by physicians as to whether the hospital is capable of changing.

Many initiatives that particular interdisciplinary teams undertake are perceived by physicians to be thwarted by home department (functional department) decisions. Interdisciplinary teams should be able to work independently, within certain parameters, to achieve their goals.

Nurses and Other Professionals

The health care system responded to external demands with more innovation, new technologies, and a new group of applied health sciences professionals. Many of these people emerged from the nursing profession and acquired unique bodies of knowledge based on science and skill. The development of experts in many expanded fields led to pressure from patients, some of whom, at times, wished to access the health care system through professionals other than physicians. The Ministry of Health responded in January 1994 by implementing the Regulated Health Professions Act, which allowed 22 categories of qualified practitioners, such as midwives, chiropodists, audiologists, to perform various functions once only provided by a physician. These developments were challenging the traditional hierarchy of health care services.

Nurses and members of applied health professions were accustomed to performing as members of teams. An organizational change would result in the need to reevaluate and address how health care providers could work together to provide integrated and efficiently delivered care.

Jennifer Jones, director of nursing, indicated at a recent focus group that nurses were very interested in "where the hospital is going" in the future. She indicated that she was aware of the hospital's desire to move toward interdisciplinary teams. She had a number of comments and concerns about the situation, including:

Nurses have historically been the co-ordinators of inpatient care and we see this as something that is unique to their function. We are concerned that, in an interdisciplinary model, others may be given this role. It seems logical that the nurse managers who currently manage a nursing unit would, in future, become managers of interdisciplinary teams.

We are also concerned about the ability of nurses to maintain their nursing practice standards in an interdisciplinary environment. A strong affiliation with the department of nursing is perceived to be important to foster professional growth and development of nurses.

Personally, I am not at all sure that any kind of organization change is required. The hospital may be overreacting to the economic environment. The downsizing the hospital has done to date should be sufficient to address Victoria's financial problems.

❑ A VISION FOR REDESIGNING THE HOSPITAL

Dr. Frelick recognized that Victoria needed to respond to the challenges it was facing. During the fall of 1994, when he undertook an assessment of the pressures facing the hospital and the many strengths within the hospital, he engaged in significant consultation with senior management,

hospital staff, and the board of directors. In January 1995, Dr. Frelick, through a series of meetings, snared a vision for a newly designed hospital with these groups.

This new version was to provide a positive environment with effective results for patients, who would move through the various phases of care (prevention in the community, pre-admission, ambulatory, in-patient, etc.) in a seamless efficient fashion. Victoria would achieve this vision by empowering self-directed care teams to:

- develop care plans across the continuum of care;
- develop new work processes to streamline operations and reduce costs; and
- focus on delivering quality care directed at meeting patients' service needs.

The vision also included re-engineered hospital-wide administrative processes that would maximize the use of technology, thereby increasing hospital efficiency. In addition, Dr. Frelick envisioned new entrepreneurial initiatives that would create additional revenue streams as government funding decreased.

Strategies to Achieve the Vision

Many Ontario hospitals which faced similar situations were developing a variety of approaches for coping with increasing economical cutbacks. The most straightforward strategy was an upfront massive downsizing of the organization, i.e., a "slash and burn" strategy. Dr. Frelick believed that, although this method would produce immediate financial results, it was only a short term solution. He concluded that hospitals would have to undergo a fundamental change in how they delivered care, in conjunction with carefully planned restructuring. Therefore, he developed a plan which called for three fundamental business strategies to achieve the new vision.

The first strategy included bringing the organization structure into line with the way the hospital cared for patients. The goal here was to realign the organization with the primary production centres by developing highly capable interdisciplinary care teams which could meet the demands of their ever changing environments. The care teams would be clustered in groups forming "product-lines" (see Figure 1.16). The hospital would also have to build strong linkages

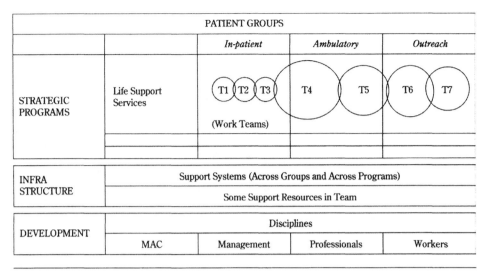

PATIENT GROUPS					
		In-patient	*Ambulatory*	*Outreach*	
STRATEGIC PROGRAMS	Life Support Services	T1 T2 T3 (Work Teams)	T4 T5	T6 T7	
INFRA STRUCTURE	Support Systems (Across Groups and Across Programs)				
	Some Support Resources in Team				
DEVELOPMENT	Disciplines				
	MAC	Management	Professionals	Workers	

Figure 1.16   General Redesign for Care Teams

and partnerships with other providers of services and supplies in the community. In its restructuring, Victoria would need to determine what work could best be done by others and then form strategic partnerships to achieve these efficiencies.

The second strategy involved the redesign of the "system of production" to bring work processes into line with current technology, expected patient outcomes, patient needs and resource constraints. For example, a project was launched to redesign the admitting process so that patients could go directly to the specific unit without going through an admitting department. The projected impact included significant dollar savings as well as improved patient/customer service.

The third strategy required the development of entrepreneurial strategies to support the vision. Opportunities for significant revenue generation through the provision of services that were no longer covered by provincial health insurance, through services which could be marketed abroad, and services for physicians and other health care practitioners affiliated with the hospital, must be devised.

The first step was to develop a few prototype interdisciplinary care teams. Support would be available in areas such as project planning and measurement development, and a corporate framework of targets would provide direction. These new teams, which could then assume self-direction

within those guidelines, would have the following goals:

- defining and clarifying targets to establish world class capability;
- developing a game plan to achieve the targets;
- planning for patient care, related education, and applied research;
- determining what resources are required to achieve their goals;
- developing patient care strategies with good outcomes at reasonable case costs; and
- developing measurement systems to determine progress.

Once the initial methodology for care team design had been tested and enhanced, other related or linked care teams would be mandated to launch the change process. Gradually, groups of care teams would be linked together to form product lines; for example, cardiovascular services, children's services or cancer services.

Careful evaluation of the infrastructure required to support the care teams would also be necessary. Some of the support systems such as porters and cleaners might be decentralized and assigned directly to each care team or program, while other services such as information systems would remain centralized. Health professional disciplines would be assigned to the care teams but would remain grouped together in some form to address certain discipline-specific concerns.

❏ IMPLEMENTATION — THE ORGANIZATION'S RESPONSE

Financial Targets

Task forces were established to design and implement the specific initiatives. Each was led by a number of senior management or a member of the senior medical staff, and staffed primarily with middle managers and some physicians, all of whom were conducting their regular duties in addition to the new challenges of the redesign initiative.

The task forces were to achieve several goals. Their initial financial targets, based on economic forecasts, had been developed to ensure that the savings achieved would be sufficient to meet the annual economic shortfalls projected to 1999 (see Figure 1.17). They also had qualitative targets, such as reduced waiting time for patients in the admitting process. The CEO asked them to validate the assigned initial targets, to develop specific implementation strategies, and to integrate their redesign plans with other key initiatives, including consolidation of operations on one site.

Board of Director's Response

Early in the process Dr. Frelick had presented the goals, the strategy for implementation, and the financial targets to the board of directors for information and support. He spent significant time discussing the difference between a "slash and burn" type of downsizing and the participative approach he had chosen. The board shared initial enthusiasm for the redesign initiative by indicating support for the values, the vision and the strategy.

However, during subsequent meetings, debate arose regarding whether or not the plan put forward by the CEO could actually meet the economic challenge facing the hospital. Friction began to develop at the board table. Some members indicated that they did not really understand the redesign initiative and were concerned that the approach might take too long to deliver the required cost savings. On the other hand, others believed that if appropriate care were taken, the organization could achieve more fundamental change through redesigning patient care teams than by "slash and burn" downsizing. Rather than give the CEO the mandate to achieve results, the board members

Overall Dollars Required (Total Target)	1995/1996 $8.3 M	1996/1997 $18.9 M	1997/1998 $16.7 M	1998/1999 $16.5 M
Task Force Cost Cutting Targets				
Overhead/Fixed Costs (Operations Benchmarking Task Force)	(2.0 M)	(1.0 M)	(1.0 M)	—
Clinical Resource Management (Optimizing Case Mix and Length of Stay)	(3.8 M)	(5.5 M)	—	—
Leadership Design (Organizational Structure)	(0.5 M)	(0.5 M)	—	—
Patient Care Innovation (Self-directed Teams and Major Clinical Processes, *e.g.*, Care Paths, Admitting) Consolidation (to one campus)	—	(6.0 M) —	(8.0 M) To Be Determined	— To Be Determined
Task Force on Revenue Enhancement (Ambulatory Care, Preferred Accommodation, Land leases)	2.0 M	4.0 M	10.0 M	10.0 M
TOTAL IMPACT (Improved by)	$8.3 M	$17.0 M	To Be Finalized	To Be Finalized

Source: Victoria Hospital (CEO's office)

Figure 1.17   Financial Target

sought more detailed financial projections to ensure the feasibility of the project Eventually, they asked the CEO to provide a detailed implementation plan prior the task forces' presentation of their unit based strategies.

Tension continued to grow at the board level. Members debated whether consolidating the hospital from two sites to one site was more important than the redesign initiative. At times, it was unclear whether some of the specific tensions were directed generally toward the administration and concerns about their capabilities to lead the organization through major change or toward internal conflicts among board members.

The Administration

From the beginning, the CEO had involved the vice presidents in his vision of building a new hospital organization and a new way of conducting business. He conducted a series of planning sessions with the senior team to seek their input and counsel regarding strategies for change. However, after several months of discussion, there remained varied amounts of "buy-in" from the senior team members. At this point, Dr. Frelick asked for the support and leadership of each team member. To use their skills and to ensure the active involvement of each individual in sponsoring the initiative, he placed each vice president in charge of a major aspect of the plan.

Once the initiatives had been launched, the vice presidents worked at different levels of enthusiasm and speed to lead their part of the change. In some cases, commitment was unclear and other priorities occupied their attention. Some thought that consolidation should be the single agenda for change; others appeared to avoid change by moving their task forces into endless cycles of analysis.

One of the significant aspects of the redesign involved breaking out of traditional silos and moving to an interdisciplinary team organization. Some members of senior management were hesitant to embrace this new design, as it required taking significant risks. A great deal of discussion took place, but designated leaders did not appear to rise above the traditional discipline tensions.

The External Community

The Ministry of Health continued to put direct and indirect pressure on the hospitals in the region to come to terms with the apparent duplication and perceived waste in the system, and continued to press for system-wide change. The ministry withheld support for some of Victoria's specific change initiatives, such as specific program shifts in collaboration with other hospitals and consolidation to one site, on the basis it would not support changes at one hospital without a city-wide plan for change.

❏ THE PROBLEM

Dr. Frelick realized that he had a significant problem on his hands. He was firmly committed to his redesign vision. He believed that, although a downsizing strategy coupled with a single focus on consolidation to one campus might prove popular to some board members and staff, it would not serve Victoria Hospital's long-term needs. He needed to implement a plan for his vision and find a way to acquire a reasonable level of support from board members, vice presidents, physicians, professionals, and workers.

Understanding How Organizations View Change

❏ CHAPTER AT A GLANCE

Highlights of this chapter include the following:

1. The change management literature describes several important change models that are useful in guiding managers in implementing major change in organizations.

2. We introduce a typology of change that will enable us to classify change. This will provide a framework to help simplify the complex forces at work in change initiatives.

3. Theories of change are frameworks that describe how to initiate and implement meaningful change in firms. Lewin's Change Model provides a foundation and an excellent framework for analyzing a complex change initiative.

4. Nadler's Congruence Model is an organizational performance framework that views organizations as systems where optimal performance derives from congruence between the various organizational subsystems.

5. Kotter's Eight Stage Model provides a way of looking at the actual stages of the change process, which enables us to map our organizational system with the process of change itself.

6. Corporate performance has long been measured almost exclusively by financial accounting measures. The Balanced Scorecard proposes that the traditional financial accounting measures, with their emphasis on return on investment and payback periods, are incomplete and they should be augmented with data that reflects other criteria of performance.

7. The impact of globalization and technology on today's business environment requires that organizations become more flexible and responsive so that they can learn and adapt to change.

❏ VIGNETTE[1]

In late 2005, Intel announced a sharp departure from the company Andy Grove had built. Essentially, top management proposed to blow up Intel's brand, the fifth best-known in the world. Intel's new Chief Marketing Officer Eric B. Kim declared that Intel must "clear out the cobwebs" and kill off many Grove-era creations. Intel Inside? Dump it, he said. The Pentium brand? Stale. The widely recognized dropped "e" in Intel's corporate logo? A relic.

This moment signaled an historic shift for one of the world's most powerful technology companies. The iconic Intel would leave the Grove era behind and head into uncharted territory. Central to the effort will be the first new corporate logo in more than three decades and a $2.5 billion advertising and marketing blitz.

The changes go far deeper than the company's brand. Intel's current CEO, Paul S. Otellini, is tossing out the old model. Instead of remaining focused on PCs, he's pushing Intel to play a key technological role in a half-dozen fields, including consumer electronics, wireless communications, and health care. And rather than just microprocessors, he wants Intel to create all kinds of chips, as well as software, and then meld them together into what he calls "platforms." The idea is to power innovation from the living room to the emergency room. "This is the right thing for our company, and to some extent the industry," he says. "All of us want [technology] to be more powerful and to be simpler, to do stuff for us without us having to think about it."

Why the shift? Stark necessity. PC growth is slowing, even as cell phones and handheld devices compete for the *numero uno* spot in people's lives. Otellini must reinvent Intel—or face a future of creaky maturity.

Since Otellini took over as CEO in May 2005, he has reorganized the company top to bottom, putting most of its 98,000 employees into new jobs. He created business units for each product area, including mobility and digital health, and scattered the processor experts among them. He has also added 20,000 people in the past year. The result? Intel is poised to launch more new products than at any time in its history.

Intel's culture is changing, too. Under the charismatic Grove, who was CEO from 1987 to 1998 and then chairman until 2005, the company was a rough-and-tumble place. Grove's motto was "Only the paranoid survive," and managers frequently engaged in "constructive confrontation," which any outsider would call shouting. Engineers ruled the roost.

The shake-up hasn't helped company morale, though. Especially hard-hit were the engineering teams in California and Texas, which had been working on the Pentium 4 until Otellini canceled it. Some of the design specialists have quit for new jobs, often with AMD or TI.

Intel's transformation presents a daunting task, especially for a company that has never had much success outside the computer industry. Companies that have been good at transforming themselves, from Nissan and Apple to Texas Instruments, typically need a crisis to precipitate change, says management expert Jay R. Galbraith of Galbraith Associates. "Change is really hard when you're solidly on top," says Galbraith. "He'll have to bring in new people who have new skill sets."

❏ CHAPTER PERSPECTIVE

In the final analysis, if we really want to understand how organizations approach change, we need to comprehend how management decisions are aligned with strategy. This perspective will provide us with the window into the world of organizational change.

We will see that every organization has a unique *corporate culture* based on its assumptions, values, and beliefs of the world in which it resides. Cultures create acceptable and predictable behaviors within organizations so that employees do not need to continually reevaluate and negotiate what is expected; daily practice is understood. Corporate culture serves the firm's strategic goals and objectives by enabling it to be adaptive and flexible in responding to changing opportunities and threats.

The organization will also view change through the prism of its *structure*, which can include a traditional vertical hierarchy, a project-management/matrix structure, a functional or divisional design, or a product or process-oriented structure. Successful firms select structures that are compatible with the strategies and behaviors necessary to achieve the firm's goals.

We will see how relationships with a firm's stakeholders are a prerequisite of successful strategy implementation. Premier firms understand how to create and sustain high-quality stakeholder relationships, be it with customers, employees, shareholders, suppliers, the community in which they operate, even competitors.

Today's organizations need to be able to work cooperatively and collaboratively, both within work groups and across departments and functions. Therefore, team building and group dynamics are important management responsibilities. As we will learn in Chapter 7, corporate cultures either contribute to or take away from effective cooperation and collaboration, so managing the corporate culture is an effective way to encourage successful teamwork.

Thus, understanding how organizations view change ultimately focuses on those systems and processes that managers and leaders control, such as linking career development to career goals, aligning individual and organizational goals, open communication, focusing on core competencies, driving home strategy with performance measures, and total compensation programs.[2] Although it is not the intention of this text to elaborate each of these systems and processes in detail, we will introduce a managerial framework that will reveal how these and similar systems and processes fit into the organization as a whole, and how they impact one another as part of a larger system.

Using Change Models in Organizational Analysis

As illustrated in the section vignette, Intel's success in addressing its business realities and related transformation depends heavily on execution. The devil is in the details. These details reside in the process Intel or any company follows in managing change. Without a comprehensive roadmap or model for guiding the change process, organizational leaders may fall short in implementing their strategies for change.

The change management literature has a variety of change models that are useful in guiding managers in implementing major change in firms. These models instruct us in managing the change process. The change models we will look at are all grounded in theory and practice and are well accepted by both scholars and practitioners in the field.[3] We will examine Lewin's Change Model, Nadler's Congruence Model, Kotter's Eight-Stage Change Process, and the Balanced Scorecard. Each of these approaches is designed to provide us with unique perspectives on how organizations manage and view change.

The change models we examine share several features in common. Each model focuses on the leader's role in creating urgency for the change, and they all build upon the notion of the three basic stages of *unfreezing, movement,* and *refreezing*. The leader is further expected to design and communicate the vision for change, inspire followers to embrace the vision, measure the results, and institutionalize or anchor the changes in the culture. Each of our models depends upon managing the design features of the firm, including the resources, systems, and processes.

As we shall see, Lewin's Change Model is the foundation upon which many other models are built. All of the models include a healthy dose of creativity and innovativeness to foster the atmosphere of a "learning organization," where the culture of the firm encourages challenging assumptions and looking outside for new ideas and trends.

Before we turn to a review of the change models, let us first discuss several important imperatives related to change, a basic typology of change, and change agent management style.

❑ CLASSIFYING ORGANIZATIONAL CHANGE

Why should we care about managing organizational change? As a manager, leader, or organization member, it is important to understand several "imperatives" that influence organizational change. Let us explore these issues further.

Take a look around you. What have you seen in the worldwide business community during the last few years? Although there are many success stories, there are also numerous highly publicized collapses, including Enron, World Com, and other once-great firms that self-destructed because of the way top management led their organizations. Running organizations is a complex business, and the better we understand what to look out for, the better our chances to prosper as employees, managers, and leaders.

Enron's collapse, and the profound organizational control issues that it raised, have seriously impacted how organizations view their internal and external environments. Managers, boards of directors, and executive management rethought their management processes with an eye to assuring that the problems that the Enron's of the world created don't befall their firms. Price Waterhouse identified several "imperatives for change" in a post-Enron world, designed to help firms create the right cultures, structures, and politicized environments to achieve their business strategies but in an ethical, moral, way.[4]

First, there is a need for close and constant communication. Enron demonstrated that even the best educated, highly paid executive managers in the world can fall out of touch with what is taking place on the shop floor. A disturbing communications gap exists at many large organizations between executive managers and the average, technical employee.

It is imperative to communicate regularly and on the important, significant issues and topics. Internal communication should seek opportunities for dialogue, creating a strong connection between the firm's mission and the company's strategic threats and opportunities.

Next, it is essential that firms realign to meet stakeholder expectations. The Enron debacle has clearly impacted the ways in which executive management view key systems, processes, and activities. The organization may believe it has a firm grasp on stakeholder requirements, but if they haven't reexamined those needs since Enron, they need to do so soon.

Third, it is critical that all organizational members think and act strategically. Each department and function must deal with significant strategic business issues and understand the risks involved. Many departments and members think only tactically. By embedding departments strategically within the organization, it reflects management's perspectives regarding the value of each function and department.

When appropriately positioned, each department must resemble and behave like a strategic business unit within the firm. To accomplish, this requires a strategic foundation designed to

- Articulate the mission and role of each department, laying the groundwork for a fit with the organization's mission and strategy.

- Identify each department's primary stakeholders, starting with external customers and extending to internal relationships.

- Clarify organizational risk priorities

- Identify specific departmental activities that create value for all stakeholders

- Profile critical internal processes and practices, comparing them with worldwide best practices.

To accomplish these and other imperatives, we first introduce a typology of change that will enable us to categorize various types of change. We then examine some important analytical frameworks that will help you understand the component parts of the organizational change process and how they fit together. Our purpose is to help you extract from each of these frameworks what is most important to your specific situation, fashioning them into your personal approach to understanding change.

A Typology of Change: Categorizing Types of Change

Typologies or classification systems are often useful devices for helping us simplify complex concepts, and the field of organizational behavior relies heavily upon typological analysis. Change tends to be viewed from two perspectives: the first is the scope of the change, whether the change targets subsystems of the firm or the entire organization. We label change that focuses on individual components with the purpose of maintaining fit between the components as *incremental* change. Jick provides an example of incremental change, such as adapting reward systems to changing factor market conditions, because this is an incremental, system-enhancing change.[5]

Changes that affect the entire firm, including strategy, are labeled *strategic* changes. These strategic changes often entail smashing out of set congruence patterns and establishing a completely new configuration. Incremental changes maintain the current context of the current mix of organizational strategies and elements. They do not seek to address fundamental shifts in the focus of the business, changes of structure, culture change, or similar issues. Strategic change, however, does break that frame, although sometimes only bending it, but always creating something fundamentally new through system-wide changes.

The second perspective of change pertains to how change is positioned in relation to external events. Changes that are in response to events that have already occurred are known as *reactive* changes, while other changes are initiated in anticipation of future events; these are known as *anticipatory* changes. Figure 2.1 illustrates the four classes of change that arise through the intersection

	Incremental	*Strategic*
Anticipatory	Tuning	Reorientation
Reactive	Adaptation	Recreation

Figure 2.1   *Types of Organizational Change*

of the two main axes (Scope of Change versus Timing of Change).[6]

1. *Tuning*. Tuning refers to the incremental change that anticipates future developments. Its focus is on enhancing efficiency to meet anticipated changes, not in response to past problems.

2. *Adaptation*. Adaptation, like tuning, is incremental change, but it is made in response to past events; thus it is *reactive*. Some examples are competitive changes, demand for new products or services, introduction of new technologies, or other developments that require a response to stay competitive. These responses, however, may not require fundamental changes throughout the organization, only changes in certain parts of it.

3. *Reorientation*. This is a type of strategic change that involves fundamental realignment of the organization but has been made in anticipation of future trends; in other words, it is the result of future thinking but does not indicate a radical break with the past. It is focused on facilitating major change without a major frame-break with the existing organizational structure, culture, or politicized system. These changes are sometimes known as "framebending" changes.[7]

4. *Recreation*. This type of strategic change is brought about by external changes, often very serious ones that threaten the well being of the firm. As such, these external changes usually necessitate a drastic departure from past ways of doing things, including replacing top management, culture change, vision and values, and other major reactive changes. These are known as "framebreaking" changes.

It is also useful to view these changes in the context of their *intensity*. Intensity describes how severe the change is and how much traumatic shock is inflicted on the firm as a consequence of the change. It is intuitively logical that strategic changes would be more intense than incremental changes, which often don't even require fundamentally altering the organization's essential management processes. Reactive changes are experienced more intensely than anticipatory changes because they necessitate compressing a lot of activity into a shorter time frame without the luxury of preparing people for the shocks that are coming. We should also emphasize how much less room for error and correction exists in reactive change.

The intensity of different types of change is increased as we move from 1 to 4 below:

1. Incremental proactive change (tuning) — change made in anticipation of future events.

2. Incremental reactive change (adaptation) — change made in response to external events such as actions of competitors.

3. Strategic proactive change (reorientation) — change made with the luxury of time afforded by having anticipated the external events that will require a fundamental redirection of the organization.

4. Strategic reactive change (recreation) — change necessitated by external events that threaten the existence of the organization.

Departments within an organization make incremental changes; strategic changes require fundamental change and are implemented across the entire organization.

We next need to examine the final dimension on which organizational change can vary — *organizational complexity*. Organizational complexity denotes the size of the organization in terms of how many employees it has, and how many product lines and businesses are a part of the entire organization. Geographic dispersion is also an element of complexity. It is easier to implement change in a smaller organization with less programmatic and geographic dispersion than it is in large, multidimensional, global organizations. Types of change management vary along the two conceptual axes of *intensity of change* and *organizational complexity*. Low-intensity changes are easier than high intensity, or strategic changes, with the least difficult being those that are low in organizational complexity. The higher the levels of intensity and organizational complexity, the more difficult will be the change, with *recreations* being the highest risk, most traumatic type of change in our typology. Given the natural risk aversion of managers, it is normal to assume they would like to avoid these riskier and costlier types of change if possible; the key to doing so is anticipating future trends and initiating reorientations in anticipation of them.

Manager Style and Scale of Change

The manager style that a change agent would use during the change process can be categorized as either collaborative and consultative or directive and coercive. Figure 2.2 relates the types of manager styles that are used to accomplish the incremental or strategic change referred to in Figure 2.1. If employees are working together with management in a collaborative and consultative manner, we can expect that there will be both short and long-term gains to the organization because the team addresses issues and concerns and makes decisions in the best interest of the overall organization. When management determines that it is in the best interest of the organization to direct or coerce the change (for example, the organization must change quickly to survive), employees may not be allowed to participate in the decision-making process.

Four Distinct Categories of Projects

Organizations need to view strategic change as projects to help ensure that these initiatives are provided the appropriate time and attention. Four distinct categories of projects have been identified by Cicmil:[9]

1. Engineering
2. New product development
3. System development; and
4. Organizational change projects.

The *organizational change initiatives* generally are strategic in nature with three types of projects:

a. Process/system improvement or some other form of business process reengineering (BPR)

b. Product/service improvement or development, or various other quality initiatives; and

c. Employee/management development, education, training, and total quality management (TQM).

These projects have varied levels of ambiguity and complexity and the project manager/change agent needs competencies and skills necessary to negotiate, manage, and decrease uncertainty around objectives during project start-up and implementation.[10]

Figure 2.3 provides the success rates for different types of organizational change projects.[11] The measure of success can be categorized in the following manner:

• Overall success — satisfaction with change, stakeholder expectations are met

• Project management — project completed on time, on budget, with promised features

• Operations performance — cost reduction, productivity gain, product/service quality

• Enterprise performance — earnings, return on equity, operating profit, competitive edge.[12]

When evaluating success, more than one of the above measures should be used to determine what was accomplished. Organizations need to learn from the planning and implementation of each strategic change initiative so that the next change can be addressed in a more efficient and effective manner.

Manager Style of Change Management		
Collaborative and Consultative (work together)	PARTICIPATIVE EVOLUTION	COLLABORATIVE TRANSFORMATIONAL
Directive and Coercive (directed)	FORCED EVOLUTION	DICTATE TRANSFORMATIONAL
Scale of Change	**Incremental**	**Strategic**

Figure 2.2   Manager Style versus Scale of Change[8]

Type of change (description)	Number of projects	Success rate (%)
Strategy deployment (building or changing the capabilities of the organization)	562	58
Restructuring and downsizing (rearranging organizational units and/or the workforce)	4830	46
Technology change (implementation of large hardware/ software systems purchased from vendors)	1406	40
Mixed collection of change efforts	23	39
Total quality management driven (aimed at continuous improvement of organization's operations)	863	37
Mergers and acquisitions (ownership and the operations of two companies being integrated to form one organization)	395	33
Reengineering and process design (design of a new business process or the radical redesign of an existing process)	3442	30
Software development and installation (developing and installing software)	31,480	26
Business expansion (expanding a business through product development, new lines of business, and selling to new markets)	200	20
Culture change (changing the prevailing behavior patterns of employees)	225	19
All	43,426	33

Figure 2.3   *Success Rates for Different Types of Organizational Change*

❏ LEWIN'S CHANGE MODEL

One of the earliest and key contributions to organizational change is Kurt Lewin's three-step change model. While theories of planned change tend to focus on how to implement change in organizations, which are sometimes called **"theories of changing,"** they are frameworks that describe how to initiate and implement meaningful change in firms.[13] Lewin's framework serves as the foundation of planned change.

Lewin's change model conceived of change in terms of a modification of the forces that stabilize a system's behavior. In particular, he envisioned a dynamic where there are two sets of opposing forces—those that are focused on maintaining stability and the status quo and those militating for change. We can view particular sets of behavior at a moment in time through these two lenses. When we have a balance between these two opposing forces, we have what Lewin called a state of "quasi-stationary equilibrium." To alter that state, it is possible to decrease the forces that oppose the change while simultaneously increasing the forces for change, or some combination of the two. Think of the example of a work group that is stable because the group's behavioral norms (standards of behavior) are equivalent to a supervisor's pressures to produce at higher levels. In order to change that level, it could be increased by changing the group behavioral norms to encourage higher levels of performance or by increasing supervisory pressures to increase output. Lewin suggested that the path of least resistance, i.e., modifying those forces maintaining the status quo would produce less tension and resistance than would increasing the forces for change; thus, the former (encouraging performance) is a more effective change strategy than the latter (increasing supervisory pressure).

Lewin's basic change model of *unfreezing-→ changing/movement-→refreezing* is a framework that has been very influential in the field of change management over the last 50 years. The key to understanding this approach, at the individual level, is to see change as a profound psychological dynamic process.[14] This psychological process involves painful unlearning and difficult relearning as one cognitively attempts to restructure one's thoughts, perceptions, feelings, and attitudes. Lewin viewed these three steps as follows:

1. **Unfreezing.** This step usually involves reducing those forces maintaining the organization's behavior at its present level. Unfreezing is sometimes accomplished through a process of "psychological disconfirmation." By introducing information that shows discrepancies between behaviors desired by organization members and those behaviors currently exhibited, members can be motivated to engage in change activities.

2. **Changing/Moving.** This step shifts the behavior of the organization, department, or individual members to a new level. It involves intervening in the system to develop new behaviors, values, and attitudes through changes in organizational structures and processes.

3. **Refreezing.** This step stabilizes the organization at a new state of equilibrium. It is frequently accomplished through the use of supporting mechanisms that reinforce the new organizational state, such as organizational culture, norms, policies, and structures.

Lewin highlighted the observation that stability of human behavior was supported by a large "force field" of driving and restraining forces. If change was to occur, this force field had to be altered under dynamic psychological conditions because as soon as we add an additional driving force to change, a countervailing restraining force arises. These restraining forces are usually embedded in the personal psychological defenses or group norms in the culture or individual.

Take an example where a supervisory program teaches individual supervisors how to empower employees and then sends them back into an organization that supports only defensive, autocratic behavior. The point is that new behavior must be congruent with the rest of the behavior of the learner or it will create cognitive dissonance (psychological conflict) that may lead to the unlearning of the very thing one learned in the first place. Lewin's classic study was the attempt to change eating habits by using an educational program that taught housewives how to use meats such as liver and kidneys and then sent them back into the community in which the norms are that only poor folks who can't afford good meat would use such poor meat.[15] (Nota Bene: Lewin's sample was British housewives in postwar England in the late 1940s, hence the example.)

Lewin's change model has clear implications for *personal* change as well as *team-based* change. For group-based change management, it is appropriate to train the entire group in how their traditional norms support the old behavior. In this way, Lewin's basic model of change leads to an entire range of insights and new concepts that make change dynamics more comprehensible and manageable.

Applying Lewin's Change Model

At the end of the chapter, we include a case study and an article that help illustrate how to apply the concepts contained in Lewin's Change Model. The British Airways case details the transformation of its corporate culture from one of government ownership to one of the private ownership, forgoing its government subsidies for the push-and-pull of the competitive marketplace.

The authors of the case apply Lewin's Change Model to this transformation of BAs culture, beginning with an explication of how the three stages of the model, unfreezing — changing/movement — refreezing, look in the context of BAs transformation. In the first stage of *unfreezing*, we see the massive restructuring involved in reducing the workforce by almost half. Instead of decimating BAs performance, a year after the restructuring all their performance measurement indices were up, not down. The new organization had become more flexible, adaptive, and responsive to customer demands.

In the next stage, *changing/movement*, BAs change agents led the initiative in the new direction. This involved a series of new structures, processes, and behaviors that will be examined in our review of change models in a later section, and which include the major initiatives, "Managing People First" and "Leading the Service Business," both of which were programs that depended on individual participation and feedback throughout British Airways.

The last stage, *refreezing*, reveals how BAs leadership team anchored the changes in the culture through programs such as the "Open Learning" initiative and the "Top Flight Academies" program that helped executives and senior managers embrace the new culture. New performance management systems were created, and even cultural artifact such new uniforms, the corporate coat-of-arms, and slogans were introduced to reinforce a new perspective.

As we see through the case and the accompanying article, Lewin's Change Model provides an excellent framework for analyzing a complex change initiative, even one as comprehensive as a culture change effort.

Change Equation Formula

A useful tool for getting an initial impression of the forces impacting change in an organization, the Beckhard and Harris Change Equation Formula provides a good perspective on how to conceptualize the forces at work in Lewin's Change Model.[16]

The Change Equation holds that change will occur where

$$(D*V*F) > R,$$

where D = Dissatisfaction
V = Vision
F = First steps, or Plan, and
R = Resistance to change

Referring back to Lewin's "Force Field Analysis," D, V, and F are all "forces for change," while R represents the "forces against change." It provides a simple and straightforward perspective that reveals the possibilities and conditions at work in organizational change. Note that *all three components must be active to offset the forces against the change*, which is usually manifested as resistance to change from organizational members. The change program must address *dissatisfaction* with the present situation, a clear *vision* of the future and what is possible, and knowledge of the first *steps* (or Plan) toward reaching this vision.

If any one of the three is missing, the product of the equation will tend toward zero and the *resistance to change* will dominate.

We now turn to another useful model for understanding and managing change: Nadler's Congruence Model.

❏ NADLER'S CONGRUENCE MODEL

Where Lewin's change model provided us with a general framework and foundation for understanding organizational change, David Nadler and his colleagues developed a useful model that has at its core the concept of "organizational fit"(see Figure 2.4).[17] Nadler's Congruence Model is an organizational performance model that is built on the view that organizations are *systems* and that only if there is congruence between the various organizational subsystems can there be optimal performance. If Lewin's theories provide the theoretical underpinning of the field of change management, Nadler's model is a hands-on, how-to approach that will help you to diagnose the current state of your organization.

According to the organizational performance model, firms experience problems when they discover that their outcomes are different from those that they thought they had designed into their systems. In order to comprehend those problems, it is necessary to investigate the areas of congruence and incongruence among the system's subcomponents. In this view, real change is an integrated process that unfolds along a time continuum, and impacts every aspect of the organization. It is a dynamic, not static, model that necessitates constant revision of the elements of an overarching model driven by strategic objectives.

Nadler provides the example of Sun Microsystem's design of a "loosely coupled, tightly aligned" organization to reflect his model. Sun's formal structure was designed to encourage an independent, entrepreneurial, innovative culture, with a healthy dose of competition thrown in for good measure. This was consistent with Sun's corporate strategy. The physical infrastructure was designed to facilitate the shaping of this kind of culture; it fostered an antibureaucratic atmosphere with no assigned parking places, executive dining rooms, or other artefacts of status differentiation. The purpose was to

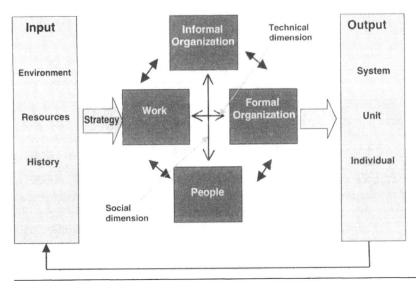

Figure 2.4   *The Congruence Model*

attract top engineers who couldn't waste time on hierarchical formal relationships when they were supposed to be creating breakthroughs for the company. The change in the formal and physical setting of Sun Microsystems helped shape the operating culture of the firm, which in turn attracted candidates with the right mix of skills, abilities, and knowledge to move the organization toward its goals.

The Three Basic Challenges Confronting Business Leaders

Nadler emphasized that there are three basic challenges confronting business leaders:[18]

1. ***Recognition:*** Can the firm anticipate changes that are going to happen in the business environment, or that may be happening already? If so, can the firm do so early enough to develop a response, before the organization is swamped by the reality of the new competitive environment?

2. ***Strategic choice:*** Given all the strategic choices that are available to the firm, can it make the correct ones that will enable the firm to prosper and survive?

3. ***Organizational redesign:*** How does management reshape the organizational components in order to implement the strategic imperatives?

Nadler astutely observes that, for each of these three critical challenges, there are three correlative potential failures:[19]

1. ***Failure of recognition:*** Big business is replete with examples of once-great competitors failing to recognize their customer's tastes and preferences. One example is Detroit's failure to recognize the American consumer's interest in smaller, fuel-efficient cars in the wake of the 1973 OPEC oil embargo. Ten years later the big three were fighting for their lives.

2. ***Make the wrong choice:*** What happens if you see what's coming down the track, lay out the optional choices in response, but pick the wrong one? In the 1980s, Apple Computer chose to maintain a closed operating system even though it recognized computers were moving into an open system world. Apple barely survived that flawed decision.

3. ***Failure of organizational redesign:*** In this scenario, the managers recognize the changes that are coming, make the correct strategic choices, but neglect to make the necessary changes to the structure, systems, processes, and skills/abilities of the workforce. It's not enough to have a well-formulated strategy; to implement that strategy correctly requires developing the appropriate organizational capabilities to make the strategy work.

Five Stages of Discontinuous Change

With the Congruence Model providing a conceptual framework, Nadler introduces a set of tools and techniques for making organizational changes.[20] These tools include *Diagnosis and Preparation, Implementation, and finally, Consolidating and Sustaining the Change.*

Stages 1 and 2: *Diagnosis and Preparation.*
Initiating change requires anticipating and preparing for change. This begins by keeping abreast of changes in the external environment that help the firm to anticipate change and more effectively position themselves to meet these changes. Having done this, the firm next looks at the strengths and weaknesses inside the firm to identify the internal adjustments that will need to be made in order to capitalize on the opportunities, or minimize the threats, arising in the external environment.

Having diagnosed the change, the next task is to plan for change, which entails developing a shared direction. The leadership team needs to develop a vision of change and communicate it to the rest of the organization. Consistency is the key here, coupled with frequency; "we more often need to be reminded than informed."

Stage 3: *Implementation of Change.*
The underlying theme of the Congruence Model is that the greater the congruence of the component parts of the system, the more effective the firm will be in achieving its strategic goals. These changes take place in the transformational subsystem of the organization, what we label the *Work, Formal Organization, Informal Organization, and People* subsystems. Within these transformation components, leaders are urged to execute change by

a. Building a new strategy
b. Redesigning the organizational hardware
c. Aligning strategy and culture, and
d. Finding the right people.

Stages 4 and 5: *Consolidating and Sustaining Change.*
In this final cluster of activities, the organization institutionalizes the changes. This occurs through a process of *assessment*, where the progress of the change is monitored and measured, to *refinement*, where the change agenda is refined to capitalize on successes and minimize failures. Finally, it is recommended that these changes should be *baked-in* to the formal structures and processes of the firm, so the once radical changes become accepted ways of doing things.

The Congruence Model makes a significant contribution to our understanding of organizational change by showing us the role of leadership in championing change and providing an operational model for managing the process.

❏ KOTTER'S PROCESS OF LEADING CHANGE

While the Congruence Model depicts the organization as an "open system" where changes in one part of the system impact other parts, Kotter introduced an eight-stage model as a way of looking at the actual stages of the change process itself. This enables us to map our organizational system (The Congruence Model) with *the process* of change.

In any change effort, managing the change process is clearly important. However, competent management is required to keep change efforts on track. But for most organizations, the much bigger challenge is leading change. Only leadership can blast through the many sources of corporate inertia and only leadership can motivate the actions needed to alter behavior in any significant way. Only leadership can get change to stick, by anchoring it in the very culture of the organization. But leadership cannot be confined to one larger-than-life individual who charms thousands into being obedient followers. Modern organizations are far too complex to be transformed by a single giant. The leadership effort must have support from many people who assist the leadership agenda within their sphere of activity.

Kotter's model was developed after studying over one hundred organizations. He was perplexed over the fact that the majority of change efforts failed, and he sought to identify the common mistakes in the change process (see Figure 2.5).[21] Kotter's eight-stage model offers a process to successfully manage change and avoid the common pitfalls that beset failed change programs. We can view his approach as a vision for the change process, one that calls attention to its key phases. The model provides two key lessons, first that the change process goes through a series of phases, each lasting a considerable period of time, and, second, that critical mistakes in any of the phases can have a devastating impact on the momentum of

1. **Not establishing a great enough sense of urgency.** Getting a transformation program started requires the aggressive cooperation of many individuals. Kotter claims that well over 50% of the companies fail in this first step.

2. **Not creating a powerful enough guiding coalition.** Large processes often start with one or two people, but in successful cases the leadership coalition continued to grow over time.

3. **Lacking a vision.** In unsuccessful cases, the leadership team failed to develop a picture of the future that is relatively easy to communicate and is attractive to insiders and others.

4. **Undercommunicating the vision by a factor of 10.** In unsuccessful projects, the leaders failed to use all existing channels and every opportunity to communicate the vision to their people.

5. **Not removing obstacles to the new vision.** All obstacles are not obvious from the beginning. The process of removing them is an ongoing one.

6. **Not systematically planning for and creating short-term wins.** Real transformation takes time and a renewal effort loses momentum if there are no short-term goals to meet and celebrate.

7. **Declaring victory too soon.** Premature victory celebrations kill momentum before the process is actually finished.

8. **Not anchoring changes in the corporation's culture.** Change is not permanent until it becomes "the way we do things around here." Until the group norms of the various units change and the organizational culture is altered, the changes are likely to be abandoned when the pressure for change is removed.

Figure 2.5   *Eight Errors Common to Organizational Change Efforts*

the change process. Kotter's model focuses on the strategic, not tactical, level of the change management process.

If we compare each of the eight stages in Kotter's eight-stage model (see Figure 2.6) with one of the eight fundamental errors summarized in Figure 2.5, we see that the model proposes a specific response to each of the errors.

The Eight-Stage Change Process[22]

The first four stages have to do with the practices associated with "thawing out" or "unfreezing the organization."

1. Establishing a greater sense of urgency.
   a. Getting people to examine seriously the competitive realities

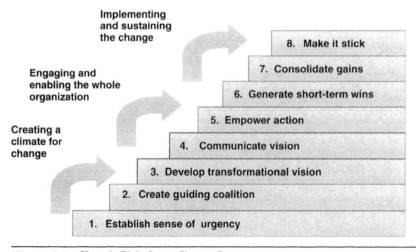

Implementing and sustaining the change

8. Make it stick

7. Consolidate gains

6. Generate short-term wins

Engaging and enabling the whole organization

5. Empower action

4. Communicate vision

Creating a climate for change

3. Develop transformational vision

2. Create guiding coalition

1. Establish sense of urgency

Figure 2.6   *Kotter's Eight-Stage Change Process*

b. Identifying crises, potential crises, or major opportunities

2. Creating the guiding coalition.
   a. Putting together a group with enough power to lead the change
   b. Getting the group to work together like a team

3. Developing a transformational vision and strategy.
   a. Creating a vision to help direct the change effort
   b. Developing strategies for achieving that vision

4. Communicating the change vision.
   a. Using every vehicle possible to constantly communicate the new vision and strategies
   b. Role modeling needed behavior by the guiding coalition

The next three stages introduce many new practices ("change/moving");

5. Empowering a broad base of people to take action.
   a. Getting rid of blockers
   b. Changing systems or structures that seriously undermine the change vision
   c. Encouraging risk taking and nontraditional ideas, activities, and actions

6. Generating short term wins.
   a. Planning for some visible performance improvements
   b. Creating those wins
   c. Visibly recognizing and rewarding people who made the wins possible

7. Consolidating gains and producing even more change.
   a. Using increased credibility to change all systems, structures, and policies that don't fit together and don't fit the transformation vision
   b. Hiring, promoting, and developing people who can implement the change vision
   c. Reinvigorating the process with new projects, themes, and change agents

Finally, the last stage is required to ground the changes in the corporate culture ("refreezing") and make them stick.

8. Institutionalizing new approaches in the culture.
   a. Creating better performance through customer and productivity oriented behavior,

more and better leadership, and more effective management
   b. Articulating the connections between new behaviors and firm success
   c. Developing means to ensure leadership development and succession

The Eight-Stage Model requires that all of the stages must be worked through in order, and completely, to successfully change. Skipping even a single step or getting too far ahead without a solid base almost always creates problems. People under pressure to show results will often skip the warm-up or defrosting activities (the first four steps). In this case you rarely establish a solid enough base on which to proceed. Failure to reinforce earlier stages as you move on results in the urgency dissipating, or the guiding coalition breaking up. Without the follow-through that takes place in the final step, you may never get to the finish line and make changes stick.

Kotter's Change Model is the most widely used model for change because it provides us with a framework and guidance; however, we need to go further into each stage to better understand how it can increase the probability of success for the strategic change initiative project. Figures 2.7 and 2.8 provide additional insight into important aspects of Kotter's Eight Stage Change Model, which we present following Lewin's unfreeze, move, and refreeze perspective.[23] Figure 2.7 indicates that organizations need to provide information to show busy managers the importance or urgency of the change; the coalition must have credibility to be taken seriously; the vision for the change effort must inspire employees; and effectively communicate the vision! Figure 2.8 shows that leadership starts with establishing a goal with employees; that short-term wins let organizational members know that the sacrifices are worth it; that whenever you let up before the job is done, critical momentum can be lost; and finally that once positive change happens, management must work to make it a part of the culture. It is important to note that all of Kotter's Stages need to be followed sequentially to most efficiently and effectively plan and implement strategic change.

❏ THE BALANCED SCORECARD

Corporate performance has long been measured by financial accounting measures, quite often to the

Stage	Sources of Complacency	Direct Response
1. *Establish a Sense of Urgency*	• The absence of a major and visible crisis • Too many visible resources • Low overall performance standards • Measurement of the wrong performance indexes	• Provide "visuals" of what will happen without the change • Sell the corporate jet; close the executive dining hall • Establish "stretch" goals for everybody in the organization • Reevaluate how the organization measures "success"
2. *Create a Guiding Coalition*	• The coalition needs key players, including board members and line managers • The coalition must have credibility, based on members' reputations, to be taken seriously	• The coalition needs the expertise and diversity necessary to make informed, intelligent decisions • The coalition must have proven leaders
3. *Develop a Vision and Strategy for the Specific Change*	• The change leader should actively elicit participation from all of the coalition members • The vision for the specific change effort must inspire organizational members	• This participation provides valuable input into the decision-making process, plus it gives the coalition members a sense of ownership in the plan • Six characteristics should be present in an effective vision: Imaginable, desirable, feasible, focused, flexible, and communicable
4. *Communicate the Change Vision and Strategic Plan*	**Suggestions for effectively communicating the vision:**	
	a. Simplicity—Employees will not be inspired by a vision they do not understand	**b.** Multiple forums and repetition—The vision should be communicated through training sessions, meetings, memos, press releases, the company's intranet, and so on
	c. Leadership by example—otherwise employees will not take the message seriously	**d.** Explanation of inconsistencies and give and take—to maintain an open, interactive organizational culture

Figure 2.7 *Key Points for Each of Kotter's Eight Stages: 1–4 Unfreeze*

exclusion of everything else. Two management scholars, Robert Kaplan and David Norton, proposed an approach to measuring firm performance: the Balanced Scorecard (BSC).[24] They proposed that the traditional financial accounting measures, with their emphasis on return on investment and payback periods, were incomplete and outdated in their attempts to accurately depict business performance.

The Balanced Scorecard, suggests that financial measures are important but they should be augmented with data that reflects other criteria of

5. *Empower Employees for Broad-Based Action*		
	Leadership starts with establishing a goal with the employee	Then the leader's remaining responsibility is to help clear the path so that the employees can accomplish the goal
6. *Generate Short-Term Wins*		
	Three characteristics of good short-term wins: it's visible, unambiguous, and clearly related to the change effort	Short-term wins let organizational members know that the sacrifices are worth it. These wins also "turn neutrals into supporters." It is important to build and maintain momentum for the change effort.
7. *Consolidate Gains and Produce More Change*		
	Whenever you let up before the job is done, critical momentum can be lost and regression may follow	The credibility of short-term wins can be used to push forward faster, tackling even more or bigger projects
8. *Anchor the New Change in the Culture*	Once positive change happens, management must work to make it part of the culture	The New organizational culture must be reinforced by the policies for recruiting, selecting, promoting, compensating, evaluating, and training

Figure 2.8 *Key Points for Each of Kotter's Eight Stages: 5–8 Change/Moving-→ Refreezing*

performance such as customer satisfaction, internal business processes, and the ability to foster the characteristics of a "learning organization" (which is the ability to learn and grow as a firm.). We now turn to reviewing the four key perspectives of the balanced scorecard.

The Four Perspectives of the BSC

1. Financial Perspective — Is the firm meeting the expectations of its shareholders?
2. Customer Perspective — is the firm satisfying, or more, its customers?
3. Internal process perspective — is the firm doing *the right things* and *doing them right?*

4. Learning and growth perspective — is the firm prepared for the future?

Executives and managers in charge of the change process would be well advised to ask themselves these four questions, and to work through these four processes. These perspectives can be extended from the corporate level to specific work units, and even individual projects can be assessed using this methodology.

Why is the balanced scorecard important for change managers? Primarily because it points out that financial measurements are a necessary-but-not-sufficient condition of performance. Financial measurements do not fully account for intangible assets or the knowledge, skills, and abilities of the workforce, including leadership. If you are in a knowledge-based industry, financial perspectives are insufficient to adequately measure everything that needs to be measured.

By using the balanced scorecard, each functional area (engineering, marketing, etc.) within an organization defines how it will utilize its resources to help support the strategic change initiative and therefore becomes accountable for those actions. Each functional area must understand the goals and objectives of the strategic change initiative, how they can effectively support those goals and objectives, and do their part to support the strategic change objective.

The balanced scorecard doesn't dispense with financial measurements; it supplements them with other indicators that are considered to be predictors of future financial performance. The BSC is sometimes depicted metaphorically as a pilot in an airplane viewing his or her instrument panel. The pilot requires all of the instruments to land the plane. Furthermore, there is considerable research indicating that the nonfinancial BSC indicators accurately predict financial performance, i.e., that they are leading indicators predicting the lagging indicator of financial performance.

There is a common cliché in business, "what is measured is performed." That is one of the reasons why too great an emphasis on financial indicators can be a problem; they can promote a preoccupation with short-term results. As we know, managers have a strong incentive to pursue short-term financial results if their compensation is weighted with bonuses and stock options tied to periodic revenue and income figures. A balanced scorecard spreads

the focus around, so that financial indicators do not become disproportionately significant. They are seen in the context of customer satisfaction, learning, and internal processes.

Balanced Scorecard Project examples of how different parts of the organization can help meet objectives of the strategic change initiative are shown in Figure 2.9.[25] An organization can grow revenues with a new pricing program and build customer loyalty with a frequent purchase program. Please note that the projects listed help support the four perspectives of the Balanced Scorecard and recognize the importance of all areas of the organization doing their part to support the change!

Why Adopt a Performance Measurement system?

According to experts at the Balanced Scorecard Institute, there are ten reasons for a Performance Measurement system:[26]

1. It improves the bottom line by reducing process costs and improving productivity and mission effectiveness.

2. A performance measurement system such as the Balanced Scorecard allows an organization to align its strategic activities to the strategic plan. It permits — often for the first time — real deployment and implementation of the strategy on a continuous basis. With it, an organization can get feedback needed to guide the planning efforts. Without it, an organization is "flying blind."

Perspective	Objectives	Project Initiatives
FINANCIAL	Grow revenue Increase asset utilization	New pricing programs Benchmarking and Just-in-Time Mfg.
CUSTOMER	Increase partnering Build loyalty	Partner program Frequent purchase program
INTERNAL PROCESS	Develop customer information Reduce downtime	IT Tools and Training Maintenance overhaul and ISO 9002
EMPLOYEE LEARNING AND GROWTH	Develop core competencies Increase empowerment	Global communications Decision training

Figure 2.9 *Balanced Scorecard Project Level Example*

3. Measurement of process efficiency provides a rational basis for selecting what business process improvements to make first.

4. It allows managers to identify best practices in an organization and expand their usage elsewhere.

5. The visibility provided by a measurement system supports better and faster budget decisions and control of processes in the organization. This means it can reduce risk.

6. Visibility provides accountability and incentives based on real data, not anecdotes and subjective judgments. This serves as a basis for reinforcement and the motivation that comes from competition.

7. It permits benchmarking of process performance against outside organizations.

8. Collection of process cost data for many past projects allows us to learn how to estimate costs more accurately for future projects.

9. For many organizations, including federal agencies, it's the law. The Government Performance and Results Act of 1993 requires a strategic plan, and a method of measuring the performance of strategic initiatives.

10. It can raise your firm's TQM quotient, which can serve to increase its long-term chances of survival.

Implementing the BSC

As we learned earlier, transformational change begins at the top of the organization, with the leader taking three discrete actions: (1) establishing a sense of urgency, (2) creating the guiding coalition, and (3) developing and communicating a vision and strategy. These steps suggest that the leaders of successful companies utilizing the Balanced Scorecard follow this approach. Many companies adopt the Balanced Scorecard because they are experiencing difficulties, including the threat of failure and job loss. These kinds of dangers can create the receptivity for change. But we shouldn't limit the use of the Balanced Scorecard to desperate times; thoughtful executives think proactively, and make adjustments in anticipation of possible future changes, ensuring that the firm doesn't become complacent. They use the scorecard, then, to communicate their vision for a more vibrant future, one that is better than the present.

There are four areas that we need to pay attention to when learning how to implement the BSC:[27]

1. Make the strategy explicit
2. Choose the measures
3. Define and refine
4. Deal with people.

This may seem easy, but it's not. It is important to realize that organizations are similar on many dimensions but dissimilar on others, i.e., we can view them as related but distinct entities.

In order to successfully implement the BSC, one must assess how the organization stacks up on six dimensions or issues: *strategy map, dialogue, roles, interfaces, incentives, and IT support.*[28]

In creating a *strategy map*, Olve et al. note that one of their clients who was using the BSC stated that "The balanced scorecard is a follow-up system . . . I would like to see more effects of it, to see how the different parts affect each other."[29] The authors opined that the employee who stated this opinion saw the BSC as a multidimensional tool, rather than merely the unidimensional concept that some others might see. In other words, the BSC is not just a "reporting tool," it is a full-blown management concept, incorporating planning, organizing, conducting, and controlling.

As Olve et al. suggest, "the most important benefit of the scorecard is its use in facilitating communication about strategy, not just at the top level, but throughout the organization. In order to achieve this, the departure point for any scorecard project should be strategy visualization."[30]

Thus, the first issue in preparing to implement a BSC should be strategy visualization. Each organizational member needs to determine how *strategy maps* can be used, and how they coexist with existing strategies.

We use the concept of "dialogues" to envision the scorecard as a communication tool. Can you envision using the BSC scorecard as a strategic tool to communicate goals and initiatives? We can use "*dialogues*" to.[31]

1. Discuss the strategy map
2. Validate the conjectured links
3. Set targets together
4. Analyze results
5. Use outcome metrics to spur action

As we will see in our analysis of British Airways in the chapter reading, managers use the scorecards each month to measure performance and as a strategic tool to facilitate communicating strategic initiatives and long-term goals.

Most change efforts have a change agent who "owns" the change initiative. How do you assign *roles* to stakeholders in order to implement the BSC. There is a concept in the organizational behavior literature known as "equifinality." What equifinality means is that "there is no one-correct way," i.e., there are usually several correct approaches to solving a given problem. There is no single right way for roles to be assigned as well. The most important thing to remember is that a *change agent* needs to be responsible for casting the firm members to play their assigned roles in the BSC implementation process.

In is important to have "*interfaces*" between the various scorecards in the organization. Two ways of ascertaining how to divide work up in an organization are to examine its level of **differentiation and integration.** Work is divided by formal structures into functions (accounting, finance, marketing, etc.), or by product or service (Cadillac, Buick, Chevrolet), or by a combination of the two (using a matrix structure). **Differentiation** refers to the degree of similarity or difference represented by the design of the work-units or subunits of the firm. Reflecting the major differences in design in a highly differentiated organization, we see that some are highly formalized with numerous policies, rules, and procedures, while others are more organic, flexible, and informal.[32]

The way an organization coordinates the work across work-units is called **integration**, which requires paying attention to the "interfaces" mentioned above. Integration/interfaces can be achieved in diverse ways, further reflecting the principle of equifinality mentioned above, i.e., there are many 'right' ways to achieve integration in a firm. We can use plans and schedules, budgets, assigning roles such as project managers or change champions, or cross-functional workgroups and teams. The more uncertainty there is in an environment, the more important is integration. Also, the higher the level of differentiation and the greater the interdependence among departments, the more integration is required.

Finally, it is important to consider whether your human resource systems support the implementation of the BSC in your firm. Specifically, do you provide the appropriate *incentives* to motivate members to care about the work involved in implementing a change initiative? Human resource systems influence the mix of skills, personalities, and behaviors of the firm's members. The knowledge, skills, and abilities required to implement the strategy are measured through the performance management process. Reward systems are the concluding part of the process by acknowledging performance and its contribution to goal accomplishment. Reward systems can be tied to BCS measurement systems so that rewards are allocated on the basis of achieving BSC results. However, we need to keep in mind Peter Drucker's representation of bonuses and stock options as "bribery" for short-term results. Drucker opines that knowledge workers should be "treated and managed as volunteers who work for a not-for-profit organization:

"The first thing such people want to know is what the company is trying to do and where it is going. Next they are interested in personal achievement and personal responsibility... Above all, they want respect..."[33]

The Balance Scorecard: Prospects for the Future

The balanced scorecard is a tool of modern management, one of several in our portfolio. The scorecards are not a "magic bullet" that guarantees success, anymore than TQM or Culture Change or any of the other concepts that can either help or hinder a firm's development, depending on how they are used. If the members don't perceive the scorecard to be meaningful to their jobs and daily lives, it will prove to be a wasted endeavor. Above all else, make sure the stakeholders participate in the process from beginning to end, and that they provide feedback about what's working, and what's not working, so that the process can be improved over time.

❏ GLOBALIZATION AND TECHNOLOGY REQUIRE FLEXIBLE AND ADAPTABLE ORGANIZATIONS

Many industries and organizations are moving to operate an a global scale. In the process of going global, organizations are transformed in terms of their strategies, operations, management, and marketing, as well as their human and material resources and services. In the process of becoming more global, organizations are forced to reengineer, redesign, and reevaluate their systems, processes, procedures, and products, as well as their financial and human resources, services, and public relations.[34]

Global Expansion and Technology

Globalization is revolutionizing our world. It has provided the globe with the possibility of greater prosperity and greater social justice. However, like all revolutions, the globalization processes will take some time to develop. Innovations in technology and global communications impact organizations, industries, and governments everywhere. They provide ready access to knowledge, products, and services worldwide. As a result there are new levels of freedom and exchange, especially with the development of the Internet and Web sites.[35]

Information Technology (IT) is a powerful tool for spreading globalization. Both science and business depend on the rapid and open flow of information, facilitated by new, cheaper hardware and software.[36] So when organizations are looking to change, they must consider how this powerful tool can assist them in becoming more competitive in a global business environment. As we will discuss in Chapter 3, when organizations evaluate the four

dimensions of change, technology is an important vehicle to help them meet their goals and objectives.

Organizations Need to Be More Organic Not Mechanistic

Over the last 10–15 years, organizations have been required to deal with more strategic change than they have in the past. Therefore, it is necessary for organizations to reevaluate how they operate to better address change. One framework for analysis and evaluation is organizational structure and how one part of an organization relates to the others. For many years, organizations have operated with *mechanistic* characteristics; central control functions, vertical communication channels, and high formalization and task definitions. With a need to learn and adapt to change and be more flexible in getting things done, organizations need to move more toward *organic* characteristics, where the organizational structure is more like a network, where communications is more lateral and where task definitions are more fluid and flexible.

Figure 2.10 relates characteristics of both a mechanistic and organic organization. The organic organization focuses on teamwork, employee empowerment, and verbal communications; all focused on issues and concerns and getting the job done! From another perspective, where the mechanistic features task-centered approaches to training, the organic features more on the development of the individual; working on a strategic

MECHANISTIC	*ORGANIC*
• *Individual specialization*: Employees work separately and specialize in one task	• *Joint specialization*: Employees work together and coordinate tasks
• *Simple integrating mechanisms*: Hierarchy of authority well defined	• *Complex integrating mechanisms*: Task forces and teams are primary integrating mechanisms
• *Centralization*: Decision making kept as high as possible. Most communication is vertical.	• *Decentralization*: Authority to control tasks is delegated. Most communications is lateral
• *Standardization*: Extensive use made of rules and standard operating procedures	• *Mutual Adjustment*: Face-to-face contact for coordination. Work process tends to be unpredictable
• Much written communication	• Much verbal communication
• Organization is a network of positions, corresponding to tasks. Typically each person corresponds to one task	• Organization is network of persons or teams. People work in different capacities simultaneously and over time

Figure 2.10   Organic versus Mechanistic Organizations[37]

MANAGEMENT OF CHANGE
- The organization will spend another 6 months to a year with the "eye off the ball."
- There is a lack of change/implementation expertise and skills.
- The executive management team tends to get "bored with the detail" quickly and therefore may lose interest and impetus and let both the transition and the transformation peter out.

COMMUNICATIONS
- Staff may see this as "yet another restructure" not tackling the real problems, and therefore becoming demotivated.

PEOPLE
- We need to ensure the best people possible for each job. We need to ensure that we keep the people we want to keep.

MANAGEMENT OF SYNERGIES
- Loss of knowledge—we need to capture and transfer knowledge of, for example, strategy formulation and implementation.
- We need to ensure best practice in one part of the company is transferred across the company.

ROLES, RESPONSIBILITIES, AND INTERDEPENDENCIES
- We need to ensure those in the center are motivated and their performance measured.
- We need to establish levers other than the policeman role and the threat of regulators, and so on.

Figure 2.11 *Risks Inherent to Managing Change*[38]

change initiative provides employees a professional development opportunity. What organizations learn when going through the change process must be applied to the next change!

By being aware of what may occur during change, organizations, groups, and individuals can better deal with the uncertainty of change. Figure 2.11 provides a list of inherent risks when managing change. As we discussed in Chapter 1, there is a lack of change management competencies and skills in organizations. In addition, staff may view the change as "yet another restructure" and not tackling the real problem. Finally, organizations need to ensure that they keep the right people, those that can help the change evolve. If we are aware of risks inherent to change, we can deal with them in an orderly manner and move on to the next phase of change.

❑ **READING AND CASE**

We explore the application of the chapter concepts through the British Airways case, which discusses a large-scale transformational change that took place at BA. These ideas will be reinforced through our reading on "Creating Successful Organizational Change." Together, the reading and case provide us with alternative perspectives on how organizations view change.

Reading

2-1 Goodstein, L., Burke, W. 1991 **Creating Successful Organization Change**, *Organizational Dynamics*, Spring, 1991.

Focus: This case discusses the challenges in executing a successful organizational change and includes the strategies employed by British Airways, the models and methods of organizational change, and Lewin's Change Model.

Questions

1. According to Lewin, the first step to achieving lasting organizational change is to deal with resistance to change by unblocking the present system, or *unfreezing* the system. How is this step reflected in the British Airways case?

2. The second stage of Lewin's change model is *change/movement*, or developing dynamic energy toward a new state. In the context of the British Airways case, what are some of the structures, systems, processes, and skills and abilities of the workforce that come into play in the *movement* stage?

3. The third and final stage of Lewin's model is the *refreezing* stage, where the changes are anchored in the organization. Again drawing on our British Airways case, how did BA accomplish the goal of institutionalizing the changes and anchoring them in the culture?

4. What are the advantages and disadvantages of using a single model such as Lewin's Change Model to analyze the current state of an organization?

Linkage to Chapter

1. Application of social psychology principles to change management.

2. Provides multidimensional perspective on change management, demonstrating the need to focus at all levels (individual — group — organizational) and on structures, systems, processes.

3. Provides empirical support for Lewin's Change Model; takes it out of the realm of just theory and puts it into the realm of practice too.

4. Provides a basis for a longitudinal analysis of BA; instructor can provide opportunities for follow up, i.e., how is BA doing today, and so on.

Case

2-1 **Changing the Culture at British Airways,** 1993, Leahey & Kotter, Case 9-491-009.

Focus: The BA case introduces us to how to judge the success of a change effort. This is a crucial question for change managers. Of course, the answer depends upon the criteria originally set for the change — levels of customer satisfaction or revenue growth, or cost savings. It is pretty clear the case, for example, that BAs progress from 1983 to 1990 constituted a successful change: satisfaction, revenue, productivity, and profits all increased, and the airline became a model for the industry.

Students should follow up on the case by researching BAs subsequent competitive pro-

blems. Although BAs change effort was successful, the organization slid back into competitive problems a few years later the question becomes, "Because the success of that change did not last, must we now judge the change to be unsuccessful in retrospect?"

Questions

1. What was life like at the "old" BA? What was difficult about making changes? (You may wish to focus on topics such as the characteristics of the culture, the need for change, what type of change was needed, and the barriers to change.)

2. What were the critical factors in the successful transformation? (You may wish to consider factors such as their vision, what they wanted to become, and how they transformed themselves, such as key steps and sequences, risks, or things you might have done differently.)

Linkage to the Chapter

1. The BA case links directly to Lewin's Change Model via the Goodstein and Burke article.

❏ ENDNOTES

1. Adapted from Edwards, C. (2006, January 9). Inside Intel. *BusinessWeek Online*. Retrieved February 27, 2007, from http://www.businessweek.com/print/magazine/content/06_02/b3966001.htm?chan=gl. Hesseldahl, A. (2006, September 6). Intel Digs Out from a Pile of Chips. *BusinessWeek Online*. Retrieved February 27, 2007, from http://www.businessweek.com/print/technology/content/sep2006/tc20060906_613217.htm.

2. Simonson, P. (1997). Promoting a Development Culture in Your Organization. Davies-Black Pub.

3. Mento, A. J., Jones, R. M., & Dirndorfer, W. (2002). A change management process: grounded in both theory and practice. *Journal of Change Management*, Vol. 3, No. 1, pp. 45–59.

4. Price-Waterhouse (1997). *CFO: Architect of the Corporation's Future*. Price-Waterhouse Coopers Financial & Cost Management Team. John Wiley & Sons, 1997.

5. Jick, T., & Peiperl, M. (2002). *Managing Change*, 2nd edn. McGraw-Hill Custom Publishing.

6. Jick (2002), op. cit., pp. 206–08.

7. Ibid. p. 207.

8. Adapted from Dunphy, D., & Stacy, D. (1993). The strategic management of corporate change, *Human Relations*, Vol. 46, No. 8, pp. 905–921.

9. Cicmil, S. (1998, March–April). Implementing organizational change projects: impediments and gaps. *Strategic Change,* pp. 119–129.

10. Ibid, p. 122.

11. Smith, M. E. (2002). Success rated for different types of organizational change. *Performance Improvement,* Vol. 41, No. 1, p. 27.

12. Ibid.

13. Cummings, T. G., & Worley, C. G. (2005). *Organization Development and Change,* South-Western Press, p. 22.

14. Schein, E. (1990). Kurt Lewin's change theory in the field and in the classroom: notes toward a model of managed learning, Occasional paper, MIT Sloan School of Management. See http://www.solonline.org/res/wp/10006.html

15. Schein, E. (1987). *Process Consultation,* Vol II. Wokingham, Addison Wesley.

16. Beckhard, R., & Harris, R. (1987). *Organizational Transitions: Managing Complex Change.* 2nd edn. Reading, MA: AddisonWesley.

17. Nadler, D. A. (1998). *Champions of Change.* San Francisco: Jossey-Bass, p. 41.

18. Nadler (1998), op. cit., p. 74.

19. Nadler (1998), op. cit., pp. 74–75.

20. Nadler (1998), op. cit., pp. 75–82.

21. Kotter, J. P. (1996). *Leading Change.* Boston: Harvard Business School Press, p. 16.

22. Ibid.

23. Beitler, M. A. (2006). *Strategic Organizational Change.* 2nd edn. Greensboro, NC: Practitioner Press International, pp. 39–48.

24. Kaplan, R., & Norton, D. (2001). *The Strategy Focused Organization.* Boston: HBS Press.

25. Niven, P. R. (2006). *Balanced Scorecard Step-By-Step: Maximizing Performance and Maintaining Results.* Hoboken, NJ: John Wiley & Sons, p. 191.

26. Arveson, P. (1998). Top ten reasons for a performance measurement system. *Balanced Scorecard Institute.* Retrieved March 2, 2007, from http://www.balancedscorecard.org/appl/top_ten.html.

27. Olve, N. G., Petri, C. J., Roy, J., & Roy, S. (2004, May/June). Twelve years later: understanding and realizing the value of balanced scorecards. *Ivey Business Journal Online.* Retrieved March 2, 2007, from http://www.iveybusinessjournal.com/view_article.asp?intArticle_ID=487, p. 1.

28. Ibid, pp. 2–7.

29. Olve (2004), op. cit., p. 2.

30. Olve (2004), op. cit., p. 2.

31. Olve (2004), op. cit. p. 3.

32. Cummings (2005), op. cit.

33. Olve (2004), op. cit., p. 6.

34. Harris, P. R. (2002). European Challenge: Developing Global Organizations. European Business Review, Vol. 14, No. 6, p. 418.

35. Ibid, p. 422.

36. Ibid, p. 418.

37. Organic vs Mechanistic Structures (n.d.). Retrieved March 2, 2007, from http://www.analytictech.com/mb021/organic_vs_mechanistic_structure.htm?userid=Givesmart&userip=76.100.63.15&useragent=Mozilla%2f4.0+(compatible%3b+MSIE+7.0%3b+Windows+NT+6.0%3b+SLCC1%3b+.NET+CLR+2.0.50727%3b+Media+Center+PC+5.0%3b+.NET+CLR+3.0.04506)

38. Extracted from Cameron, E., & Green, M. (2004). Making Sense of Change Management. London: Kogan Press, p. 176.

Reading 2-1

Creating Successful Organization Change

LEONARD D. GOODSTEIN
W. WARNER BURKE

Even with its survival at stake, getting an organization to change itself is no easy task. Here's why and how to do so, replete with examples from such a change successfully made by British Airlines.

BUFFETED AT HOME AND abroad by foreign competition that appears to produce higher-quality goods at lower prices, corporate America has now largely forsaken (at least publicly and momentarily) the traditional analogy of the organization as a machine and its organizational members as parts designed to work effectively and efficiently. Instead, many American corporations are accepting the "New Age" view of organizations as "a nested set of open, living systems and subsystems dependent upon the larger environment for survival."

What is surprising about this quote is not its viewpoint, which has been normative in the organizational psychology and behavioral literature for several decades, but its source: *The Wall Street Journal*. And it is typical to find such articles in virtually every issue of most recent American business publications: articles on corporate culture, on the changing attitudes of American workers, on the need for greater employee participation in managerial decision making, and on the place of employees as an important (if not the most important) asset of the corporation.

We are not suggesting that traditionally managed organizations are now extinct in America. Corporate executives, however, have definitely begun to recognize that managing the social psychology of the workplace is a critical element in the success of any organization.

❏ ORGANIZATIONAL CHANGE

Organizations tend to change primarily because of external pressure rather than an internal desire or need to change. Here are a few all-too-familiar examples of the kinds of environmental factors requiring organizations to change:

- A new competitor snares a significant portion of a firm's market share.
- An old customer is acquired by a giant conglomerate that dictates new sales arrangements.
- A new invention offers the possibility of changing the organization's existing production technology.

Other examples include (1) new government regulations on certain health-care financing programs and (2) economic and social conditions that create long-term changes in the availability of the labor force. The competent organization will be alert to early-warning signs of such external changes so that it can move promptly to make internal changes designed to keep it viable in the changing external world. Competent organizations are those that continue to change and to survive.

Thus, it is practically a cliche to state that change in organizations today is a way of life. And clearly it is not saying anything new to comment that executives and managers today are more finely attuned to change or that they

71

more frequently view their role as that of change agent.

But even though we often state the obvious and spout cliches about change, this does not mean that we have an in-depth understanding of what we are talking about. We are only beginning to understand the nature of change and how to manage the process involved, especially with respect to organizations. The purpose of this article is to improve our understanding of organizational change by providing both some conceptual clarification and a case example that illustrates many of the concepts involved.

It is possible to conceptualize organizational change in at least three ways — levels of organizational change, strategies of organizational change and, more specifically and not mutually exclusive of strategies, models and methods of organizational change. (First we will present the concepts, second the case example, and finally some implications.)

❑ LEVELS OF ORGANIZATIONAL CHANGE

A broad distinction can be made between (1) fundamental, large-scale change in the organization's strategy and culture — a transformation, refocus, reorientation, or "bending the frame," as David A. Nadler and Michael L. Tushman have referred to the process — and (2) fine-tuning, fixing problems, making adjustments, modifying procedures, etc.; that is, implementing modest changes that improve the organization's performance yet do not fundamentally change the organization. By far most organizational changes are designed not to transform the organization but to modify it in order to fix its problems.

In this article we address more directly the large-scale, fundamental type of organizational change. (A word of caution: "Organizational transformation," "frame bending," and other expressions indicating fundamental change do not imply wholesale, indiscriminate, and complete change. Thus when we refer to "fundamental change," we do not mean "in any and all respects.")

We are concerned with transformation when an organization faces the need to survive and must do things differently to continue to exist. After polio was licked, for example, the March of Dimes had to change its mission in order to survive as an organization. Although its mission changed from one of attacking polio to one of trying to eradicate birth defects, the organization's core technology — fund raising — remained the same.

A corporate example of transformation is seen in the transition of International Harvester to Navistar. Facing bankruptcy, the company downsized drastically, completely restructured its financial situation, and overhauled its corporate culture. Although many of the company's technologies were sold off, it too retained its core technology: producing trucks and engines. Once internally focused, its culture is now significantly market-oriented — and the company is operating far more efficiently than it did in the past.

Although organizational members experience such transformations as a complete change, they rarely if ever are. Theory would suggest that if fundamental — or even significant — change is to occur with any success, some characteristic(s) of the organization must *not* change. The theory to which we refer comes from the world of individual change: psychotherapy. For organizational transformation to be achieved — for the organization to survive and eventually prosper from such change — certain fundamentals need to be retained. Some examples: the organization's ultimate purpose, the previously mentioned core technology, and key people. The principle here is that for people to be able to deal with enormous and complex change — seeming chaos — they need to have *something* to hold on to that is stable.

Conceptually, then, we can distinguish between fundamentally changing the organization and fine-tuning it. This distinction — which is a matter of degree, not necessarily a dichotomy — is useful in determining strategies and methods to be used in the change effort. When fine-tuning, for example, we do not necessarily need to clarify for organizational members what will not change — but in the case of transformation, such clarity is required for its successful achievement.

❑ STRATEGIES OF ORGANIZATIONAL CHANGE

Organizational change can occur in more than one way. In a 1971 book, Harvey A. Hornstein and colleagues classified six ways: individual change strategies, technostructural strategies, data-based strategies, organization development, violent and coercive strategies, and nonviolent yet direct action strategies. All of these strategies have been used to attempt, if not actually bring about, organizational change. Senior management usually chooses any one or various combinations of the first four and manages them internally. The last two — violent, coercive strategies and nonviolent yet direct-action strategies — are more often than not initiated by actions outside the organization, and the organization's executives typically manage in a reactive mode.

In this article we address some combination of the first four strategies. Yet, as previously indicated, we are assuming that the overwhelming majority of organizational changes are motivated by *external* factors — that executives are responding to the organization's external environment. But even when it is not a reaction to some social movement, organizational change is nevertheless a *response* — a response to changes or anticipated changes in the marketplace, or changes in the way technology will affect the organization's products/services, or changes in the labor market, etc.

The assumption is based on the idea that an organization is a living, open system dependent on its environment for survival. Whether it is merely to survive or eventually to prosper, an organization must monitor its external environment and align itself with changes that occur or will occur in that environment. Practically speaking, the process of alignment requires the organization to change itself.

❏ MODELS AND METHODS OF ORGANIZATIONAL CHANGE

Models of change and methods of change are quite similar in concept and often overlap — so much so that it is not always clear which one is being discussed. Kurt Lewin's three-phase model of change — unfreeze, move (or change), refreeze — also suggests method. Organization development is based on an action-research model that is, at the same time, a method.

More on the model side is the relatively simple and straightforward framework provided by Richard Beckhard and Reuben T. Harris. They have suggested that large-scale, complex organizational change can be conceptualized as movement from a present state to a future state. But the most important phase is the in-between one that they label *transition state*. Organizational change, then, is a matter of (1) assessing the current organizational situation (present state), (2) determining the desired future (future state), and (3) both planning ways to reach that desired future and implementing the plans (transition state).

Methods of implementing the change — for example, a new organizational strategy — include the following:

- Setting up a comprehensive training program individual change strategy).

- Modifying the structure, individuals' jobs, and/or work procedures (technostructural strategy).

- Conducting a companywide survey to assess organizational culture for the purpose of using the data to pinpoint required changes (data-based strategy).

- Collecting information from organizational members about their views regarding what needs to be changed and acting accordingly (organization development strategy).

- Combining two, three, or all of these methods.

The case example we will discuss here illustrates organizational transformation in response to change initiated in the institution's external environment — excluding, however, the violent, coercive strategies and the nonviolent, direct ones. The example, which is analyzed according to Lewin's three-phase model/method, highlights the use of multiple methods for change — in fact, it presents in one form or another a specific method from each of the four other change strategies mentioned earlier.

❏ CASE EXAMPLE

In 1982 Margaret Thatcher's government in Great Britain decided to convert British Airways (BA) from government ownership to private ownership. BA had regularly required large subsidies from the government (almost $900 million in 1982), subsidies that the government felt it could not provide. Even more important, the Conservative government was ideologically opposed to the government's ownership of businesses — a matter they regarded as the appropriate province of private enterprise.

The growing deregulation of international air traffic was another important environmental change. Air fares were no longer fixed, and the resulting price wars placed BA at even greater risk of financial losses.

In order to be able to "privatize" — that is, sell BA shares on the London and New York Stock Exchanges — it was necessary to make BA profitable. The pressures to change thus exerted on BA by the external environment were broad and intense. And the internal organizational changes, driven by these external pressures, have been massive and widespread. They have transformed the BA culture from what BA managers described as "bureaucratic and militaristic" to one that is now described as "service-oriented and market-driven." The success of these efforts over a five-year period (1982–1987) is clearly depicted in the data presented in Figure 2.12.

This exhibit reflects BA's new mission in its new advertising slogan—"The World's Favorite Airline." Five years after the change effort began, BA had successfully moved from government ownership to private ownership, and both passenger and cargo revenues had dramatically increased, leading to a substantial increase in share price over the offering price, despite the market crash of October 1987. Indeed, in late 1987 BA acquired British Caledonian Airways, its chief domestic competitor. The steps through which this transformation was accomplished clearly fit Lewin's model of the change process.

❏ LEWIN'S CHANGE MODEL

According to the open-systems view, organizations — like living creatures — tend to be homeostatic, or continuously working to maintain a steady state.

This helps us understand why organizations require external impetus to initiate change and,

indeed, why that change will be resisted even when it is necessary.

Organizational change can occur at three levels — and, since the patterns of resistance to change are different for each, the patterns in each level require different change strategies and techniques. These levels involve:

1. Changing the *individuals* who work in the organization — that is, their skills, values, attitudes, and eventually behavior — but making sure that such individual behavioral change is always regarded as instrumental to organizational change.

2. Changing various organizational *structures and systems* — reward systems, reporting relationships, work design, and so on.

3. Directly changing the organizational *climate or interpersonal style* — how open people are with each other, how conflict is managed, how decisions are made, and so on.

According to Lewin, a pioneer in the field of social psychology of organizations, the first step of any change process is *to unfreeze* the present pattern of behavior as a way of managing resistance to change. Depending on the organizational level of change intended, such unfreezing might involve, on the individual level, selectively promoting or terminating employees; on the structural level, developing highly experiential training programs in such new organization designs as matrix management; or, on the climate level, providing data-based feedback on how employees feel about certain management practices. Whatever the level involved,

	1982	**1987**
Ownership	Government	Private
Profit (loss)	($900 million)	$435 million
Culture	Bureaucratic and militaristic	Service-oriented and market-driven
Passenger load factor	Decreasing	Increasing — up 16% in 1st quarter 1988
Cargo load	Stable	Increasing — up 41% in 1st quarter 1988
Share price	N/A	Increased 67% (2/11/87–8/11/87)
Acquisitions	N/A	British Caledonian

Figure 2.12   *The British Airways Success Story: Creating the "World's Favorite Airline"*

each of these interventions is intended to make organizational members address that level's need for change, heighten their awareness of their own behavioral patterns, and make them more open to the change process.

The second step, *movement,* involves making the actual changes that will move the organization to another level of response. On the individual level we would expect to see people behaving differently, perhaps demonstrating new skills or new supervisory practices. On the structural level, we would expect to see changes in actual organizational structures, reporting relationships, and reward systems that affect the way people do their work. Finally, on the climate or interpersonal-style level, we would expect to see behavior patterns that indicate greater interpersonal trust and openness and fewer dysfunctional interactions.

The final stage of the change process, *refreezing,* involves stabilizing or institutionalizing these changes by establishing systems that make these behavioral patterns "relatively secure against change,"

as Lewin put it. The refreezing stage may involve, for example, redesigning the organization's recruitment process to increase the likelihood of hiring applicants who share the organization's new management style and value system. During the refreezing stage, the organization may also ensure that the new behaviors have become the operating norms at work, that the reward system actually reinforces those behaviors, or that a new, more participative management style predominates.

According to Lewin, the first step to achieving lasting organizational change is to deal with resistance to change by unblocking the present system. This unblocking usually requires some kind of confrontation and a retraining process based on planned behavioral changes in the desired direction. Finally, deliberate steps need to be taken to cement these changes in place — this "institutionalization of change" is designed to make the changes semipermanent until the next cycle of change occurs.

Figure 2.13 presents an analysis of the BA change effort in terms of Lewin's model. The

Levels	*Unfreezing*	*Movement*	*Refreezing*
Individual	Downsizing of workforce (59,000 to 37,000); middle management especially hard-hit. New top management team. "Putting People First."	Acceptance of concept of "emotional labor". Personnel staff as internal consultants. "Managing People First." Peer support groups.	Continued commitment of top management. Promotion of staff with new BA values. "Top Flight Academies." "Open Learning" programs.
Structures and systems	Use of diagonal task forces to plan change. Reduction in levels of hierarchy. Modification of budgeting process.	Profit sharing (3 weeks' pay in 1987). Opening of Terminal 4. Purchase of Chartridge as training center. New, "user friendly," MIS.	New performance appraisal system based on both behavior and performance. Performance-based compensation system. Continued use of task forces.
Climate/ interpersonal style	Redefinition of the business: *service,* not *transportation.* Top management commitment and involvement.	Greater emphasis on open communications. Data feedback on work-unit climate. Off-site, team-building meetings.	New uniforms. New coat of arms. Development and use of cabin-crew teams. Continued use of data-based feedback on climate and management practices.

Figure 2.13   Applying Lewin's Model to the British Airways (BA) Change Effort

many and diverse steps involved in the effort are categorized both by stages (unfreezing, movement, and refreezing) and by level (individual, structures and system, and climate/interpersonal style).

Unfreezing. In BA's change effort, the first step in unfreezing involved a massive reduction in the worldwide BA workforce (from 59,000 to 37,000). It is interesting to note that within a year after this staff reduction, virtually all BA performance indices had improved — more on-time departures and arrivals, fewer out-of-service aircraft, less time "on hold" for telephone reservations, fewer lost bags, and so on. The consensus view at all levels within BA was mat the downsizing had reduced hierarchical levels, thus giving more autonomy to operating people and allowing work to get done more easily.

The downsizing was accomplished with compassion; no one was actually laid off. Early retirement, with substantial financial settlements, was the preferred solution throughout the system. Although there is no question that the process was painful, considerable attention was paid to minimizing the pain in every possible way.

A second major change occurred in BA's top management. In 1981, Lord John King of Wartinbee, a senior British industrialist, was appointed chairman of the board, and Colin Marshall, now Sir Colin, was appointed CEO. The appointment of Marshall represented a significant departure from BA culture. An outsider to BA, Marshall had a marketing background that was quite different from that of his predecessors, many of whom were retired senior Royal Air Force officers. It was Marshall who decided, shortly after his arrival, that BA's strategy should be to become "the World's Favorite Airline." Without question, critical ingredients in the success of the overall change effort were Marshall's vision, the clarity of his understanding that BA's culture needed to be changed in order to carry out the vision, and his strong leadership of that change effort.

To support the unfreezing process, the first of many training programs was introduced. "Putting People First" — the program in which all BA personnel with direct customer contact participated — was another important part of the unfreezing process. Aimed at helping line workers and managers understand the service nature of the airline industry, it was intended to challenge the prevailing wisdom about how things were to be done at BA.

Movement. Early on, Marshall hired Nicholas Georgiades, a psychologist and former professor and consultant, as director (vice-president) of human resources. It was Georgiades who developed the specific tactics and programs required to bring Marshall's vision into reality. Thus Georgiades, along with Marshall, must be regarded as a leader of BA's successful change effort. One of the interventions that Georgiades initiated — a significant activity during the movement phase — was to establish training programs for senior and middle managers. Among these were "Managing People First" and "Leading the Service Business" — experiential programs that involved heavy doses of individual feedback to each participant about his or her behavior regarding management practices on the job.

These training programs all had more or less the same general purpose: to identify the organization's dysfunctional management style and begin the process of developing a new management style that would fit BA's new, competitive environment. If the organization was to be market-driven, service-based, and profit-making, it would require an open, participative management style — one that would produce employee commitment.

On the structures and systems level during the unfreezing stage, extensive use was made of diagonal task forces composed of individuals from different functions and at different levels of responsibility to deal with various aspects of the change process — the need for MIS (management information systems) support, new staffing patterns, new uniforms, and so on. A bottom-up, less centralized budgeting process — one sharply different from its predecessor — was introduced.

Redefining BA's business as service rather than transportation represented a critical shift on the level of climate/interpersonal style. A service business needs an open climate and good interpersonal skills, coupled with outstanding teamwork. Offsite, team-building meetings — the process chosen to deal with these issues during the movement stage — have now been institutionalized.

None of these changes would have occurred without the commitment and involvement of top management. Marshall himself played a central role in both initiating and supporting the change process, even when problems arose. As one index of this commitment, Marshall shared information at question-and-answer sessions at most of the training programs — both "to show the flag" and to provide his own unique perspective on what needed to be done.

An important element of the movement phase was acceptance of the concept of "emotional labor" that Georgiades championed — that is, the high energy levels required to provide the quality of service needed in a somewhat uncertain environment, such as the airline business. Recognition that such service is emotionally draining and often can lead to burnout and permanent psychological damage is critical to developing systems of emotional support for the service workers involved.

Another important support mechanism was the retraining of traditional personnel staff to become internal change agents charged with helping and supporting line and staff managers. So too was the development of peer support groups for managers completing the "Managing People First" training program.

To support this movement, a number of internal BA structures and systems were changed. By introducing a new bonus system, for example, Georgiades demonstrated management's commitment to sharing the financial gains of BA's success. The opening of Terminal 4 at Heathrow Airport provided a more functional work environment for staff. The purchase of Chartridge House as a permanent BA training center permitted an increase in and integration of staff training, and the new, "user friendly" MIS enabled managers to get the information they needed to do their jobs in a timely fashion.

Refreezing. During the refreezing phase, the continued involvement and commitment of BA's top management ensured that the changes became "fixed" in the system. People who clearly exemplified the new BA values were much more likely to be promoted, especially at higher management levels. Georgiades introduced additional programs for educating the workforce, especially managers. "Open Learning" programs, including orientation programs for new staff, supervisory training for new supervisors, and so on, were augmented by "Top Flight Academies" that included training at the executive, senior management, and management levels. One of the Academies now leads to an M.B.A. degree.

A new performance appraisal system, based on both behavior and results, was created to emphasize customer service and subordinate development. A performance-based compensation system is being installed, and task forces continue to be used to solve emerging problems, such as those resulting from the acquisition of British Caledonian Airlines.

Attention was paid to BA's symbols as well — new, upscale uniforms; refurbished aircraft; and a new corporate coat of arms with the motto "We fly to serve." A unique development has been the creation of teams for consistent cabin-crew staffing, rather than the ad hoc process typically; used. Finally, there is continued use of data feedback on management practices throughout the system.

Managing change. Unfortunately, the change process is not smooth even if one is attentive to Lewin's model of change. Changing behavior at both individual and organizational levels means inhibiting habitual responses and producing new responses that feel awkward and unfamiliar to those involved. It is all to easy to slip back to the familiar and comfortable.

For example, an organization may intend to manage more participatively. But when a difficult decision arises, it may not be possible to get a consensus decision — not at first, at least. Frustration to "get on with" a decision can lead to the organization's early abandonment of the new management style.

In moving from a known present state to a desired future state, organizations must recognize that (as noted earlier) the intervention *transition* state requires careful management, especially when the planned organizational change is large and complex. An important part of this change management lies in recognizing and accepting the disorganization and temporarily lowered effectiveness that characterize the transition state.

In BA's change effort, the chaos and anger that arose during the transitional phase have abated, and clear signs of success have now emerged. But many times the outcome was not at all clear, and serious questions were raised about the wisdom of the process both inside and outside BA. At such times the commitment and courage of top management are essential.

To heighten involvement, managing such organizational changes may often require using a transition management team composed of a broad cross-section of members of the organization. Other techniques include using multiple interventions rather than just one — for example, keeping the system open to feedback about the change process and using symbols and rituals to mark significant achievements. The BA program used all of these techniques.

Process consultation. In addition to the various change strategies discussed above, considerable use was made of all the usual organization development (OD) technologies. Structural changes, role clarification and negotiations, team building, and process consultation were all used at British Airways to facilitate change.

In process consultation — the unique OD intervention — the consultant examines the pattern of a work unit's communication. This is done most often through direct observation of staff meetings and, at opportune times, through raising questions or making observations about what has been happening. The role of the process consultant is to be counternormative — that is, to ask why others never seem to respond to Ruth's questions or why no one ever challenges Fred's remarks when he is clearly off target. Generally speaking, process consultation points out the true quality of the emperor's new clothes even when everyone is pretending that they are quite elegant. By changing the closed communication style of the work teams at British Airways to a more open, candid one, process consultation played an important role in the change process.

❏ THE RESEARCH EVIDENCE

Granted that the BA intervention appears to have been successful, what do we know generally about the impact of OD interventions on organizations and on their effectiveness? Over the past few years, the research literature has shown a sharp improvement in both research design and methodological rigor, especially in the development of such "hard criteria" as productivity and quality indices. The findings have been surprisingly positive.

For example, Raymond Katzell and Richard Guzzo reviewed more than 200 intervention studies and reported that 87% found evidence of significant increases in worker productivity as a result of the intervention. Richard Guzzo, Richard Jette, and Raymond Katzell's meta-analysis of 98 of these same studies revealed productivity increases averaging almost half a standard deviation — impressive enough "to be visible to the naked eye," to use their phrase. Thus it would appear that the success of BA's intervention process was not a single occurrence but one in a series of successful changes based on OD interventions.

The picture with respect to employee satisfaction, however, is not so clear. Another meta-analysis — by Barry Macy, Hiroaki Izumi, Charles Hurts, and Lawrence Norton — on how OD interventions affect performance measures and employee work satisfaction found positive effects on performance but *negative* effects on attitudes, perhaps because of the pressure exerted by new work-group norms on employee productivity. The positive effects on performance, however, are in keeping with the bulk of prior research. A recent comprehensive review of the entire field of OD by Marshall Sashkin and W. Warner Burke concluded, "There is little doubt that, when applied properly, OD has substantial positive effects in terms of performance measures."

❏ IMPLICATIONS AND CONCLUDING REMARKS

We very much believe that an understanding of the social psychology of the change process gives all of us — managers, rank-and-file employees, and consultants — an important and different perspective for coping with an increasingly competitive environment. Our purpose in writing this article was to share some of this perspective — from an admittedly biased point of view.

The change effort at BA provides a recent example of how this perspective and this understanding have been applied. What should be apparent from this abbreviated overview of a massive project is that the change process at BA was based on open-systems thinking, a phased model of managing change, and multiple levels for implementing the change. Thus both the design and the implementation of this change effort relied heavily on this kind of understanding about the nature of organizations and changing them.

The change involved a multifaceted effort that used many leverage points to initiate and support the changes. The change process, which used transition teams with openness to feedback, was intentionally managed with strong support from top management. Resistance to change was actively managed by using unfreezing strategies at all three levels — individual, structural and systems, and interpersonal. Virtually all of the organizational change issues discussed in this article emerged in some measure during the course of the project.

It is quite reassuring to begin to find empirical support for these efforts in field studies and case reports of change efforts. Moreover, the recent meta-analyses of much of this work are quite supportive of what we have learned from experience. We need to use such reports to help more managers understand the worth of applying the open-systems model to their change efforts. But we also need to remember that only when proof of the intervention strategy's usefulness shows up on the firm's "bottom line" will most line managers be persuaded that open-systems thinking is not necessarily incompatible with the real world. The BA success story is a very useful one for beginning such a dialog.

As we go to press, it seems clear that many of the changes at British Airways have stabilized the company. Perhaps the most important one is that the company's culture today can be described as having a strong customer-service focus — a focus that was decidedly lacking in 1982. The belief that marketing and service with the customer in mind will have significant payoff for the company is now endemic to the corporate culture. Another belief now fundamental to BA's culture is that the way one manages people — especially those, like ticket agents and cabin crews, with direct customer contact — directly impacts the way customers will feel about BA. For example, during 1990, Tony Clarry, then head of worldwide customer service for BA, launched a leadership program for all of his management around the globe to continue to reinforce this belief.

Yet all is not bliss at British Airways, which has its problems. Some examples:

- American Airlines is encroaching upon BA's European territory.
- The high level of customer service slips from time to time.
- Those who can afford to ride on the Concorde represent a tiny market, so it is tough to maintain a consistently strong customer base.
- Now that BA has developed a cadre of experienced managers in a successful company, these managers are being enticed by search firms to join other companies that often pay more money.

Other problems, too, affect BA's bottom line — the cost of fuel, effectively managing internal costs, and the reactions of the financiers in London and on Wall Street, to name a few. It should be noted that since 1987 and until recently, BA's financials have remained positive with revenues and profits continuing to increase. During 1990 this bright picture began to fade, however. The combination of the continuing rise in fuel costs, the recession, and the war in the Persian Gulf have taken their toll. Constant vigilance is therefore imperative for continued success.

It may be that BA's biggest problem now is not so much to manage further change as it is to manage the change that has already occurred. In other words, the people of BA have achieved significant change and success; now they must maintain what has been achieved while concentrating on continuing to be adaptable to changes in their external environment — the further deregulation of Europe, for example. Managing momentum may be more difficult than managing change.

❏ SELECTED BIBLIOGRAPHY

The Wall Street Journal article referred to at the outset, "Motivate or Alienate? Firms Have Gurus to Change Their 'Cultures,'" was written by Peter Waldbaum and may be found on p. 19 of the July 24, 1987 issue.

With respect to levels of organizational change, see the article by W. Warner Burke and George H. Litwin, "A Causal Model of Organizational Performance," in the 1989 Annual published by University Associates of San Diego. These authors describe the differences between transformational and transactional change. Along the same conceptual lines is the article by David A. Nadler and Michael L. Tushman — "Organizational Frame Bending: Principles for Managing Reorientation" (*The Academy of Management Executive,* 1988, August, 194–204).

Regarding strategies of organizational change, see Harvey A. Hornstein, Barbara B. Bunker, W. Warner Burke, Marion Gindes, and Roy J. Lewicki's *Social Intervention: A Behavioral Science Approach* (The Free Press, 1971).

Concerning models and methods of organizational change, the classic piece is Kurt Lewin's chapter "Group Decisions and Social Change," in the 1958 book *Readings in Social Psychology* (Holt, Rinehart & Winston), edited by Eleanor E, Maccobby, Theodore M. Newcomb, and Eugene L. Hartley. For an explanation of organization development as action research, see W. Warner Burke's *Organization Development: Principles and Practices* (Scott, Foresman, 1981). The framework of present state-transition state-future state is explained in *Organization Transitions: Managing Complex Change,* 2nd Ed. (Addison-Wesley, 1987), by Richard Beckhard and Reuben T. Harris. A recent article by Donald C. Hambrick and Albert A. Cannella, Jr. — "Strategy Implementation as

Substance and Selling" (*The Academy of Management Executive*, 1989, November, 278–285) — is quite helpful in understanding how to implement a change in corporate strategy.

A point made in the article is that for effective organizational change, multiple leverage is required. For data to support this argument, see W. Warner Burke, Lawrence P. Clark, and Cheryl Koopman's "Improving Your OD Project's Chances of Success" (*Training and Development Journal*, 1984, September, 62–68). More on process consultation and team building may be found in two books published by Addison-Wesley: Edgar H. Schein's Process Consultation, Vol. 1: *Its Role in Organization Development*, 1988, and W. Gibb Dyer's Team Building: Issues and Alternatives, 1987.

References for the research evidence are: Richard A. Guzzo, Richard D. Jette, and Raymond A. Katzell's "The Effects of Psychologically Based Intervention Programs on Worker Productivity: A Meta-Analysis" (*Personnel Psychology,* 1985, 38, (2), Summer, 275–291); Raymond A. Katzell and Richard A. Guzzo's "Psychological Approaches to Worker Productivity" (*American Psychologist,* 1983, 38, April, 468–472); Barry A. Macy, Hiroaki Izumi, Charles C. M. Hurts, and Lawrence W. Norton's "Meta-Analysis of United States Empirical Change and Work Innovation Field Experiments," a paper presented at the 1986 annual meeting of the Academy of Management, Chicago; John M. Nicholas's "The Comparative Impact of Organization Development Interventions on Hard Criteria Issues" (*The Academy of Management Review,* 1982, 7(4) October, 531–543); John M. Nicholas and Marsha Katz's "Research Methods and Reporting Practices in Organization Development" (*The Academy of Management Review,* 1985, October (4), 737–749); and Marshall Sashkin and W. Warner Burke's "Organization Development in the 1980s" (*Journal of Management,* 1987, (2), 205–229).

Leonard D. Goodstein, Ph.D. — a consulting psychologist based on Washington, DC — specializes in organization and executive development, especially in strategic planning and the assessment and restructuring of organizational culture. He recently completed a three-year term as executive vice-president and chief executive officer of the American Psychological Association (APA), located in Washington, DC. His Ph.D., in psychology, is from Columbia.

Dr. Goodstein has held professorships at the Universities of Iowa, Cincinnati, and Arizona State, where he served as chair of the department of psychology. At the Vrije Universiteit in The Netherlands, he served as Fulbright Visiting Professor. After leaving academia and before joining APA, he was president and later chairman of the board of University Associates, Inc., an international consulting and publishing company based in San Diego.

He is a licensed psychologist in California and DC and a Distinguished Practitioner of the National Academy of Practice, and he holds the Diploma in Clinical Psychology of the American Board of Examiners in Professional Psychology. A frequent speaker before executive, management, and human resources professional groups, he is the author, coauthor, or coeditor of 12 books and more than 200 articles.

W. Warner Burke, Ph.D., is professor of psychology and education at Teachers College, Columbia University, and director of that school's graduate program in organizational psychology. He is also president of W. Warner Burke Associates, Inc. His Ph.D. is from the University of Texas, Austin.

From 1966 to 1974, he worked full time with the NTL Institute for Applied Behavioral Science, and from 1967 to 1974 he was executive director of the OD Network. A former editor of both *The Academy of Management Executive* (1986–1989) and *Organizational Dynamics* (1979–1985), he is a member of the American Psychological Society and has served on the board of governors of both the Academy of Management and the American Society for Training and Development (ASTD). He is the author of more than 50 articles and book chapters on organization development, training, and social and organizational psychology; he is also the author, coauthor, editor, or coeditor of 12 books.

Dr. Burke is a Diplomate in Industrial/Organizational Psychology, American Board of Professional Psychology. In 1989 he received the Public Service Medal from the National Aeronautics and Space Administration and, in 1990, the Distinguished Contribution to Human Resource Development Award from ASTD.

Case 2-1

Changing the Culture at British Airways

I remember going to parties in the late 1970s, and if you wanted to have a civilized conversation, you didn't actually say that you worked for British Airways, because it got you talking about people's last travel experience, which was usually an unpleasant one. It's staggering how much the airline's image has changed since then, and, in comparison, how proud staff are of working for BA today.

> — British Airways employee,
> spring 1990

I recently flew business class on British Airways for the first time in about 10 years. What has happened over that time is amazing. I can't tell you how my memory of British Airways as a company and the experience I had 10 years ago contrasts with today. The improvement in service is truly remarkable.

> —British Airways customer,
> fall 1989

IN JUNE 1990, British Airways (BA) reported its third consecutive year of record profits, £345 million before taxes, firmly establishing the rejuvenated carrier as one of the world's most profitable airlines (See Fig. 2.14). The impressive financial results were one indication that BA had convincingly shed its historic "bloody awful" image. In October 1989, one respected American publication referred to it as "bloody awesome,"[1] a description most would not have thought possible after pretax losses totalling more than £240 million in 1981 and 1982. Productivity had risen more than 67% during the 1980s.[2] Passengers reacted very favorably to the changes. After suffering through years of poor market perception during the 1970s and before, BA garnered four "Airline of the Year" awards during the 1980s, as voted by the readers of *First Executive Travel*. In 1990 the leading American aviation magazine, *Air Transport World*, selected BA as the winner of its Passenger Service Award. In the span of a decade, British Airways had radically improved its financial strength, convinced its work force of the paramount importance of customer service, and dramatically improved its perception in the market. Culminating in the privatization of 1987, the carrier had undergone fundamental change through a series of important messages and events. With unprecedented success under its belt, management faced an increasingly perplexing problem: how to maintain momentum and recapture the focus that would allow them to meet new challenges.

---

[1] *Business Week*, "From 'Bloody Awful' to Bloody Awesome," October 9, 1989, p. 97.

[2] As measured by available ton-kilometers per employee, or the payload capacity of BA's aircraft multiplied by kms flown, the industry standard for productivity. BA's ATKs per employee were 145,000 in 1980 and 243,000 in 1989.

	1977	1978	1979	1980	1981	1982	1983	1984	1985	1986	1987	1988	1989	1990
Year End March 31														
Turnover (revenues) in £ billions	1.25	1.36	1.64	1.92	2.06	2.24	2.50	2.51	2.94	3.15	3.26	3.76	4.26	4.84
Operating profit in £ millions (airline only)	96	57	76	17	(102)	5	169	274	303	205	183	241	340	402
Pre-tax profit in £ millions	96	54	90	20	(140)	(114)	74	185	191	195	162	228	268	345
Net profit in £ millions	35	52	77	11	(145)	(545)	89	216	174	181	152	151	175	245
Revenue per passenger kilometer (pence)	2.98	3.24	3.28	3.35	3.74	4.20	4.89	5.57	5.87	5.80	6.00	5.82	5.96	6.37
Number of employees (000s)	54	55	56	56	54	48	40	36	37	39	40	43	49	50
ATK per employee (000s)	121	123	135	145	154	158	182	199	213	221	222	236	243	247

Figure 2.14   British Airways' Results, 1977–1990

❏ CRISIS OF 1981

Record profits must have seemed distant in 1981. On September 10 of that year, then chief executive Roy Watts issued a special bulletin to British Airways staff:

British Airways is facing the worst crisis in its history . . . unless we take swift and remedial action we are heading for a loss of at least £100 million in the present financial year. We face the prospect that by next April we shall have piled up losses of close to £250 million in two years. Even as I write to you, our money is draining at the rate of nearly £200 a minute.

No business can survive losses on this scale. Unless we take decisive action now, there is a real possibility that British Airways will go out of business for lack of money. We have to cut our costs sharply, and we have to cut them fast. We have no more choice, and no more time. . . .[3]

[3]Alison Corke, *British Airways: Path to Profitability* (London: Pan Books Ltd., 1986) p. 82.

Just two years earlier, an optimistic British government had announced its plan to privatize British Airways through a sale of shares to the investing public. Although airline management recognized that its staff of 58,000 was too large, they expected increased passenger volumes and improved staff productivity to help them avoid complicated and costly employee reductions. While the 1978–1979 plan forecasted passenger traffic growth at 8% to 10%, an unexpected recession left BA struggling to survive on volumes that instead decreased by more than 4%. A diverse and aging fleet, increased fuel costs, and the high staffing costs forced the government and BA to put privatization on hold indefinitely. With the airline technically bankrupt, BA management and the government would have to wait before the public would be ready to embrace the ailing airline.

❏ THE BA CULTURE, 1960–1980

British Airways stumbled into its 1979 state of inefficiency hi large part because of its history and culture. In August 1971, the Civil Aviation Act became law, setting the stage for the British Airways Board to assume control of two state-run airlines, British European Airways (BEA) and British Overseas Airways Corporation (BOAC), under the name British Airways. In theory, the board was to control policy over British Airways, but in practice, BEA and BOAC remained autonomous, each with its own chairman, board, and chief executive. In 1974, BOAC and BEA finally issued one consolidated financial report. In 1976, Sir Frank (later Lord) McFadzean replaced the group division with a structure based on functional divisions to officially integrate the divisions into one airline. Still, a distinct split within British Airways persisted throughout the 1970s and into the mid-1980s.

After World War II, BEA helped pioneer European civil aviation. As a pioneer, it concerned itself more with building an airline infrastructure than it did with profit. As a 20-year veteran and company director noted, "The BEA culture was very much driven by building something that did not exist. They had built that in 15 years, up until 1960. Almost single-handedly they opened up air transport in Europe after the war. That had been about getting the thing established. The marketplace was taking care of itself. They wanted to get the network to work, to get stations opened up."

BOAC had also done its share of pioneering, making history on May 2, 1952 by sending its first jet airliner on a trip from London to Johannesburg, officially initiating jet passenger service. Such innovation was not without cost, however, and BOAC found itself mired in financial woes throughout the two decades following the war. As Chairman Sir Matthew Slattery explained in 1962, "The Corporation has had to pay a heavy price for pioneering advanced technologies.... "[4]

For most who were involved with BEA and BOAC in the 1950s and 1960s, success had less to do with net income and more to do with "flying the British flag." Having inherited numerous war veterans, both airlines had been injected with a military mentality. These values combined with the years BEA and BOAC existed as government agencies to shape the way British Airways would view profit through the 1970s. As former Director of Human Resources Nick Georgiades said of the military and civil service history, "Put those two

together and you had an organization that believed its job was simply to get an aircraft into the air on time and to get it down on time."[5]

While government support reinforced the operational culture, a deceiving string of profitable years in the 1970s made it even easier for British Airways to neglect its increasing inefficiencies. Between 1972 and 1980, BA earned a profit before interest and tax in each year except for one. "This was significant, not least because as long as the airline was returning profits, it was not easy to persuade the work force, or the management for that matter, that fundamental changes were vital."[6] Minimizing cost to the state became the standard by which BA measured itself. As one senior manager noted, "Productivity was not an issue. People were operating effectively, not necessarily efficiently. There were a lot of people doing other people's jobs, and there were a lot of people checking on people doing other people's jobs..." As a civil service agency, the airline was allowed to become inefficient because the thinking in state-run operations was, "If you're providing service at no cost to the taxpayer, then you're doing quite well."

A lack of economies of scale and strong residual loyalties upon the merger further complicated the historical disregard for efficiency by BEA and BOAC. Until Sir Frank McFadzean's reorganization in 1976, British Airways had labored under several separate organizations (BOAC; BEA European, Regional, Scottish, and Channel) so that the desired benefits of consolidation had been squandered. Despite operating under the same banner, the organization consisted more or less of separate airlines, carrying the associated costs of such a structure. Even after the reorganization, divisional loyalties prevented the carrier from attaining a common focus. "The 1974 amalgamation of BOAC with the domestic and European divisions of BEA had produced a hybrid racked with management demarcation squabbles. The competitive advantages sought through the merger had been hopelessly defeated by the lack of a unifying corporate culture."[7] A BA director summed up how distracting the merger proved: "There wasn't enough management time devoted to managing the changing environment because it was all

[4]Corke, p. 39.

[5]Corke, p. 116.
[6]Company document, p. 2.
[7]Duncan Campbell-Smith, *The British Airways Story: Struggle for Take-Off* (Coronet, 1986), p. 10.

focused inwardly on resolving industrial relations problems, on resolving organizational conflicts. How do you bring these very, very different cultures together?"

Productivity at BA in the 1970s was strikingly bad, especially in contrast to other leading foreign airlines. BA's productivity[8] for the three years ending March 31, 1974, 1975, and 1976 had never exceeded 59% of that of the average of the other eight foreign airline leaders. Service suffered as well. One human resources senior manager recalled the "awful" service during her early years in passenger services: "I remember 10 years ago standing at the gate handing out boxes of food to people as they got on the aircraft. That's how we dealt with service." With increasing competition and rising costs of labor in Britain in the late 1970s, the lack of productivity and poor service was becoming increasingly harmful. By the summer of 1979, the number of employees had climbed to a peak of 58,000. The problems became dangerous when Britain's worst recession in 50 years reduced passenger numbers and raised fuel costs substantially.

❏ LORD KING TAKES THE REINS

Sir John (later Lord) King was appointed chairman in February 1981, just a half-year before Roy Watts' unambiguously grim assessment of BA's financial state. King brought to British Airways a successful history of business ventures and strong ties to both the government and business communities. Despite having no formal engineering qualifications, King formed Ferrybridge Industries in 1945, a company that found an unexploited niche in the ball-bearing industry. Later renamed the Pollard Ball and Roller Bearing Co. Ltd., King's company was highly successful until he sold it in 1969. In 1970 he joined Babcock International, and as chairman led them through a successful restructuring during the 1970s. King's connections were legendary. Handpicked by Margaret Thatcher to run BA, ling's close friends included Lord Hanson of Hanson Trust and the Princess of Wales' family. He also knew personally Presidents Reagan and Carter. King's respect and connections proved helpful both in recruiting and in his dealings with the British government.

One director spoke of the significance of King's appointment. "British Airways needed a chairman who didn't need a job. We needed someone who could see that the only way to do this sort of thing was radically, and who would be aware enough of how you bring that about." In his first annual report, King predicted hard times for the troubled carrier. "I would have been comforted by the thought that the worst was behind us. There is no certainty that this is so." Upon Watts' announcement in September 1981, he and King launched their Survival plan, "tough, unpalatable and immediate measures" to stem the spiraling losses and save the airline from bankruptcy. The radical steps included reducing staff numbers from 52,000 to 43,000, a 20% decrease, in just nine months, freezing pay increases for a year, and closing 16 routes, eight on-line stations, and two engineering bases. It also dictated halting cargo-only services and selling the fleet, and inflicting massive cuts upon offices, administrative services, and staff clubs.

In June 1982, BA management appended the Survival plan to accommodate the reduction of another 7,000 staff, which would eventually bring the total employees down from about 42,000 to nearly 35,000. BA accomplished its reductions through voluntary measures, offering such generous severance that they ended up with more volunteers than necessary. In total, the airline dished out some £150 million in severance pay. Between 1981 and 1983, BA reduced its staff by about a quarter.

About the time of the Survival plan revision, King brought in Gordon Dunlop, a Scottish accountant described by one journalist as "imaginative, dynamic, and extremely hardworking," euphemistically known on Fleet Street as "forceful," and considered by King as simply "outstanding."[9] As CFO, Dunlop's contribution to the recovery years was significant. When the results for the year ending March 31, 1982 were announced in October, he and the board ensured 1982 would be a watershed year in BA's turnaround. Using creative financing, Dunlop wrote down £100m for redundancy costs, £208 million for the value of the fleet (which would ease depreciation in future years), even an additional £98m for the 7,000 redundancies that had yet to be effected. For the year, the loss before taxes amounted to £114 million. After taxes and extraordinary items, it totalled a staggering £545 million.

[8]In terms of available ton-kilometers per employee, taken from annual reports.

[9]Campbell-Smith, p. 46.

Even King might have admitted that the worst was behind them after such a report. The chairman immediately turned his attention to changing the airline's image and further building his turn-around team. On September 13, 1982, King relieved Foote, Cone & Belding of its 36-year-old advertising account with BA, replacing it with Saatchi & Saatchi. One of the biggest account changes in British history, it was King's way of making a clear statement that the BA direction had changed. In April 1983, British Airways launched its "Manhattan Landing" campaign. King and his staff sent BA management personal invitations to gather employees and tune in to the inaugural six-minute commercial. Overseas, each BA office was sent a copy of the commercial on videocassette, and many held cocktail parties to celebrate the new thrust. "Manhattan Landing" dramatically portrayed the whole island of Manhattan being lifted from North America and whirled over the Atlantic before awestruck witnesses in the United Kingdom. After the initial airing, a massive campaign was run with a 90-second version of the commercial. The ad marked the beginning of a broader campaign, "The World's Favourite Airline," reflecting BA's status as carrier of the most passengers internationally. With the financial picture finally brightening, BA raised its advertising budget for 1983–1984 to £31 million, compared with £19 million the previous year, signalling a clear commitment to changing the corporate image.

❏ COLIN MARSHALL BECOMES CHIEF EXECUTIVE

In the midst of the Saatchi & Saatchi launch, King recruited Mr. (later Sir) Colin Marshall, who proved to be perhaps the single most important person in the changes at British Airways. Appointed chief executive in February 1983, Marshall brought to the airline a unique resume. He began his career as a management trainee with Hertz in the United States. After working his way up the Hertz hierarchy in North America, Marshall accepted a job in 1964 to run rival Avis' operations in Europe. By 1976, the British-born businessman had risen to chief executive of Avis. In 1981, he returned to the United Kingdom as deputy chief executive and board member of Sears Holdings. Fulfilling one of his ultimate

career ambitions, he took over as chief executive of British Airways in early 1983. Although having no direct experience in airline management, Marshall brought with him two tremendous advantages. First, he understood customer service, and second, he had worked with a set of customers quite similar to the airline travel segment during his car rental days.

Marshall made customer service a personal crusade from the day he entered BA. One executive reported, "It was really Marshall focusing almost on nothing else. The one thing that had overriding attention the first three years he was here was customer service, customer service, customer service — nothing else. That was the only thing he was interested in, and it's not an exaggeration to say that was his exclusive focus." Another senior manager added, "He has certainly put an enabling culture in place to allow customer service to come out, where rather than people waiting to be told what to do to do things better, it's an environment where people feel they can actually come out with ideas, that they will be listened to, and feel they are much more a part of the success of the company." Not just a strong verbal communicator, Marshall became an active role model in the terminals, spending time with staff during morning and evenings. He combined these actions with a number of important events to drive home the customer service message.

❏ CORPORATE CELEBRATIONS, 1983–1987

If Marshall was the most important player in emphasizing customer service, then the Putting People First (PPF) program was the most important event BA introduced PPF to frontline staff in December 1983 and continued it through June 1984. Run by the Danish firm Time Manager International, each program cycle lasted two days and included 150 participants. The program was so warmly received that non-frontline employees eventually asked to be included, and a one-day "PPF II" program facilitated the participation of all BA employees through June 1985. Approximately 40,000 BA employees went through the PPF programs. The program urged participants to examine their interactions with other people, including family, friends, and, by association, customers. Its acceptance and impact was extraordinary, due primarily to the honesty of its message, the excellence of its delivery, and the strong support of management.

Employees agreed almost unanimously that the program's message was sincere and free from manipulation, due in some measure to the fact that BA separated itself from the program's design. The program emphasized positive relations with people in general, focusing in large part on non-workrelated relationships. Implied in the positive relationship message was an emphasis on customer service, but the program was careful to aim for the benefit of employees as individuals first.

Employees expressed their pleasure on being treated with respect and relief that change was on the horizon. As one frontline ticket agent veteran said, "I found it fascinating, very, very enjoyable. I thought it was very good for British Airways. It made people aware. I don't think people give enough thought to people's reaction to each other.... It was hard hitting. It was made something really special. When you were there, you were treated extremely well. You were treated as a VIP, and people really enjoyed that. It was reverse roles, really, to the job we do." A senior manager spoke of the confidence it promoted in the changes: "It was quite a revelation, and I thought it was absolutely wonderful. I couldn't believe BA had finally woken and realized where its bread was buttered. There were a lot of cynics at the time, but for people like myself it was really great to suddenly realize you were working for an airline that had the guts to change, and that it's probably somewhere where you want to stay."

Although occasionally an employee felt uncomfortable with the "rah-rah" nature of the program, feeling it perhaps "too American," in general PPF managed to eliminate cynicism. The excellence in presentation helped signify a sincerity to the message. One senior manager expressed this consistency in saying, "There was a match between the message and the delivery. You can't get away with saying putting people first is important, if in the process of delivering that message you don't put people first." Employees were sent personal invitations, thousands were flown in from around the world, and a strong effort was made to prepare tasteful meals and treat everyone with respect. Just as important, BA released every employee for the program, and expected every one to attend. Grade differences became irrelevant during PPF, as managers and staff members were treated equally and

interacted freely. Moreover, a senior director came to conclude every single PPF session with a question and answer session. Colin Marshall himself frequently attended these closing sessions, answering employee concerns in a manner most felt to be extraordinarily frank. The commitment shown by management helped BA avoid the fate suffered by British Rail in their subsequent attempt at a similar program. The British Rail program suffered a limited budget, a lack of commitment by management and interest by staff, and a high degree of cynicism. Reports surfaced that employees felt the program was a public relations exercise for the outside world, rather than a learning experience for staff.

About the time PPF concluded in 1985, BA launched a program for managers only called, appropriately, Managing People First (MPF). A five-day residential program for 25 managers at a time, MPF stressed the importance of, among other topics, trust, leadership, vision, and feedback. On a smaller scale, MPF stirred up issues long neglected at BA. One senior manager of engineering said, "It was almost as if I were touched on the head.... I don't think I even considered culture before MPF. Afterwards I began to think about what makes people tick. Why do people do what they do? Why do people come to work? Why do people do things for some people that they won't do for others?" Some participants claimed the course led them to put more emphasis on feedback. One reported initiating regular meetings with staff every two weeks, in contrast to before the program when he met with staff members only as problems arose.

As Marshall and his team challenged the way people thought at BA, they also encouraged changes in more visible ways. In December 1984, BA unveiled its new fleet livery at Heathrow airport. Preparations for the show were carefully planned and elaborate. The plane was delivered to the hangar-turned-theater under secrecy of night, after which hired audio and video technicians put together a dramatic presentation. On the first night of the show, a darkened coach brought guests from an off-site hotel to an undisclosed part of the city and through a tunnel. The guests, including dignitaries, high-ranking travel executives, and trade union representatives, were left uninformed of their whereabouts. To their surprise, as the show began, an aircraft moved through the fog and laser lights decorating the stage and turned, revealing the new look of the British Airways fleet. A similar presentation continued four times a day for eight weeks for all staff to see. On its heels, in May 1985, British Airways unveiled its new uniforms, designed by Roland Klein. With new leadership, strong communication from the top, increased acceptance by the public, and a new physical image, few on the BA staff could deny in 1985 that his or her working life had turned a corner from its condition in 1980.

Management attempted to maintain the momentum of its successful programs. Following PPF and MPF, they put on a fairly successful corporatewide program in 1985 called "A Day in the Life" and another less significant program in 1987 called "To Be the Best." Inevitably, interest diminished and cynicism grew with successive programs. BA also implemented an "Awards for Excellence" program to recognize outstanding contributions, and a "Brainwaves" program to encourage employee input. Colin Marshall regularly communicated to staff through video. While the programs enjoyed some success, not many employees felt "touched on the head" by any successor program to PPF and MPF.

❏ PRIVATIZATION

The financial crisis of 1981 rendered irrelevant the 1979 announcement of privatization by the British government until BA's return to profitability in 1983. Unfortunately for BA, a number of complicated events delayed the selling of shares to the public for almost four more years. On April 1, 1984, the government passed legislation that made BA a public limited company. Still, the minister maintained control of the shares. Before a public sale, BA first had to weather an antitrust suit against it and a number of other airlines by the out-of-business Laker airline chief Freddie Laker. They were also confronted by complicated diplomatic difficulties with the United States concerning UK-US flight regulations, and increased fears of terrorism. Finally, they faced a challenge at home by British Caledonian over routes, a challenge that ironically turned out to be the final ingredient in the cultural revolution.

In 1984, British Caledonian management persuaded some influential regulators, civil servants, and ministers that the government should award the smaller airline some of BA's routes for the sake of competition. In July the Civil Aviation Authority

(CAA) produced its report recommending the changes. Arguing that substitution was a poor excuse for competition, Lord King led BA into a fierce political battle. Against the odds, King managed to extract a non-threatening compromise. Called The White Paper, the October report recommended increased competition but rejected forced transfers from BA to British Caledonian. Instead, it approved of a mutually agreed transfer between BA and BCal by which BCal attained BA's Saudi Arabia routes and BA attained BCal's South American routes. Perhaps just as important as the results, King led BA through a battle that both bound staff together and identified their cause with his board. Over 26,000 British Airways employees signed a petition against the route transfers. Thousands sent letters to their MPs and ministers. King's battle may have been the final stake in the heart of the lingering divisions that existed from the BEA and BOAC merger more than a decade earlier. The organization had been offered a uniting motive and a leader with whom to identify. As BA's legal director offered, King "took his jacket off, and he had a most fantastic punchout with [the government] about keeping the route rights. He got the whole of this organization behind him because they could see that he was fighting for them."

With its CAA review, diplomatic concerns with the United States, and Freddie Laker legal battle finally resolved, BA was ready for privatization in 1986. In September of that year, newly-appointed Secretary of State for Transport John Moore announced the intention to sell shares to the public in early 1987. With the offer 11 times oversubscribed, the public clearly displayed its approval of the changed British Airways.

After privatization, King and Marshall made globalization a major thrust. In 1987, BA took a 26% stake in Galileo, an advanced computer reservation system also supported by KLM Dutch Airlines and Swissair. That same year, BA arranged a partnership with United Airlines, allowing each carrier to extend its route coverage without stretching its resources. In early 1988, British Airways finally outmuscled Scandinavian Airlines System (SAS) to acquire British Caledonian. Finally, in December 1989, BA concluded a deal with Sabena World Airlines through which it secured a 20% stake in the Belgian carrier. Combined, the steps bolstered British Airways' global power and prepared it for what analysts expected to be a post-1992

European marketplace in which only the strongest carriers would survive. They also put an exclamation point on an evolving shift from a strongly British, engineering, and operationally-driven culture to one that emphasized global marketing through customer service.

❏ REACTION AT BA

Although not unanimously, by 1990 staff and management at BA felt that the culture at the airline had changed for the better since the 1970s. There was near complete agreement on the positive feelings generated by success.

The general atmosphere of the company is a much more positive one. There is an attitude of "we can change things, we are better than our competitors...." I'm not certain if there's a relationship which is that a good culture leads to a successful company, but there is certainly the converse of that, that a successful company leads to a better culture. We are a more successful company now, and as a result of that it's easier to have a positive culture. (Senior Manager, Marketing)

I think the core difference is that when I joined this was a transport business. And I now work for a service industry. (Senior Manager, formerly of Cabin Services)

You start to think not just as an engineering department, where all my concerns are just about airplanes and the technical aspects. My concerns have developed into what the operation requires of me, and the operation is flight crew, cabin crew operations, ground operations. ... What do I need to do to help British Airways to compete aggressively against all the other operators? (Senior Manager, Engineering)

Fifteen years ago, you just did one thing, and only went so far with the job, and the next bloke would do his bit. Now, I can go and do the lot, whatever I need to do. I don't call someone else to do the job. Now, you just get on with it. A job that could have taken eight hours is done in two hours. (Veteran engineer)

In the late 1970s, it was very controlled, a lot of rules and regulations. It stifled initiative.... We've become very free, and that's nice. There's not so much personal restriction. You can now talk to your boss. When I first started, it was definitely officers and rank. Now you've got more access to managers. (Ticketing supervisor)

In terms of both its superficial identity, its self-confidence, and also the basic service and product, there's an enormous difference to 10 or 11 years ago. Its management is perceived as more professional and its business is perceived to be more competent and effective. (Executive, Human Resources)

❏ CHALLENGES FOR THE 1990s

Despite the enormous change in the culture over the 1980s, BA still faced huge challenges. Management and staff agreed that, while the new culture fostered a strong commitment to service, a much higher morale, and a better market image, certain pockets within BA still needed to institutionalize change.

I like it much better now, but I think it's still got a long way to go.... The trust and the belief in this organization is not quite there. We can see the problems, but we still don't have any input.... We waste so much time waiting for spares, waiting for airplanes.... We still think of ourselves as little areas. The five shifts here are five little outfits. We still don't quite think of ourselves as British Airways. (Veteran engineer)

I don't think the culture change by any means has taken place as much as the public perceives. I think a lot has been done, but I don't feel it has become the norm. There is in places a lack of recognition of emotional labor, and the management and leadership requirements of emotional labor. I suspect we've gone a long way compared to many organizations, but it would be very easy to lose it. Eight years is a relatively short period of time to establish that, particularly when the economic pressure comes back on.... (Executive, Human Resources)

If you all pull together, then you get more out of it. The problem is getting everyone pulling gether. You never get 100%, obviously, but I suppose if you get 80% pulling together, then you're not doing too bad. There will always be a percentage that won't be pulling together. (Veteran engineer)

Ironically, attacking those pockets was more difficult because of the strong impact of the 1983–1985 corporate celebrations. Employees as a group were changed by those celebrations, and to some degree by successive programs, but excessive repetition risked rebellion. Management had to make a judgment of whether the communication programs of the 1980s were worn out.

I think that the fundamental message has not changed over the last decade. We're restating old values. When the message was first heard, people did listen and read and absorb, because it was new, and it was radically different from the previous decade. So they had an incentive. The difference is there is no longer the incentive. First, because it's old news. Second, because there is a degree of cynicism about the sincerity. (Senior Manager, Passenger Services)

You go on a million courses to see how wonderful you are and how wonderful British Airways is, and you get back to work and nothing changes. . . . The larger you are, it has to be more and more impersonal. You are always going to find that the lower levels feel so far removed from the upper levels that pulling together is almost an impossibility. (Veteran ticket agent)

You can't go on selling the same old socks. In terms of messages and themes and something to focus the company around, it's a bit difficult to repackage in another way, and put all the sort of support mechanisms around it that we did in the 1980s, and do it all again in a way that captures the imagination in the 1990s. (Executive, Marketing and Operations)

Increasing costs complicated the effort to fine-tune the cultural changes. In the mid- and late-1980s there was a gradual drift toward higher ratings and higher pay scales. Added to that was an increase in sheer numbers, due to the 1987 merger with British Caledonian and the loss of focus.

When this all started five years ago, the idea was to cut out levels of management, and they did one night — that night of the long knives, they called it. Forty managers, hundreds of years of experience were chopped. We've doubled those managers now. (Ticket supervisor)

We're trying to get our cost base down. We're trying to find out why it is that as we try to grow, somehow or other our costs rise faster than our revenue generation. How do you manage all those issues, get them under control, as well as keeping the people in the business focused upon delivering quality consistently over time? (Executive, Marketing and Operations)

BA also faced both a loss of focus and a contradictory new message. The apparent contradiction between cutting costs and driving customer service may have been the most difficult challenge of all.

During the early- and mid-1980s period, there were some specific challenges for us to overcome, and they are less obvious now than they have been in the past. (Executive, Internal Business Consulting).

The real challenge in a people culture and a service culture is when the pressure's on. How do you manage change which requires you to get more productivity or more cost-efficiency or whatever, but still maintain a degree of trust, a respect for the individual, which I still think underpins service? (Executive, Human Resources)

Today, there is the unrelenting almost fanaticism about being able to deliver customer service. It's the thing staff remember above all else. And the frustration they talk about now in terms of their ability to deliver that customer service and some of the difficulties that we as a company are having in trading off still needing consistent customer service, but also needing to do it at a cost. We're struggling with a way of putting that message across to the work force that doesn't some way get returned to us as "you don't care about service anymore" because we've generated that single focus over the last seven or eight years. (Executive, Marketing and Operations)

In less than 10 years, British Airways had lifted itself out of bankruptcy to become one of the world's most respected airlines. The financial crisis of 1981 and the drive to ready itself for privatization had given the people of BA a focus that led to many changes. Still, there were obviously parts of the organization in which new beliefs were not institutionalized by the tornado of change. And in looking for a new focus, management dealt with the seemingly unattractive alternative of trying to get staff to identify with an issue as glamorless as cost-cutting. Yet, without increasing the value the culture placed on productivity and profits, while maintaining or increasing the value placed on customer service, King and Marshall could not guarantee BA's continued success in an increasingly competitive global marketplace.

3

Dimensions of Change Management and Using a Project Management Approach

❏ CHAPTER AT A GLANCE

Highlights of this chapter include the following:

1. The range or dimensions of managing organizational change can be addressed with strategy as a foundation upon which resources, systems, and culture operate on a daily basis to enable the organization to accomplish its goals and objectives.

2. When an organization's capabilities reside primarily in its people, changing capabilities to address new problems is relatively simple. However, when the capabilities have come to reside in processes and values, and especially then they have become embedded in culture, change can be extraordinarily difficult.

3. Strategic change is a continuous process using change managers to analyze, formulate, and implement change initiatives by addressing content (what), process (how), and context (where and what strategy).

4. The strategic direction chosen by a company must be supported by competent and compatible employees who have the necessary

talent to implement organizational goals and objectives.

5. Both systems and processes must be flexible to support employees' ability to adapt to changing tasks.

6. An organization's values can be defined as the standards by which employees set priorities that enable them to make a judgments and where employees flexibility, information sharing, cooperation, communication are encouraged, the probability of a successful change initiative will increase.

7. A strategic change initiative can be split into project management (plan and implement) and operations (manage) components.

8. Developing a project plan for the strategic change initiative is critical to starting out in the right direction with employee involvement ensuring buy-in and better decisions as changes occur during the implementation.

9. Managing the implementation of change initiatives by using a project management approach is necessary so that we can monitor and control what is going on and make necessary adjustments.

To set the stage for what we will cover in this chapter, the following vignette gives you a sense of how important it is to address the four dimensions of change while using a project management approach to plan and implement a strategic change initiative.

❏ VIGNETTE

So you want me to manage a strategic change initiative? You have been asked to consider taking on the responsibility to manage a large project that has the potential to contribute significantly to the organization's bottom line. Bob, the sponsor of the strategic change initiative, is now ready to see you to discuss the scope of the project. You come highly recommended because of your years of service in a number of the function areas of the organization. An ability to integrate this change initiative across functional areas is seen as critical to its success.

"Not only will the outcome of this project impact organization profitability, it will also impact the way business is conducted, the relationship with suppliers, overall customer satisfaction, and cycle time

of core processes," said Bob. "We expect that we will have to reorganize some of our functional areas in order to better match our resources to the needs of our customers." In fact, marketing, sales, operations, accounting, engineering, and customer service will all be required to reevaluate their processes and systems as a part of this initiative.

A small group of company executives, with input from front-line managers and employees, have determined that this initiative must be in-place within 2 years. If not, they expect that significant market share will be lost, so there is a sense of urgency. "First, we will have to take the work that the executive group has done and fully develop our strategy," said Bob. This means that we will have to define where we want to be in 2 years and then determine what additional resources and/or new systems are needed. In addition, Bob stated, "Our strategy requires that we change our attitude and behavior when working with our suppliers and customers, we need to develop better working relationships."

You have been the project manager for a number of smaller initiatives and have developed good working relationships with members of the different functional areas. Your question to Bob is, "What resources will be available to plan and implement this initiative?" You recognize that while a direction has been set, there is uncertainty associated with this initiative and that there will likely be many adjustments to the plan as it is implemented. Bob's response is, "You will start out with a representative from each of the functional areas and then add or remove as needs change."

What other questions do you have? Are you ready to start?

Many change agents find themselves in the above situation, the material covered in this chapter will help you get a better sense of what needs to be addressed to successfully plan, implement, and manage a strategic change initiative!

❏ CHAPTER PERSPECTIVE

Because of differences in the way organizations operate, managing change is different than it has been in the past. Today, organizations need to be able to evaluate the overall effectiveness of their change process and make necessary adjustments to increase the probability of sustainable success. By addressing four dimensions of change, we can increase your understanding of important issues in the fundamental aspects of change, as well as your approaches to the process of managing change in groups and your organization. Specifically, a plan that addresses strategy, resources, systems, and culture, will enable you to make better decisions during the planning and implementation of the strategic change initiative as it evolves over time.

Chapter 3 also addresses establishing a plan for the future and implementing that plan. It will also show you how to determine readiness to change and discuss the benefits of utilizing a project management approach. A Managing Change Questionnaire (Subset MCQ) will be used to provide you feedback on your perspectives of the key concepts of change management in organizations. We will cover the development of an integrated plan, managing the implementation of a change project, and monitoring and controlling activities and resources in sections that deal with utilizing the project management approach. The tools and techniques addressed in this chapter will enable you and your organization to successfully adapt to changes in today's business environment.

An example of a failure to adapt (Lucent) and the successful adaptation to the business environment (IBM) provide a real-world perspective on how businesses operate.

Failure to Adapt — Lucent

When Lucent was spun off from AT&T in 1996, the new company also faced significant change in the external environment. At the outset it seemed that the Telecommunications Act of 1996 would be a boon for Lucent as customers decided to modernize their networks while they still had access to their monopoly revenues. These companies turned to Lucent for new equipment (when it was still part of AT&T), and much of it would work only with upgrades from the original manufacturer. Despite this apparent advantage, Lucent ran into problems. The company failed to adapt to significant changes in the industry, including the shift from electrical to optical switching, the shift from voice to data networks, and the shift from specialty to commodity markets. Lucent was aware of these changes but was not able to respond as quickly as new competitors.[1]

Success in Adaptation — IBM

As the external environment changes in significant ways, a company may find that it is necessary to emphasize a different core competency or develop new ones. IBM appears to be succeeding in its attempt to transform itself from a producer of computer software to a one-stop provider of all the information technology needs of its clients. The new CEO, Sam Palmisano, feels confident that there is a unique opportunity to help clients integrate the IT processes of their divisions and link them to suppliers, partners, and customers. Instead of just selling computers to customers, IBM now provides IT services as needed, on a variable, pay-as-you-go basis, sometimes to remote locations. Such Fortune 500 firms as American Express and JPMorgan Chase have already signed on for the service.[2]

As the two examples above indicate the ability to adapt to an ever-changing business environment is the key to success.

❑ WHY ORGANIZATIONAL CHANGE TODAY IS DIFFERENT FROM THE PAST

In today's business environment, change is inevitable and everywhere. An organization's ability to deal successfully with change is critical to its survival. As described above, Lucent failed to adapt to its business environment, while IBM was able to transform itself into a new company. With that said, we will look at why organizational change is different now than in the past to better understand what today's change leaders must address.

Planned organizational change has been around for many years; however, today it is much different from in the past for five primary reasons:[3]

1. Change is initiated by the leaders of the organization, rather than consultants or human resource specialists.

2. Change is closely linked to strategic business issues, not just questions of organizational process or style.

3. Change can be traced directly to external forces, such as new sources of competition, new technology, deregulation or legal initiatives, changes in ownership, or shifts in fundamental market structure.

4. Change affects the entire organization (whether it be a corporation or a business unit), rather than individual SBUs (strategic business units) or departments.

5. Change is profound for the organization and its members because it usually influences organizational values regarding employees, customers, competition, or products.

	Twentieth	*Twenty-first*
Structure	• Multileveled • Bureaucratic • Characterized by policies and procedures that complicate interdependencies	• Limited to fewer levels • Nonbureaucratic, fewer rules and employees • Characterized by policies and procedures that produce minimal interdependencies to serve customers
Systems	• Few performance information systems • Performance data to executives only • Management training and support systems to senior leadership only	• Many performance information systems • Performance data distributed widely • Management training and support systems to widely available
Culture	• Inwardly focused • Centralized • Slow to make decisions • Political • Risk averse	• Externally focused • Empowering • Quick to make decisions • Open communication • Risk tolerant

Figure 3.1   *Operating Twentieth Versus Twenty-first Century Organizations*[4]

The internal and external business focus for the above reasons reflects the importance of an organization's ability to better match the company's resources to customer needs. Therefore, organizations today need to continually review and make adjustments so that they can increase their probability of success.

From an organizational perspective, there are significant differences in how an organization operates on a daily basis today versus the twentieth century. Figure 3.1 addresses twentieth versus twenty-first century differences in how organizations operate.

A flatter organization with fewer layers reduces bureaucracy and allows decisions to be made in a timely manner. An increased amount of performance data and associated metrics provides managers with the information they need to make continuous adjustments to improve how the organization operates. An externally focused organization can be more competitive by empowering its employees to make timely decisions when dealing with customers.

With the above focus on the internal and external environment and the significant changes in the daily operating environment, it is critical that an organization and its members take more control over their destiny. With the proper planning and

appropriate attention to implementation, organizations can be successful with sustainable change initiatives.

❏ FACTORS THAT AFFECT WHAT AN ORGANIZATION CAN AND CANNOT DO

As an organization grapples with changes in business strategy to better match where it wants to be in the marketplace, it must also evaluate its present capability. This will enable the organization to determine gaps between where it is and where it wants to be. Research has shown that three factors affect what an organization can and cannot do: its resources, its processes, and its values.[5] These factors are part of the daily operations that enables the organization to succeed.

The operational capabilities of organizations evolve over time based on their resources, systems (including processes), and culture. This evolution has been described as follows:[6]

The factors that define an organization's operational capabilities and disabilities evolve over time: They start in resources; then move to visible, articulated processes and values; and migrate finally to culture. As long as the organization continues to face the same sorts of problems that its processes and values were designed to address, managing the organization can be straightforward. But because those factors also define what an organization cannot do, they constitute disabilities when the problems facing the company change fundamentally. When the organization's capabilities reside primarily in its people, changing capabilities to address the new problems is relatively simple. But when the capabilities have come to reside in processes and values, and especially when they have become embedded in culture, change can be extraordinarily difficult.

The successful alignment of strategy and culture is highly dependent on what an organization can do with its resources and systems and how well it integrates them.

Despite what some change management programs claim, processes are not nearly as flexible or adaptable as resources are, and values are even less so. Therefore, it may be necessary for managers to create a new organization where necessary capabilities can be developed. There are three possible ways to do that:[7]

1. Create new organizational structures within corporate boundaries in which new processes can be developed.

2. Spin out an independent organization from the existing organization and develop within it the new processes and values required to solve the new problem.

3. Acquire a different organization whose processes and values closely match the requirements of the new task.

Managers who are confronting change must first determine whether they have the resources required to succeed. Then, they must determine if the organization has the process and values needed in this new situation. Today, a major responsibility of management is to ensure that capable people are in their organization.

In the next few sections, we will address the four dimensions of change. This provides you a perspective on their scope and importance so that you can understand how an integrated plan can be developed when we focus on the usage of the project management approach later in the chapter.

❑ FOUR DIMENSIONS OF CHANGE

We define the four dimensions of change as *strategy*, *resources*, *systems*, and *culture*. Figure 3.2 shows the components of each dimension and indicate how they relate to using a project management approach to plan and implement with subsequent management of the operation of the strategic change initiative. Organizations define a change project by developing an appropriate strategy and then manage that initiative on a daily basis by utilizing resources, systems, and culture to enable the organization to accomplish its goals and objectives. In most cases, these goals and objectives relate directly to improved performance and competitiveness.

By linking the four dimensions of change to a project management approach, we address the change process in an organized and systematic manner. This will help ensure that we meet our performance goals and objectives.

❑ STRATEGY

Wheelwright defines strategy as follows:[8]

An organization's strategy is not a matter of simply changing a few decisions or even making one major

PROJECT MANAGEMENT (Plan and Implement)	OPERATIONS (Manage)		
Strategy (Strategy and Structure)	**Resources** (Human and Other)		
	Systems (Systems and Processes)		
Note: Strategy and structure define resource, systems, and culture requirements	**Culture** (Values and Beliefs)		
Timeline = Plan → Implement → Manage			

Figure 3.2 *Four Dimensions of Change and Linkage to Project Management and Operations*

issue or event the focal point of change. Rather it requires a change in the process of management, encompassing a broad range of behaviors, practices, and decisions as well as philosophies and values

The above statement reflects the fact that the process of changing an organization's **corporate** (what businesses should we be in) and **business** (how should we compete) **strategy** is an ongoing one that uses change agents to formulate and implement change initiatives. It occurs in a given internal context consisting of resources, systems, and culture, and external context of economic, political, and social constructs. In addition, the content focus is on the assessment and selection of products or services and markets based on the organization's objectives (supported by underlying assumptions). Experience has shown that strategic changes are seldom made by well-defined successive stages of analysis, choice, and implementation. An iterative process is followed as managers evaluate, learn more about their options, understand their situation and determine what is best for their organization.

Assessment, Formulation, and Implementation Study

The Centre for Corporate Strategy and Change recently investigated the process of assessment, formulation, and implementation of strategic and operational change in four mature industry and service sectors: automobile manufacturing, book publishing, merchant banking, and life insurance. The study concluded that higher performing firms are more effective when addressing the following factors than lower performing firms:[9]

1. Environmental assessment — The process of competition often begins from the understanding a firm develops of its environment. Strategy creation tends to emerge from the way a company, at all levels, processes information about its environment.

2. Leading change — Leadership is acutely sensitive to context. Early and bold actions can be counter-productive. More promising is the construction of a climate for change while at the same time laying out new directions, but prior to precise action being taken.

3. Linking strategic and operational change — An organization must justify the need for change, build capacity for appropriate action, supply necessary visions, values and business direction, break emergent strategy into actionable items, and use an appropriate reward system.

4. Human resources as assets and liabilities — An organization must demonstrate the need for business and people change and identify the total set of knowledge, skills, and attitudes that the firm needs to compete.

5. Coherence in the management of change — A given strategy should be characterized by *consistency* (not present inconsistent goals); *consonance* (by an adaptive response to its environment); *advantage* (provide for the maintenance of competitive advantage); and *feasibility* (the strategy must not create unsolvable problems).

The integration of these five factors was also critical in differentiating the high versus low performing firms. The study noted that reliance on only a few of the factors placed those firms at a significant disadvantage.[10] By recognizing the importance of these factors and asking a series of questions, as defined in the following sections, you will have a better sense of how to undertake strategic change.

Questions that Need to Be Asked

Pettigrew and Whipp suggest that strategic change should be viewed from three perspectives with an associated focus and addressing the following questions:[11]

1. Content (objective, purpose, and goal) — What is to be changed?

2. Process (implementation) — How is the change to be made?

3. Context (internal and external environment) — Where and what strategies are most appropriate and useful for accomplishing the change?

Since the organization is "Who" needs to change and the "Why" is to be competitive, by focusing on these perspectives, all of the key (who, why, what, how, and where) questions have been addressed. Success in doing strategic assessment, formulation, and implementation requires that managers continually evaluate these questions.

In order to properly evaluate the competitive position of an organization, recognizing that destabilizing forces and opportunities have been identified; three questions (consistent with the three perspectives suggested above by Pettigrew and Whipp) need to be asked:

First, "What" is to be changed? Four major organizational properties are typical objects of change:[12]

1. Frequently, the way a person performs a particular job needs to be modified. Different raw materials, new equipment, better procedures — these all can serve to alter *individual task behaviors*. [Resources]

2. At the organizational level, methods of control, information transmittal, and decision making may need revising in the face of new circumstances. Such *organizational processes* as these are therefore a second object of change. [Systems]

3. More broadly, management may need to modify the organization's *strategic direction* — what services it will provide, to what clients; what markets it will compete in, with what products. [Strategy]

4. Finally, management may decide that certain critical organizational assumptions, norms, ideas, and customs need revising. The enterprise's *organizational culture* thus becomes an object of change. [Culture]

Second, "How" is the change to be made? Four distinct methods are available:[13]

1. The way in which materials, intellectual resources, and production operations are treated may be altered. These are *technological* methods.

2. Relationships can be modified — for example, functional, role, or reporting relationships. These are *structural* methods.

3. Administrative actions also can be taken. For example, the organization's reward system can be use to stimulate a change, or labor-management cooperation can provide a means for change to occur in a positive and constructive manner. These are examples of *managerial* methods.

4. Finally, human beings can be selected, retrained, transferred, replaced, or fired. We call these "people" methods of change.

The third question is "Where and What Strategies" are most appropriate and useful for accomplishing that change? There are four major strategies that managers can use in conducting organizational change:[14]

1. The people on whom the change is having a direct impact are called "change targets." *Facilitative* strategies make it easier for change targets to accomplish a given change or series of changes. For example, change targets may be offered resources that will aid them in making the change. Basically, facilitative strategies are used in situations in which the change targets have some sense of what they want to do, but lack the means to do it.

2. When using *informational* strategies, change managers offer knowledge, facts, and opinions so that change targets can make rational decisions and take the resulting action. Change managers assume that targets will act rationally in the face of facts, and given adequate information will recognize the problem and develop solutions in agreement with one another because the facts are so compelling.

3. *Attitudinal* strategies are based on the belief that people's attitudes determine their actions in any situation. To change an action we must change an attitude. These strategies focus on changing attitudes both of individuals and groups.

4. Political activities in organizations concern acquiring, developing, and using resources to accomplish one's purpose. *Political* strategies rely on this notion. They involve giving, withholding, competing for, or bargaining for scarce resources so as to accomplish the change program's objectives.

By addressing these questions, organizations and their leaders will be able to determine the appropriate course and direction for change. Organizations will also have a much better understanding of where they are and where they want to be!

An analysis of the competitive environment, if done jointly by the management team in collaboration with other members of the organization, can produce an understanding of and commitment to the strategic tasks of the organization. Strategic tasks such as development of product extensions, improved product quality, reduced cost, improved customer service, or the introduction of new products are means by which the business will compete. By focusing on the previously mentioned objects and methods of change, these tasks become the strategic initiatives for change.

It should also be noted that strategic change may alter employee's fundamental patterns of action and behavior as the change process evolves over time. Managers and workers must learn to work in a new way. That new way leads to learning about what the new organizational intention really means and what it demands in attitudes, behavior, and skills. This learning and the new patterns of actions and behaviors become the base for the eventual alignment of culture and strategy that will be discussed further in Chapter 7.

By developing a strategy using the above guidance, you and your organization will better understand what is important to them. In the next section, we will address the role that resources play in supporting that strategy.

❏ RESOURCES

Consider the following example of strategy and technology (organizational resource) and Wal-Mart:

In 2002, Wal-Mart had $ 217.8 billion in sales and employed 1.3 million people, making it the largest company in the world. Sam Walton started Wal-Mart with one store in 1962, and today the company has over 3,500 stores worldwide. By holding fast to the founding principles of customer satisfaction and low prices, Wal-Mart has ascended to one of the top-ranked companies in the world.

Wal-Mart focuses on the efficient operation and execution of strategy in every facet of the business. Walton's growth-oriented strategy of placing stores in areas that were a few miles outside of towns and allowing suburban expansion to come to the store, described as "stretch out and back fill," allowed Wal-Mart to save money on start-up costs. As it grew larger, Wal-Mart upgraded its technology to stay organized and efficient. By linking inventory in stores across the nation to suppliers, manufacturers can plan production and delivery schedules, allowing efficient and reliable supply to the Wal-Mart stores. The application of technology has been vital to the survival of the ever-growing company.[15]

As the example above shows, the application of technology as an organizational resource can play a significant role in making a company more competitive. As will be shown below, organizational resources help define what a company can do!

When they ask the question, "What can this company do?" most managers look for the answer in its resources — both the tangible ones like people, equipment, technologies (as shown above), and cash, and the less tangible ones like product designs, information, brands, and relationships with suppliers, distributors, and customers.[16] Without a doubt, access to high-quality resources increases an organization's chances of coping with change. Therefore, a continuous review of the existing resources and their ability to perform at necessary levels is an absolute necessity as the organization moves through the change process.

Competent and Compatible Employees

The strategic direction chosen by a company must be supported by competent and compatible employees who have the necessary talent to implement organizational goals and objectives. An iterative process should be undertaken to enable management to determine what human resources are required to meet a defined strategy. In most cases, there is a gap between what human resources an organization has today and what is required to support the chosen strategy. Therefore, an implementation plan, must address what resources are no longer required and those that need to be acquired.

Financial Strength and Appropriate Facilities and Equipment

An organization must also determine what other resources are required to support its chosen strategy. Other resources include the financial strength to support daily operations (financial resources), the acquisition of necessary facilities and equipment (physical resources), and the purchase of statistics, forecasts, and reports (information resources). As with human resources, this is a process where a gap is determined between where a firm is today and where it wants to be. Again, an implementation plan must address the deletion or addition of other resources.

Based on a defined strategy with identified resources, an organization will next look at what systems and processes are required. In the next section, we will address how systems and processes support an organization's operational objectives.

❏ SYSTEMS

Consider this systems and processes example at Dell Computer:

Dell Computers has become a byword in its industry for efficiency and reliability and is one of the great American success stories. When Michael Dell started marketing his computers, the competition regarded him as just another cut-price reseller. However, his build-to-order model and elimination of the retailer revolutionized the business. Manufacturing PCs that had already been purchased and eliminating virtually all inventory enabled him to unseat such giants as Digital and Compaq from the top of the heap.

The Dell model of dealing with customers directly through the Web or on the telephone saves both money and time. Costs are further reduced by the company's inventory practices. Dell has no warehouses to store parts; instead parts are delivered straight to the factory only when needed to fill specific orders. Because each PC or other product is assembled by one person, direct accountability helps to keep quality high. Finally, Dell spends much less than its competitors on product research and development — a mere $440 million a year, compared to Hewlett-Packard's $4 billion. Dell's many patents tend to be for manufacturing processes, which is an indication of the importance placed on both efficiency and process reliability.[17]

As one of the four dimensions, systems include the processes required to support operational objectives and enable timely decisions to be made. Since it is critical that employees be able to adapt during the implementation of a change initiative, both systems and processes must be flexible so that we can effectively address the risks and uncertainties of change. By providing flexible systems and process to competent and capable employees, you will be able to place your organization in a situation that increases the probability of success.

Systems that Support Operational Objectives

Systems are established to provide the information necessary for an organization to operate on a daily basis. As a part of developing a strategy, an organization must determine the information required to support decision making. The gathering, dissemination, and access to this information are critical in supporting operational objectives. In addition, there must be an integration of system and processes to make information available when a process requires it, so that decisions can be made.

Processes that Allow Timely Decision Making

Processes are the patterns of interaction, coordination, communication, and decision making that employees use to convert resources into products and services of higher value. These processes support and govern both internal (product development, procurement, and manufacturing) and external (marketing, sales, and customer service) activities. Some processes are formal, in the sense that they are explicitly defined and documented. Others are informal: they are routines or ways of working that evolve over time.

An organization's systems and associated processes must be established to support strategic goals and objectives. In some cases, however, management must recognize a dilemma:[18]

One of the dilemmas of management is that processes, by their very nature, are set up so that employees perform tasks in a consistent way, time after time. They are meant not to change or, if they must change, to change through tightly controlled procedures. *When people use a process to do what it was designed for, it is likely to perform efficiently. But when the same process is used to tackle a very different task, it is likely to perform sluggishly.*

In the case of handling a different task, which can often occur during change, employees must be able to adapt, recognize this difference, and make necessary adjustments. As change agents monitor the progress of the change initiative, this adaptability and the associate learning that occurs are critical to success. The last of the four dimensions, culture, will be discussed in the next section.

❏ CULTURE

Let's begin with a culture and system example at MetLife:

When Robert Benmosche took over as chairman of Metropolitan Life Insurance Company (MetLife) in 1998, he and his senior team had to contend with a long history of virtually guaranteed lifetime employment, which, together with the free lunches offered to employees for decades, has earned the company the half-contemptuous nickname "Mother Met." The business had been showing poor returns relative to the rest of the industry for years — return on equity was just 7 percent in 1997 — and was planning to go public. Obviously, dramatic change was needed.

Some of that change took the form of massive cost-cutting efforts (including unprecedented firings), the restructuring of the business, and the launch of new products and services. But Benmosche and his senior team were just as concerned with developing a culture that, unlike the old MetLife, would encourage and reward excellent performance. Formerly, performance reviews had tended to be, in the words of one commentator, frequently just "meetings of mutual admiration societies," while bonuses where predictably awarded to virtually everyone each year, with little differentiation between strong and weak performers.[19]

Lisa Weber, senior VP and chief administrative officer, oversaw the change to a system that developed, promoted, and encouraged high performance. The new system called for employees to be measured on a five-point scale against their peers and given an annual grade. Bonuses are awarded according to performance ratings. Those who exceed expectations (people rated four or five on the scale) can expect to receive bonuses 46 percent higher that Grade Three employees, who in turn can expect to see bonuses 68 percent higher than their colleagues in Grades One or Two. "When you treat your top performers like the stars they are, you will get their loyalty forever, and that's what it's all about," Weber says. "When you have the loyalty, you get the production, and that is how the company can win from within." While overall turnover for the company is 17 percent, the turnover among the highest grade of employee is only 7 percent.[20]

In addition, the message about improving productivity was reinforced by week-long training programs for managers at all levels, and Benmosche himself spent a full day working with program attendees to address the management dilemmas they faced. Such a commitment on the part of the chairman of the organization served to send a clear message that this was an important initiative, just as the revisions to the performance management system and the new kind of training managers received were an unmistakable signal that the old culture was no more.[21]

Culture is the values and beliefs of an organization; the standards by which employees set priorities that enable them to make a judgment. Some examples of judgment are whether an order is acceptable or unacceptable, whether one customer is more important or less important than another, and whether an idea for a new product is attractive or unattractive. Employees at every level within an organization make these kinds of decisions.

Organizational culture is a complex adaptive system that uses coherence as a potent binding force. This coherence is developed where employee flexibility, information sharing, cooperation, and communication are encouraged, resulting in a higher probability of a successful change.

The larger and more complex a company becomes, the more important it is for managers to train employees throughout the organization to make independent decisions about priorities that are consistent with the strategic direction and the business model of the company. A key metric of good management, in fact, is whether such clear, consistent values have permeated the organization.[22]

The development of relationships and trust among employees and with customers is critical to establishing a culture that supports organizational goals and objectives. A cultural characteristics template lets us assess how these relationships and the associated trust are working. The template focuses on the following attributes:[23]

1. We respond quickly to customer needs
2. We create value by delivering quality products on time on schedule
3. We share knowledge
4. We always act as a team, not alone
5. We meet our commitments
6. We respect our diverse skills

The scale for each item addresses whether the attribute was present and then whether it was positive, negative, or neutral. These performance metrics can be very helpful in understanding progress with strategic change initiatives because they address the relationship that we have with our customers.

❑ INCORPORATING EXTERNAL TRENDS INTO INTERNAL STRATEGIES

We have addressed the four dimensions of change to provide a framework for determining the new direction of the organization. Let us now look further into what needs to be done to link an assessment of the external business landscape with an awareness of how an organization can become more competitive. So how should an organization look at the external business environment to consider change? Figure 3.3 provides a process on how to look at what is happening in the world, consider what others are doing, work to recognize opportunities, define prerequisites to success, and then

Six steps to linking an insightful assessment of the external business landscape with a keen awareness of how to become more competitive with internal strategies!	
FIRST: What is happening in the world today? *(The most significant trends affecting business transcend company and industry.)*	For example, the Internet has made it easy for corporations to link operations in Manhattan and Mumbai, and exposed villagers in India to Western brands such as Dell and Levi's.
SECOND: What does it mean for others? *(Put the organization in other's shoes.)*	For example, the typical classified advertiser was finding new outlets like eBay for used goods and Monster.com for job listings.
THIRD: What does it mean for us? *(Are there new market opportunities, investment priorities, or unpalatable risks?)*	For example, emerging-market economies (like China and India), in general, are forecast to grow faster than developed nations. GE would have much to offer in products and services (reliable energy and clean water).
FOURTH: What would have to happen first? *(Are there steps along the way, prerequisites that enable the future to occur?)*	For example, Apple Computer's iPod digital music player was relatively easy to design and produce. However, consumers needed a broad selection of music and a price point where consumers and studios would be comfortable.
FIFTH: What do we have to do to play a role? *(What could the organization do to become an important player?)*	For example, for GE to become a general store for emerging markets, it have to recognize that selling infrastructure products and services in those countries was not the same as selling power plants to utilities in America. GE would need to deal with Government agencies that are fragmented and where key people turn over regularly.
SIXTH: What do we do next? *(Need to begin to execute new priorities with a plan for the next 12 months.)*	For example, pinpointing acquisitions, determining pricing, or developing new competencies.

Figure 3.3   *Incorporating External Trends into Internal Strategies*[24]

determine what the organization could do to become an important player! Critical to this process are identifying significant trends, putting the organization in other's shoes, recognizing new market opportunities, determining prerequisites for establishing the trend as significant, and determining what the organization would have to do to be a key player. Examples of the different steps are provided to give you a sense of what would need to occur for an organization to incorporate external trends into internal strategies for success.

No single aspect of managerial skill is more important than an organization's assessment of the external landscape and how patterns and trends fit together. If this assessment is wrong or inaccurate, the organization's strategic positioning will likely be wrong. The focus of such an assessment and determination of a subsequent strategy is to set up an organization to succeed! This is another example of how organizations need to learn and adapt to change.

In this chapter, we have addressed the four dimensions of change (strategy, resources, systems, and culture) and how to incorporate external trends into internal strategies. We have also reviewed several real-world examples, stated how these dimensions are related to the overall change process, and suggested how information can be gathered to better understand the direction in which an organization is headed. In the next section, we provide a means of determining readiness to move through the change process.

❏ ASSESSING CHANGE AGENT READINESS AND PLANNING CHANGE

The ability to perform as a change agent (one who helps facilitate, implement, and manage change to improve performance) requires competencies in the following areas:[25]

1. Individual response to change: concerning the nature, prevalence, and utility of resistance to change.

2. The general nature of change: concerning whether effective large system change is evolutionary or revolutionary in nature and the characteristic patterns that typifies change efforts in organizations.

3. Planning change: concerning the causes of change in organizations, articulation of the vision, how to get from the present to the future, and barriers to effective transition.

4. Managing the people side of change: concerning how, when and how much to communicate about change within the organization, and psychological issues related to transition.

5. Managing the organizational side of change: concerning the design and structural issues of systemic and long-term change efforts.

6. Evaluating the change effort: concerning indicators of a change effort's effectiveness.

Items 1 and 2 address your knowledge of the fundamental aspects of change and items 3 through 6 address your knowledge of the change process. In the following section we will review a questionnaire that was developed to focus on these knowledge areas.

Assessing Manager Readiness for Change

Critical to plan development and implementation is the ability to assess the readiness for change within the organization. One instrument that may be used to assess readiness for change is a subset of Dr. Warner Burke's, Managing Change Questionnaire (Subset MCQ).[26] The instrument provides feedback to managers and executives regarding their perspectives on key concepts of change management in organizations and groups (see Figure 3.4). The Subset MCQ also indicates respondents' familiarity with, or knowledge about, important aspects of change management in organizations.

The Managing Change Questionnaire (Subset MCQ)

Figure 3.4 depicts the Subset MCQ. It includes 12 True–False statements about the nature of change in organizations. You may complete the questionnaire and compare your responses with those provided in Appendix B (including comments to support the correct answer). Please read each statement carefully, and then indicate whether the statement is true or false in the associated answer slot. You may utilize the following grading scale to evaluate your readiness: A = 11 or 12 correct, B = 10 correct, C = 9 correct, D = 8 correct, and E = 7 or less correct. Please note that this questionnaire provides an indication of how prepared you are to take on a change initiative.

This Subset MCQ questionnaire focuses on individual response to change (questions 3 and 7), general nature of change (questions 6 and 12), planning change (questions 1, 4 and 10), managing the people side of change (questions 2 and 5), managing the organizational side of change (questions 9 and 11), and evaluating the change effort (question 8).

Past usage of the Managing Change Questionnaire (MCQ) for managers who have managing organizational change responsibilities is described below:[27]

The instrument has been administered to over 2,500 managers. Almost 60 per cent of the individuals were 40 years of age or older. Of the participants 72 per cent were male and 13 per cent were female; the

True or False	#	Subset MCQ Questions
	1.	The articulation of the organization's future state by its leaders is one of the most important aspects of a successful change effort.
	2.	The most difficult aspect of any change effort is the determination of the vision for the future state.
	3.	Lacking freedom of choice about change usually provokes more resistance than change itself.
	4.	A highly effective, early step in managing change is to surface dissatisfaction with the current state.
	5.	A common error in managing change is providing more information about the process than is necessary.
	6.	Despite differences in organizational specifics, certain clear patterns typify all change efforts.
	7.	Managing resistance to change is more difficult than managing apathy about change.
	8.	With little information about the progress of a change effort people will typically think positively.
	9.	A change effort routinely should begin with modifications of the organization's structure.
	10.	Organizational change is typically a response to external environmental pressures rather than internal management initiatives.
	11.	In managing change, the reduction of restraints or barriers to the achievement of the end state is more effective than increased pressure toward that end state.
	12.	Effective organizational change requires certain significant and dramatic steps or "leaps" rather than moderate incremental ones.

Figure 3.4   Managing Change Questionnaire (Subset MCQ)*

remaining 15 per cent did not indicate gender. Regarding education, almost eight out of ten participants had completed at least a college education; specifically, 43 percent had obtained their Bachelor's degree or the equivalent, 24 per cent had obtained a Master's degree, and 11 per cent had a doctoral level or other advanced degree (e.g. PhD, MD, JD). The diversity of this large sample provides an opportunity for learning about how managers' different perspectives on change management vary with personal and organizational characteristics. The average level of agreement on the

MCQ was approximately 70 per cent. If the instrument is viewed as normative, this score can be described as roughly equivalent to a grade of 'C' in the subject of change management.

Based on these results, most managers responsible for managing organizational change require additional education and training. This likely means that most employees in an organization require education and training on how to deal with organizational change! Please note that Appendix B provides the correct responses to the Subset MCQ Questionnaire with comments that explain the reasoning behind the answer.

*Used by permission of Dr. Warner Burke (Burke, 1990).

What Makes Organizational Change Work?

A recent 5-year study focused on the planning and implementation of a variety of major change programs: from acquisition integration to turnaround to major cultural change (which can take as long as 3–5 years). The study also evaluated both the sequencing and timing of organizational change. Results of the study showed that successful change occurs when sufficient speed and mass are generated quickly enough so that enough momentum is created to move the organization quickly, from its state of rest — the status quo — in the desired direction.[28]

The study also raised a concern that many organizations treat change as a part-time undertaking, something to be taken care of after the "day-job" is done. This mentality, the study suggests, almost inevitably leads to slow progress, a lack of momentum and ultimately, failure.[29] Another disturbing theme from the study reflects the following:[30]

We don't make the tough calls. We try to accomplish far too much, spread our resources way too thin, and then wonder why everything moves forward at a snail's pace.

The study also concluded that management must establish a set of winning conditions that create the context for successful execution of organizational change. A reading on this study, "Fast forward: A new framework for rapid organizational change,"

by Elspeth Murray and Peter Richardson, including these conditions, can be found at the end of this chapter.

Direction Setting and Planning Process Linkages and Timetable

Now that we have discussed the four dimensions of and readiness for change, we need to provide a perspective on the timetable for the direction setting and planning process associated with the change and linkages between the two. This will set the stage for our discussion (in the next section of this chapter) on using a project management approach to plan and implement a strategic change initiative

Based on experience, Kotter provides a perspective on the creation of a timetable for the direction-setting strategy and subsequent planning of a strategic change initiative. Figure 3.5 depicts the relationship between direction setting and the planning process of change:[31]

Note: The steps in the managing organization change process are as follows for the above context and Figure 3.2:

Plan

1. Identify the Need to Change
2. Set the Direction of Change
3. Plan for the Change

		Timetable
Direction Setting Process Creates	Vision — the kind of organization people aspire to create in the long-term	3 to 20 years
	Strategies — what needs to be done to achieve the vision	1 to 5 years
Planning Process Creates	Formal/Written plans	6 months to 2 years
	Unwritten plans	1 day to 1 year
Relationships	Direction setting provides focus to the planning process	
	Planning process provides a "reality check" to the direction setting process	

Figure 3.5 *Direction Setting & Planning Process Relationships*

	Goal or Objective:
"The Change"	To ***improve the organization*** in some fashion — for instance reducing costs, improving revenues, solving problems, seizing opportunities, aligning work and strategy, streamlining information flow within the organization
Change Management	To ***apply a systematic approach to helping the individuals*** impacted by "the change" to be successful by building support, addressing resistance and developing the required knowledge and ability to implement the change (*managing the 'people' side of the change*)
Project Management	To ***develop a set of specific plans and actions*** to achieve "the change" given time, cost and scope constraints and to utilize resources effectively (*managing the 'technical' side of the change*)

Figure 3.6   *Linkages Between Change & Project Management*[32]

Implement

4. Implement the Change

As with Kotter's Eight-Stage Model, if these steps are not followed with the appropriate attention, the probability of success will be decreased. An organized and structured approach is an absolute necessity when dealing with the uncertainties of the change process. By recognizing the importance of the steps in the change process and understanding a likely timeline, we can utilize a project management approach to planning and implementing our strategic change initiative and as shown in Figure 3.6 address both the "people" and "technical" side of the change process. The next two sections of this chapter address the planning and implementation and monitoring and control necessary for you to successfully implement a strategic change initiative.

❏ USING A PROJECT MANAGEMENT APPROACH TO IMPLEMENT STRATEGIC INITIATIVES

Today's business environment is changing tremendously due the redesign of systems to decrease cost, the need to speed up product development, and the focused attention on satisfying customers. These types of changes support the use of project management as a way to introduce change to an organization. A general definition of ***project management*** is that *it is an efficient and effective means for achieving a specific, one-time, usually unique*

requirement within a strictly defined period of time. Because a strategic change initiative is so important to an organization and it must be done in a timely fashion, using the project management approach is an absolute necessity. Organizations should use project management to translate strategy into a project and then implement that project. Figure 3.7 provides four examples (growth market, quality service, risk reduction, and operating efficiency) of how an organization can improve itself by going through a change process.

Please note that Appendix C — *Effective Project Management To Help Achieve Business Success*, provides a case study that shows how an organization used a project management approach to bring key employees together to achieve organizational goals and objectives.

Project Management Focus

Project management is one of the most important management developments in the second half of the twentieth century. The 1970s and 1980s saw a continual increase in the use of project management in U.S. industry as the superior quality of foreign products eroded U.S. market share, and U.S. companies fought for their corporate lives. Use of project management concepts has continued to expand throughout the world, and these concepts are now an integral part of global market competition. Following its evolution as a management discipline over the last 50 years, project management is now a pervasive and important part of the larger field of management.

EXAMPLE 1			
GROWTH MARKET: A transportation service company			
CHANGE PROJECT:	**WHY**	**WHAT**	**HOW**
Development of a new service within the portfolio	A long-term goal of growth with a new service where the company already enjoys an excellent reputation for its core business	Design and implement a new transportation service that will address a new customer market	Dedicate a competent person to the project to lead a multi-specialist team of people from the beginning (sales and marketing, operations, accounting, etc.)
EXAMPLE 2			
QUALITY SERVICE: A financial services organization			
CHANGE PROJECT:	**WHY**	**WHAT**	**HOW**
Implement a new IT system across the organization	To create a dynamic working environment that would support higher quality service in a market where product differentiation as a competitive strategy has a very limited scope	Design and implement a new IT system to enhance quality of service: speed, satisfaction, the volume of loans processed, value added to customers at a cost lower than its competitors	First step would be to establish a cross-functional team to determine the scope of the project and user requirements
EXAMPLE 3			
RISK REDUCTION: Manufacturing division of an overseas company			
CHANGE PROJECT:	**WHY**	**WHAT**	**HOW**
Implementation of a system of procedures and standards for an "Environmental Management System"	To ensure financial stability and reputation by preventing pollution	Study the 12 elements of the standard and create procedures (including training) to meet certification requirements, then implement	Establish a project team and develop a project plan to address system design and operating processes
EXAMPLE 4			
OPERATING EFFICIENCY: Selling and renting machines, equipment and parts, and offering service			
CHANGE PROJECT:	**WHY**	**WHAT**	**HOW**
Utilize a six-sigma to improve operating systems and processes	Efficiently process payments and invoices, address disputes and create a mutual respect between the company and the customer	Review existing systems and processes to determine what could be streamlined or automated	Utilize the six-sigma process, DMAIC (define, measure, analyze, improve and control) to evaluate and change existing systems and processes

Figure 3.7 *Examples of Strategic Change Projects.*[33] *The Why, What, and How of change projects!*

Developing a plan for the strategic change initiative or project is critical to starting out in the right direction. By using the discipline of project management, a group develops a plan for implementation of the change initiative. Since the group develops the plan, members buy-in to the plan and also are able to make better decisions as changes occur during the implementation. From a management perspective, the project manager or change agent is responsible and accountable for all project activities. Since experience has shown that one major reason why strategic change initiatives have failed is the lack of responsibility and accountability, organizations need to have one point of contact to find out the status of activities. In simple terms, being more organized, committed, and better informed plus having one point of contact are key characteristics of a project management approach.

Develop an Integrated Plan

In most cases a cross-functional group or project team develops the plan to implement the strategic change initiative. Therefore, an integrated plan that addresses multiple functional areas is required to clarify strategies, tasks, responsibilities, and time frames so that there is a focused and organized approach to accomplishing the strategic change initiative or project. Figure 3.8 addresses the major components of a strategic change initiative project plan by providing a table of contents with nine sections: project overview, the organization, usage of project management, work breakdown, training, communication, risk management, budget, and schedule.

The Integrated (or Project) Plan is a detailed description of the major aspects of a comprehensive implementation, including (but not limited to) the following:[34]

1. Implications of status quo
2. Implications of desired future state
3. Description of the change
4. Outcome measures
5. Disruption to the organization
6. Barriers to implementation
7. Primary sponsors, change agents, targets, and advocates
8. Tailoring of announcement for each constituency

Generic Project Plan

1.0 Project Overview

  1.1 Description
  1.2 Scope
  1.3 Key Constraints
  1.4 Major Milestones
  1.5 Key Assumptions

2.0 Project Management Organization

  2.1 Sponsors
  2.2 Co-Project Managers, Project Coordinator, Project Office Manager
  2.3 Core Team
  2.4 Field Team
  2.5 Headquarter's Resources

3.0 Project Management Approach

4.0 Functional Work Breakdown

  4.1 Administration
  4.2 Operations
  4.3 Systems
  4.4 Other

5.0 Training Plan

6.0 Communications Plan

  6.1 Employees
  6.2 Stakeholder Group 1
  6.3 Stakeholder Group 2
  6.4 Stakeholder Group 3

7.0 Risk Management Plan

8.0 Project Budget

9.0 Master Schedule

  9.1 Schedule Overview
  9.2 Detailed Schedule

Attachment 1—Example of Approach for Documents

Attachment 2—Example of Detailed Activities

Attachment 3—Administration/Operations Scope of Work

Attachment 4—Systems Work Breakdown and Timeline (original)

Figure 3.8 *Generic Change Initiative Project Plan Table of Contents*

Project Terms

Project: Specific set of tasks related to the strategic change initiative.

Change Leader: Individual directly responsible and accountable for project tasks. This individual will also be responsible for development of appropriate metrics.

Major Tasks: Major components of a project that define what needs to be accomplished.

Plan: Schedule or timeline established to complete identified major tasks.

Status: Monthly reporting on what has been completed compared to "Plan" (ahead, on or behind schedule, and WHY?). Task 1 was completed one month prior to Plan and is Ahead of schedule because additional resources were utilized.

Exceptions Report: The focus of this report is to identify significant deviations from the "Plan" with a brief explanation so that management has the option to make adjustments.

Metrics: Measures that provide an indication of the successful implementation of the project that support initiative objectives.

Variances from PLAN: Deviations from PLAN that may reduce the probability of project success.

Issues: Circumstances that are barriers or restrictions and need to be resolved in order to accomplish project tasks.

Accomplishments: Highlights of completed activities that significantly support project activities.

Comments: Clarification or additional information on the "Variance from PLAN," status of "Issues" and "Accomplishments" and why tasks are delayed.

Figure 3.9   *Example Definition of Terms — Change Initiative Project*

9. Management of the transition state
10. Level of commitment needed from which people
11. Alignment of project and culture
12. Strategies to improve synergy
13. Training for key people
14. Major activities
15. Sequence of events

Note: These items should be embedded in the Figure 3.8 components.

In addition to using the above list, you should brainstorm with the project team to determine what other aspects of the project need to be listed. A listing of the definitions of terms, similar to those shown in Figure 3.9 should also be developed to help ensure that all stakeholders understand key characteristics of the project.

Please note that the terms stated in Figure 3.9 are also reflected in the Figure 3.10 and in Figure 3.11, reporting documents. These terms and documents not only help clarify what is planned but also provide a status report, including metrics, on what is happening on an ongoing basis.

Figure 3.10 is a sample plan and monthly reporting document. It effectively establishes a commitment to complete stated activities by a scheduled time. In addition, it allows for the reporting of project metrics and an explanation of project variances.

By stating what needs to be done and placing a schedule on when it will be complete, the individual(s) who prepare a Figure 3.10 document make a commitment to completing those activities. In addition, by having a plan you are able to monitor how you are doing against that plan and if necessary make adjustments. The next section will focus on how you can monitor and control your strategic change initiative as it evolves over time.

❏ MANAGING THE IMPLEMENTATION OF CHANGE PROJECTS

Managing the implementation of a change project focuses on applying change management concepts,

PLAN AND MONTHLY REPORTING DOCUMENT

Report Date: _____   Submitted by: _____

Dept.: _____

Project:	Change Agent:	

MAJOR TASKS (to complete project)	PLAN (scheduled completion of MAJOR TASKS)	STATUS (compared to PLAN – ahead, on or behind schedule & WHY?)
PLAN	Completion Date	
— Activities	Completion Date	
IMPLEMENT	Completion Date	
— Activities	Completion Date	

METRICS (may attach data summaries, as appropriate):		
— Quantitative	Example, numeric data	
— Qualitative	Example, survey data	

ASSOCIATED ITEMS:		
Variances from Plan	Comments	
Issues	Comments	
Accomplishments	Comments	

Figure 3.10   Example: Change Initiative Project Plan & Monthly Report Document

techniques, and philosophy to build sponsor commitment, develop pain management strategies (to relieve employee stress and frustration), increase synergy, decrease resistance, apply reframing skills, and build the appropriate culture.[35] Figure 3.11 is a sample monthly exceptions report that provides management with exceptions or deviations from the Plan (Figure 3.10) with appropriate explanations. Please note that this report may reflect both behind and ahead of schedule activities. Based on the potential impact of the exception, management may be required to make adjustments to the Plan.

Monitor and Control Activities and Resources

Execution of the "Plan" through the implementation of tasks and activities requires monitoring and then control over what is going on by making necessary adjustments. As with any project, things change or don't go according to the Plan. These changes should be regularly shared with management (see Figure 3.11) to keep them advised of progress, seek their advice or approval where needed, and to continue to build and maintain their support for the project. The project manager should ensure that the following occurs:[36]

1. Actively monitor project implementation and conduct assessments at regular intervals after implementation starts

2. Review implementation–monitoring plans and assessment results with management and make necessary revisions

3. Ensure that team members have the required skills and knowledge to perform their roles

Change Initiative Project

MONTHLY EXCEPTIONS REPORT

Report Date: _____   Prepared by: _____

Project # _____   Dept: _____

Expand table as needed.

Exception Number	Tasks					
	1	**2**	**3**	**4**	**5**	**6**
Exception # 1		Delay				
Exception # 2						Ahead
and so on						

Entries: *OK = As Planned E 1 = Exception # 1 (accomplishment highlight, variance from plan or constraint)*
NA = Not Applicable

EXCEPTIONS LISTING & EXPLANATION:

Exception Number	Explanation
# 1	Delay in receiving system software (will implement with next version upgrade)
# 2	Received process chart ahead of schedule (will input into system next week)
and so on	

Figure 3.11   *Example Monthly Exceptions Report*

4.   Work with management to communicate the status of the change project to the affected groups

Once the implementation process begins, it's critical that the project manager and his or her sponsor monitor what is happening. It is likely that other management representatives will also become involved when appropriate revisions to the Plan need to be made and implemented. Revisions to the Plan will be required throughout the implementation process. The project manager must continually balance competing demands among scope, schedule, cost, and quality. In addition, the different needs and expectations of stakeholders and those affected by the change project must be considered. The role of the project manager is to proactively anticipate critical issues or negative situations so that actions may be taken to dampen their impact. This includes providing necessary leadership to the change initiative that will be discussed at length in Chapter 4.

Allow Plan to Evolve

In many cases it is necessary to organize change projects into *"Phases."* This enables the project manager, sponsor, and management to reflect on what has occurred as they complete one phase so that lessons learned and appropriate changes can be made to the *"Plan."* Major change initiatives will evolve over a number of years with ongoing adjustments and changes. The project manager and his or her team will have many emotional ups and downs as they move in the required direction; however, the sponsor and other management representatives should provide the necessary leadership to stay the course. Failure should not be an alternative!

Lessons Learned from Previous Change Projects

Using lessons learned is an important component of using a project management approach. Organizations need to identify what they have done well and determine what they could have done better and how! Figure 3.12 focuses on the preparation, communication, objectives, implementation, and monitoring of strategic change initiative project activities. Items range from the "people" or change management perspective (check for significant top-level support) to the "technical" or project management perspective (build in a process of automatic review).

Recognizing the uncertainties of strategic change initiatives, it is important that we also understand how different they can be when compared to traditional projects. Figure 3.13 identifies a number of characteristics that reflect the added complexities of a strategic change initiative project. For example, shared views are the case for a traditional well understood project: however, conflicting perceptions are found with strategic change projects. An additional difference of major concern is that most traditional projects have realistic top management expectations; yet for strategic change initiative projects top management expectations are demanding and unrealistic. This is another reason why there is so much stress and frustration associated with the planning and implementation of strategic change projects!

In order to get an indication of potential problems with the planning and implementation of a strategic change initiative, Figure 3.14 provides a profile tool that can be used to determine if you are in trouble and if you are venerable to failure! A brief

Change and Project Management Perspective	
PREPARATION	• Check for false assumptions. • Always do a potential problem analysis. • Check for significant top-level commitment.
COMMUNICATION	• Ensure earliest possible involvement of stakeholders. • Ensure consistent message across the organization. • Harness energy and enthusiasm across the organization
OBJECTIVES	• Lack of focus produces failure. • Have clear objectives. • Differentiate between the "what" and the "how"
IMPLEMENTATION	• It helps to have people who have been through similar projects before. • Network of people and resources. • Build the change management team.
MONITORING	• Build in a process of automatic review. • Always evaluate, financially and otherwise. • To ensure sustainability have follow-through.

Figure 3.12   Learning from Previous Change Projects[37]

Traditional Projects	Strategic Change Projects
Operational changes	Strategic changes
Few extra resources needed	Significant resource commitment
Realistic top management expectations	Unrealistic top management expectations
Certainty of means	Uncertain means
Self-contained	Multiple "ripples"
Shared views	Conflicting perceptions
Single function system	Multipurpose changes
Stable goals	Unstable goals
Clear ownership of process and outcomes	Confused responsibilities for process and outcomes

Figure 3.13 *Characteristics of Traditional versus Strategic Change Projects*[38]

Change Profile Tool

Project managers/change agents can review the change project they are managing against the six features identified below as important.

Circle the numbers below which most accurately describe your change project!

SIGNIFICANCE

Core	5	3	1	margin

SOLUTION

Novel	5	3	1	familiar

OUTSIDE LINKS

Many	5	3	1	few

SENSE OF OWNERSHIP

Low	5	3	1	high

SENIOR MANAGERS STANCE

Ambiguous	5	3	1	supportive

CHANGING GOALS

Often/Major	5	3	1	rare/minor

Figure 3.14 *Strategic Change Project Profile Tool*[39]

description of the six features covered in the tool follow:

Significance — core changes in the way we do things versus marginal change

Solution — innovative and novel approach to change versus something we are very familiar with

Outside links — the project is highly dependent on other departments changing the way they work

Sense of ownership — responsibility for project components is unclear, leaving the change agent without backing at critical times

Senior stance — senior managers have ambiguous and unrealistic expectations versus an understood and supportive involvement

Changing goals — the project is only halfway through implementation and we are already implementing significant changes to cope with new areas of the business

High scores indicate where trouble is most likely to arise. The higher the total, the more vulnerable you are.

❏ READING AND CASE

The following Reading and Case provide an opportunity to apply the concepts and theory discussed in this chapter to real-world situations. They reflect an organization's need to be flexible during the change process, to recognize working conditions that can lead to success, to continually evaluate the matching of customer needs to organizational resources, and involve staff in every step of the change process.

Reading

3-1 Fast forward: A new framework for rapid organizational change, Elspeth Murray & Peter Richardson, Ivey Business Journal, March/April 2003.

Focus: Successful change occurs when sufficient speed and mass are generated quickly enough so that enough momentum is created to move the organization quickly from a state of rest in the desired direction. We discovered that it was not so much what people did that led to success, but rather the fact that certain conditions were established during the change process.

Questions

1. When addressing organizational change, why are the following key questions?
   What activities?
   What sequence?
   What are the best ways to perform activities?

2. From your experience, provide examples that are aligned with the following statements and explain why they are counterproductive to the change process?
   "We don't make the tough calls. We try to accomplish far too much, spread our resources way too thin, and then we wonder why everything moves forward at a snail's pace."

3. Review the "winning conditions", select a condition, and then explain: (a) what must occur to move "toward" that condition, and (b) what is a barrier or constraint to attaining the condition?

4. Please explain what can be done to avoid the following (page 5)? "Many organizations treat change as a part-time undertaking, something to be taken care of after the 'day-job' is done.

Linkage to Chapter

1. Successful change initiatives need a plan and monitoring devices (create guidance), to generate and maintain speed (build momentum), and to provide critical mass (commitment and successes)

2. Change leaders must be proactive, anticipate problems, and use a project management approach

3. By following the "winning conditions" an organization can set itself up for a successful change process

4. How critical it is to get off to a good start

Case

3-1 Competition drives changes in organizational structure, William Leban, PM Network, November, 1996.

Focus: Success depended on providing efficient and cost-effective services. A better matching of resources to customer needs (internal and external) was required to make the organization more competitive. The project management approach provided a focal point of responsibility and accountability and enabled activities to be completed in a timely fashion.

Questions

1. Please explain how the selected organizational structure fits the company's strategy?

2. Why was the new workflow pattern more efficient and effective than the old?

3. What are some of the employee benefits that resulted from the change?

4. Based on the information provided, did internal and external customers receive the same benefits and why?

Linkage to the Chapter

1. Change in structure is most often the first step when implementing a new strategy

2. A change in the competitive environment resulted in a change in the way the company operated

3. Systems are needed to support a defined strategy

4. Using a project management approach enabled this company to keep up the pace

❑ ENDNOTES

1. Watts, R. M. (2002, May). Strategies for market disruptions. *Journal of Business Strategy*, p. 19.
2. Eisenberg, D. (2003, January 20). There's a new way to think of big blue. *Time*, p. 48.
3. Nadler, D. A., & Tushman, M. L. (1989). Organizational frame bending. *Academy of Management Executive*, Vol. 3, No. 3, p. 194.
4. Kotter, J. P. (1996). *Leading Change*. Boston, MA: HBSP, p. 172.
5. Christensen, C. M., & Overdorf, M. (2000, Mar-Apr). Meeting the challenge of disruptive change. *Harvard Business Review*.
6. Christensen (2000), op. cit., p. 71.
7. Ibid. p. 73.
8. Wheelwright, S. (1987). Restoring competitiveness in us manufacturing. In D. J. Teece (ed.), *The Competitive Challenge: Strategies for Industrial Innovation and Renewal*. Cambridge, Mass.: Ballinger, p. 83–100.
9. Pettigrew, A., & Whipp, R. (1993). *Managing Change For Competitive Success*. Oxford, UK: Blackwell Publishing, p. 106.
10. Ibid.
11. Ibid, p.6.
12. Connor, P. E., Lake, L. K., & Stackman, R. W. (2003). *Managing Organizational Change*. Westport, CT: Praeger Publishers, p. 8.
13. Ibid.
14. Ibid, p.9.
15. Yukl, G., & Lepsinger, R., (2004). *Flexible Leadership*. San Francisco, CA: Jossey-Bass, p. 34.
16. Christensen (2000), op. cit.
17. Govidarajan, V., & Gupta, A. K. (2001, July). Strategic innovation: a conceptual road map. *Business Horizons*, p. 3.
18. Christensen (2000), op. cit., p. 68.
19. Yukl (2004), op. cit., p.206.
20. Hillman, J. (2001, December 11). *Metlife's Cultural Transformation Increases Productivity*. A. M. Best Newswire.
21. Yukl (2004), op. cit., p. 207.
22. Christensen (2000), op. cit.
23. Livigni, R. (2003, January). *Creating An Adaptive Organizational Culture*. Academy of Management, Organization Development and Change Submission, p. 15.
24. Charan, R., (2006, March). *Sharpening Your Business Acumen*. Strategy + Business enews, pp. 4–9.
25. Siegal, W., Church, A. H., et.al. (1996). Understanding the management of change. *Journal of Organizational Change Management*, Vol. 9, No. 6, p. 59.
26. Ibid.
27. Ibid, p. 60.
28. Murray, E. J., & Richardson, P. R. (2003, March–April). Fast forward: a new framework for rapid organizational change. *Ivey Business Journal*.
29. Ibid, p. 5.
30. Ibid, p. 2.
31. Kotter, J. P. (1990). *A Force for Change*. New York, NY: The Free Press, p. 39.
32. Creasey, T. (2007). Defining change management. PROSCI Change Management Learning Center. Retrieved on March 6, 2007, from http://www.change-management.com/tutorial-defining-change-management.htm.
33. Cicmil, S. (1998, March–April). Implementing organizational change projects: impediments and gaps. *Strategic Change*, 8, pp. 123–127.
34. Harrington, H. J., Conner, D. R., & Horney, N. L. (2000). *Project Change Management*. New York: McGraw-Hill, p. 124.
35. Ibid.
36. Harrington (2000), op. cit., p. 128.
37. Cameron, E., Green M., (2004). *Making Sense of Change Management*. London: Kogan Press, p. 177.
38. Buchanan, D. A., (1991). Vulnerability and agenda: context and process in project management. *British Journal of Management*, Vol. 2, No. 3, p. 130.
39. Boddy, D., (1993, October). Managing change. *Management Services*, vol. 37, No. 10, p. 24.

Reading 3-1

Fast Forward: A New Framework for Rapid Organizational Change

BY ELSPETH J. MURRAY AND PETER R. RICHARDSON

Organizations don't necessarily need five or ten years to change. In fact, as these authors discovered, speed, focus and unstoppable momentum can make organizational change succeed — and last. They also discovered, and discuss below, that there are ten winning conditions that must be in place to make organizational change work.

"Cultural change takes a long time, 3 to 5 years at a minimum."

"Don't challenge people with radical change. Take an incremental approach and give them time to adjust."

THE STATEMENTS ABOVE are typical of the conventional wisdom on the pace and style of organizational change. But like some conventional wisdom, these statements are wrong, and this case, dangerously wrong. In fact, if organizational change is to be successful, it must happen rapidly and it must create momentum. The trouble is, most organizations don't know how to effect and manage change properly.

Just why is it that a few organizations can consistently make major changes rapidly and successfully, yet many others have limited, if any, success? To understand what separates winners from losers, we undertook a five-year study of 30 organizations. During this time, we developed and tested a model of organizational change that addresses three key questions:

- What activities lead to successful organizational change?
- In what sequence do these activities need to occur?
- What are the best ways to undertake these activities?

Our findings have led us to identify *ten conditions* that are necessary for rapid change to be successful. The first three create guidance for a change initiative, the next three generate and maintain *speed,* and the remaining four provide *critical mass.* Together, these *winning conditions* create the momentum required for success. We discuss these winning conditions, and the requirements to put them into place, in this article.

Elspeth J. Murray is associate professor of strategic management, School of Business, Queen's University, Kingston, Ontario. Peter R. Richardson is professor of strategic management, School of Business, Queen's University. They are co-authors of *Fast Forward: Organizational Change in 100 Days,* Oxford University Press, October 2000.

❏ THE CHALLENGE OF RAPID CHANGE

Some organizations can initiate and implement significant change only when a crisis occurs. In many others, where there is no crisis, change usually happens slowly, if at all, particularly if it is significant change such as a cultural transformation or perhaps a new business model. Most executives we met believe that significant change takes a long time, perhaps five years or a decade, if it happens at all. Many have been led to believe that radical changes are bad, and that slow, incremental change, allowing employees time to adjust, is preferable. Yet, for the most part, these executives reported that they are highly frustrated with their change initiatives.

How to make major organizational change happen quickly, without a crisis, and make it last, are challenges that have bedeviled managers for decades. In fact, these challenges remain some of the most important and difficult tasks that face leaders and managers in any kind of organization — public, private, or not-for-profit. In our research and work with organizations over the last five years, we have identified a dramatically different and more successful approach than the one preferred by most executives. This approach stresses focus, speed and unstoppable momentum, and is capable of producing significant, lasting change, without a crisis.

In his groundbreaking book, *New Directions for Organization Theory* (Oxford University Press, New York, 1997), Jeffrey Pfeffer identified one of the major challenges facing organizations as the elimination of inertia, which he defined as an inability to change as fast as the environment. We know that many companies appear unable to do so, and are increasingly challenged by the task of implementing organizational change. Why is this so? Our work has yielded a common set of reasons, as summarized below:

- Organizations implement "shallow" changes which do not address the real causes of poor performance.
- Executives fail to maintain and consolidate crisis-driven change.
- Too many changes occur at one time.
- Inadequate resources are allocated to major initiatives.
- Poor rates of progress lead to frustration and a loss of momentum.

- Insufficient personal time is devoted to leading strategic initiatives.
- Senior executives fail to provide appropriate leadership behavior patterns.

Our work with rank and file employees where major change initiatives have been unsuccessful echoes many of the concerns expressed by executives:

- Lack of information about the expectations for the roles and responsibilities that will change.
- Failure to deal with saboteurs or non-performers.
- Lack of positive reinforcement for employees committed to the change initiatives.
- Poor communication about progress — are our efforts all in vain?
- Failure to remove organizational barriers such as structural constraints.
- Perceived lack of commitment by the executive team, or a failure to "walk the talk".

❏ THE IMPORTANCE OF ESCAPE VELOCITY

Over the years, working in our 'living laboratories' with numerous CEOs and senior managers in variety of industries and firm sizes, we were struck by the fact that these individual failings, taken together, add up to a much more critical problem, the of lack of momentum. For in addition to sustaining forward movement, momentum must also act to tear down organizational barriers. As cases in point, consider the following three typical quotes from people we have interviewed:

The CEO of a major telecommunications provider observed:

No matter how hard we try, it seems to me that with many significant opportunities, where I thought we had alignment, we obviously didn't. Promised commitments never materialized, and agreed to high-priority projects were starved of necessary resources. We're still finalizing the design specs and we find out that one of our smaller, nimbler competitors is actually getting ready to go to market.

An entrepreneurial division manager in a major packaged goods company complained:

We're stuck in the Stone Age, Halfway through the year, one of my brand managers comes up with a great new product idea, and we're told to stick it in next year's budget. It's the 21ˢᵗ century and my company has yet to realize that great ideas don't coincide with budget cycles.

Another theme that we heard countless times in many different ways was neatly represented by this cry from the heart:

We don't make the tough calls. We try to accomplish far too much, spread our resources way too thin, and then we wonder why everything moves forward at a snail's pace.

A failure to develop its own internal source of energy is devastating for any change initiative. All too often, big initiatives fail to reach "escape velocity" and eventually die a slow, lingering death, often destroying careers and hard-earned reputations in the process. Even if they eventually succeed, they do so at a cost that is disproportionate to whatever benefits are realized.

Understanding why change efforts fail is interesting but not terribly useful. It is far more interesting to understand why change efforts, those that achieve escape velocity, overcome organizational inertia and succeed. While there has been a great deal of study on why change programs do, in fact, work, there has been relatively little work done to help understand the effects that pace and sequencing have on change success. As Andrew Pettigrew concluded, "Until very recently, scholars of innovation and change have been curiously uncurious about the pace and sequencing of change." (Linking Change Processes to Outcomes, in Michael Beer and Nitin Nohria, *Breaking the Code of Change,* Harvard Business School Press, Cambridge, Mass., 2000.

In our research we have been very curious about the effects of both pace and sequencing on the success of change programs. The specific questions we set out to answer are:

- What activities lead to success?

- In what sequence do these activities need occur?

- When specifically do these activities matter most in the overall change program?

In our five-year study, we worked with, observed and collected data from the executive teams, senior management ranks, and rank-and-file employees,

as they planned for and implemented a variety of major change programs — from acquisition integration to turnaround to major cultural change. Through this research program, we developed, refined and tested a model of organizational change that incorporates both sequencing and timing. We further validated the model through a series of interviews with 20 Fortune 500 CEOs who have implemented significant organizational change rapidly and successfully.

❏ THE WINNING CONDITIONS FOR CHANGE

When we started to review what is known about why change programs work, the first and most obvious conclusion was that success was linked to the elimination of organizational inertia. Physics 101 teaches us that organizational inertia is overcome only by generating sufficient momentum to overcome the natural inclination to stay at rest. Physics 101 further teaches us that momentum is the product of velocity and mass. And finally, from physics we know that velocity is speed with a specific direction or vector. Thus, in terms of today's fast paced business environment, successful change occurs when sufficient speed and mass are generated quickly enough so that enough momentum is created to move the organization quickly, from its state of rest — the status quo — in the desired direction. With these basic laws of motion as the theories underpinning our equation for success, we set out to identify those activities that are focused on generating sufficient speed, those that are primarily concerned with developing critical mass, and to identify which of those activities needed to happen and when.

We discovered that it was not so much *what* people did that led to success, but rather the fact that certain conditions were established during the change process. We called these conditions the *winning conditions.* By chance, and not by design, there are ten winning conditions:

1. Correct diagnosis of the change challenge — its nature, depth, breadth and the forces at play.

2. Early establishment of a shared understanding of the change challenge among the leadership team — a sense of vision, success measures, key programs and projects, and of the change process itself.

3. Multiple and ongoing opportunities to enrich this shared understanding — frequent progress reviews and action plan updates.

4. A sense of urgency — emphasizing speed when building an awareness and understanding of the need for change, without a crisis, and insisting on early tangible deliverables.

5. A limited and focused agenda for change — identifying 2, 3, or 4 major priorities, at a maximum, and driving them hard and fast.

6. Rapid, strategic decision-making and resource deployment — essential to build both speed and, subsequently, momentum.

7. A human flywheel of commitment — engaging the early adopters very rapidly, and bringing along the "fence-sitters" in a timely manner.

8. Identifying the sources of resistance and dealing with them ruthlessly — eliminating the 'drag' in the process that can prevent the build up of momentum, and waste valuable executive time.

9. Effective follow-through on changing key organizational enablers — ensuring that structure, communications, performance evaluation and recognition/reward are aligned with the new direction.

10. Demonstrating strong and consistent leadership — appropriate behaviours that provide tangible,early evidence of true commitment to the change process and the relentless pursuit of the new direction.

❏ THE FIRST 100 DAYS

Specifically, we wanted to understand when the winning conditions mattered most and why? In what sequence do these winning conditions need to be established? The first three create what we refer to as an intelligent direction or guidance for the change program. The next three are primarily concerned with generating and maintaining speed. The remaining four provide the critical mass. Taken together, these three sets of winning conditions lead to the unstoppable momentum that is required for successful organizational change.

In addition to understanding why the *winning conditions* matter, we wanted to find out when they were most critical in the overall change timetable. In words echoed by several of the CEOs we studied, we found that, "It is largely in the first 100 days that the game is won or lost." As Craig Conway of Peoplesoft noted, "The stakes are higher now. There is a dimension of speed, too. Not only are there fewer survivors, the difference between winning and losing can happen in a very short window of time. Companies that were regarded as the hottest plays in high technology three to 24 months ago could be downsizing or in reorganization or bankruptcy today."

We also concluded that the first 100 days were critical to success. Just as the American public and the media watch what every new president plans for and executes in the first 100 days in office, so too do employees in organizations. The "show me" ' phenomenon prevails, with a very short window of opportunity to do so. Furthermore, we found that the first 100 days are critical to the establishment of sufficient speed in the process — getting up a head of steam if you will. To borrow from the space ship analogy, successful launches result from proper fuel ignition, enough force generated to achieve lift off and sufficient acceleration — ever increasing speed — to provide a good shot at breaking out of the earth's gravitational force.

Consider Cisco's approach to acquisitions. The company aims to have the products of the acquired company integrated into its own product line as soon as the deal is closed. A pre-determined integration team, often headed by an employee of the acquired company, swings into action immediately. The new employees are made to feel as though they are Cisco employees as fast as possible, often with enhanced benefits. Major systems integration projects are completed within the first 100 days. Little wonder that Cisco is relatively more successful than its competitors at deriving value from its acquisitions.

❏ THE SECOND 100 DAYS

The second 100 days are important in terms of consolidating the progress made during the initial 100 days. This is the critical period during which momentum is building. Along with increasing the mass of resources now in place around the initiative, the accelerating speed is building momentum to the point where it cannot be stopped. By the end of the second hundred days, tangible results should be starting to flow.

Take, for example, Acklands Grainger, an industrial distributor we studied extensively, and that undertook a significant repositioning enabled by a major change in its culture. By the end of the second hundred days, several major steps had been taken. First, over five hundred of the company's employees had been through one-day sessions in which they had reviewed the new strategy, had an opportunity to ask questions of Doug Harrison, the CEO and his executive team, and consider the implications for their own operations. Almost to a person, they expressed enthusiasm for the new approach. However, there was still a palpable sense of 'Is this all talk, or are things really going to change? ' across the company. Even at this point, Harrison could report that the company's growth rate had risen to nearly 20 percent on an annualized basis. However, recognizing the understandable skepticism in the organization, the strategy team made a commitment to deliver five things by the end of the first 200 days. The five would demonstrate to all employees that things were changing. Although their delivery was not perfect, these initiatives, each a first step in one of the organization's five key initiatives, accelerated the momentum that was being created and felt throughout the organization.

❑ SUCCESSFUL CHANGE: ESTABLISHING AND MAINTAINING THE WINNING CONDITIONS

Many organizations treat change as a part-time undertaking, something to be taken care of after the 'dayjob' is done. Our research has shown that this mentality almost inevitably leads to slow progress, a lack of momentum and ultimately, failure. Organizational change follows the laws of motion, requiring mass, speed and momentum if it is to be effective. Our paper has presented what we believe are the requirements for establishing these *winning conditions* for change. The deeper the level of change that is desired, the more important it is that executives recognize the critical importance of the first 100 days in creating speed, and the second 100 days in building momentum. As usual, there is no one silver bullet, no simple formula that will bring about success in this situation. Rather, executives have to establish a set of *winning conditions* that create the context for the successful execution of rapid organizational change.

Case 3-1

Competition Drives Changes in Organizational Structure
How One Utility Responded to a New Reality

WILLIAM V. LEBAN, PH.D., PMP, ROOP

DIRECTOR OF BUSINESS MANAGEMENT PROGRAMS AT DEVRY UNIVERSITY

NATURAL GAS PIPELINE COMPANY (Natural) owns and operates almost 13,000 miles of interstate pipeline. Its natural gas transmission system has two major subsystems, the Amarillo and Gulf Coast Systems, interconnected by the A/G line. Both systems terminate in the Chicago area. In addition, Natural owns various gas storage fields in Iowa, Illinois, and Texas and leases storage capacity in Oklahoma (see map).

Natural maintains approximately eight percent of the U.S. natural gas transmission industry market share. Prior to recent changes in regulation, Natural had provided natural gas sales, storage, and transportation services to gas distribution companies as well as to producers, marketers, industrial and commercial end users, power plants, and other pipelines.

Natural's success depends upon its ability to provide efficient and cost-effective services. By adding pipeline to attach to new markets or upgrading facilities to reduce operating costs, the company enhances its competitive position. Since the Engineering function determines what new facilities should be installed to meet customer (internal and external) needs, it plays a major role.

Changes in the natural gas transmission industry have resulted in less regulation and more competition; in response, Natural's Engineering function moved from sequential to simultaneous work flow to address increased competitive pressure.

Regulation and Change

Until 1993 interstate pipeline operations were subject to extensive regulation by the Federal Energy Regulatory Commission (the "FERC"). The FERC regulated, among other things, rates and charges for the resale and transportation of gas in interstate commerce, the construction and operation of interstate pipeline facilities, and the accounts and records of interstate pipelines.

In 1993 the FERC issued Order 636, which mandated a role change for natural gas transmission companies. Their traditional merchant function (buying and reselling natural gas) was changed to one of natural gas transporter. Natural's throughput, sales plus transportation, is approximately 1,550 billion cubic feet per year. Sales dropped from 70 percent of throughput in 1984 to zero in 1994, transportation increased from 30 percent of throughput in 1984 to 100 percent in 1994.

William V. Leban, Ph.D., PMP, RODP is Director of Business Management Programs at DeVry University.

This article is reprinted from the November 1996 *PM Network* magazine with permission of the Project Management Institute, 130 South State Road, Upper Darby, PA 19082 USA, a worldwide organization for advancing the state-of-the-art of project management. Phone 610/734-3330 Fax 610/734-3266.

Thanks to changes in federal regulations, the natural-gas pipeline industry was suddenly faced with market pressures. Using project management to achieve simultaneous workflow allowed this company to keep up the pace.

Natural gas procurement has become the responsibility of local utilities and other customers, with pipelines transporting and storing natural gas. While the gas transmission industry has existed for many years (the initial parts of Natural's system were constructed in the 1930s), the introduction of competition with reduced regulation has occurred over the last several years.

The Competition

Natural's transportation competitors consist of interstate pipelines (Fig. 3.15) that own facilities in the vicinity of the Chicago metropolitan area.

Competition for gas transportation and storage may be provided by one or more other pipelines, depending on how each pipeline markets its services to meet customer needs. For example, Natural has the lowest priced 100-day storage service; 50 versus 60 cents per MMBtu charged by its competitor, American Natural Resources (ANR). However, Natural's average firm transportation rate from the Mid-Continent (MidCon) gas supply region to Chicago is higher; 61 versus 53 cents per MMBtu when compared to ANR.

Transportation rates, adequate pipeline capacity, and the availability of storage services are key factors in determining Natural's ability to compete for particular transportation business. By upgrading pipeline facilities to reduce operating costs and adjusting flow patterns on Natural's system to better utilize spare capacity, Natural enhances its competitive position.

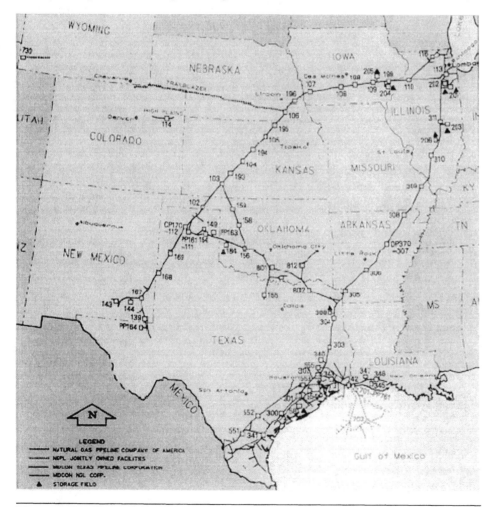

Figure 3.15   Natural's Facilities

Business Situation

Natural follows traditional business lines with Marketing, Accounting, Transmission, Rates, and Engineering vice-presidential areas. The Transmission area is responsible for operating the interstate natural gas transmission system, with all other areas performing support functions. Engineering plays a major role in deciding how facilities are utilized and determines what new facilities should be installed to meet customer needs.

With changes introduced by the FERC, Natural moved from a monopolistic market with geographic boundaries to one of price-sensitive, competitive services. Therefore, Natural's Engineering area redefined its role in 1993. Prior to 1993, Natural had been more reactive in responding to well-developed, long-term customer needs in a captive market, with a high probability of cost recovery. The new competitive environment requires a more proactive role in recognizing and reducing pipeline system operating inefficiencies (to reduce cost) and developing more individualized customer-based strategies (to make gas transportation and storage services more attractive to the customer).

Engineering Responsibilities and Organizational Structure

Natural's Engineering area (approximately 140 staff with an annual $100 million capital expenditure budget) performs three main functions in supporting project activities: design, drafting, and construction administration. These functions had traditionally been accomplished under a functional organization structure. Activities include engineering, specification, procurement and construction of replacement, upgrade or new facilities. Specific projects vary in scope, from designing a gas dehydration tower to developing a major gas storage facility.

Under the original functional organizational structure (Figure 3.16), four distinct departments had well-defined project responsibility when given a preliminary project definition. As described in the figure, each of these areas performed specific technical and administrative-type tasks in support of project activities. Departments were broken down into tasks, with each group of tasks dependent on completion by the previous group. Projects had a sequential line of development, meaning tasks were handled one at a time, with each one completed before moving onto the next. Groups such as Environmental, Land, Corrosion, Metallurgy, etc., maintained a support role.

Human Resource Background

Engineers in the departments had company experience that could be classified in one of two types: Type 1 engineers, those with pipeline field operating or facility construction experience, were routinely assigned to Construction, while Type 2 engineers, those experienced in engineering equipment design, cost estimating, drafting, and procurements, were assigned to Design. Some engineers in the Engineering area are considered experts based on their years of field experience working on pipeline or station facilities. Other engineers have technical experience in such specialized areas as electric power design, gas processing, structural engineering, controls, and automation programming.

❏ THE CHALLENGE OF CHANGE

In 1993, as a result of the change in business environment, Natural's Engineering area determined that it must address the issues of:

1. *Focal Point of Responsibility and* Accountability. The planning and implementation of project activities require a focus point of responsibility. A stronger tie to customers (internal/Transmission area or external/Marketing services) to provide better project definition and continuity.

2. *Matching Company Resources to Customer Needs.* Projects are evaluated, selected, and planned based on their contribution to meeting company and customer objectives. Establishing project priorities and schedules should be based on matching company resources to customer needs.

The alternatives developed to address these issues by increasing the effectiveness of work flow were:

Alternative 1. Maintain Existing Functional Organization and Categorize Projects

Categorize projects so that tasks are distributed and processed based on established criteria. Field

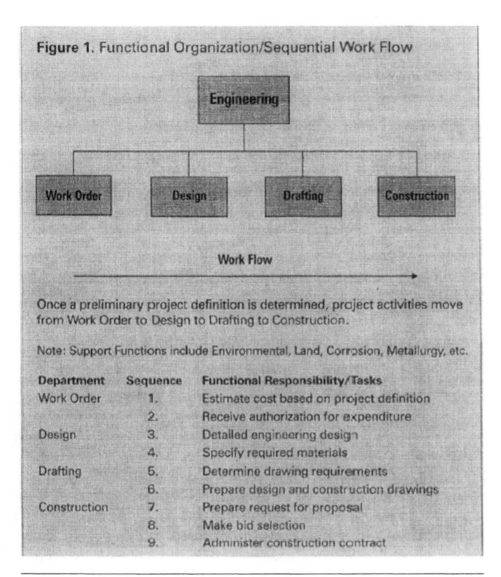

Figure 1. Functional Organization/Sequential Work Flow

Work Flow

Once a preliminary project definition is determined, project activities move from Work Order to Design to Drafting to Construction.

Note: Support Functions include Environmental, Land, Corrosion, Metallurgy, etc.

Department	Sequence	Functional Responsibility/Tasks
Work Order	1.	Estimate cost based on project definition
	2.	Receive authorization for expenditure
Design	3.	Detailed engineering design
	4.	Specify required materials
Drafting	5.	Determine drawing requirements
	6.	Prepare design and construction drawings
Construction	7.	Prepare request for proposal
	8.	Make bid selection
	9.	Administer construction contract

Figure 3.16 *Functional Organization/Sequential Work Flow*

personnel or central office design engineers would be assigned projects based on the categories shown in Figure 3.17. Personnel would receive assignments based on their experience and skills.

The design engineer, for Category II and III projects, would prepare the job scope and required material specifications. Work Order would prepare the necessary cost estimates to support the project approval process. A sequential work flow would continue, as information would next be sent to Drafting and then on to Construction for implementation. In addition, projects would be prioritized within each department.

Alternative 2. Establish a Project Management Control for All Projects

Establish project teams to plan, organize, monitor, and control all aspects of project activities. Teams would be assigned projects based on the project categories stated in Alternative 1. A project team, headed by a project manager who is assigned to project engineers, would be responsible for all aspects of a project: design, cost estimation, drawings, material procurement, and contract administration. Projects would evolve with parallel lines of development, meaning that several tasks,

Table 1. Categories of Capital Expenditure Activities

Listed below are categories of the capital expenditure activities performed in Natural's Engineering area:

Category I   Field Recognition and Implementation

(30 percent of the number of projects/approximately $2.5 million/year)

No safety system involved.

No design required.

No environmental considerations.

Under $25,000.

Example: Install cathodic protection devices along the pipeline.

Basis: Well-defined guidelines.

Category II   Design and Operating Experience Required

(10 percent of the number of projects/approximately $3.5 million/year)

Design required. Sketches and material specifications.

No drawings required.

No environmental considerations.

Under $100,000.

Examples: Install air compressor, liquid pump or drip tank.

Basis: Experienced designer approves activities.

Category III   Detailed Design and Formal Contracts

(60 percent of the number of projects/approximately $94 million/year)

Design and drawings required.

Environmental permits, etc., required.

Engineering to prepare al Bills of Material.

Formal contract.

Unlimited expenditure.

Examples: Install pipeline loop or gas compressor units.

Basis: Applicable standards and company procedures must be followed.

Figure 3.17   Categories of Capital Expenditure Activities

addressing different functional areas, could be handled simultaneously. Project activities could be accomplished by the engineer and support personnel in the manner shown in Figure 3.18.

Project engineers would be the catalysts in coordinating project tasks. Decisions would be made based on their impact on all facets of the project. Team members would work together in a group to assist each other based on their experience.

Alternative 3. Field Extension, Engineering Services Group and Project Teams

Utilize field personnel to plan and implement Category I projects. Establish an Engineering Services

Table 2. Alternative Work Flow Plan

Work Flow	Tasks	Previous Functional
A	1. Estimate cost/receive approval	Work Order
	3. Detailed engineering design	Design
	5. Determine drawing requirements	Drafting
B	2. Receive authorization for revised activities	Work Order
	4. Specify required materials	Design
	6. Prepare design and construction drawings	Drafting
C	7. Prepare request for proposal	Construction
	8. Make bid selection	Construction
	9. Administer construction contract	Construction

Figure 3.18 Alternative Work Flow Plan

Group (ESG) for Category II projects. Utilize project teams for all Category III projects. Figure 3.19 illustrates the organizational structure of Alternative 3. The ESG would include specialists with field experience, who could answer questions and address problems on the operation and maintenance of existing facilities. If technical specialists (electrical or gas processing, for example) were required, they would be available from the Functional Support Group.

Selecting an Alternative

Management determined that the best alternative would be a structure in which:

- Engineering can focus on internal customer (pipeline operating) needs by utilizing field personnel and the Engineering Services Group.

- Project teams, addressing external customer needs, would handle activities that require a broader, less-defined role of coordinator over project activities, and thereby act as a focal point.

- Technical specialists directly support project team activities.

Alternative 3, Field Extension, Engineering Services Group and Project Teams, met these criteria and was implemented in Natural's Engineering area. A comparison of the sequential versus simultaneous work flow, as shown in Figure 3.20, illustrates the broader focus on project activities found under the project organization.

The selection of Alternative 3, Field Extension, Engineering Services Group and Project Teams, impacts the Engineering area's focus of change in two ways:

A Focal Point of Responsibility and Accountability. By placing the experienced experts in the Engineering Services Group, internal customers such as Transmission have direct access to individuals who can most likely satisfy their needs. By forming project teams, engineers can work directly with Marketing to analyze and develop the best project alternative for external customers.

By maintaining a Functional Support Group, which reports to project managers, technical experts focus on specific engineering disciplines to address problems. In addition, this group provides consistent responses. Project managers, as leaders of the project teams, have the responsibility

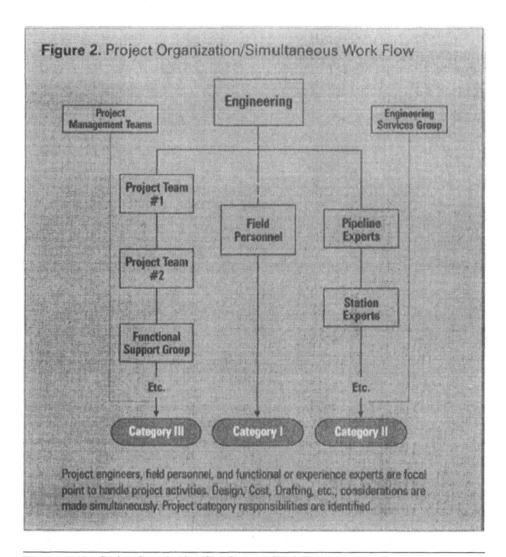

Figure 2. Project Organization/Simultaneous Work Flow

Figure 3.19   Project Organization/Simultaneous Work Flow

and authority to make decisions on project activities. Therefore, they have the primary responsibility to plan, direct, monitor, and control project activities.

Matching Company Resources to Customer Needs. By categorizing projects, Category 1 activities that maintain pipeline integrity are handled directly by field personnel. Engineering standards are implemented by field personnel. By assigning Category II projects to an "experience" expert, projects gain an advocate to work with field personnel to assist in development and direct implementation. These maintenance and replacement projects no longer directly compete with the larger-dollar activities. By assigning Category III projects to a team that

has technical support, there is a focal point of coordination and resources are matched to needs. Project cost, scheduling, and performance goals are the focus of the team.

Implementation

Placement on a project team or within an Engineering Services or Functional Support Group was made based on an engineer's experience, knowledge, and ability. Some engineers were promoted to the new "project manager" position and sent to leadership training sessions to fine-tune their skills. Project engineers were encouraged to upgrade their skills with technical training courses.

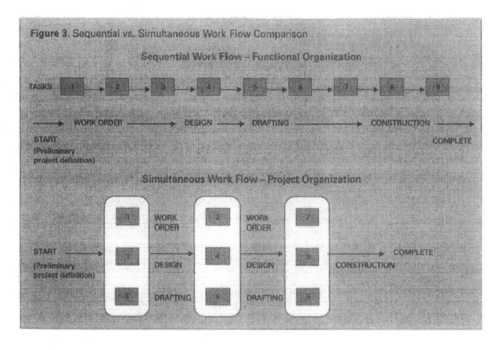

Figure 3.20 *Sequential vs. Simultaneous Work Flow Comparison*

Job experience and training have enabled engineers to develop into a valuable resource for the company. Focus groups met every two weeks to address problems with procedures, communications, etc. A continuous review of how the new organization operated revealed an upgrading of services and a better utilization of human resources.

Competitive forces dictated the need for proactive project coordination in meeting the demands of Natural's internal and external customers. Alternative 3, Field Extension, Engineering Services Group, and Project Teams, has provided an organizational design and the proper allocation of human resources necessary to meet Engineering's focus of change.

4

Leading Change and Empowering Employees

❏ CHAPTER AT A GLANCE

Highlights of this chapter include the following:

1. Management skills are required to address the daily operations of a business. Leadership skills are required to provide direction and guidance to strategic change initiatives. Change agents need to have both management and leadership skills.

2. Recent concepts of leadership emphasize the emotional aspects of influence much more than reason or the rational, cognitive process.

3. A transactional leader would lead incremental change (fine tuning or adapting) and a transformational leader would lead strategic change (fundamental changes that develop a new configuration). As with management and leadership, transformational leadership

is not an alternative for leadership, but augments transactional leadership.

4. A transformational approach to leadership, combining path finding with people problem-solving skills to introduce organizational change and using employee empowerment are more effective in overcoming barriers to change than a transactional leadership approach, which concentrates on technical problem-solving, often to the neglect of people and organizational issues.

5. Leading change through application of the four "Cs" (coordination, competencies, commitment, and communication) will enable you to extend a network, focused on the change initiative, to others within your organization. Your ability to focus on these factors and utilize this network to plan, implement, and operate the strategic change initiative will determine your success.

6. Critical to the successful leadership of a strategic change initiative is your ability to understand the external environment, build coalitions, question existing organizational assumptions, communicate a vision, and shift ownership to a working team.

7. Change agents can create change by providing a vision that is attractive to followers rather than creating dissatisfaction with the status quo.

8. The integration of five "Core Roles" (entrepreneur, coordinator, mentor, advocate, and visionary) enables a change agent to help employees facilitate, implement, and manage change to improve performance.

9. In situations of organizational change, where consultation and participation are advocated, soft skills and emotional intelligence are important for leadership effectiveness.

10. Leadership is the influencing process of leaders and followers to achieve organizational objectives through change.

The following vignette provides us a perspective on how leaders within an organization determine the limitations of their old mindset and style of leading and focus on new ways to see themselves, one another, their role in the organization, and their opportunities. Only after leaders have defined their roles and responsibilities can they lead others!

❏ VIGNETTE

"The transformation of DTE Energy from a regulated to a "fiercely competitive" deregulated business was mindset driven. When we began supporting this effort, both the CEO and president realized that even though they could not yet specify all the changes required in their business strategy and organization, they could and must begin shifting their culture from entitlement to an entrepreneurial, service-oriented style. Early on, they realized that this responsibility began with them.

The strategy for dealing with the leaders' mindsets was developed in partnership with DTE Energy's internal change leaders. We agreed to provide the top executives with a four-day breakthrough experience aimed at "walking the talk of change." This session was designed to wake the leaders up to the limitations of their old mindset and style of leading and introduce them to new ways to see themselves, one another, their role in the organization, and the opportunities in deregulation.

The overall strategy went far beyond the four-day workshop. Our experience of delivering breakthrough training has demonstrated to us that, although the multiday workshop is a central component, the tangible results required to support the organization's transformation comes from a much larger, integrated process. For DTE, this included presession interviews of each of the participants by the facilitators to establish clear personal objectives, follow-up sessions, pre- and postsessions meetings between bosses and subordinates, large group meetings, executive coaching, on-the-job feedback, and team development. Each of these reinforced and extended the insights from the initial program.

Every follow-up session included the executives, who shared with their managers their own personal development experiences from the program. The executives modeled telling the truth, being vulnerable and openly correcting their relationships with one another, various management groups, and the union.

During these sessions, vital information was shared in a safe environment, the healing of old wounds began, and movement toward greater collaboration was established. Over time, a number of leaders began to see the importance of operating openly and "consciously" with one another. Both the CEO and the president felt strongly that the values and principles "taught" in the breakthrough training were to be modeled overtly in the organization. As feedback among the leaders increased in real time, they set better conditions for the overall organization to become faster acting and more entrepreneurial — and to be a healthier place to work. This established a valuable foundation for the organization's transformation.

Transformational change strategy must attend to changing mindset, style, and behavior across the entire system. Beyond the leadership breakthrough training rollout, examples of interventions that catalyze and reinforce mindset and behavioral change include

- Sharing the case for change featuring mindset and behavioral change as primary drivers;
- Determining the desired culture as a reflection of the new mindset and style;
- Creating high participation in revisioning the organization's future;
- Employing whole-systems meeting technologies to design the future state;
- Building the teams required to implement the future state in ways that address mindset, style, behavior, and relationships; and
- Performing an impact analysis comparing the desired state scenarios and the current organization using the new mindset and culture criteria.

Each of these can be delivered through a cascade or large group approach (See Endnotes 31, pages 62–64).

The vignette above provides us a perspective on the extent to which one organization went to establish a new mindset and behavior by enabling their leaders to see both the positive and negative effects of their current mindset, style, and behavior. While your organization may not be as large, you will still need to go through a similar process if you want your leaders to better understand the current situation so that they can lead the movement to the future state.

❏ CHAPTER PERSPECTIVE

Leadership is critical to the success of any change initiative. By understanding differences between management and leadership, attributes of transactional and transformational leadership styles, and key factors in leading change, you can better understand what needs to be done to successfully lead change. Critical to the successful leadership of a strategic change initiative is your ability to understand the external environment, build coalitions, question existing organizational assumptions, and communicate a vision and shift ownership to a working team. In addition, Kanter (See Endnotes 28, page 4) states:

'The most important things a leader can bring to a changing organization are passion, conviction, and confidence in others. Too often executives announce a

plan, launch a task force, and then simply hope that people find the answers — instead of offering a dream, stretching their horizons, and encouraging people to do the same.'

As a leader, you must offer a better tomorrow so that followers will stretch beyond what they have seen as possible in the past and extend their capabilities to build a better future!

In Chapter 4 we will also cover the required competencies of a change agent and provide you a self-assessment instrument that will enable you to determine your strengths and weaknesses in each of five core roles. A change agent's function during organizational change will also be addressed. Finally, a series of leadership and change quotes are provided so that you can further analyze and evaluate your understanding of leadership and change in today's business environment.

❏ MANAGEMENT VERSUS LEADERSHIP

There has been much discussion on the definitions of and differences between management and leadership. From a managing organizational change perspective, individuals in today's companies need to perform both roles as appropriate to the situation. There is also an ongoing need for both managers and leaders to learn and adapt to a changing environment.

Multiple Responsibilities

A change agent is one who develops relationships designed to help employees facilitate, implement, and manage change to improve performance. We will define management skills as those required to address the daily operations of a business and leadership skills as those required to provide direction and guidance to strategic change initiatives. Therefore, since change agents implement and manage change, they need to have both management and leadership skills. Figure 4.1 depicts differences in the responsibilities of management versus leadership.

To further clarify these differences, we know that management provides a high degree of predictability and order and is likely to produce the short-term results expected by various stakeholders. In addition, we know that leadership facilitates and provides change, often to a significant

Management Responsibilities	Leadership Responsibilities
Planning and Budgeting	Establishing Direction
Organizing and Staffing	Aligning People
Controlling and Problem Solving	Motivation and Inspiring

Figure 4.1   Management versus Leadership Responsibilities[1]

degree, and has the potential to produce extremely useful change. Since there has been an increasing amount of change in today's business environment, organizations need employees to provide more leadership!

Definition of Leadership

Most definitions of leadership are formed around a number of elements including influence, group, and goal.[2] *Influence* means that the leader has an impact on others by inducing them to behave in a certain way. *Group* focuses on supporting the fact that the leader has some responsibility to members of the group. *Goal* focuses on recognizing that the leader influences the behavior of the group members in the direction of goals. Stogdill states that leadership may be considered as the process (act) of influencing the activities of an organized group in its efforts toward goal setting and goal achievement.[3] Most of the earlier definitions of leadership seem to emphasize rational, cognitive processes. For many years, it was common to view leadership as a process wherein leaders influence followers to believe it is in their best interest to cooperate in achieving a shared task objective, a transactional relationship. Until the 1980s, few conceptions of leadership recognized the importance of emotions as a basis of influence, which would be more of a transformational relationship.

Different from the past, many recent conceptions of leadership emphasize the emotional aspects of influence, i.e., motivate and inspire, much more than reason or the rational, cognitive processes mentioned above. According to this view, only the emotional, value-based aspects of leadership influence can account for the exceptional achievements of individuals, groups, or organizations. Leaders inspire followers to willingly sacrifice their selfish interests for a higher cause.[4] Kotter suggests that leadership tends to be an informal, flexible, inspirational, and future-oriented process.[5] A recent performance-based definition states that leadership is the ability of an individual to influence, motivate, and enable others to contribute toward the effectiveness and success of the organization.[6]

Role of the Leader

When discussing leadership, the role of the leader should also be addressed. For example, Wheatley makes the point that leaders need to (a) help us develop the clear identity that lights the dark moments of confusion, (b) support us as we learn how to live by our values, and (c) understand that we are best controlled by concepts that invite our participation, not policies and procedures that curtail our contribution.[7] During the past several years, there has been enough research to demonstrate the need for leader vision[8] and the enduring strength and resiliency of companies that have strong values.[9] In addition, some believe that cognitive or skills performance embedded in a distinctly social context, encouraging participation, has always been a key aspect of leadership and is likely to become progressively more important as we move into the twenty-first century.[10]

When addressing the changing needs of the business environment, organizations must emphasize the advantages of flexibility, adaptability, and the development and nurture of relationships. Common to all of these desirable traits and skills are emotional competencies. In addition, we also find that organizations are looking for leadership influence as a powerful tool in the creation and implementation of positive change and goal realization.[11]

In today's highly competitive and complex business environment, decisions need to be made in a timely manner and change initiatives need to move forward under the direction of many. Therefore, we find that leadership is required at all levels of an organization, especially when it is necessary to address the evolution of change throughout the organization.

❏ TRANSACTIONAL VERSUS TRANSFORMATIONAL LEADERSHIP STYLE

By understanding leadership style, we can begin to address the everyday actions or behaviors of a leader or manager. We will define transactional leadership style or behaviors as those typically found in the day-to-day activities of a manager and transformational leadership style or behaviors as those typically found to be future and change oriented. The major difference between the two styles is that transformational leadership is required for a change agent to be successful with a strategic change initiative because transactional leadership does not focus on a future state. From another perspective, a transactional leader would lead incremental change (fine tuning or adapting) and a transformational leader would lead strategic change (fundamental changes that develop a new configuration). See Chapter 2 for a more detailed description of incremental and strategic change.

Figure 4.2 provides us a listing of the attributes of transactional managers and transformational leaders. Please note the orientation of daily operations for transactional managers and future and change orientation for transformational leaders.

Transformational leaders provide direction and guidance on what needs to be done when working toward an uncertain future. Transactional managers provide rational and minimum direction in a stable work environment. Since some things stay the same (transactional) during the implementation of a change initiative while other things change (transformational) as we move to a new future, a change agent takes on the role of both a transformational leader and transactional manager.

Prior to 1985 most leadership research focused on transactional leadership or an exchange framework of leader-follower relationships, whereby managers clarify for subordinates the tasks that must be accomplished and the rewards for successful task completion. However, this exchange of rewards for effort was not an adequate explanation for levels of effort and performance that exceeded ordinary expectations. Therefore, transformational leadership was developed to explain subordinate performance **beyond expectations** based on commitment to the leader, a trust in mission, and a desire to fulfill the leaders vision.[13]

How Leadership Has Changed

Consistent with the concept of leadership at all levels is the "Full Range of Leadership" concept where leaders exhibit each style (transactional to transformational) to some degree and thereby use the leadership style that is most appropriate for the situation.[14] As with management and leadership, transformational leadership is not an alternative for leadership, but augments transactional leadership.[15] In addition, transformational leaders change organizational environments,

Managers (Transactional Leaders)	Transformational Leaders
• Are goal and strategy oriented	• Are visionary and mission oriented
• Bargain or contract for the exchange of effort/output for rewards as primary way to motivate others	• Use inspiration, charisma, and inherent excitement of the vision to enroll and motivate others
• Stress and value rationality, limiting options and choices, problem solving	• Are individually and developmentally oriented
• Are day-to-day and operationally oriented	• Look at old problems in new ways
• Generally accent established norms, values, culture, and beliefs	• Stress and value intellectual ability, problem exploration, experimentation
• Are risk controllers	• Are future and change oriented
	• Question existing culture, norms, values, and beliefs
	• Are risk takers

Figure 4.2   *Attributes of Transactional Managers and Transformational Leaders*[12]

Transactional Leadership
(Relates Well With a Manager's Daily Operating Role)

- Makes clear what I can expect to receive, if my performance meets designated standards
- Provides me with assistance in exchange for my efforts
- Discusses in specific terms who is responsible for achieving performance targets
- Expresses his/her satisfaction when I do a good job
- Keeps track of all my mistakes
- Directs his/her attention toward failure to meet standards

Transformational Leadership
(Relates Well With a Leader's Guidance and Direction Role)

- Instills pride in me for being associated with him/her
- Displays a sense of power and confidence
- Emphasizes the importance of having a strong sense of purpose
- Emphasizes the importance of having a collective sense of mission
- Reexamines critical assumptions to question whether they are appropriate
- Suggests new ways of looking at how we do our jobs

Figure 4.3   *Transactional versus Transformational Leadership Styles/Behaviors*

provide new realities, are proactive, and create emotional relationships with followers, as opposed to transactional leaders who accept the status quo, are reactive, and focus on creating material relationships with followers.[16] Figure 4.3 indicates the types of actions or day-to-day behaviors that would be taken with the transactional and transformational leadership styles.[17] Beatty and Lee suggest that a transformational approach to leadership, combining pathfinding with people problem-solving skills to introduce organizational changes, is more effective in overcoming barriers to change than a transactional leadership approach, which concentrates on technical problem solving, often to the neglect of people and organizational issues.[18]

Differences in Behavior

Leaders engaging in transformational behaviors have been shown to produce a variety of positive outcomes in organizational settings. Transformational leadership has consistently been linked to high levels of effort, performance, and satisfaction

with the leader. Transformational leadership has also been found to be associated with an employee's affective commitment to the organization, intention to leave the organization, and trust in the leader. *When followers have developed trust and confidence in their leader, and are in step with the organizational mission, they are able to achieve exceptional levels of performance.*[19] Given this wide variety of positive outcomes associated with transformational leadership, the development of transformational leaders in organizations should be a priority.

Even though transformational leadership behavior has been observed at lower organizational levels, it is likely to occur more frequently at the higher organizational levels because organizations provide a greater scope for visioning (or mission formulation and implementation) behavior at the higher rather than the lower levels.[20]

Figure 4.4 provides an overview based on information provided in the previous sections of this chapter of the differences between the change agent's role as management versus leadership. Based on the situation they face, the change agent

Role	Management	Leadership
Responsibilities	High Degree of Predictability	Change of Significant Degree
Type of Change	Incremental	Strategic
Attributes	Day-to-Day and Operationally Oriented	Future and Change Oriented
Objective	Exchange of Rewards for Effort	Subordinate Performance Beyond Expectations
Style/Behavior	Transactional — Provides me with assistance in exchange for my efforts	Transformational — Emphasizes the importance of having a strong sense of purpose
Approach	Technical Problem Solving	Pathfinding and People Problem Solving

Figure 4.4   *Change Agent's Role as Management versus Leadership*

will take on either role in support of the strategic change initiative.

When reviewing Figure 4.4, please note the alignment between the type of change, (strategic), attributes (future state), objective (performance beyond expectations), and approach (people and problem solving). Leaders guide and assist subordinates to perform beyond what has been expected in the past so that they can move to a better future state.

Visionary Leaders

A significant component of the transformational leadership style is that which addresses vision, mission, and purpose. The transformational leadership model portrays the leader's strategic vision as playing a central role in animating and empowering followers. In addition, transformational theories have concerned themselves with follower outcomes. Sashkin suggests that

'Visionary leaders boost the sense of self-worth of those around them by expressing unconditional positive regard, paying attention, showing trust, sharing ideas, and making clear how important and valued organizational members are.'[21]

Visionary leadership states that the key function of leadership is to communicate a compelling vision, or picture of where the organization is going. By having a clear and attractive picture of the future, people transform thought into reality and intention into action. They are energized or empowered because they have a sense of purpose or direction, combined with an enhanced belief in their ability to achieve their purpose.

Empowering Employees to Help Lead Change

Empowerment is the key to unlock the energy and talents that reside within an organization and make it competitive. Leadership must be involved in a continuous challenge to give up control over the work and unlock the potential capabilities of employees by promoting empowering initiatives. This process gives employees the power to control their own destiny and should release creative energy and initiative at every level (See Endnotes 22, page 44). However, when an employee is given authority through empowerment, the supervisor relinquishes control. Therefore, with empowerment there is a critical balance between the supervisors giving up control and the employee taking control. The best way to handle this balance is to have the supervisor and employee work together to set expectations and establish a boundary of power. As the supervisor and employee build trust over time, this boundary can be expanded.

In an empowered environment, jobs must have two main components. The *first* is the core activities, which are what the employee must achieve as the basic purpose of the job. The *second* component is an area of flexibility based on the employee's competency and interests. Job overlap, rather than being avoided, becomes an opportunity for sharing information and innovation.[22] To help establish this

1. Material Rewards	Seeking possessions, wealth and a high standard of living
2. Power/Influence	Seeking to be in control of people and resources
3. Search for meaning	Seeking to do things that are believed valuable for their own sake
4. Expertise	Seeking a high level of accomplishment in a specialized field
5. Creativity	Seeking to innovate and be identified with original output
6. Affiliation	Seeking nourishing relationships with others
7. Autonomy	Seeking to be independent and able to make decisions for oneself
8. Security	Seeking a solid and predictable future
9. Status	Seeking to be recognized, admired, and respected by the community at large

Figure 4.5   Nine Key Motivators of Employees[24]

empowered environment, a major emphasis should be placed on a new performance appraisal system to reward employees and training programs help employees to develop their full potential. These actions should be enhanced by truly open communication to welcome and involve everyone in the implementation of changes and in the learning and adapting process.[23]

An important component of empowerment is using inspiration, charisma, and inherent excitement of the vision to enroll and motivate employees, an attribute of transformational leadership (see Figure 4.2). Figure 4.5 provides a listing and description of nine key motivators that can be used in an empowered environment. If the result of these motivators is aligned with the organization's goals, it should provide a powerful combination where the employee helps meet individual, group, and organizational objectives. It should also be noted that this would also help enhance the organization's network in support of the change.

❏ KEY FACTORS IN LEADING CHANGE

In this section, we will address the key factors that a leader must focus on when integrating a strategic change initiative into an organization.

The following situation provides one organization's perspective:[25]

'A manufacturing company revamped its business strategy, structure, management processes, culture, and decision making to create strategic business units. After the majority of the organization's changes were in place, we designed a system-wide integration strategy to unify the whole and fortify the leaders' collective understanding of how the new organization worked.

Every functional leader was asked to prepare a creative presentation of his or her purpose, contribution, responsibilities, and assets. In addition, they presented their views of what services or resources they offered to other key functions and what they needed from others to carry out their roles effectively. They also identified the relationships they had with other leaders that were in good working order and those that were in need of clarification or support. Everyone was encouraged to ask for the participation of their staff to widen the organization's involvement.

In the logical sequence of business workflow, the leaders presented their input. As the organization's total functioning was pieced together like a complex puzzle, the beauty of the whole picture began to take shape. Rather than understanding just the theory behind the new design, the leaders saw how each of them was essential to the success of the whole. They saw that the total organization needed their individual functions to work optimally. And they pinpointed where new relationships were required, how to improve their effectiveness, and how the culture of shared responsibility and teamwork was essential to the company's new business direction.

The senior leaders used the meeting to reinforce their new expectations of management, to put some old negative political and behavioral patterns to rest, and to reward examples of breakthrough thinking and acting. The participants went away with a much broader perspective and much sharper directives to share with their staffs.'

The need for shared responsibility and teamwork referred to in the above situation requires that a leader focus on a number of critical factors. In this section, we will address those factors.

The direction and guidance that a leader provides during the planning and implementation of a strategic change initiative must be focused on a number of critical factors. *Coordination* or teamwork is required to identify, develop, and implement strategic project plans. Required *competencies* must be defined and compared to existing resources so that any gaps can be identified and appropriate resources acquired. Individuals and teams must make a *commitment* or "buy into" the established direction of change. Finally, *communication* of the new vision and strategic direction must be appropriately defined and consistently communicated. A change agent's ability to lead with a focus on these factors will help increase the probability of successful change.

Coordination

The coordination or teamwork required to support a strategic change initiative means that members from across the organization must work together to integrate their functional area knowledge into a comprehensive plan. Based on the scope of the strategic initiative, they must first identify the activities required to meet strategic goals and objectives. Secondly, they must develop a plan that addresses required resources, performance requirements, and an appropriate schedule of activities. Finally, they must direct, monitor, and control these activities as the project is implemented. A coordinated effort is an absolute necessity for a change initiative since many adjustments to the plan will likely be made as the change evolves.

Competencies

With changes to vision, mission statement, and strategic objectives, which result from an iterative process of review of the external and internal environments human and other resources that are not a part of the existing structure will be identified. Therefore, the addition of these resources and their associated competencies must be added to the organization. Please note that these human and other resources are included in the comprehensive plan that is developed through the coordination factor. It should also be noted that decisions would need to be made on existing resources that are no longer required.

Commitment

Individual and team commitment to the strategic change initiative is another factor that the change agent leader must focus on to be successful. In most cases this can be accomplished by utilizing individuals and teams to help evaluate and determine the best direction for the organization to proceed. By being a part of those that determined the future direction of the organization, they will have a better understanding of the "who, what, why, when, and how" questions associated with the strategic change initiative. This will enable them to make important decisions and adjustments as the plan is implemented.

Communication

The clear, concise, and consistent communication of the new vision and what it means to the organization is another important factor that the change agent leader must address. During the identification, development, and implementation of the strategic change initiative, the change agent must help ensure that the reason for change, the new direction, and how the change will affect individuals and groups within the organization are communicated in a trusting and honest manner. It is also important to note that these communications may not answer all of the stakeholder questions. However, as the strategic change initiative evolves, ongoing communications should provide sufficient information on the state of affairs.

Leading change through application of the four "Cs" (coordination, competencies, commitment, and communication) will enable you to extend a network, focused on the change initiative, to others within your organization. Your ability to focus on these factors and utilize this network to plan, implement, and operate the strategic change initiative will determine your success.

In the next few sections, we will address how effective leadership can be derived from understanding the external environment, building coalitions, questioning existing organizational assumptions, communicating a vision, and shifting ownership to a working team. By focusing on the key factors stated above and taking actions appropriate to the next few sections, you can help make yourself an effective leader!

❏ UNDERSTANDING THE EXTERNAL ENVIRONMENT

An organization's understanding of its external environment is critical to making it competitive. A leader needs to take advantage of the fact that all levels of an organization process information about its external environment and actively collect information that suggests new approaches. By gathering information from an organization's customers and suppliers, for example, leaders will not only better understand today's competitive position but also gain some insight into what the organization might want to be in the future.

Recognize Destabilizing Forces and Opportunities

By gathering information on an organization's competitors and from customers and suppliers, leaders within an organization can begin to recognize destabilizing forces and opportunities; for example, is there a need to improve response time in the customer service area, are there new alternatives to using our product, or should we add new features to our product? The next set of questions would include "what" is to be changed and "how" the change is to be made. The answers to these questions would result in a review of the existing organizational and human capabilities to determine what additional resources would be required.

Creating an Agenda

The identification of destabilizing forces and opportunities provides support for a new direction or agenda. A successful strategic change initiative means that the organization has been able to develop a strategically aligned vision of how they should organize and manage to remain competitive. Leaders will develop a vision for the future and strategies for producing the changes needed to

achieve that vision. Managers will establish detailed steps and timetables for achieving needed results and then allocate the resources necessary to make that happen.

❏ BUILDING COALITIONS

Leaders need the involvement of people who have the resources, the knowledge, and the political clout to get things done. You want the innovators, the experts, and the value leaders involved in the planning process. That sounds obvious, but coalition building is probably one of the most neglected steps in the change process.

Identify Key Supporters

It is important that the leader communicate the new direction by words and actions to all those whose cooperation may be needed so as to influence the creation of teams and coalitions that understand the vision and strategies, and accept their validity. In addition, they can provide valuable feedback and input to the vision and strategies. Because they assisted in the development of the vision and associated strategies, they are committed to the strategic change initiative and can become part of a system-wide network supporting the change.

Understand the Politics of Change

In the early stages of planning change, leaders must identify key supporters and sell their vision with the same passion as an entrepreneur. A leader will have to reach into and outside the organization to find key influencers and must also be willing to reveal an idea before it is fully developed. Secrecy denies the opportunity to get feedback, and when things are given to people with no warning, the easiest answer is always no! Coalition building requires an understanding of the politics of change, and in any organization those politics can be formidable.

Identify and Acquire Key Resource Needs

A strategic change initiative plan (as described in Chapter 3), identifying the required resources, timeline, and costs, is the roadmap to implementation. In most cases, leaders will select members of the organization who they feel will be able to learn and adapt to the change as the project is implemented. These individuals are seen as key resources for moving the organization through the next phase of change. Those that succeed will likely be rewarded and also move on to the next change initiative.

❏ QUESTIONING EXISTING ORGANIZATIONAL ASSUMPTIONS

To create a new direction, a broad range of information about organizational activities must be gathered from customers, suppliers, and other stakeholders. An evaluation of this information should enable leaders to question conventional wisdom and analytically look for patterns that answer some very basic questions about activities. Based on this analysis, discussion should lead to new ideas or opportunities for the organization. In today's business environment, these brainstorming sessions should be a proactive and ongoing part of how the organization evaluates its competitive position.

Question Assumptions and Test Solutions

An organization must look for patterns to address some basic questions: "What is required to succeed? and "How do our suppliers and customers view our products/services?" The next step is to generate and test alternative directions against this understanding, possibly experimenting with some options. Finally, the object is to choose one that is both *desirable* and *feasible*. Doing this with an iterative process that never really ends, supports the proactive nature of defining a new direction for organizational change.

Trigger New Ideas

An ongoing review of the existing organization in view of the external environment is critical to having a better understanding of the competition. With input from employees, customers, suppliers, and other stakeholder, new ideas should be a constant part of discussion. *One sure way to better understand what you are working with is to change it!*

❏ COMMUNICATING A VISION

The responsibilities of a leader in communicating a vision can be described as follows:[26]

'Leaders need to establish direction, provide a description of the future (a vision), and a strategy for getting there. A good vision statement satisfies two tests: desirability and feasibility. *Desirability* means the needs of the constituencies that support the business or organization (e.g., customers, shareholders, and employees) are met. *Feasibility* means there is a sensible strategy for getting there, one that takes into account the competition, the organization's strengths and weaknesses, technological trends, etc. A firm's direction can be very novel but often is not.'

By monitoring what employees say and do, the leader will be able to determine if the change initiative can be successfully implemented (feasible) and has been accepted as a future state (desirable). The communication of a vision should be an educational experience for both leaders and followers, enabling them to better understand and clarify what is being done as the change initiative evolves.

Make a Compelling Case

Leaders need to make a compelling case to support the vision. Individuals and groups should then move to a common understanding of the vision and set of strategies, to accept the validity of that direction, and work toward making it a reality. This aligned group of individuals and groups have the potential of making significant progress toward the vision.

Communicate an Aspiration

The ability to align members of the organization is accomplished by ongoing and continuous communication that can take a number of forms:[27]

Communicating the direction as often as possible (repetition is important) to all those people (subordinates, subordinates of subordinates, bosses, suppliers, etc.) whose help or cooperation is needed; doing so, whenever possible, with simple images or symbols or metaphors that communicate powerfully without clogging already overused communications channels and without requiring a lot of scarce managerial time; making the message credible by using communicators with good track records and working relationships, by stating the message in as sensible a way as possible, by making sure the words and deeds of the communicators are consistent, and generally demonstrating an unswerving dedication to the vision and strategies (so-called "leadership by example").

The above stated process will enable members of the organization to develop and establish relationships that support the change initiative as it evolves. Both the emotion and motivation associated with the vision and direction of the change initiative should enable an individual and groups to become powerful forces of change. We will discuss communicating a vision more fully in Chapter 6.

❏ SHIFTING OWNERSHIP TO A WORKING TEAM

With a coalition in place and a well-communicated message sent to stakeholders, leaders can now shift ownership to a working team. However, you cannot simply ask managers to execute a change agenda; you must instead develop a broad list of expectations, using your internal and external environmental information plus asking lots of questions, from which people can conduct a series of "feel their way" initiatives. That approach not only confers team ownership, but also allows people to explore new possibilities.

Link Team to Necessary Resources

Critical to the success of any change initiatives is the availability of sufficient and appropriate resources. Kanter argues that,

'It is not just the team process that determines success, it's whether or not the team is linked appropriately to the resources they need in the organization. One of the temptations leaders must resist is to simply pile responsibility on team members. While it is fashionable to have people wear many hats, people must be given the responsibility – and the time – to focus on the tasks of change.'[28]

For example, if team members become overwhelmed by being required to do their "normal" job plus the change initiative, they will quickly become ineffective at both. Additionally, if necessary expertise or experience is not in place, the right things will never be accomplished.

Allow Teams to Form Their Own Identity

Leaders must allow teams to establish their own identity and build a sense of membership and commitment to the change initiative. However, the primary role of the leader is to support the team, provide coaching and resources, and control the boundaries within which the team can freely operate. Only then will the team be empowered to implement the change initiative.

❏ CHANGE AGENTS CAN ENACT CHANGE

Changes do not always result from "pushes" or pressure to move away from the present state, but instead can result from being "pulled" toward or attracted to a new state. Brown and Eisenhardt identified three key characteristics of successful managers in continuously changing organizations:[29]

1. Successful change agents must provide clear responsibility and priorities with extensive communication and freedom to improvise. Analogous to jazz improvisation, these managers created an environment that supports intensive communication in real time, within a structure of a few, very specific rules.

2. Exploration of the future by experimenting with a wide variety of low-cost probes. They argue that low-cost probes enhance learning about future possibilities. This learning opportunity is critical because, while the future is uncertain, it is possible to learn something about it.

3. Link current projects to the future with predictable (time-paced rather than event-paced) intervals and choreographed transition procedures. Familiar routines are created by predictable timing and by transition procedures that link the present to the future.

By utilizing these characteristics, a change agent enables the change process to evolve over time. Employees have clear responsibilities and priorities, experiment with low-cost options to learn, and link current projects to the future by following familiar routines. Change agents can create change by providing a vision that is attractive to followers rather than creating dissatisfaction with the status quo.[30]

The importance of leadership to the change management process is underscored by the fact that change, by definition, requires creating a new system and then institutionalizing the new approach. Change agents play an integral role in the change process!

❏ COMPETENCIES OF A CHANGE AGENT

The following situation relates how one organization established the leadership performance criteria for their strategic change initiative:[31]

'In one Fortune 500 company, we brought the executives together to kick off their change process and define their role as change leaders. After appropriate education about change strategy and the change process, the senior vice president, to whom they all reported, told the leaders they would be held accountable for their influence on the change process and that 20 percent of their annual executive incentive would be attached to their change performance. To make their accountability as change leaders tangible and observable, we gave the executives the task of collectively identifying their own performance standards for excellent change leadership in specific actionable terms.

After a few minutes of predictable resistance, they saw and accepted the inherent challenge and proceeded to take the information they had just learned about the change process and create a set of realistic change leadership standards for themselves. Their list included:

Achievement of specific goals;

• Effectiveness of their communications for creating behavior supportive of the change in the workforce;

• Visibility as a model of the desired behavior;

• Knowledge about the status of the transformation;

• Creation of an effective change infrastructure and conditions for success;

• Timely execution of change decisions; and

• Ability to find adequate resources to support their part of the overall change.

The senior vice president used the list as his guide for evaluating their performance and, in fact, kept his word on tying it to their annual bonus. In hindsight, the executives clearly recognized the power of determining their own requirements for change leadership, which deepened their understanding of the value of wrestling with their own performance standards.'

Leaders in the above organization were able to increase their understanding of the change process by establishing a set of criteria against which their performance would be measured. Please note that almost all of the criteria are objective, not subjective!

Figure 4.6 depicts a listing of characteristics associated with an effective change agent. This list includes *establishing goals* (using a project management approach), *defining roles* (establishing an effective team), *developing communication messages* (to inspire and motivate), *negotiating* (to get things done), and *managing up* (understanding the political environment and how to use it to

benefit the project). An effective change agent is required to perform in such a manner to help the change evolve in a positive direction.

The essence of the change process involves a relationship designed to help an employee facilitate, implement, and manage change to improve performance. Change agents are directed to plan and implement some form of change — to enable the organization or employee to achieve a previously unattainable outcome. Achieving that goal depends on your ability to develop personal resources and then draw on them as you operate within five core roles (with competencies) as a change agent, derived from Gilley:[33]

1. *Entrepreneur* — Master your business as well as the tools of your profession. (stakeholder relationship, systems thinking, and industry experience)

2. *Coordinator* — Integrate and facilitate the strategic change initiative (plan, implement, and control activities)

3. *Mentor* — Meet your employees' needs for growth, both personally and professionally. (set expectations, values accountability, emotional empathy, and humility)

4. *Advocate* — Encourage and support your employees to strive for excellence throughout the change process (change alignment, conflict resolution, intervener, and learning facilitation)

5. *Visionary* — Assist your employees in defining the long-term future of the organization. (reflective learning, comfort with uncertainty and visualization)

Each core role is independent of each other, yet interdependent at the same time. While each provides the change agent with a separate platform from which to direct change, it is required that each role be performed to integrate all the important components of change.

❑ SELF-ASSESSMENT FOR CHANGE AGENT EXCELLENCE

Figure 4.7 provides a series of questions designed to assess where you currently stand in your quest to remain or become a change agent. For each statement answer "yes" or "no." Be honest. Each "yes" is worth five points. Then add up your score and

Goals	• Sensitivity to changes in key personnel, top management perceptions and market conditions, and to the way in which these impact the goals of the project. • Clarity in specifying goals, in defining the achievable. • Flexibility in responding to changes not within his/her control, perhaps requiring major shifts in project goals and management style and risk taking.
Roles	• Team-building activities, to bring together key stakeholders and establish effective working groups and clearly to define and delegate respective responsibilities. • Networking skills in establishing and maintaining appropriate contacts within and outside the organization. • Tolerance of ambiguity, to be able to function comfortably, patiently, and effectively in an uncertain environment.
Communication	• Communication skills to transmit effectively to colleagues and subordinates the need for changes in project goals and in individual tasks and responsibilities. • Interpersonal skills, across the range, including selection, listening, collecting appropriate information, identifying the concerns of others, and managing meetings. • Personal enthusiasm, in expressing plans and ideas. • Stimulating motivation and commitment in others involved.
Negotiation	• Selling plans and ideas to others, by creating a desirable and challenging vision of the future. • Negotiating with key players for resources or for changes in procedures and to resolve conflict.
Managing Up	• Political awareness, in identifying potential coalitions and in balancing conflicting goals and perceptions. • Influencing skills, to gain commitment to project plans and ideas from potential skeptics and resisters. • To stand back from the immediate project and take a broader view of priorities.

Figure 4.6   Goals, Roles, Communication, Negotiation, and Managing Up of Effective Change Agents[32]

check your current standing using the scale at the bottom.

As with any self-assessment instrument, your responses provide an indication of your areas of strength and weakness. Based on your point total in each of the five core areas, this information provides you a self-development opportunity.

❏ USING EMOTIONAL INTELLIGENCE TO BUILD GOOD WORKING RELATIONSHIPS

Globalization, deregulation, virtual teams, telecommuting, outsourcing, insourcing, e-commerce — employees throughout the business world have either adapted or been forced to adapt to new ways of doing things, i.e., organizational change! In situations of organizational change, where consultation and participation are advocated, soft skills are important for leadership effectiveness.[34] Emotional intelligence (EI) has been identified as one way to improve an individual's soft skills and leadership effectiveness.

"Emotional intelligence" refers to the capacity for recognizing our own feelings and those of others, for motivating ourselves, and for managing emotions well in ourselves and in our relationships.[35] Therefore, EI focuses on managing our relationships with *ourself* and with *others*. When

Change Agent Assessment	
Operating in the Core Role of Entrepreneur	Points (0 or 5)
I am currently developing at least three project opportunities.	
I can describe, in detail, the work flow process for my organization.	
I can recreate a higher level organizational chart, including division and department titles and responsible managers, for my organization.	
I am an expert in at least two competencies that are critical to the success of my organization.	
Operating in the Core Role of Coordinator	
I have been selected as the group or team leader for two of my last three assignments.	
I maintain a detailed plan for all projects that I manage.	
I make resource allocation assignments and set timelines for projects that I am assigned.	
I have a tracking instrument that I use to monitor and control my project's activities.	
Operating in the Core Role of Mentor	
I set expectations for all my direct reports.	
I am a good listener and work hard to understand others' perspectives.	
I believe that we all are motivated by the work that we do and the success that we derive from our accomplishments.	
I have shared my feelings and emotions with a colleague.	
Operating in the Core Role of Advocate	
I have developed and used strategies and tactics for effectively managing organizational change.	
I have defused at least five personal or organizational conflicts in the last 3 months.	
I have removed barriers or provided additional resources to every strategic change initiative in which I have participated.	
At least five separate colleagues/employees can point to specific things that they have learned from me over the last 6 months.	
Operating in the Core Role of Visionary	
I view the uncertainty and ambiguity associated with organizational change as an opportunity to make a better future.	
I keep a personal journal or log chronicling significant personal and professional events in my life.	
I make daily decisions on change initiatives by using my intuition.	
I can describe a product or service that my organization will be offering 10 years from now.	
SCORING SCALE: Your Total Score _____ 80 to 100 = Highly Competent Change Agent 55 to 75 = Transitional Change Agent (making the transition from a manager to a leader) 35 to 50 = Follower (follows others during change initiatives) 0 to 30 = Resistor (resists or is a barrier to change)	

Figure 4.7 Change Agent Assessment

considering ourself, do we try to do too much, do we understand our limitations and work within those? When considering others, do we understand others situations and work them to accomplish both their goals and ours? EI is all about establishing a good working relationship with ourself and with others to get things done!

EI is predicated on the notion that individuals should relinquish short-term benefits for long-term gains, strive for positive personal emotions and interpersonal relationships, and display individual considerations to others.[36] In times of change, leaders with high EI may generate an atmosphere of cooperation and trust by aligning themselves with the goals of the organization and considering the long-term needs of the organization and its members over personal needs. These actions would conceivably promote quality interpersonal relationships with employees and contribute to a leader's ability to influence emotions and attitudes toward change. When leaders are able to influence their employees' emotions, they may induce employees to reevaluate negative feelings or resistance to change. For example, if an employee feels concerned or anxious about impending change, an emotionally intelligent leader may be able to recognize these emotions, persuade the employee that the response is unwarranted and propose an alternative view of the change process.[37]

Figure 4.8 provides a framework for better understanding and managing yourself by using emotional intelligence. For example, under self-awareness, an accurate assessment of knowing one's strengths and limits would result in *not* taking on too much work and assigning some of the work to others. Another example, under self-regulation, means that you can adapt to change, looking at things in new ways, and searching for new solutions. Finally, under motivation, being proactive and optimistic means that you would be persistent in pursuing goals despite obstacles and setbacks (a part of the proactive approach used with project management). Using EI to control the "what" and "how" of responsibilities you take on, can make you a more effective change agent!

A framework to better managing your relationships with others by using emotional intelligence is shown in Figure 4.9. For example, under empathy, understanding others means sensing others' feelings and perspectives, and taking an active interest in their concerns by removing barriers to get work done, recognizing that you will likely need their

help to get things done in the near term. Finally, under social skills, working with other toward shared goals in a collaborative and cooperative manner (another aspect of using a project management approach). Using EI to control your relationships with others, helps get things done!

Role of Emotional Intelligence in Change Management

The underlying assumptions of EI are linked to a leader's ability to manage change. Figure 4.10 depicts a matrix of EI skills and their relationship to change management competencies from two perspectives:

1. Emotional perception and understanding, and
2. Emotional utilization and management.

These aspects are defined by the leader's focus on both self and others. The subdimensions of the matrix show various competencies and traits of an emotionally intelligent leader and how these may translate into specific change management skills.

Figure 4.10 also shows how leaders who possess the EI ability to utilize and manage emotions may be more effective change agents. Because leaders who are high on the emotional intelligence scale can manage their own emotions, they may be better able to adapt to multiple and changing conditions. Finally, emotionally intelligent leaders are also able to set challenging goals and take calculated risks during the change process.

Emotional Intelligence Linkage To Transformational Leadership

Transformational leadership style or behavior as previous described in this chapter help change organizational environments, provide new realities, are proactive, and create emotional relationships with followers.[41] The change agent leadership roles described in Figure 4.4 are enhanced by the abilities to manage oneself and others associated with emotional intelligence found in Figures 4.8 and 4.9. Just as transformational leadership is required to support strategic change, emotional intelligence is required to support transformational leadership. Studies have shown that transformational leadership and emotional intelligence are positively related to project success. In addition,

SELF-AWARENESS	*Knowing one's internal states, preferences, resources, and intuitions*
Emotional awareness	Recognizing one's emotions and their effects
Accurate self-assessment	Knowing one's strengths and limits
Self-confidence	A strong sense of one's self-worth and capabilities
SELF-REGULATION	*Managing one's internal states, impulses, and resources*
Self-control	Keeping disruptive emotions and impulses in check
Trustworthiness	Maintaining standards of honesty and integrity
Conscientiousness	Taking responsibility for personal performance
Adaptability	Flexibility in handling change
Innovation	Being comfortable with novel ideas, approaches, and new information
MOTIVATION	*Emotional tendencies that guide or facilitate reaching goals*
Achievement drive	Striving to improve or meet a standard of excellence
Commitment	Aligning with the goals of the group or organization
Initiative	Readiness to act on opportunities
Optimism	Persistence in pursuing goals despite obstacles and setbacks

Figure 4.8 *Framework for Emotional Intelligence: Better Understanding and Managing Yourself* [38]

studies have shown that emotional intelligence supports and enhances transformational leadership! [42]

❏ LEADERSHIP AND ORGANIZATIONAL CHANGE

Consider this contemporary definition of leadership articulated by Lussier and Achua:

'Leadership is the influencing process of leaders and followers to achieve organizational objectives through change.' [43]

In addition, leadership has more to do with establishing relationships than with position. Therefore, the expectations of today's leaders are much different than in the past. A change agent's role and function in today's organizational change can be specified according to four primary phases (as shown in Figure 4.11): [44]

These are the roles and responsibilities of a change agent as they work through the change process to implement strategic change initiatives. The complexity of the change process makes this challenge an opportunity to go beyond what business and organizations have expected in the past; therefore, the change agents of today must have a transformational leadership style.

❏ LEADERSHIP AND CHANGE QUOTES

The following quotes help us further think about and evaluate leadership and change based on what we have covered in the first four chapters of this text:

It is not the strongest of the species that survive, nor the most intelligent, but the ones most responsive to change. Charles Darwin

Plans are nothing, planning is everything. Dwight D. Eisenhower

Before everything else, getting ready is the key to success. Henry Ford

EMPATHY	Awareness of others' feelings, needs, and concerns
Understanding others	Sensing others' feelings and perspectives, and taking an active interest in their concerns
Developing others	Sensing others' development needs and bolstering their abilities
Service orientation	Anticipating, recognizing, and meeting customers' needs
Leveraging diversity	Cultivating opportunities through different kinds of people
Political awareness	Reading a group's emotional currents and power relationships
SOCIAL SKILLS	Adeptness at inducing desirable responses in others
Influence	Wielding effective tactics for persuasion
Communication	Listening openly and sending convincing messages
Conflict management	Negotiating and resolving disagreements
Leadership	Inspiring and guiding individuals and groups
Change catalyst	Initiating or managing change
Building bonds	Nurturing instrumental relationships
Collaboration and cooperation	Working with others toward shared goals
Team capabilities	Creating group synergy in pursing collective goals

Figure 4.9   Framework for Emotional Intelligence: Better Managing Relationships with Others[39]

Those who say it can't be done should stand back so others who know it is possible can do it. Anonymous

The significant problems we have created . . . cannot be solved at the level of thinking which existed when we created them. Albert Einstein

Leaders are first and foremost builders of people. James Lewis

I would rather try to persuade a man to go along, because once I have persuaded him he will stick. If I scare him, he will stay just as long as he is scared, and then he is gone. Dwight D. Eisenhower

People have one thing in common they are all different!! Robert Zend

Setting an example is not the main means of influencing another, it is the only means. Albert Einstein.

Leadership is being in the right place at the right time with the right idea and set of values, and the ability to communicate it convincingly. Richard Hart

Leadership: the ability to promote stability based on planned diversity through vision and example. Vince Hockett

Always look for the best, not the worst; concentrate on the positive, not the negative; and look for the victories, not the defeats, within the people around you. Anonymous

Think about what you have learned about leadership and change with respect to the foregoing quote. More specifically, how you would provide leadership in a changing business environment?

❑ READING AND CASE

The application of theories and concepts discussed in this chapter to real-world situations is addressed with the following reading and case. They reflect the importance of employee empowerment, a valid vision and strategy, questioning assumptions, learning and adapting, and developing relationships with all stakeholders to become an effective leader.

Reading

4-1 Change management — or change leadership?, Roger Gill, Journal of Change Management, May 2003.

EI Skill	Self	Others	Relationship to change management
• Emotional perception and understanding (knowledge of situation)	• Ability to be self-aware	• Ability to empathize • Read nonverbal and emotional cues	• Development of an appropriate vision • Predicting the link between employees' emotions and behaviors during times of change
• Emotional utilization and management (actions taken)	• Positive thinking • Self-control • Adaptability • Appropriate resource allocation	• Interpersonal skills; social and emotional • Ability to influence • Consider needs of others over personal needs	• Accepting and working with cynicism to change and resistance to change • Engage employees in consultation and decision making • Using appropriate emotionally expressive language to communicate vision • Building trust • Gaining commitment rather than compliance to change • Able to set challenging goals and take calculated risks in change process • Assisting employees to cope with change

Figure 4.10   *A Matrix of Leader Emotional Intelligence and Change Management Competencies*[40]

Focus   (statements from reading): Change programs often fail because of poor management: poor planning, monitoring and control, lack of resources and know-how, and incompatible corporate policies and practices. Change is all too often regarded as a 'quick fix.' A lack of commitment to change may be due to a lack of compelling evidence for the benefits of change.

Questions

1. Why is "Management" necessary but not sufficient to support a strategic change initiative?

2. Human and political aspects of change are often not well thought out in a change management initiative. What can be done to address this deficiency?

1st — The prelaunch phase	• Leader self-examination • Gathering information from the external environment • Establishing a need for change • Providing clarity regarding vision and direction
2nd — The launch phase	• Communication of the need for change • Initiating key activities • Dealing with resistance
3rd — Postlaunch phase or further implementation	• Multiple leverage • Taking the heat • Consistency • Perseverance • Repeating the message
4th — Sustaining the change	• Dealing with unanticipated consequences • Momentum • Choosing successors • Launching yet again new initiatives

Figure 4.11 *A Change Agent's Role and Function in Today's Organizational Change*

3. The author suggests that there are four separate tracks of leadership theory (cognitive intelligence, spiritual intelligence, emotional intelligence, and behavioral skills) that have never fully or usefully converged. Is it necessary that a leader integrate all four to be successful? Explain.

4. Is effective emotional and behavioral leadership possible without a valid vision and strategy? Explain.

5. Is employee empowerment the change management solution to increased technological and political complexity? Explain.

6. How important is effective leadership to the change management process? Explain.

Linkage to Chapter

1. Both management and leadership are needed to support a successful change initiative.

2. Rational and emotional approaches to effective leadership are both required to support successful change.

3. Employee empowerment is a critical component of effective leadership.

4. A valid vision and strategy are required to support effective leadership.

Case

4-1 Peter Browning and Continental White Cap, Mary Gentile and Todd D. Jick, Harvard Business School. 2000.

Focus (statements from case): Browning's charge was to revitalize and reposition the division to remain preeminent in the face of threatened, but not yet fully realized, changes in the competitive environment. Browning recognized two major obstacles: first, few managers or employees acknowledged the need for change, and second, White Cap had a family-style culture characterized by long-term loyalty from its employees, longstanding traditions of job security, liberal benefits, and paternalistic management.

Questions

1. From a change management perspective, in what situation did Browning find himself as he took on the challenge to change Continental White Cap? Explain.

2. What should Browning's strategy be and how should he address those above and below him when implementing that strategy?

3. What is an appropriate time frame for Browning to make necessary changes (based on directives from executive officers and the internal and external environment)? Explain.

4. What are the required characteristics of a successful change agent or leader?

Linkage to Chapter

1. Developing relationships with all stakeholders is critical to effective leadership.

2. Effective leaders identify objectives, establish a plan, and set appropriate expectations.

3. Building coalitions is a critical component of a successful change initiative.

4. Attributes of a successful change agent or leader are identified.

❏ ENDNOTES

1. Kotter, J. P. (1996). *Leading Change*. Boston, MA: Harvard Business School Press, p. 26.
2. Bryman, A. (1996). Leadership in organizations. In S. R., Cleg, C., Hardy, & W.R., Nord, (Eds.). *Handbook of Organization Studies*. Thousand Oaks, CA: Sage Publications pp. 277–292.
3. Stogdil, R. M. (1950). Leadership, membership and organizations. *Psychological Bulletin*, Vol. 47, pp. 1–14.
4. Yukl, G. A. (2002). *Leadership in Organizations* 5th ed. Upper Saddle River, NJ: Prentice Hall.
5. Kotter, J. P. (1988). *The Leadership Factor*. New York: Free Press.
6. House, R. J., Hanges, P. J., Dorfman, P. W., et al. (1999). Cultural influences on leadership and organizations: Project GLOBE. In W.H. Mobley (Ed.). *Advances in Global Leadership*. Greenwich, CT: JAI Press, Vol. 1, pp. 171–233.
7. Wheatley, M. J. (1999). *Leadership and the New Science*. San Francisco: Berrett-Koehler, p. 131.
8. Bass, B. M. (1990). *Bass and Stogdill's Handbook of Leadership: Theory, Research and Managerial Applications, 3rd ed.* New York: Free Press.
9. Collins, J. C., & Porras, J. I. (1994). *Built to Last*. New York: Harper Collins Publishers.
10. Mumford, M. D., Zaccaro, S. J., Connelly, M. S., & Marks, M. A. (2000). Leadership skills: conclusions and future directions. *Leadership Quarterly*, Vol. 11, pp. 155–171.
11. Senge, P. M. (1990). *The Fifth Discipline: The Art and Practice of the Learning Organization*. New York, NY: Doubleday Currency.
12. Schein, E. H. (2003). *DEC is Dead, Long Live DEC*. San Francisco, CA: Berrett-Koehler Publishers, Inc., p. 93.
13. Bass (1990), op. cit.
14. Bass, B. M. (1998). *Transformational Leadership: Industry, Military, and Educational Impact*. Mahwah, New Jersey: Lawrence Erlbaum Associates.
15. Ibid.
16. Bass, B. M. (1985). *Leadership and Performance Beyond Expectations*. New York: Free Press.
17. Bass, B. M., & Avolio, B. J. (2000). *MLQ Multifactor Leadership Questionnaire 2nd ed.* Technical Report for MLQ-5X. Redwood, CA: Mind Garden, Inc, pp. 53–59.
18. Beatty, C. A., & Lee, G. L. (1992). Leadership among middle managers: an exploration in the context of technological change. *Human Relations*, Vol. 45, No. 9, pp. 557–590.
19. Bass (1985), op. cit.
20. Conger, J. A., & Kanungo, R. N. (1998). *Charismatic Leadership in Organizations*. Thousand Oaks, CA: Sage Publications.
21. Sashkin, M. (1988). The visionary leader. In J. A. Conger & R. N. Kanungo (Eds.), *Charismatic Leadership: The Elusive Factor in Organizational Effectiveness*. San Francisco: Jossey-Bass, pp. 122–160.
22. Taborda, C. G., (2000, October). Leadership, teamwork, and empowerment: Future management trends. *Association of Cost Engineers*, No. 10, p. 44.
23. Ibid, p. 41.
24. Woodcock, M., Francis, D., (1992). *25 Training Activities for Creating and Managing Change*. Amherst, MA: Human Resource Development Press, Inc., p. 139.
25. Anderson, L. & Anderson, D. (2001). *The Change Leader's Roadmap*. San Francisco, CA: Jossey-Bass/Pfeiffer, p. 218.
26. Kotter (1990), op. cit., p. 47.
27. Kotter (1990), op. cit., p. 60.
28. Kanter, R. M. (2000). The enduring skills of change leaders. *Ivey Business Journal*, May/June 2000, p. 6.
29. Eisenbach, R., Watson, K., & Pillai, R. (1999). Transformational leadership in the context of organizational change. *Journal of Organizational Change*, Vol. 12, No. 2, p. 82.
30. Ibid.
31. Anderson, L. & Anderson, D. (2001). *The Change Leader's Roadmap*. San Francisco, CA: Jossey-Bass/Pfeiffer, pp. 105-06.
32. Senior, B., Fleming, J., (2006). *Organizational Change*. England: Pearson Education Limited, p. 362.

33. Gilley, J. W., et al. (2001). *The Manager as Change Agent*. Cambridge, MA: Perseus Publishing.

34. Connell, J. (1998). Soft skills: The neglected factor in workplace participation?, *Journal of Labour and Industry*, Vol. 9, No. 1, p. 69.

35. Goleman, D., (1985). *Working with Emotional Intelligence*. New York, NY: Bantam Book, p. 317.

36. Mayer, J. D., Salovey, P. (1995). Emotional Intelligence and the construction and regulation of feeling, *Applied and Preventative Psychology*, Vol. 4, p. 198.

37. Ferres, N., Connell, J., (2004). Emotional intelligence in leaders: an antidote for cynicism towards change? *Strategic Change*, March-April Vol. 13, No. 2, p. 65.

38. Goleman (1985), op. cit., p. 26.

39. Goleman (1985), op. cit., p. 27.

40. Adapted from Schmidt, D. (1997). Organizational change and the role of emotional intelligence. Paper presented at *The Annual Meeting of the Academy of Management*. Boston. Ferres (2004), op. cit.

41. Bass (1985), op. cit.

42. Leban, W. V., Zulauf, C. (2004). Linking emotional intelligence abilities and transformational leadership styles. *The Leadership and Organization Development Journal*, Vol. 25, No. 7, p. 561.

43. Lussier, R. N., & Achua, C. F. (2004). *Leadership*. Eagan, Minnesota: Thomson – Southwestern, p. 5.

44. Burke, W. W. (2002). *Organizational Change*. Thousand Oaks, CA: Sage Publications, p. 271, Figure 11.

Reading 4-1

Change Management — or Change Leadership?

ROGER GILL

Roger Gill is Director of the Research Centre for Leadership Studies at The Leadership Trust and Visiting Professor at the University of Strathclyde Graduate School of Business, where he was formerly Professor of Organizational Behaviour and Human Resource Management and Director of Executive Development Programmes. In addition to academic appointments in the UK and the USA, he has worked as a management consultant in the UK, the Middle East, and Southeast Asia and as a human resources manager in industry in the UK.

Keywords: leadership, management, change

Abstract This paper argues that, while change must be well managed, it also requires effective leadership to be successfully introduced and sustained. An integrative model of leadership for change is proposed, reflecting its cognitive, spiritual, emotional and behavioural dimensions and requirements. The model comprises vision, values, strategy, empowerment, and motivation and inspiration. The paper concludes with a brief account of the application of the model in varied strategic change situations.

. . . there is no more delicate matter to take in hand, nor more dangerous to conduct, nor more doubtful in its success, than to set up as a leader in the introduction of changes. For he who innovates will have for his enemies all those who are well off under the existing order of things, and only lukewarm supporters in those who might be better off under the new. (Machiavelli, 1469–1527)

IN THE EARLY sixteenth century, Niccolò Machiavelli clearly understood the problem of change. In *The Prince*, he points out the difficulty and risk involved in implementing change, in particular resistance to change and, at best lack, of commitment to it.[1] Some 500 years later, this is still a familiar problem. As Andrew Mayo says, "Our organisations are littered with the debris . . . of yesterday's [change] initiatives (Mayo, 2002). The reason for this, this paper contends, is not necessarily poor management of change but more likely a lack of effective leadership. While change must be well managed — it must be planned, organized, directed, and controlled — it also requires effective leadership to introduce change successfully: it is leadership that makes the difference. This paper proposes a new model of leadership which is the result of a three-year study of the burgeoning literature on the subject and which has been successfully applied in several organizations in a variety of sectors planning and implementing strategic change. The model proposes that the leadership of successful change requires vision, strategy, the development of a culture of sustainable shared values that support the vision and strategy for change, and empowering, motivating, and inspiring those who are involved or affected. This behaviour reflects the underlying dimensions and requirements of leadership: the cognitive, the spiritual, the emotional and the behavioural.

Used with permission from Henry Stewart Publications 1469-7017 (2003) Vol. 3, 4,307–318 *Journal of Change Management*

Roger Gill Director, Research Centre for Leadership Studies, The Leadership Trust, Weston-under-Penyard, Ros-on-Wye, Herefordshire HR9 7YH, UK and Visiting Professor, University of Strathclyde Graduate School of Business, 199 Cathedral Street, Glasgow G4 OQU, UK Tel: +44 (0)1989 760705; Fax: +44 (0)1989 760704; e-mail: rwtgill@aol.com

Taylor and Francis Ltd. http://www.tandf.co.uk/journals

❏ WHY "MANAGEMENT" IS NECESSARY BUT NOT SUFFICIENT

Change programmes often fail because of poor management: poor planning, monitoring and control, lack of resources and know-how, and incompatible corporate policies and practices. Good management of change is a *sine qua non*.

How change may be mismanaged is well known. Change efforts may fail because of poor planning, monitoring and control, focusing more on the objective than on the steps and process involved, a lack of milestones along the way, and failing to monitor progress and take corrective action. Change efforts often lack the necessary resources, eg budget, systems, time and information, and the necessary expertise — knowledge and skills. Corporate policies and practices sometimes remain the same and become inconsistent with the aims and strategies for change. For example, the performance criteria used in appraisal and reward policies may not support and reinforce a desired performance-driven, teamwork-oriented culture, resulting in a disincentive or lack of incentive to change behavior. A large European study found that the most successful organizations make mutually supportive changes in terms of changes in roles, governance structures and strategies (Whit-tington *et al.*, 1999).

Change is all too often regarded as a "quick fix." This fails to address the implications of the change for the organization as a whole and therefore causes unforeseen and unacceptable disruption. Change initiatives are often the result of the naïve adoption of management fads. Such fads frequently deal with only one aspect of an organization's functioning without regard to their implications for other aspects. Lack of communication or inconsistent messages and the resulting misunderstanding of the aims and process of change lead to rumours that demoralize people and to a lack of commitment to change.

A lack of commitment to change may be due to a lack of compelling evidence for the benefits of change. It shows itself in objections, unwillingness to consider options or look at process issues, and the use of "hidden agendas" or delaying tactics. Top management itself may display a lack of commitment to change. Their commitment is evident in several ways: their unequivocal acceptance of ownership and responsibility for success of the change initiative, eagerness to be involved, willingness to invest resources, willingness to take tough decisions when required, awareness of the impact of their own behavior, a consistent message, and the holding of regular reviews of progress.

Change efforts that are purely "managerial" in nature, especially those that are mismanaged, result in a lack of dedicated effort, conflict between functional areas and resistance to change. Resistance to change is a common phenomenon. Kubr (1996) provides a good account of why people resist change. A cognitive and behavioural reason is lack of know-how. A lack of conviction that change is needed — questioning the meaning and value of the change for individuals — inevitably leads to a lack of motivation to change. Perhaps the most powerful forces of resistance to change, however, are emotional:

- Dislike of imposed change.
- Dislike of surprises.
- Lack of self-confidence and confidence in others: fear of the unknown and of inadequacy and failure and the adverse consequences, such as share price decline and blame.
- Reluctance of management to deal with difficult issues (especially in the case of managers approaching retirement).
- Disturbed practices, habits and relationships: 'We've always done it this way'. Moving people from their 'comfort zone' means moving from the familiar, secure and controllable to the unfamiliar, insecure and uncertainly controllable.
- Self-interest and shifts in power and influence such as loss or change of role in the organization.
- Lack of respect and trust in the person or people promoting change and scepticism as a result of the failure of previous change initiatives.

The human and political aspects of change are often not well thought through in change management initiatives. Mulligan and Barber (1998) speak of the yin and yang of change: respectively the social and emotional considerations (leadership) and the technical aspects (management). McLagan (2002) points out that taking a purely rational and technical approach to change, "making sure it's technically sound and offers economic advantage to the organization," tends to lead to the false assumption that the organization will naturally absorb it. Kotter (1995a) says:

In failed transformations, you often find plenty of plans and directives and programs . . . [with] procedures, goals, methods, and deadlines. But nowhere was there a clear and compelling statement [a vision] of where all this was leading. Not surprisingly, most of the employees with whom I talked were either confused or alienated. [The "managerial" approach] did not rally them together or inspire change. In feet, [it] probably had just the opposite effect."

In his classic statements on management and leadership, Kotter (1990a, 1990b) says that management produces orderly results which keep something working efficiently, whereas leadership creates useful change; neither is necessarily better or a replacement for the other. Both are needed if organizations and nations are to prosper. He also says, however:

Management's mandate is to minimise risk and to keep the current system operating. Change, by definition, requires creating a new system, which in turn always demands leadership. (Kotter, 1995a)

Sadler (1997) concurs:

... we have observed dramatic transformations in British industry in recent times which appear to be due more to inspirational leadership than to good management as traditionally conceived. British Airways under Colin Marshall, and ICI under John Harvey-Jones are oft-quoted examples.

Change, therefore, is primarily about leadership.

❏ THE LEADERSHIP OF CHANGE

The keys to successful change, according to an American Management Association survey (American Management Association, 1994), are first and foremost leadership, followed closely by corporate values and communication (Figure 4.12).

If change is a process of taking an organization (or a nation) on a journey from its current state to a desired future state and dealing with all the problems that arise along the journey, then change is

	% mentioning this as important
Leadership	92
Corporate values	84
Communication	75
Teambuilding	69
Education and training.	64

Figure 4.12 Keys to Successful Change: Survey of 259 Senior Executives in Fortune 500 Companies in the USA

about leadership as well as management. Leadership, in The Leadership Trusf's view, is about showing the way: using personal power to win the hearts and minds of people to work together towards a common goal (Gill, 2001). The leadership of change, for the chief executive, Hooper and Potter (2000) say, means "developing a vision of the future, crafting strategies to bring that vision into reality [and ensuring] that everybody in the organization is mobilising their energies towards the same goals . . . the process we call emotional alignment." It can be argued that the most difficult challenges facing leaders today are making sure that people in the organization can adapt to change and that leaders can envisage where the organization is currently placed in the market and where it should be in the future (Heifetz and Laurie, 1997).

The case for alignment is made in a report by World Economic Forum (2000) in partnership with management consultants Booz Allen & Hamilton and the Center for Effective Organizations at the University of Southern California:

Alignment . . . galvanizes people around the aspirations and objectives of the company. People know what is to be done, and understand how they as individuals contribute to the whole. Adaptability enables the organisation to change rapidly and effectively in response to external threats or opportunities.

Alignment is displayed a shared understanding, common orientation, common values, and shared priorities. Adaptability is displayed by environmental sensitivity, tolerance for contrary views, a willingness to experiment, tolerate failure and learn from it, and the ability to respond quickly to change — organizational agility. Both alignment and adaptability are needed (World Economic Forum, 2000):

Alignment without adaptability results in bureaucratic, sclerotic organizations that 'can't get out of their own way' . . . Adaptability without alignment results in chaos and resources wasted on duplicate and conflicting efforts.

The former chairman of ICI, Sir John Harvey-Jones (1988), takes a radical view of alignment:

In the future the organisation will have to adapt to the needs of the individual, rather than expecting the individual to adapt to the needs of the organization.

Nixon (2002) identifies "big issues" concerning global business leaders: creating successful and sustainable workplaces, the need to be good corporate citizens and at the same time profitable, the gap between strategy makers and those not involved, products that damage the quality of life, and a yearning for meaning and balance in life, "uniting body, mind, heart and spirit". Dubrin (2001) says that "The transformational leader . . . [helps] group members understand the need for change both emotionally and intellectually." How to meet the challenge of change can be understood more broadly using a new model of transformational leadership. This model attempts to integrate the multiple dimensions and requirements of leadership — the cognitive, spiritual, emotional and behavioural.[2]

❑ THE DIMENSIONS AND REQUIREMENTS OF LEADERSHIP

Leadership theory has developed along separate tracks that have never fully or usefully converged. Nevertheless, each track provides a distinct dimension and set of requirements for effective leadership. These tracks are the study of cognitive or rational processes (cognitive intelligence), the need for meaning and worth in people's work and lives (spiritual intelligence), emotions or feelings (emotional intelligence) and volitional action or behaviour (behavioural skills) in leadership (Gill, 2002).

The Intellectual/Cognitive Dimension and Requirements of Leadership — "Thinking"

Strategic failure, especially in times of rapid change, is often the result of the inability to see a novel reality emerging: the corporate mind is wedded to obsolete assumptions that blind it to the perception of change. Effective leadership requires the intellectual or cognitive abilities to perceive and understand information, reason with it, imagine possibilities, use intuition, make judgments, solve problems and make decisions. These abilities produce vision, mission (purpose), shared values and strategies for pursuing the vision and mission that "win" people's minds.

The Spiritual Dimension and Requirements of Leadership — "Meaning"

"Spirit," according to *Webster's Dictionary* and the *Oxford English Dictionary*, is a person's animating principle. The spiritual dimension of leadership

concerns the yearning for meaning and a sense of worth that animate people in what they seek and do. Meaning and this sense of worth depend on the vision and shared values to which one is party. William W. George, chairman and CEO of Medtronic, Inc. — one of the world's leading medical technology companies, based in Minneapolis — and the Academy of Management's 2001 "Executive of the Year," argues that people at work today seek meaning and purpose in their work. When they find it," [they] will buy into the company's mission and make the commitment to fulfilling it" (George, 2001). Dess and Picken (2000) quote Xerox PARC guru John Seely Brown as saying: "The job of leadership today is not just to make money: it's to make meaning." Effective leadership "wins people's souls."

The Emotional Dimension and Requirements of Leadership — "Feeling"

Effective leadership also requires well-developed emotional intelligence — the ability to understand oneself and other people, display self-control and self-confidence, and to respond to others in appropriate ways. Emotionally intelligent leaders use personal power rather than positional power or authority. Emotional intelligence, in addition to cognitive and spiritual intelligence, is key to identifying and promoting the shared values that support the pursuit of vision, mission and strategies and to empowering and inspiring people. Emotionally intelligent leaders "win people's hearts."

The Behavioral Dimension and Requirements of Leadership — "Doing"

While the necessary behavioural skills of leadership include both using and responding to emotion, for example through "body language," they also comprise communicating in other ways through writing, speaking and listening — using personal power — and through physical behaviour, for example MBWA ('managing by walking around'). Communication is the "life blood" of the organization and the "oxygen" of change within it.

❑ A NEW MODEL OF LEADERSHIP FOR CHANGE

Effective leadership of change reflects all of these dimensions of leadership. An integrative model of leadership for successful change needs to explain the following elements of effective leadership practice: vision, values, strategy, empowerment and motivation and inspiration. Effective emotional and behavioral leadership without valid vision and strategic thinking can be misguided, even dangerous. The converse is impotent.

Vision

"Without vision, a people perish," one is told in the Bible,[3] and so does an organisation. The foundation of effective leadership is defining and communicating an appealing vision of the future. One of the best definitions of a vision comes from the *Oxford English Dictionary:* "something seen vividly in the imagination, involving insight foresight and wisdom." A vision is a desired future state: this is the basis for directing the change effort.

Kotter (1995a) suggests that the starting point in a successful change process is attaching a sense of urgency and importance to change. Kotter says it is necessary to create dissatisfaction with the status quo and an understanding of the need to change. He quotes a former CEO of a large European company as saying that successful change begins by "[making] the status quo seem more dangerous than launching into the unknown." This is the basis for developing a vision for change.

Sylvie Jackson of Cranfield University's Royal Military College of Science starkly illustrates how little vision figures in communication in organizations:

Total amount of communication going on to an employee in three months = 2,300,000 words or members. Typical communication of a change vision over a period of three months = 13,400 words or numbers. 13,400/2,300,000 = 0.0058. The change vision captures only 0.58% of the communication "market share." (Jackson, 2001)

The British government has identified leadership as key to meeting fee challenges of change in public services (Performance Improvement Unit 2001). Change starts with a vision: "The Government has to present a clear picture . . . of the kind of society it [wants] from its reforms and stop being seen as a "value-free zone," says health secretary Alan Milburn. Prime minister Tony Blair responds: "[New Labour] needs to rediscover its political vision . . . building a Britain of opportunity for all" (Waugh and Morris, 2002).

Vision needs to be meaningful, ethical and inspiring. Effective visions are imaginable, desirable,

feasible, focused, flexible and communicable (Kotter, 1995b). They are memorable and quotable. Senge (1990) sees vision as a driving force, while Covey (1992) describes vision as "true north," providing a "compass." Vision helps to create commitment, inspiration and motivation by connecting and aligning people intellectually and emotionally to the organisation; and it is associated with organizational growth and success (Baum *et al*, 1998).

A shared vision is key to successful change. Kakabadse (2002) reports fee finding from a survey at Cranfield School of Management of over 12,000 organisations that more than one-third of directors have a vision of fee future of their organisation that is different from those of their colleagues. Without a shared vision, there is no alignment. Senge (1990) puts it this way:

In a corporation, a shared vision changes people's relationship with the company. It is no longer "their company"; it becomes "our company". A shared vision is the first step in allowing people who mistrusted each other to begin to work together. It creates a common identity.

Kotter (1997) makes the point that, for organisational change, only an approach based on vision works in the long term. He says a shared vision:

- clarifies the direction of change and ensures the everything that is done (new product development, acquisitions, recruitment campaigns) is in line wife it

- motivates people to take action in the right direction, even though the initial steps in the change process may be painful to some individuals

- helps to align individuals and coordinate their actions efficiently.

Values and Culture

A Nepalese Buddhist mantra says: "Open your arms to change, but don't let go of your values." Values are principles held dear in people's hearts by which they live (and sometimes die). Covey (1992) makes the distinction between personal values, which are intrinsic, and corporate values, which he regards as extrinsic guiding principles for behaviour throughout the organization.

The challenge of change has stimulated an emphasis on values-based leadership. OToole (1995) says that there is a widespread belief among corporate executives in the need to create strong, shared values to unite people in a fragmented world. The fear, though, is the danger of "group think." Yet, if there is one organizational characteristic that provides the "glue" in uniting people, it is trust. As O'Toole suggests, trust 'emanates from leadership based on shared purpose, shared vision, and especially, shared values' (O'Toole, 1995).

Bennis and Goldsmith (1997) point out that "Leaders walk their talk; in true leaders, there is no gap between the theories they espouse and their practice." Effective leaders are role models for corporate values: they set an example. Collins and Porras (1998) contend that corporate values are "not to be compromised for financial gain or short-term expediency."

Effective leadership entails identifying and promoting shared values. Shared values are a key feature of a strong organizational culture (that includes beliefs, attitudes and patterns of habitual behaviour) that supports a common purpose and engenders commitment to it. Values that are not shared can be dysfunctional (Drucker, 1999). Shared values create a sense of belonging and may contribute positively to competitive advantage (Deetz *et al.*, 2000). Indeed, a change orientation is one of the common values among the most admired companies in the USA (Kets de Vries, 2000), and firms have become more customer and stakeholder focused, more time-competitive and more value-added and quality focused (Cannon, 2000).

Networks of power and influence and "horizontal" relationships will replace the formal hierarchies found in bureaucratic organizations (Gill *et al.*, 1998). New organizational cultures will supplant bureaucratic cultures that are characterised by hierarchy, boundaries, internal orientation, control, and the need to avoid mistakes (Hastings, 1993). Bureaucracy is a well-documented hindrance to developing a learning culture.

One of the problems of change during mergers and acquisitions is that change is exciting for those who do it and threatening for those to whom it is done. The solution that worked for one company was to get people to participate in it. When ScottishPower acquired Manweb and Southern Water in the 1990s, it created "transition teams" with managers from the acquired company to create shared values and human resource policies and practices.

Culture change programmes are about "changing hearts, minds and souls" of employees (Rajan, 2000). This takes along time, and it requires some luck: Amin Rajan says, "The "big bang" approach has the potential to inflict . . . collateral damage, "although sometimes it may be necessary. Bill Cockburn, managing director of British Telecoms' UK operations, believes that in his business, incrementalism does not work: "radical reinvention" is required (Monks, 2000). But, to be more effective, culture change requires leaders to plan and implement sequential, but incremental, changes.

An example of a culture change programme aimed at changing feelings of involvement, consultation and values is that experienced at Marks and Spencer. Marks and Spencer fell from grace at the end of 1998, with a drastic fall in shareholder value. Under a new chairman, Luc Vandervelde, in early 2000, a major initiative was introduced to revolutionise the corporate culture as part of the recovery strategy. This entailed improving consultation — on key business issues rather man "tea and toilets" — among managers and employees through Business Involvement Groups (BIGs) and training in consultation processes. The outcome, by May 2002, according to Marks and Spencer's Helen Eaton, was "a greater mutuality of interest at meetings, with managers and staff beginning to work together on key business issues . . . [and] . . . more openness, honesty, trust and professionalism" as well as a clearer sense of direction (Law, 2002).

Wendy Sullivan and her colleagues describe how aligning the values of the people in the organization — and those of the organization itself — can help to bring about rapid change, citing the case of Sellotape (Sullivan *et al*, 2002). The company significantly improved business performance, with profitability increasing from 3 percent to 10 percent over two and a half years, and significant improvements in individual job satisfaction and fulfilment and in morale and teamwork.

Strategy

Without strategies for change, vision is a dream. Strategies are ways of pursuing the vision and mission; they are informed by vision, mission and values. Strategic plans are "road maps" of a changing terrain in which a compass (vision) is needed (Covey, 1992). Effective leadership entails developing, getting commitment to and implementing rational business strategies based on possible future scenarios for the organization. A key issue with the effectiveness of strategies is where their ownership lies and commitment to them: effective strategy development taps the wisdom of people in the organization (Eden, 1993).

William W. George of Medtronic says, "Employees can adapt to major strategic shifts as long as the company's mission and values remain constant" (George, 2001). This is an important factor in maintaining trust in top management. Medtronic is "completely reinvented" every five years in terms of its business strategies. For example, between 1989 and 1994, the company was transformed from a pacemaker company into a broader cardiovascular business, with revolutionary new therapies during the following five years, and with further innovations likely over the next five to ten years reflecting its "Vision 2010."

Meanwhile, mission and values have remained, and will remain, constant. Innovation and change require structural flexibility, but with the stability to deliver products and services on time. Peters (1993) calls this "permanent flexibility." It is well established in the management literature that structure must serve strategy, not the converse. An example of how structures have changed is the introduction of short-term, high-performance teams, superseding permanent functional or departmental teams and cross-functional teams. They come together for a specific purpose and, on achieving it, disband. The consequences are roles that frequently change and temporary and varied leadership roles.

An effective strategy for change entails creating a guiding coalition — putting together a group of people with enough power to lead the change — and getting it to work together as an effective team (Kotter, 1995a). Kotter also emphasises the need to use every method possible to communicate constantly and explain the new vision and strategy and ensure the guiding coalition models the behavior expected of all employees.

Empowerment

Like so many aspects of leadership, empowerment is not a new idea. In the fifth century BC, Lao Tzu wrote:

"As for the best leaders, people do not notice their existence.
   The next best, the people honour and praise.
   The next, the people fear.
   And the next, the people hate.
   But when the best leader's work is done, the people say, 'We did it ourselves.'"[4]

Empowerment literally is giving people power. It is about making them *able to do* what needs to be done in the change process. In practice, empowerment is giving people the knowledge, skills, opportunity, freedom, self-confidence and resources to manage themselves and be accountable. Important aspects of empowerment are stimulating people's intellects and imagination, in particular their creativity in the change process, risk taking and trust. Empowering people for action in part entails getting rid of obstacles to change, removing or changing systems or structures that undermine the vision, and encouraging risk taking, new ideas and innovative activities (Kotter, 1995b).

Bennis (1999) suggests that a "shrinking" world with increasing technological and political complexity offers fewer and fewer arenas for effective top-down leadership. The key to real change, he says, is empowered teams. The need for rapid response and innovation has created a culture of "intrapreneurship" in many companies. Innovation has become the province of *all* employees, not just those in the product development department Encouraging intrapreneurship is an example of empowerment.

General Electric successfully underwent extensive restructuring in the 1980s under chairman and CEO Jack Welch, to build a network of interrelated businesses with the aim of capturing top market-share positions in their respective industries. The change process included "Work-Out," a way in which employees could participate in teams in the process, and "Town Hall Meetings" with all employees to strengthen dialogue and understanding in respect of the change process and the new roles and work habits that were needed. Managers had previously been appraised solely on their ability to manage in a "command-and-control" culture. Now, however, they were required to meet ownership, stewardship, and entrepreneurial goals. Performance expectations and rewards were therefore realigned. As a result, GE strengthened its position in several global markets and greatly increased its market value.

Empowerment is also about involving people in the change process. People are much more inclined to support what they help to create (and they resist what is forced on them). Myers (1993) writes:

Study after study finds that when workers have more control —when they can help define their own goals . . . and when they participate in decision making — their job satisfaction rises.

Tom Cannon describes how organizations have responded to the challenge of change (Cannon, 2000). They have created flatter structures with more empowered employees who are trusted more, expected to conform to shared values and encouraged to be more entrepreneurial and innovative. They have introduced flexible learning programmes to enhance competencies in initiating and achieving successful change.

Motivation and Inspiration

Effective leaders motivate and inspire people to want to do what needs to be done. In any change process, the change champions — leaders — must be credible. Credibility comes from perceptions of honesty and competence in leaders and from their ability to inspire, say Kouzes and Posner (2002). Motivation and inspiration arise from alignment of organizational goals with individual's needs, wants, values, interests, and aspirations and from the use of positive and appealing language.

Motivation also arises from short-term wins. Gaining short-term wins entails planning and creating visible improvements during the change process. It also entails visibly recognizing and rewarding people who made the wins possible (Kotter, 1995a).

Positive and appealing language is characterized by framing the message and crafting one's rhetoric. Framing the message, Conger (1999) says, is "connecting your message with the needs, interests and feelings of those whose commitment you need" and, thereby, Goodwin (1998) says, "making people feel they have a stake in common problems." Examples of framing language are:

- linking the message with the benefits for everybody involved
- reflecting their values and beliefs
- talking in their language
- matching body language with words
- moving from "I" statements to "we" statements
- making positive comparisons of their situation with that of others
- expressing confidence in people's ability to achieve.

Rhetorical crafting of language consists of giving examples, citing quotations, reciting slogans, varying one's speaking rhythm, using familiar images, metaphors and analogies to make the message vivid (Martin Luther King's allusion to "the jangling discords of our nation" comes to mind), waxing lyrical, and using repetition.

❏ APPLYING THE LEADERSHIP MODEL

This integrative model of leadership has been successfully applied in leadership development programmes in several organizations concerned with change: a manufacturing company, a private mental healthcare company, a public sector defence agency, the top management teams of two universities, a youth charity, and an insurance and emergency assistance company.

Former US president Harry S. Truman is on record as saying: "Men make history and not the other way round. In periods where there is no leadership, society stands still. Progress occurs when courageous, skillful leaders seize the opportunity to change things for the better."[5] Change requires good management, but above all it requires effective leadership.

❏ NOTES

1. Niccolò Machiavelli (1469–1527) *The Prince,* translated from the Italian by Hill Thompson, Collector's Edition, 1980, The Easton Press, Norwalk, CT, 55.
2. Roger Gill, *Defining Leadership*, Sage Publications, London, in preparation.
3. The Bible, Proverbs, 29: 18.
4. Lao Tzu (c.500BC:) *The Way of Lao Tzu,* Number 17.
5. Quoted by Dana Hield Whitson and Douglas K. Clark (2002) 'Management Audits: Passé, or a Useful Quality Improvement Tool?', *Public Management,* 84(4), 6.

❏ READING REFERENCES

American Management Association (1994) *Survey on Change Management,* AMA, New York.

Baum, J. R., Locke, E. A. and Kirkpatrick, S. A. (1998) 'A Longitudinal Study of the Relation of Vision and Vision Communication to Venture Growth in Entrepreneurial Firms', *Journal of Applied Psychology,* 83(1), 43–54.

Bennis, W. (1999) 'The End of Leadership: Exemplary Leadership is Impossible Without Full Inclusion, Initiatives, and Cooperation of Followers', *Organizational Dynamics,* 27, July, 71.

Bennis, W. and Goldsmith, J. (1997) *Learning to Lead,* Nicholas, Brealey, London.

Cannon, T. (2000) 'Leadership in the New Economy', paper presented at The National Leadership Conference, 'Leaders and Managers: Fit for the Future', The Royal Military Academy, Sandhurst, 24th May.

Collins, J. and Porras, J. (1998) *Built to Last,* Random House, London.

Conger, J. (1999) 'The New Age of Persuasion', *Leader to Leader*, Spring, 37–44.

Covey, S. (1992) *'Principle-centered Leadership,* Simon & Schuster, London.

Deetz, S. A., Tracy, S. J. and Simpson, J. L. (2000) *Leading Organizations Through Transition*, Sage, Thousand Oaks, CA.

Dess, G. G. and Picken, J. C. (2000) 'Changing Roles: Leadership in the 21st Century', *Organizational Dynamics*, 28(3), 18–34.

Drucker, P. F. (1999) 'Managing Oneself', *Harvard Business Review*, March–April, 65–74.

Dubrin, A. J. (2001) *Leadership: Research Findings, Practice, and Skills*, 3rd edn, Houghton Mifflin, Boston, MA, 76.

Eden, C. (1993) 'Strategy Development and Implementation: Cognitive Mapping for Group Support' in Hendry, J. Johnson, G. and Newton, J. (eds) *Strategic Thinking: Leadership and the Management of Change*, John Wiley, Chichester.

George, W. W. (2001) 'Keynote Address, Academy of Management Annual Conference, Washington, DC, August', in *Academy of Management Executive*, 15(4), 39–47.

Gill, R. (2001) *Essays on Leadership*, The Leadership Trust Foundation, Ross-on-Wye.

Gill, R. (2002) 'Towards an Integrative Theory of Leadership', paper presented at the Workshop on Leadership Research, European Institute for Advanced Studies in Management. Oxford, 16th–17th December.

Gill, R., Levine, N. and Pitt, D. C. (1998) 'Leadership and Organizations for the New Millennium', *The Journal of Leadership Studies,* 5(4), 46–59.

Goodwin, D. K. (1998) 'Lessons of Presidential Leadership', *Leader to Leader*, 9, 23–30.

Harvey-Jones, J. (1988) *Making It Happen*, HarperCollins, London.

Hastings, C. (1993) *The New Organization*, IBM/McGraw-Hill, London.

Heifetz, R. A. and Laurie, D. L. (1997) 'The Work of Leadership', *Harvard Business Review*, January–February, 75(1), 124–134.

Hooper, A. and Potter, J. (2000) *Intelligent Leadership*, Random House, London.

Jackson, S. (2001) *Leadership and Change Management: Leading Change*, Cranfield University Royal Military College of Science, Shrivenham.

Kakabadse, A. (2002) 'Management Teams Need to Pull Together', *Professional Manager*, September, 37.

Kets de Vries, M. (2000) 'Beyond Sloan: Trust is at the Core of Corporate Values', Mastering Management, *Financial Times*, 2nd October.

Kotter, J. P. (1990a) 'What Leaders Really Do', *Harvard Business Review*, May–June, 156–167.

Kotter, J. P. (1990b) *A Force for Change: How Leadership Differs from Management*, Free Press, New York.

Kotter, J. P. (1995a) 'Leading Change', *Harvard Business Review*, March–April.

Kotter, J. P. (1995b) *The New Rules: How to Succeed in Today's Post-Corporate World*, Free Press, New York.

Kotter, J. P. (1997) 'Leading by Vision and Strategy', Executive Excellence, October, 15–16.

Kouzes, J. M. and Posner, B. Z. (2002) *The Leadership Challenge*, 3rd edn, Jossey-Bass, San Francisco, CA.

Kubr, M. (1996) *Management Consulting: A cuide to the Profession*, 3rd (revised) edn, International Labour Office, Geneva.

Law, S. (2002) 'Getting Involved in Culture Change at M&S', *Professional Management*, May, 24–25.

Mayo, A. (2002) 'Forever Change', *Training Journal*, June, 40.

McLagan, P. (2002) 'Change Leadership Today', *Training & Development*, 56(11), 26–31.

Monks, J. (2000) 'Engaging the Workforce During Change', paper presented at The National Leadership Conference, 'Leaders and Managers: Fit for the Future', The Royal Military Academy, Sandhurst, 24th May.

Mulligan, J. and Barber, P., quoted in Sadler, P. (1998) *Management Consultancy: A Handbook of Best Practice*, Kogan Page, London.

Myers, D. G. (1993) *The Pursuit of Happiness*, The Aquarian Press, London.

Nixon, B. (2002) 'Responding Positively to the Big Issues', *Professional Consultancy*, 4, April, 24–26.

O'Toole, J. (1995) *Leading Change: Overcoming the Ideology of Comfort and the Tyranny of Custom*, Jossey-Bass, San Francisco, CA.

Performance Improvement Unit (2001) *Strengthening Leadership in the Public Sector*, Research Study by the PIY, Cabinet Office, UK Government, www.cabinet-office.gov.uk/innovation/leadershipreport.

Peters, T. (1993) *Liberation Management*, Macmillan, London.

Rajan, A. (2000) *How Can Leaders Achieve Successful Culture Change?*, Centre for Research in Employment & Technology in Europe, Tonbridge, Kent.

Sadler, P. (1997) *Leadership*, Kogan Page, London.

Senge, P. (1990) *The Fifth Discipline*, Doubleday, New York.

Sullivan, W., Sullivan, R. and Bufton, B. (2002) 'Aligning Individual and Organisational Values to Support Change', *Journal of Change Management*, 2(3), 247–254.

Waugh, P. and Morris, N. (2002) 'Ministers Warn Blair that Labour Lacks Core Values', *The Independent*, 9th March.

Whittington, R. Pettigrew, A., Peck, S., Fenton, E. and Conyon, M. (1999) 'Change and Complementarities in the New Competitive Landscape: A European Panel Study, 1992–1996', *Organization Science*, 10(5).

World Economic Forum (2000) *Creating the Organizational Capacity for Renewal*, Booz Allen & Hamilton/World Economic Forum, New York.

Case 4-1

Peter Browning and Continental White Cap (A)

ON APRIL 1, 1984, Peter Browning assumed the position of vice president and operating officer of Continental White Cap, a Chicago-based division of the Continental Group, Inc. Having completed a successful five-year turnaround of Continental's troubled Bondware Division, Browning found this new assignment at White Cap to be a very different type of challenge. He was taking over the most successful of Continental's nine divisions — "the jewel in the Continental crown," as one Continental executive described it. White Cap was the market leader in the production and distribution of vacuum-sealed metal closures for glass jars.

Browning's charge, though, was to revitalize and reposition the division to remain preeminent in the face of threatened, but not yet fully realized, changes in the competitive environment. Sales were stable and costs were up. Recent years had brought changes in the market: one competitor in particular was utilizing price cuts for the first time to build market share, and the introduction of plastic packaging to many of White Cap's traditional customers threatened sales. White Cap had not yet developed a plastic closure or the ability to seal plastic containers. After more than 50 years of traditional management and close control by White Cap's founding family, corporate headquarters decided it was time to bring in a proven, enthusiastic manager to push the business toward a leaner, more efficient, and more flexible operation — one capable of responding to the evolving market conditions.

From the very start, Browning recognized two major obstacles that he would have to address. First, few managers or employees at White Cap acknowledged the need for change. Business results for more than 50 years had been quite impressive and when dips were experienced, they were perceived as cyclical and transient. Second, White Cap had a family-style culture characterized by long-term loyalty from its employees, long-standing traditions of job security, liberal benefits, and paternalistic management. Attempts to alter these traditions would not be welcome.

Reflecting on his new assignment at White Cap, Browning recalled that at Bondware he had walked into a Ming business where he "had nothing to lose." Now he was entering "a successful business with absolutely everything to lose." One White Cap manager observed: "White Cap will be the testing period for Peter Browning in the eyes of Continental." Browning's success in refraining the business would be critical for his future in corporate leadership there. Browning thought about the stern words of caution he had received from his boss, Dick Hofmann, executive vice president of the Continental Group: "White Cap needs changes, but just don't break it while you're trying to fix it. Continental can't afford to lose White Cap."

Research Associate **Mary Gentile** *prepared* this *case under the supervision of Professor* **Todd D. Jick** *as the basis for class discussion rather than to illustrate either effective or ineffective handling of administrative situation.*

Reprinted by permission of Harvard Business School Publishing. Peter Browning and Continental White Cap (A), HBS Case No. 9-486-090 was prepared by Todd D. Jick and Mary Gentile as the basis for class discussion rather than to illustrate either effective or ineffective handling of an administrative situation. Boston: Harvard Business School Publishing, copyright © 1986 all rights reserved.

❑ WHITE CAP BACKGROUND

In 1926 William P. White and his two brothers started the White Cap Company in an old box factory on Goose Island, located in the Chicago River. From the beginning, the White Cap Company was active in many areas: in closure production and distribution, in new product development, and in the design of cap-making and capping machinery. Thus, White Cap promoted itself as not only a source of quality closures but also providers of a "Total System" of engineering and R&D support and service to the food industry. It claimed the latest in closure technology — for example, in 1954 White Cap pioneered the twist-off style of closure, and in the late 1960s it developed the popular "P. T." (press-on/twist-off) style of cap. It also took pride in its capping equipment and field operations service. White Cap's customers were producers of ketchup, juices, baby foods, preserves, pickles, and other perishable foods.

In 1956 the Continental Can Company bought White Cap, and in 1984 the Continental Group, Inc., went from public to private as it was merged into KMI Continental, Inc., a subsidiary of Peter Kiewit Sons, a private construction company. The White Cap Company became Continental White Cap, the most profitable of the parent firm's nine divisions — each of which produced different types of containers and packaging.

Despite the sale of White Cap in 1956, the White family continued to manage the organization, and its traditional company culture persisted. As the manager of human resources at the Chicago plants expressed it: "I really think that many employees felt that White Cap bought Continental Can, instead of the other way around." W.P. White, the company founder, and later his son, Bob, inspired and encouraged a strong sense of family among their employees, many of whom lived in the Polish community immediately surrounding the main plant. Once hired, employees tended to remain and to bring in their friends and relatives as well. At the two Chicago plants in 1985, 80% of the employees had over 15 years of service.

The Whites themselves acted as patrons, or father figures. Legends recounted their willingness to lend money to an hourly worker with unexpected medical bills, or their insistence, in a bad financial year, on borrowing the money for Christmas bonuses. In exchange for hard work and commitment, employees received good salaries, job security, and the feeling that they were part of a "winner." In an area as heavily unionized as Chicago, these rewards were potent enough to keep White Cap nearly union-free. Only the lithographers — a small and relatively autonomous group — were unionized.

White Cap was rife with rituals, ceremonies, and traditions. In the early days of the company, Mrs. W.P. White would prepare and serve lunch every day for the company employees in the Goose Island facility. Over the years, White Cap continued to provide a free family-style hot lunch for all salaried employees and free soup, beverage, and ice cream for the hourly workers.

A press department manager, a White Capper for 28 years, explained:

> For work in a manufacturing setting, you couldn't do better than White Cap. White Cap isn't the real world; when the economy is hurting, White Cap isn't White Cap always lived up to the ideal that "our people are important to us." They sponsored a huge family picnic every year for all White Cappers and friends. When they first instituted the second shift in the factory, they lined up cabs to take late workers home after their shift. They sponsored golf outings and a softball team. People generally felt that nothing's going to happen to us as long as we've got a White there.

But in 1982, Bob White stepped down and turned the management over to Art Lawson, who became vice president and executive officer. Lawson, 63 years old, was a veteran White Capper, and many saw him as simply a proxy for the Whites. Even Lawson would say that he saw himself as a caretaker manager, maintaining things as they had always been.

At about this time, price competition began to heat up in the closure industry. White Cap had been the market leader for over 50 years, but customers were beginning to take the Total System for granted. There were by then five significant manufacturers in the national marketplace and 70 worldwide who offered the twist-off cap. Competitors like National Can Company were beginning to slash prices, aware that the very advantage White Cap had maintained in the market (i.e., its R&D and full service) made it difficult for it to compete effectively with drastic price cutting.

Just at this time, plastic containers — requiring plastic closures — began to be available (see Figure 4.13). In 1982 the Food and Drug Administration had approved the use of a particular plastic substance as an appropriate oxygen-barrier for

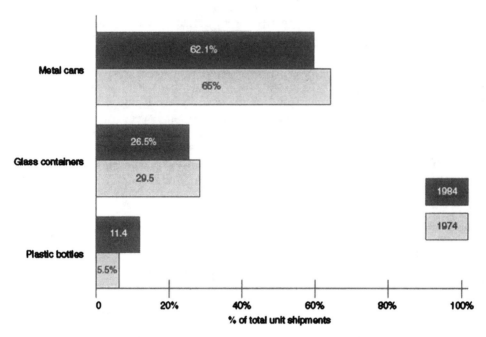

Percentage of Rigid Containers Shipped in 1974 and 1984

Source: Bureau of the Census, International Trade Administration, and *U.S Industrial Outlook 1985.*

Shipments of Plastic Bottles for Food

	Market Year			
	1978	1982	1983	1984 (estimated)
Millions of Units	260	697	798	900

Figure 4.13 *Changes in the Container Industry*

food containers. Subsequently, the American Can Company's Gamma bottle, a squeezable plastic container, was adopted by the Heinz Company for its ketchup and by Hunt for its barbecue sauce. (White Cap had held 100% of the ketchup business worldwide.) Welch's jams and jellies also adopted this new technology, and the reasons were typical:

Welch's expects the new packaging to help revitalize a relatively flat product category, having conducted research indicating that their customers are willing to pay more for the convenience of the squeezable plastic bottle.[1]

[1]Melissa Larson, "Dispensing Closures Revitalize Flat Markets," *Packaging*, August 1985, p. 25.

Another major White Cap account had announced plans to introduce a new juice line in plastic containers for the spring of 1986, as well. Without a competitive plastic closure, White Cap would continue to lose customers. Senior White Cap management, however, had been reluctant to allow R&D to commercialize plastics developments because such plastics threats in the past had never materialized.

In 1984, two years after Bob White had left, Peter Browning was named vice president and operating officer, reporting to Art Lawson. He took over a division with $175 million in gross sales, 1,450 employees (of whom 480 were salaried), 12 sales offices, and 4 plants (2 in Chicago, Illinois, 1 in Hayward, California, and 1 in Hazleton, Pennsylvania).

❏ PETER BROWNING'S BACKGROUND

I'm Peter Browning and I'm 43 years of age. I have four children — three girls, 20,16, and 12, and a seven-year old son. My undergraduate degree is in history, and while at White Cap, I earned my MBA through the Executive Program at the University of Chicago. I have been with Continental for 20 years.

This was Peter Browning's characteristic opening each time he presented himself and his ideas to a new audience. On first impression, Browning appeared enthusiastic, charming, and intellectually and socially curious. Various employees and managers described him alternately as "Mr. Energy," "ambitious," "direct," "the most powerful boss I've had," "the quintessential politician, shaking hands and kissing babies." His speeches to management and staff were peppered with inspirational aphorisms and historical, often military, metaphors, repeated as refrains and rallying cries.

In spring 1985 the Continental Group arranged for each of the nine divisional managers to be interviewed by industrial psychologists. The psychologist's report on Browning stated:

His intellectual ability is in the very superior range. . . . He is a hard-driving individual for whom success in an organization is extremely important. . . . Further, he is completely open in communicating the strategy he has conceived, the goals he has chosen, and the ongoing success of the organization against those goals. He cares about people, is sensitive to them, and makes every effort to motivate them. . . . His own values and beliefs are so strong and well-defined that his primary means of motivation is the instilling of enthusiasm and energy in others to think and believe as he does. By and large he is successful at this, but there are those who have to be motivated from their own values and beliefs, which may be different but which may nonetheless lead to productive action. These people are apt to be confused, overwhelmed, and left behind by his style.[2]

Browning's career began with White Cap and Continental Can in 1964 when he took a position as sales representative in Detroit. He continued in marketing with White Cap for nine years and then in other Continental divisions until 1979. At that time, he returned to Chicago to become vice president and general manager of Continental's Bond-ware Division. Once in the area again, Browning was able to touch base with old contacts from

[2]Alexander B. Platt & Associates Inc., May 2, 1985.

White Cap and to observe firsthand the challenges they faced.

At Bondware (producers of waxed paper cups for hot and cold beverages and food), Browning took over a business that had lost $24 million in five years (1975 to 1979) and that Continental could not even sell. Browning adopted a drastic and accelerated change program, employing what he called "radical surgery" to reduce employees by half (from 1,200 to 600), to eliminate an entire product line, to close four out of six manufacturing sites, and to turn the business around in five years.

❏ BROWNING IS REASSIGNED

Early in 1984, Browning received his reassignment orders from the executive officers of the Continental Group (Stamford, Connecticut). They wanted definite changes in the way the White Cap Division did business, and they believed Browning — fresh from his success with Bondware and a veteran of White Cap himself — was surely the person to make those changes.

Continental's executive officers had several major concerns about White Cap. First of all, they saw a competitive onslaught brewing that they believed White Cap's managers did not recognize. They believed the business instincts of White Cap's management had been dulled by a tradition of uncontested market leadership. The majority of White Cap's managers had been with the firm for over 25 years, and most of them had little intention of moving beyond White Cap, or even beyond their current positions. They were accustomed to Bob White's multilayered, formal, and restrained management style — a style that inhibited cross-communication and that one manager dubbed "management without confrontation." Some of them were startled, even offended, by the price-slashing tactics practiced by White Cap's most recent competitors, and they spoke wistfully of an earlier, more "gentlemanly" market style.

Continental's executive officers were also concerned that White Cap's long-time success, coupled with the benevolent paternalism of the White family management, had led to a padded administrative staff. They instructed Browning to communicate a sense of impending crisis and urgency to the White Cap staff, even as he reduced the salary and administrative costs which Continental perceived as inflated. Furthermore, he was to do all this without threatening White Cap's image in the marketplace or its tradition of employee loyalty.

Browning recognized that corporate attitudes toward White Cap were colored by a history of less than open and cooperative relations with Bob White:

Bob White engendered and preserved the image of White Cap as an enigma, a mystery. He had an obsession with keeping Continental at arm's length, and he used the leverage of his stock and his years of experience to preserve his independence from corporate headquarters. After all, Bob never wanted to leave White Cap or go further.

This kind of mystery, coupled with White Cap's continued success, engendered doubts and envy and misconceptions at the corporate level.

A former Continental Group manager elaborated:

White Cap has always been seen as a prima donna by the Continental Group. I'm not convinced that there aren't some in Connecticut who might want to see White Cap stumble. They have always looked at the salary and administrative costs at 13% of net sales, compared with a 3%–4 % ratio in other divisions, and concluded that White Cap was fat.

Perhaps the demand for cost cuts was fueled by the fact that the Continental Group was going through its own period of "radical surgery" at this time. Since 1984 when Peter Kewit Sons acquired the company, corporate headquarters had "sold off $1.6 billion worth of insurance, paper products businesses, gas pipelines, and oil and gas reserves" and had cut corporate staff from 500 to 40.[3] The corporate climate was calling for swift, effective action.

❏ TAKING CHARGE

In the first month of his new position, Browning turned his attention to three issues. To begin with, he felt he had to make some gesture or take some stand with regard to Bob White. White was very much alive in the hearts and minds of White Cap's employees, and although retired, he still lived in the Chicago area. Although White represented many of the values, and the style that Browning hoped to

[3] Allan Dodds Frank, "More Takeover carnage?" *Forbes,* August 12, 1985, p. 40.

change, he was also a key to the White Cap pride and morale that Browning had to preserve.

In addition, Bob White's successor, Art Lawson, was another link to White Cap's past, and his strong presence in the marketplace represented continuity in White Cap's customer relations. Since corporate headquarters was determined to maintain an untroubled public image throughout White Cap's transition, they brought Browning in reporting to Lawson — the division's vice president and executive officer and a person Browning had known for over 20 years (see Figure 4.14). Browning knew he had to give some strong messages about new directions if he was to shake up the comfortable division, but he had to do this from below Lawson and in spite of White's heritage.

A second challenge facing Browning was White Cap's marketing department. At a time when major, long-term customers in mature markets were faced with the attraction of an emerging plastic-packaging technology and were beginning to take the White Cap Total System for granted, Browning found a marketing and sales organization that, according to him, "simply administered existing programs." It was not spending constructive time with the customers who had built the business, nor was it aggressively addressing new competitive issues.

Jim Stark had been the director of marketing for the previous five years. He had a fine track record with White Cap customers and, as an individual, maintained many strong relationships in the field. Customers knew him well and relied on him. He had been with the company for 30 years and had been a regional sales manager before his transfer to marketing. In this prior position, Stark's strength had clearly been his ability to deal with the customers as opposed to his people-managing skills. Despite his strong outside presentation and selling ability, his internal relationships with his marketing staff and with the field sales force had apparently soured over the years. Team spirit was not in evidence. Stark complained that he didn't receive the support he needed to make changes in marketing.

Stark's boss, the general manager for sales and marketing and a highly competent sales professional, urged Browning to avoid any sudden personnel changes and "to give Stark a chance." Moreover, relieving a manager of his responsibilities would be unprecedented at White Cap. Yet, for some, Stark was like "a baseball coach who has

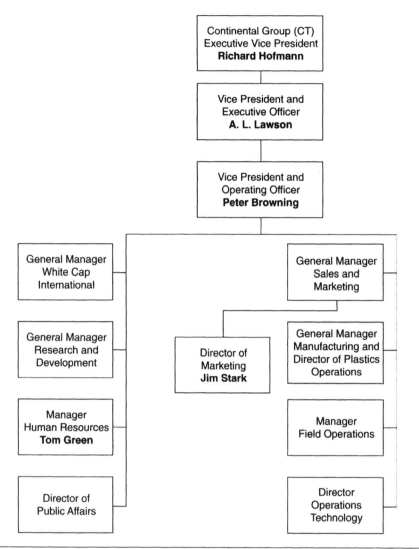

Figure 4.14   *Organization Chart, April 1984*

been with the team through some slow seasons and was no longer able to turn around his image."

Browning also inherited a manager of human resources, Tom Green, whose role and capabilities he began to question. Browning had always been a proponent of a strong human resources function. He met with Tom Green and asked him to help identify and evaluate key personnel throughout the division in terms of promotion and reassignment decisions. Green was a veteran White Capper with 20 years' seniority and 5 years in his current position. Long tenure managers were very comfortable with him and he was well-liked. He offered few surprises to employees and helped maintain all the traditional and popular benefit policies and practices that they had come to expect from White Cap.

Browning soon recognized a problem with Green:

In reviewing the personnel files with Green, I found he had few constructive ideas to offer. He seemed to do a lot of delegating and to spend a lot of time reading the *Wall Street Journal.* And a lot of managers seemed to work around him. I found myself getting involved in decisions that he should have been taking care of, such as deciding whether a departing secretary in another department needed to be replaced or not.

One possibility was to replace Green with the human resources manager from Bondware who had helped me with the changes I had made there. But

Green was also a valuable information source and someone who could be a nonthreatening conduit to and from White Cap employees.

Peter Browning pondered these initial choices and decisions carefully. He wanted to rejuvenate White Cap and yet not demoralize its loyal work force and management. Browning knew that Dick Hofmann, his boss, expected him to push for real, measurable change in the division's culture and performance. What was less clear was how far he should push — and how fast — in order to succeed. Even Hofmann acknowledged that Browning's assignment put him "smack dab between a rock and a hard place."

Managing the Evolution of Change and Engaging Employees

❏ CHAPTER AT A GLANCE

Highlights of this chapter include the following:

1. Change occurs and is accepted more frequently today than ever before; however, the new behavior is more of a personal integration into our daily lives.

2. By understanding and utilizing the behavioral "Change Curve," the change agent can recognize employee symptoms and treat them in an appropriate manner.

3. Change leaders must realize that there may be a gap between their understanding of the

change and the understanding of the rest of the organization.

4. Change programs get delayed, and leaders become frustrated by employees' failure to perceive the obvious need for change. Therefore, change agents need to work with and develop relationships with employees so that both parties understand what needs to be accomplished.

5. Employee satisfaction and engagement have been shown to be related to organization's outperforming their competition.

6. Because the planning process provides for a better understanding of and the ability to predict what may occur, change agents or leaders should be able to make better decisions when unexpected events occur.

7. There are steps that change agents can take during the different stages of change that will increase employee understanding of and commitment to the change initiative.

8. Since relationships established during the change process can be considered a foundation for long-term sustainable change, the manner in which resistance to change is addressed is very important.

9. Middle managers are essential to transforming an organization's vision to reality. They provide linkages between upper management and those that are on the front line of implementing the strategic change initiative.

10. The results-driven orientation focuses on performance metrics that are measurable and support the goals and objectives of the change initiative.

11. Employees must be able to "Pace" their work and synchronize their energies with one another, creating a focused flow of attention to enhance the performance of the strategic change initiative.

12. Organizations can determine if their strategic change projects will succeed by evaluating the four factors of the DICE framework; duration, integrity, commitment, and effort.

13. Indicators can be used to determine whether the strategic change project team is working effectively and collaboratively together.

14. Managing the evolution of change of a strategic initiative means that planning, implementation and appropriate monitoring and control are an absolute necessity. However, it should also be noted that you must have properly addressed the four dimensions of change during planning to increase your organization's probability of success.

❏ VIGNETTE[1]

In one organization we worked with, the change process leader, a very conscious and creative man, decided that the organization needed to run a pilot program. Concerned about resistance, he announced to the organization that a pilot test would be run on the desired state scenario and that two sites would have the opportunity to contribute to the organization's future by testing the desired state, as well as be a year ahead of the game if they were successful in their efforts. He invited any site that was interested in pioneering the future to tell him why and how they would proceed. Much to our surprise, more than half of the thirty potential sites submitted proposals. At the time, the desired state scenario was defined through the managerial level of design, requiring the chosen test sites to complete their own operational-level design as they figured out how to implement. Two sites were chosen; the test period was to be one year.

The two sites represented two very different leadership styles and cultures within the organization. One was more controlling, conservative, and pressured; the other was more facilitative, open, and risk taking. The conservative site rolled out its implementation with no consulting help, little margin for error, and minimal foundation setting. The innovative site used the internal organization development consultants, selected its own change team to design the change strategy, spent considerable effort to identify and create conditions for success, and involved the front-line teams that were most impacted by the desired state design.

Upon completion of the pilot program, both sites reported important findings about the desired state, the change strategy used for their rollout, and the receptivity of the various target audiences in the organization. The results of the pilots revealed predictable outcomes — the more innovative site that took a proactive and participative approach proved to be the more positive. The conservative site was also considered successful, although the culture, morale, and performance of the innovative site had observably more vitality, commitment, and buy-in. It was clearly the preferred wave of the future.

❑ CHAPTER PERSPECTIVE

Each one of us will deal with change in both a rational and emotional manner. In this chapter, we will discuss rational support for change and the behavioral states that one goes through, how different levels of the organization move through change, and how employees and management can work together during change. In addition, we will address questions that need to be asked to monitor and control the evolution of change and how change agents can proactively address resistance to change. We will also discuss the role of middle manager who provides a critical linkage between top-down and bottom-up change, the importance of focusing on results during change, the pace and extent of change, and trust in times of change. Finally, we will review the positive and negative factors and tactical strengths and weaknesses of a reengineering change initiative and perform a simulation exercise. All of the material in this chapter should not only increase your ability to move through change but also enable you to help others in your organization.

❑ CONTEMPORARY APPROACH TO ORGANIZATIONAL CHANGE

In today's business environment, Lewin's three-stage change process could simply be described by

1. A series of management training sessions where the need for change (old behavior is not acceptable) is revealed,
2. Moving to a new level of behavior, and
3. Ensuring that the new level of behavior is secure.

Movement from the old to the new behavior reflects what the organization has determined is the need for change. Change occurs and is accepted more frequently today than ever before; however, the new behavior is more of a personal integration into our daily lives. In the following paragraphs, Schein provides an example of a contemporary approach to organizational change that develops from Lewin's three-stage process as an alternative:[2]

Unfreezing is the process of creating motivation and readiness for change. In general, Schein's *first step* states that there are three ways of accomplishing this:

1. Disconfirmation, when members of the organization experience a need for change which, in turn, motivates them to embrace change
2. Induction of guilt or anxiety involving the establishment of a perceived gap between what is not currently working well and a desired future state
3. Creation of psychological safety, providing an environment in which people feel safe enough to experience disconfirmation and induction

An understanding or experience of the need to change, recognition of a desired future state, and a comfort level with the future state are all required. In most cases, the rational and emotional impact or consequences of change must both be understood and accepted.

The *second step* for Schein is changing (or cognitive restructuring), which is akin to movement in Lewin's model. This is the process of helping people to see things differently and react differently in the future. Changing can be accomplished by identification with a new role model, mentor, boss or consultant, which enables one to see things from another's viewpoint, or by scanning the environment for new and relevant information. In this step, the individual determines that the new state is both desirable and feasible to them. If they have had input to or provided feedback to the development of the new direction, this will likely be an easy step!

The *third step*, refreezing, involves integrating the change process through personal refreezing, which involves taking the new, changed way of doing things and fitting it comfortably into one's total self-concept, and relational refreezing which involves successfully integrating the new behavior in interactions with significant others. The individual's role becomes part of the initiative and the individual accepts this role based on what they are expected to do!

Schein has provided us with steps that enable an individual to create motivation and a readiness for change, recognize that the new state is both desirable and feasible, and integrate the new state into what needs to be done. An individual must move through these steps to participate in and become committed to the change initiative.

❑ THE CHANGE CURVE

A change agent should expect that there will be some employee dissatisfaction with the change initiative. Therefore, by understanding and utilizing the behavioral "Change Curve," the change agent can recognize employee symptoms and

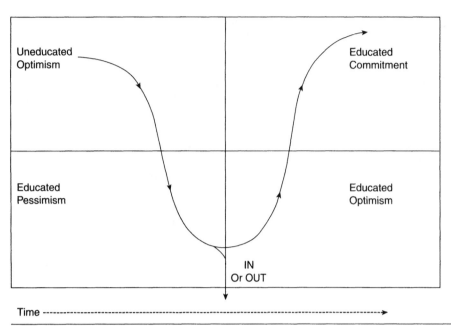

Figure 5.1   The Change Curve

treat them in an appropriate manner. The Change Curve has four quadrants that reflect a behavior state from "Uneducated" to "Committed" (see Figure 5.1).[3] Description of each quadrant follow.

Uneducated Optimism — The upper left corner describes a behavior expressed by "Others may be required to change, but not me." Employees feel enthusiastic because they believe that the change they have been hearing about will have little, if any, impact on them. When the change is perceived to be something that will happen to others, these non-impacted employees feel comfortable. Based on employee lack of knowledge related to the change, a change agent should provide as much information as possible and tell employees why the change is happening.

Educated Pessimism — The lower left quadrant is where reality sets in and behavior is expressed by "They cannot make me change." Once employees start receiving specific information about the implementation effort, they begin to realize that they will be impacted in some way by the change. Consequently, many employees begin to actively resist change. Recognizing this resistance, a change agent should continue to provide information and help the employee stay focused on what the future

should bring, not dwell on the past. Please note that the very information employees seek will typically throw them, at least temporarily, into a state of pessimism. In addition, change agents need to recognize that employees need to go through this portion of the change curve before they can move toward accepting and supporting change.

OUT or IN — There is a critical point in the change curve which is located at the very bottom of the curve. This is typically where some employees choose to move themselves OUT of the change process, emotionally and even physically, in a state of anger, frustration, and disappointment. As a change agent, you obviously want to minimize the number of employees that choose to move OUT. On the other hand, change agents need to accept the reality that, in some cases, this is ultimately the best solution for everyone. What you cannot afford is to have employees the move OUT mentally and emotionally, but to physically remain in the organization.

Educated Optimism — The third quadrant, in the lower right corner, is where progress can be realized and there is movement toward acceptance of change. In this quadrant, the realities of change are perceived more positively than negatively. Employees enter a period of adoption, where

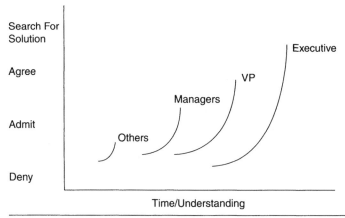

Figure 5.2   *The Change Cycle Gap*[5]

they accept the reality of the change that is occurring and can start seeking positive outcomes.

Educated Commitment—The upper right quadrant, the final stage is where employees accept the change and are fully committed to the new way of doing things. This is where the change agent can utilize collective energies and finally realize the full positive impact of your change initiative. Employee behavior is expressed by "Things are better this way." In this stage, the change agent should recognize employees' efforts and reflect on what they have learned and how that can help them manage future change.

    "The speed with which employees move through the Change Curve and the severity of disruption in productivity stemming from change will vary, depending on how significant the change is, whether the person chooses the change and what other changes are also going on in the person's life."[4] By understanding the behavioral state of individuals moving through the Change Curve, the change agent can both evaluate the need for information and education and also get a sense of the "pace of change" within the organization. As we will discuss later in this chapter, the "pace of change" is another critical aspect of the change process.

❏ THE CHANGE CYCLE GAP

Change leaders interact with individuals and groups in the organization to explain the who, what, when, where, why, and how of the change. They utilize every opportunity to interact with others to legitimize necessary change and to encourage challenges and answer questions. In addition, they realize that people are skeptical; while some are early adopters of change, others need much convincing. Change leaders realize that there is a gap between their understanding of the change and the rest of the organization (see Figure 5.2).

Every change initiative in an organization sets in motion a cycle of resisting change, recognizing the need for change, agreement as to the type of change required, and finally development of implementation strategies. As leaders we are often reluctant initially to admit that a change is needed. ***Change is very costly!*** We seek to convince ourselves that if we just stick to the current plan we will weather the storm. As the storm grows worse and the roof starts to leak, we start to admit that a change may be needed.[6]

    After this admission stage has been passed we start a process to get others to recognize that a change is needed. We build support for a new direction. Then we begin the search for strategies and solutions.[7]

    The executive group goes through this cycle first, and then layer by layer the rest of the organization follows. The first one through this cycle becomes impatient with the rest of the organization as it necessarily goes through its own deny, admit, agree, and solve cycle. We tend to forget our own reactions. We become more and more impatient and then try to speed up the process. People feel we are trying to push or sell them a concept they have yet to fully understand or feel a need to embrace. If leaders try to push past the organization's limits to change of purpose, identify or master, they do so at their own and the organization's peril.[8]

    Change leaders must create an environment where people involved in the change process can open themselves up to new ideas and concepts, challenge old assumptions, adopt new assumptions, and overcome their hostility and resistance to change. Change leaders must provide tools, techniques, and laboratory settings to allow people to synthesize new concepts and align them to the new way (and vice versa!).[9]

Change leaders recognize that they are always trying to balance stability and change. It is a delicate balance to accomplish since employees desire order and stability, while organizations must be ready to adapt to changing conditions quickly.[10]

By understanding the change gap that occurs in organizations, change leaders can better control the "pace of change" during the planning and implementation of a change initiative. In a later section of this chapter, we will discuss the importance of moving together through change.

❏ CREATING DISSATISFACTION WITH THE CURRENT STATE

Change programs get delayed, and leaders become frustrated by employees' failure to perceive the obvious need for change. In successful change efforts, the top leader's desire for change was inevitably followed by providing information and reasons for change that diffused dissatisfaction in moving to a future state. This information and reasons for change can be organized into four methods: competitive information, external environmental factors, internal environmental factors, and mandated dissatisfaction.

Competitive information is the most common way that organizations inform their employees that things need to change. As is shown in Chapter 3, Figure 3.1, organizations today have many more performance systems than they did in the past and the resultant performance data is now more widely distributed to employees. The main drawback to this reactive method is that it likely finds the organization in a disadvantaged competitive position.

The costs of raw materials or services which may increase dramatically (energy prices, services to meet regulatory requirement, etc.) represent an external environmental factor. While one might assume that this would impact all competitors equally, that may not be the case. For example, the raw material or service contract terms for one organization can be much different than those of another. Today, leaders within an organization must be tuned into the external environment.

Examples of internal environmental factors include outdated equipment, inefficient processes, antiquated systems, lack of expertise, and many other factors that may significantly reduce an organization's capability to compete. While many of these factors do not occur overnight, the ability to meet the needs of your customers, similar to what your competition provides, can change quickly. In addition, this can significantly impact the financial strength of an organization if a number of these must be addressed at one time.

Sometimes it is necessary for leaders in an organization to take a drastic approach and mandate dissatisfaction. In that case, one might state, "You must change according to my determination of what needs to be done or leave the organization." In other words, you will lose your job if you continue to support the status quo!

We need to recognize that in most cases a good rational argument supports the need for change. An organization must provide sufficient information and reasoning to enable employees to understand and recognize the need to change. In the following section, we will address situations where there is significant uncertainty that makes it more difficult for employees to accept the *feasibility* and *desirability* of the future state.

❏ CHANGING THE EMPLOYMENT CONTRACT AND MOBILIZE TO DO ADAPTIVE WORK

The following sections focus on the new set of expectations that are forced upon employees due to the change effort.[11] These sections provide us a perspective on the importance of change leaders working with employees so that both parties understand what needs to be accomplished.

Companies are in danger of losing the voluntariness that makes possible much of a business's ability to compete. As whole industries undergo restructuring, psychological contracts — those unwritten commitments made between workers and their employers — need to change in order to be kept. Service, quality, and innovation require higher contributions from people and, therefore, a new psychological contract involving commitment and trust. In high contribution work settings, that means change the deal while keeping the people. Changes that violate a contract or fail to substitute another effective one in its place won't do. And, even though the psychological contract is not legally binding, today's executive must know how successful firms transform it.[12]

Effectively changing a psychological contract depends on two things: how similar is the proposed change to the current contract, and how good is the relationship between employee and employer? Asking people to use a new work system or work a few extra hours can simply mean to modify, clarify, substitute, or expand an existing contract. However, asking people to redefine themselves–as professionals rather that job holders, customer service providers rather than technicians, or as leaders rather than middle managers–is far more complicated.[13]

Challenge the Old Contract

Contracts are challenged when discrepant information is available regarding their underlying assumptions. All contracts are based on certain assumptions, including the nature of the business and good faith efforts to obtain mutual benefits. Shifts in the nature of the business, especially those not directly under organizational control, can create severe costs to either party of continuing the contract. A contracts framework suggests that it is important to ask how the change process was legitimated and whether externally anchored reasons were offered. Challenging the contract requires creating a deep understanding of the reasons why change is necessary. The stress and disruption of this change should be addressed with an intervention that provides new discrepant information that educates the employee.[14]

Prepare for Change

Change breeds uncertainty. Reactions to it may vary from overt displays of emotion and frustration to passive withdrawal. Ending the old contract can involve employee information gathering (send them out to talk with customers and benchmark successful firms). By recognizing deficiencies of the existing operation, employees can bridge to the new contract by acknowledging the end of the old contract (celebrate good features of old). It may even be necessary to create a transitional structure or cross-functional task force to manage the change. During this transition, managers need to remain readily available for questions and to convey whatever information they know when they know it.[15]

Generate New Contract

Understanding new contract terms requires employees to act like newcomers, regardless of how long they have been with the organization. Employees will sign-on only after they have made sense of the new situation. Therefore, employees should be encouraged to be actively involved in new contract creation.[16]

Live the New Contract

Solidifying the new contract means that for a while the organization has to strive to be incredibly consistent. Until employees know with certainty that the 'old deal is over', the new contract is not reality. Focus groups and informal networks can help test whether the new contract is well understood. Until the new deal is taken for granted, the organization cannot afford to send mixed messages.[17]

Change cannot be legitimated if people don't understand the reasons for it, nor can they effectively participate in crafting appropriate new terms. The present and future psychological contract is increasingly a balanced one where adjustments are inevitable on both sides. The most powerful contacts of all are those that can be both changed and kept.[18]

The ability of an organization to move from an old to a new state is highly dependent on being able to move employees to a new state that they find feasible and desirable plus one where they can adapt to the environment. At times this can be difficult because a change initiative may satisfy the needs of one group but will reduce the satisfaction of others. Change agents must develop relationships with these groups and individual employees that enable both parties to understand what needs to be accomplished to meet the goals and objectives of the entire organization. These expectations then become the new psychological contract.

❏ EMPLOYEE ENGAGEMENT IN THE CHANGE PROCESS

An engaged employee is one who is fully involved in and enthusiastic about the work they do! Engaged employees, during a change process, care about the future of the company and are willing to invest the discretionary effort to see that the organization succeeds. Employee satisfaction and engagement have been shown to be related to organizations outperforming their competition. Employee engagement cannot only make a real difference, but it can also set the great organizations apart from the merely good ones.[19]

A combination of the right business environment and a culture that creates wants instead of

CONNECT	Leaders must show that they value employees.
CAREER	Leaders should provide challenging and meaningful work with opportunities for career advancement.
CLARITY	Leaders must communicate a clear vision.
CONVEY	Leaders clarify their expectations about employees and provide feedback on their functioning in the organization.
CONGRATULATE	Exceptional leaders give recognition, and they do so a lot; they coach and convey.
CONTRIBUTE	Employees want to know that their input matters and that they are contributing to the organization's success in a meaningful way.
CONTROL	Employee's value control over the flow and pace of their jobs and leaders can create opportunities for employees to exercise this control.
COLLABORATE	When employees work in teams and have the trust and cooperation of their team members, they outperform individuals and teams which lack good relationships.
CREDIBILITY	Leaders should strive to maintain an organization's reputation and demonstrate high ethical standards.
CONFIDENCE	Good leaders help create confidence in an organization by being exemplars of high ethical and performance standards.

Figure 5.3   *The 10 C's of employee engagement*[20]

requirements places few limits on what employees can achieve. Empowering employees can engage them in meeting their individual, as well as, organizational goals. Figure 5.3 relates several actions that can be taken to challenge, provide feedback, recognize, coach, inspire, motivate, and engage employees. Please note that all of these actions are directly related to managing organizational change!

Organizations Must Deploy Employees in New Ways

To be able to learn and adapt to the changing business environment, organizations must deploy employees in new ways by maintaining the right mix of PEOPLE, with the right SKILLS, available at the right TIME.[21] The right COMBINATION will enable the organization to do the right THINGS to survive. Barriers against allowing organization to deploy resources in such a manner are rising labor costs, increased stress and frustration, increased employee mobility,

and a lack of trust in today's business world. Organizations can do a number of things to offset these barriers: improve employee attitudes about their work situation by empowering and engaging them in the development of a better tomorrow and recognizing, rewarding, and compensating (pay for performance) them for their efforts.

Rational and Emotional Aspects of Employee Engagement

As employee engagement markers, Towers Perrin uses a set of nine key "indicative responses" that have been developed and tested statistically over a number of years with many different employers. The items examine both "emotional" and "rational" aspects of the employee's relationship with the organization.[22]

The first five items, the "emotional" aspects, relate to people's personal satisfaction and the sense of inspiration they get from their work and being part of the organization:

1. I really care about the future of my organization.
2. I am proud to tell others I work for my organization.
3. My job provides me with a sense of personal accomplishment.
4. I would recommend my organization to a friend as a good place to work.
5. My organization inspires me to do my best work.

The remaining four "rational" markers relate to the relationship between the individual and the organization:

6. I understand how my unit/department contributes to the success of my organization.
7. I understand how my role is related to my organization's overall goals, objectives, and direction.
8. I am willing to put in a great deal of effort beyond what is normally expected to help my organization succeed.
9. I am personally motivated to help my organization be successful.

High scores on all nine items indicate a state of true "high engagement." When an organization is moving through a change, these indicators have an even greater significance, recognizing that employees are asked to go above and beyond what they have done in the past!

❏ ADDRESSING THE UNEXPECTED

The planning and implementation of strategic change initiatives will bring many unexpected situations and events. These are inevitable and represent varying degrees and levels of resistance that you should expect to encounter in any major change initiative. You need to be proactive in identifying these situations and events and then select from a variety of ways to deal with them. The next sections provide you some guidance in how to deal with these changes.

Questions a Change Leader Must Ask

In order to proactively monitor the strategic change initiative, change leaders must ask questions that enable them to get a sense of the "pulse" of what is going on so that they can determine if things are proceeding as planned. These questions can be focused in four areas:

1. What is the employees' perspective?
2. Do employees receive satisfactory responses to their questions?
3. Have we communicated to employees at both an overview and detail level?
4. Have employees accepted the vision as "Ours."

Change initiative implementation strategies must include employee interaction and feedback to enable the organization to determine the level of employee comprehension and commitment. The end of chapter reading, *The 10 Questions Change Leaders Must Answer First*, provides some additional insight on what the change leader needs to ask to assess the status of a change initiative.

Unexpected Events and Changes in Scope

Unexpected events can include anything from a change in employee assignment to changes in the business that identified the need for strategic change. A change leader's ability to address these events is dependent on how well the change leader understands the change initiative and what has been learned during the planning process. Because the planning process provides for a better understanding of and the ability to predict what may occur, change leaders should be able to make better decisions when unexpected events occur.

The scope creep that is found with most projects should not always be viewed as detrimental to the change initiative; it may be an opportunity.[23]

There is probably no one who has escaped scope creep, where the magnitude of change initiative deliverables increases with no additional provision of resources. Unfortunately, most scope creep is subtle. It slithers, almost invisibly, into the final list of change initiative expectations and is rarely clearly identified and stated. In many cases, scope creep is not necessarily an outward attempt to get more freebies out of you. It is more the result of the employees becoming excited about the prospects of the change initiative once they begin to see the positive impacts it might have on their business. You don't want to stifle that enthusiasm, but you certainly want to prepare your employees for potential negative impacts.

Our experience with change initiatives has also shown that members of the team will bring their "pet projects" or activities that they have not been able to accomplish and attempt to make them part of the change initiative. Once we recognize that this is what is happening, I stop the meeting and remove the pet project. We then repeat the importance of focusing on the objectives and goals of the change initiative.

❑ ADDRESSING RESISTANCE TO CHANGE

As we have discussed, change leaders need to be proactive in addressing strategic change initiatives. This is also the case when addressing resistance to change. There are steps that change leaders can take during the different stages of change that will increase employees' understanding of and commit-ment to the change initiative. In addition, there is some advice that we can provide when dealing face-to-face with resistance to change. Both these steps and advice should assist those dealing with resistance to change.

Steps a Change Agent Can Take

Figure 5.4 lists eight steps that change agents can deploy to help reduce employee resistance to change. These eight steps are embedded into Lewin's three stages of change and will enable the change agent to not only reduce employee resistance but also integrate the employee into the change process in a positive manner.

Advice for Dealing with Change

Since relationships established during the change process can be considered a foundation for

STAGE 1—Unfreeze (loosening up the employee's attitude, such that they become more open-minded to the possibility there might be a better way).
Step 1 — Provide Your Rationale (share your reasoning with the employees — why the change will be beneficial to the company).
Step 2 — Be Empathetic (show the employees you appreciate the difficulties such a change will create for them).
Step 3 — Communicate Clearly (communicate all the particulars as simply, clearly, and extensively as possible, both verbally and in writing).
STAGE 2 — Make the Transition (move to the desired state).
Step 4 — Explain the Benefits (show how the change will benefit them — it gives them an incentive to help implement the new way).
Step 5 — Obtain Participative Input (allow those affected to offer their input and to express their needs; show how you have incorporated their ideas)
Step 6 — Provide Training (training is needed to ensure the employees feel competent and confident in the new way).
STAGE 3 — Refreeze (institutionalize the new state)
Step 7 — Indicate Top Management's Support (employees focus on what top management does, not what they say).
Step 8 — Publicize Successes and Make Corrections (it is imperative that praise be given when recognition is deserved and make adjustments based on input from employees).

Figure 5.4   Eight Steps to Reduce Employee Resistance to Change[24]

1. Keep your cool in dealing with others.
2. Handle pressure smoothly and effectively.
3. Respond nondefensively when others disagree with you.
4. Develop creative and innovative solutions to problems.
5. Be willing to take risks and try out new ideas.
6. Be willing to adjust priorities to changing conditions.
7. Demonstrate enthusiasm for and commitment to long-term goals.
8. Be open and candid in dealing with others.
9. Participate actively in the change process.
10. Make clear-cut decisions as needed.

Figure 5.5   Advice to Reduce the Stress of Face-to-Face Confrontations

long-term sustainable change, the manner in which resistance to change is addressed in very important. When one is confronted face-to-face with employee resistance to change, how should they react? Figure 5.5 highlights some fundamental recommendations to reduce the stress of those face-to-face confrontations:[25]

This list focuses on one's ability to be empathetic, patience, creative, flexible, open and informative, but also addresses the need to be decisive and committed to the strategic change initiative. By following the above advice, a change agent can help reduce the stress and anxiety of change for both themselves and the employee.

❑ MIDDLE MANAGERS AND CHANGE

Middle managers are essential to transforming an organization's vision to reality. They provide linkages between upper management and those that are on the front line of implementing the strategic change initiative. To identify middle managers that can take on the role of an effective change agent, organizations should look for the following characteristics:[26]

1. Early volunteers eager to participate in change initiatives
2. Positive critics who can spot an initiative's potential problems and suggest solutions
3. People whom others seek out informally for advice and help

4. Versatile individuals who have previously adapted to major change

By selecting middle managers that have these characteristics, an organization can help ensure the success of a strategic change initiative. In addition, to support the strategic change initiative, these change agents will take on the following roles: entrepreneur, communicator, therapist, and tightrope artist. A brief description of the actions that these change leaders will take and the effect they will have on the change initiative for each of these roles is stated below:[27]

Entrepreneurs — As an entrepreneur, the change leader will be close enough to the front lines to spot problems, yet far enough away to see the big picture and new possibilities. The individual will likely be diverse in work experience, geography, gender, ethnicity, and can generate better, richer ideas than their bosses. For example, of 117 change-program projects at a large telecom company, 80% of senior-executive-initiated projects failed, while 80% of middle managers' succeeded — generating $300 million in annual profits.

Communicators — As a communicator, the change leader will have strong credibility, plugged into broad and deep social networks. The individual will sell change initiatives and fire up people in non-threatening ways and be more tenured, know who gets things done, how, and exert strong but informal leverage. For example, a middle manager at a large airline realized that senior executives were computer-illiterate. He developed a reverse-mentoring program where younger employees taught executives about the Internet in return for exposure to higher-level business concerns. The program protected executives' pride — and helped them make complex strategic decisions about e-commerce.

Therapists — As a therapist, the change leader will keep anxious employees productive during radical change by addressing emotional needs. The individual will prevent alienation and paralyzing chaos and provide one-on-one problem solving and support. For example, in a company facing relocation, a middle manager persuaded the firm to pay for employee visits to the new site months in advance. Each family received a welcoming-committee sponsor to locate needed resources in the area.

Tightrope Artists — As a tightrope artist, the change leader will balance radical change with needed continuity. The individual will avoid the chaos of too much change too quickly, and the inertia of too little change too slowly and will keep the company working. For example, in one company implementing a 13,000-person downsizing, middle managers' work with union representatives averted a strike and slowed turnover. This continuity let the firm generate revenue during a difficult time–and funded many change projects.

The challenge of the change agent is to figure out how to hold on to core values and capabilities while simultaneously changing how work gets done and shifting the organization in a new strategic direction.[28]

❑ FOCUS ON RESULTS, NOT ACTIVITIES

For many change initiatives, organizations mistake means for ends and process for outcome. In essence, organizational members focus on completing activities with the hope that this will enable them to meet their goals. For example, activities such as assessment of customer satisfaction or training employees to problem solve do address key aspects of the change initiative. However, did they impact the bottom line performance improvements? The focus should really be on results![29]

Comparing Improvements Efforts

While activity-centered and results-driven share some common methodologies for initiating change, they differ in very significant ways. The lack of a bottom line result orientation is reflected in the activity-centered effort versus the results-driven effort, which has specific timetable and performance objectives (see Figure 5.6).

The results-driven orientation focuses on performance metrics that are measurable and support the goals and objectives of the change initiative. By following this focus, organizations can recognize that progress is being made. Figure 5.7 provides some examples of performance factors and the types of performance metrics that can be used.

The focus of the performance metrics should be both objective and subjective. Objective to provide quantifiable results that can be measured over time so that trends can be determined and subjective to provide qualitative results that can fill in the gaps between what objective data cannot provide.

Institutionalize the Results-Driven Focus

There is no reason for change agents to acquiesce when their employees plead that they are already accomplishing just about all that can be accomplished or that factors beyond their control, like company policy, missing technology, or a lack of resources are blocking performance improvements.[31] By being results-driven, employees will bring up these factors so that management can act to remove these barriers or restrictions. This results-driven focus can be institutionalized by using the following guidelines:[32]

1. Ask each unit to set and achieve a few ambitious short-term performance goals. To begin with, managers can ask unit heads to commit

Activity-Centered	The improvement effort is defined mainly in long-term, global terms. ("We are going to be viewed as number one in quality in our industry.")
Results-Driven	There are measurable short-term performance improvement goals, even though the effort is a long-term, sustaining one. ("Within 60 days, we will be paying 95% of claims within 10 days.")"

Figure 5.6   Activity-Centered versus Results-Driven Effort[30]

Performance	Metrics
Efficiency	Productivity, time to produce products/services, production/services costs, and cost of raw materials or labor
Quality	Number of rejects, product/service reliability over time, and number of returns
Responsiveness	Number of repeat customers, level of customer service, and level of on-time deliveries
Innovation	Number of new products/services introduced, cost of product/service development, and time to introduce upgraded products/services

Figure 5.7 *Performance and Metrics*

to achieve in a short time some improvement targets, such as faster turnaround time in responding to customers, lower costs, increased sales, or improved cash flow.

2. Periodically review progress, capture the essential learning, and reformulate strategy. In scheduled work sessions, change leaders should review and evaluate progress on the current array of results-focused projects and learn what is and what isn't working.

3. Institutionalize the changes that work — and discard the rest. In this way, an organization can gradually build successful innovations into its operations and discard unsuccessful ones before they do much harm.

4. Create the context and identify the crucial business challenges. Change agents must establish the broader framework to guide continuing performance improvement in the form of strategic directions for the business and a "vision" of how it will operate in the future.

By focusing on both long-term strategic objectives with short-term improvement projects, management can translate strategic direction into reality and resist the temptation to include non-productive activity-centered programs.

❏ THE "PACE AND EXTENT" OF CHANGE

The following case study can be used as an example of how important it is to monitor and control change.

We worked with one organization that had over thirty 'priority' change efforts underway simultaneously. The people of the organization were exhausted and frustrated with their leaders. The executives engaged us to help organize, prioritize, and coordinate their many initiatives into one unified approach and build the organization's understanding of its transformation. Consistency and integration of the discrete efforts were desperately needed across the organization, as many of the initiatives were competing with each other when their outcomes could only be achieved through synergistically working together. Nearly every one of the initiatives was being run using a different change model, if one could even be deciphered. This made collaboration nearly impossible. Like different computer platforms, the initiatives could not talk to each other. They needed a common language and approach.

We helped the change leaders prioritize their top initiatives and educated them and their internal consultants about the change process. The training was all 'case-based', and the change leaders applied the same model to each of their top initiatives as they learned it. Having a change process operating system became a strategic advantage that provided them a basis for consistency, integration, and flexibility. With this approach, their multiple changes could coexist, work in tandem, and be communicated as one overarching transformation. The methodology allowed them to lead all of the changes in a coherent, yet customized fashion. With continuous follow-up, application clinics, and coaching, the leaders created a system that met the majority of their needs as well as accomplishing their transformation.[33]

The "Pace and Extent" of change should continually be monitored for an acceptable pace of movement across the organization and for symptoms of repetitive change syndrome, initiative over-load, change-related chaos, employee cynicism, and burnout. Employees must be able to "Pace" their work and synchronize their energies with one another, creating a focused flow of attention to enhance the performance of the strategic change initiative. Another consideration for organizations is that they may pursue too much change too fast, potentially causing significant disruption and a negative impact.

We Need To Move Together

Employees and groups don't want to be too far out in front or too far behind. The organization must implement phases of the change initiative in a timely fashion to allow for the evaluation of the status of change, so that adjustments can be made and the next phase of change undertaken. Because the change process is such an important learning experience, it important that "we need to move together." Only then can we make appropriate modifications to our plan and move forward with the next phase of change. From another perspective, too large a gap between one group and another cannot only cause isolation and frustration but also reduce the incentive for the rest of the organization to keep up.

How Much is Too Much Change?

Many organizations have a tendency to increase the speed of change until they are going danger-ously fast. Recognizing the competitive need to change and the energized "Vision" for change, organizations may also undertake too many change initiatives. Organizations should moni-tor their rate of change by surveying change leaders and also keep track of the number of change initiatives. If they don't, employees can become overwhelmed and customers can be harmed.

❑ TRUST IN TIMES OF CHANGE

One of the paradoxes of change is that trust is hardest to establish when you need it the most.[34] There are some companies that employees trust, but if a company is in trouble, or if it is in the middle of a change effort, lack of trust automatically emerges as a serious barrier.

Trust in a time of change is based on two things that change leaders must focus on: both predict-ability and capability.[35]

Predictability — Know What to Expect

In any organization, people want to know what to expect; they want predictability. That's why, in the middle of change, trust is eroded when the ground rules change. This is particularly true in large, previously successful corporations. Under the old psychological contract between the company and its employees, predictability consisted of an implicit agreement: in return for years of service, tenure, and loyalty, the employee could count on employment. The career path was also pre-dictable. For example, an engineer knew that his or her work life would progress with certain regularity, starting by working on a small project, then a larger project, leading to an assignment as an assistant man-ager, then on to being a manager. There was a map that people could follow to rise within the organization. With layoffs and downsizing, the old contract has been broken. Not only is the guaranteed career path gone, but so is the guarantee of employment.[36]

In this new context, people are still looking for pre-dictability. But predictability has to take a different form and apply to different situations. Predictability consists of intention and ground rules: what are our general goals and how will we make decisions? The more leaders clarify the company's intentions and ground rules, the more people will be able to predict and influence what happens to them — even in the middle of a constantly shifting situation.[37]

The predictability of the situation also means that managers and employees must determine if they can work in the new style. For example, some may come forward and say that they cannot operate in the new style while others are identified as non-performers in the new situation. These individuals must then be moved to another area so that they don't negatively impact the strategic change initiative.[38]

Capabilities — Roles and Responsibilities

To trust an organization, both managers and their reports must define the capability that each is provid-ing; and each side has to believe that the other is cap-able of playing the new role. In the old organization, capability was defined in terms of deliverables. Bosses would say, 'I don't care how you get it done; just pro-duce the results I want.' Now managers realize that if their processes are aligned and in control, the desired result will follow. To make this happen, managers and employees must identify needed capabilities and nego-tiate the roles and responsibilities of those involved in the process before each will trust the situation.[39]

Organization and Employees are Interdependent

Rather than just checking on milestones and timetables, managers should ask how the work would get done. They may occasionally attend cross-functional team meetings to listen to the participants talk about how the project is going, or they may talk with others across the different functions to get feedback on the project. And, by the same token, those understanding the project may want to negotiate with the manager or others to access different capabilities, perspectives, and experiences. When each side understands the needs, capabilities, and objectives of the other, trust can be built.[40]

One of the consequences of this new approach is to shift to interdependency. Employees are not longer dependent on the company in a hierarchical relationship. Now the company and its employees themselves are interdependent. In essence, the company is creating a new team and offering its people a fair shot at playing on the team. The only real security the company has to offer is a chance for people to work together to create the future and to achieve their goals.[41]

While organization's relationship with employees is much different than in the past, by focusing on predictability and required capabilities, both employees and management can develop relationships that can address short-term situations with a long-term perspective.

❑ GAUGING THE SUCCESS OF A STRATEGIC CHANGE INITIATIVE

As we learned in Chapter 3, the final measures of success for a strategic change initiative can be categorized as overall success, project management, operations performance, and enterprise performance. However, what should an organization do to measure success and the end of each phase of a strategic change initiative project so that necessary adjustments can be made? Organizations can determine if their strategic change projects will succeed by evaluating the four factors of the DICE framework; duration, integrity, commitment, and effort.[42] By using DICE, organization can gauge its ability to succeed at any point in time, not just at the end of the strategic change initiative project.

Using The DICE Framework

Organizations must pay as much attention to the hard side of change management as they do to the soft aspects. By rigorously focusing on four critical elements, organizations can stack the odds in favor or success.[43] With the DICE framework, organizations can determine if they are headed in a direction that will lead to success.

A study of 225 companies by Sirkin revealed a consistent correlation between the outcomes (success or failure) of change projects and four hard factors: project *duration*, particularly the time between project reviews; performance *integrity*, or the capabilities of project team; the *commitment* of both senior executives and the staff whom the change will affect the most; and the *effort* that employees must make to cope with the change. They are called DICE factors because organizations can load them in favor of project success. Figure 5.8 identifies **various measures** (time between formal reviews, for example) and **comments related to these measures** (more often the better; should be no less than two months apart, for example). Please note that these measures can be indicators of success or failure and should be used to make adjustments (more formal review meetings, for example) when necessary.

Evaluating the Project Team and Collaboration

The project team is a critical driving force behind managing organizational change. Figure 5.9 lists individual and team components that can be used to recognize whether there is support for or barriers to project success. As with the DICE framework, this listing (mission clarity, commitment, etc.) enables an organization to view indicators and gain insight into whether the team is working effectively and collaboratively in such a manner that the strategic change initiative will be successful. The focus here is to build resources and use them efficiently so that the team will be successful.

❑ SALES PROCESS REENGINEERING ANALYSIS

The following strategic initiative example provides insight into the evolution of an organizational change by identifying positive and negative factors and tactical strengths and weaknesses of a reengineering project:[47]

The Situation — Following a period of declining profits, McCorman Construction, a large construction company, underwent a major shake-up. A new president was

	Measure	*Comments*
D = DURATION	Do formal reviews occur regularly?	More often the better, should be less than two months apart.
I = INTEGRITY	Is the team leader capable? How strong are team members' skills and motivations? Do team member have sufficient time to spend on the change initiative?	Team leader must be respected by peers. Team members must have skills and motivation to complete the project! Team members must have time to complete the project in the stipulated timeframe.
C = COMMITMENT	Does top management regularly communicate the reason for change and its importance? Is the message consistent? Has top management devoted enough resources to the change?	Does top management, through actions and words clearly communicate about the change? If some top management appears to be neutral or are reluctant to support the change this means they are highly unlikely to contribute to success.
E = EFFORT	What is the increased effort that employees must make to implement the change effort?	If less than 10% extra work, it can be done successfully. If greater than 30% extra work, it cannot be done successfully.

Figure 5.8   DICE Framework For Evaluating Success[45]

brought in from the outside, and half of the executive team was replaced with outsiders in a matter of a few months. Approximately 20% of the workforce was laid off. The ratio of sales expense to sales revenue was significantly exceeding industry average. Attempts to reverse a trend toward increasing operating costs caused the president to focus on the sales process.

The Organizational Change — The consultant hired to advise the president verified the problem through an analysis of financial reports, and then moved to identify the factors contributing to the cost control problem. Through interviews with the executive team and a cross-section of midlevel managers, the consultant concluded that there were few measures for tracking and controlling sales expenses on a timely basis. The control issue was complicated by the absence of defined sales or marketing processes. These deficiencies meant that the sales and marketing approaches were different for each sales effort.

Further complicating the issue, the executive team was divided into two functions: the "veterans" were invested in the status quo, while the "new guys" wanted to reinvent everything. Recommendations included:

1. Design a marketing/sales process

2. Develop a measurement plan for tracking and controlling projects with emphasis on cost control and timeliness

3. Specify the roles and responsibilities of the personnel involved in the new process

The executives formed a steering team to oversee the design efforts. Four teams of managers and employees would design the new process and measurement plan. The teams were assigned different sections of the marketing-proposal-selling process.

Planning — The "process" team began by identifying performance inhibitors with the current mode of operation. Next, the team listed the features and capabilities that should be part of the new process, and defined essential outputs and inputs. The team then went through several iterations of flowcharting the new process, with each succeeding version becoming more detailed. The process design was checked to ensure that all performance inhibitors were addressed.

Using information from the process flowcharts, the first step was to develop quality, cost, and timeliness measures for the process outputs. The team worked backwards from the output measures to identify the

	Individual	*Team*
MISSION CLARITY	I am not certain what we are trying to accomplish as a team	Our team leader(s) have a clear vision of where we are going as a team We have a clear overall team purpose
COMMITMENT	Team members put their own personal interests before the interests of the team	Our team works hard We are committed to superior team performance We all accept personal responsibility for the success of the team
COMPETENCE	This team suffers from a lack of training or experience	Members of our team have been carefully selected to create the right mix of skills There are team members who have the skill or knowledge to back me up, if necessary Our team members are skilled and competentTeam members strive to develop their own skills that can benefit the team
MATERIAL RESOURCES	I would be more effective if I had certain tool, resource, or piece of equipment I work under unpleasant conditions, such as crowding, dirt, noise, or poor lighting	We have easy access to the equipment we need We have enough money and other material resources to do our work
TIME & STAFFING	I am burdened by other responsibilities that reduce my ability to contribute to this team I just do not have enough time to give to this team	We have enough time and people to perform well We are overwhelmed with things to do

Figure 5.9   *Components of A Project Team Evaluation*[46]

steps and subprocesses that were important for controlling quality, cost, and timeliness. Measures were defined for each point within the process that had an impact on the final process outputs. These intermediate measures formed the basis for managing the process performance on a real-time basis.

The steering team approved the new designs. A project manager was appointed to coordinate implementation plans. Five teams were appointed to do the detailed work of making the new designs operational. The vice presidents of Sales and Marketing accepted roles as "process owners" for the processes that corresponded to their areas of responsibility. The two process owners were to make sure that the implementation teams had the resources they needed.

Implementation — The implementation phase began with training the team leaders on how to develop detailed plans. The project manager and team leaders met regularly to ensure that each team's activities supported the efforts of other teams. The project manager assisted team leaders in thinking through problems, reported progress to the executive steering team, and advised the process owners about problems that needed to be addressed.

All told, it took seven months from the beginning of the implementation phase to put the new process and metrics into operation. The president held a "town hall meeting" to introduce employees to the new process and answer questions. This session was followed by departmental training sessions in which the details of the new process were discussed. In particular, the process design incorporated job-level details so that training could deal with job responsibilities and appropriate measures for evaluating job performance. Throughout the implementation period, employees could access a Web site that described the new process and the measurement plan, and offered a status report and schedule. A monthly newsletter distributed to employees featured a question-and-answer column in which the president and other executives addressed questions posted at the Web site.

Monitor and Control — Performance measurement and feedback were key aspects of daily operations. Employees and their supervisors met regularly to discuss performance against specific objectives. Sales and process activity data were compiled monthly for the president and executive team to review the process, discuss performance issues, and forecast future sales and marketing activities.

Several issues hampered progress throughout daily operations:

1. Team members were under severe time pressures due to the combination of project demands and the need to support ongoing sales proposals. Progress in implementing the new process and metrics was slower than expected.

2. Some team members were junior employees and lacked the information and skills required for the process design work.

3. Delays in "freezing up" a programmer to produce the software for compiling measurement reports cost the project at least two months of implementation time.

4. One process owner was ambivalent about the project and was not as active in addressing roadblocks as the other process owner.

Results — The new process and metrics enabled the organization to achieve a dramatic improvement in the ratio of sales expense to sales revenue. According to the president, the company realized "over 100 percent improvement in efficiency in just one year," as measured by "dollars spent versus dollars sold." Morale also improved, as measured by surveys before and after the project. Significant gains were observed for such items as "felt I understood the strategy of the organization," "felt I could have an impact on the strategy," and "satisfied with communication."

Assessment — Positive factors outnumbered negatives eight to five. The most critical negatives were the leadership issues, an unrealistic schedule, and the lack of recognition for the substantial effort of employees who served on the various teams.

Positive factors:

1. There was a strong project manager.

2. There was continued support from the sponsor throughout the project.

3. The change was part of the stated business strategy.

4. The change was a response to a crisis.

5. The effort was adequately staffed and funded.

6. There was a detailed plan.

7. There was a dedicated, capable project team.

8. Progress toward the goals was tracked and publicized.

Negative factors:

1. IT (systems) support was not available or failed to deliver on schedule.

2. The schedule was unrealistic or changed frequently.

3. The change effort increased workloads without rewarding the effort.

4. Key executives did not support the change.

5. Executives had other priorities.

Observations on some of the tactics used included strengths in putting an infrastructure in place, working from an implementation plan, and translating the change into job-level details. Weaknesses included not building alliances and not recognizing implementation efforts.

Tactical strengths:

1. Defined change as a compelling element of organizational strategy because the project supported company goals for controlling operational costs and profit margin.

2. Put an infrastructure in place including a steering team to oversee the project, teams to design the new process and measurement plan, a consultant who contributed the methodology and facilitated the work, and a project manager and team leaders who coordinated the implementation phase and ensured that each team supported the efforts of other teams.

3. Worked from an implementation plan that included the deployment of a marketing/sales process, deployment of a measurement plan for tracking and controlling projects, specification on the roles and responsibilities of the personnel involved in the new process, and specific measures to introduce the changes such as a town hall session, training, a Web site, and a newsletter.

4. Translating the change into job-level details so that training could deal with job responsibilities and appropriate measures for evaluating job performance. Specific performance objectives were developed for each job involved in the new process. The objective setting also set up a review schedule for employees and their supervisors to discuss performance against objectives.

5. Integrated the change into management systems where activity data were complied monthly for the president and executive team to review the functioning of process. These reviews were opportunities to discuss performance issues and forecasts of future sales and marketing activities.

6. Follow up was relentless. The project manager and team leaders met regularly to ensure that the activities of each team supported the efforts of the other teams. The manager assisted the team leaders in thinking through problems. The project manager also reported progress to the executive steering team and advised the process owners about problems that needed to be addressed. Unfortunately, one of the process owners was ambivalent about the project and was not as active in addressing roadblocks as the other process owner.

Tactical weaknesses:

1. Did not recognize the investment and commitment for the long haul. Commitment to the new process and measurement plan was initially strong, especially on the part of the president. However, the commitment apparently was not shared by all the executives, and corporate events diverted attention to other issues.

2. There was no particular effort to make the project small and manageable.

3. Key executives divided into factions, so it was difficult to build alliances in support of the change.

4. The project was punishing for junior staff assigned to the implementation teams with no recognition for this effort.

After a review of the information provided on the reengineering project example mentioned above, focus your attention on the positive and negative factors and the tactical strengths and weaknesses and how they relate to what has been covered in this and previous chapters. Managing the evolution of change of a strategic initiative means that planning, implementation, and appropriate monitoring and control are an absolute necessity. However, it should also be noted that you must have properly addressed the four dimensions of change during planning to increase your organization's probability of success.

❏ STRATEGIC CHANGE INITIATIVE SIMULATION

In order to enable students to develop a learning relationship with the concept of uncertainty and to

become excited about the topic of change, an experiential exercise is part of this chapter. The experiential activity involves the merger of two hospitals. Employee and management groups are given various tasks to perform throughout the exercise. The next three sections provide a brief description of the focus of this simulation.[48]

Develop Learning Relationship with Uncertainty

The exercise engages students in analyzing a change, making decisions based on the change, and communicating information regarding the change as either a member of the management team or the employee team. In addition, the activity explores issues such as organizational justice, survivor reactions, psychological contracts, communication, and leadership.[49]

Generation of Emotional Responses

This exercise generates an emotional response from students. The ambiguity surrounding the change frequency causes students to make up information while others exploit their lack of knowledge. It is important that leaders at all levels of the organization understand the human issues surrounding change.[50]

Strategies and Tactics During Organizational Transition

Even in the short timeframe of the simulation, participants discover that organizational transitions and uncertainty lead to the social construction of organizational realities or sense making,[51] where people develop theories and explanations to account for their organizational experiences. The exercise naturally introduces the skill of framing, or managing meaning for others, as supervisors assert that their interpretations should be taken as real over other possible interpretations."[52]

This simulation exposes you to a sense of what emotions may emerge during a period of uncertainty and change. In addition, the exercise also helps you recognize the importance of communications during a strategic change initiative, something that we will cover in the next chapter.

❏ READING AND CASE

The reading and case will enable you to apply the concepts and theory discussed in this chapter.

They address questions that a change leader should ask, how to avoid employee cynicism and burnout and resistance to change, and the importance of middle managers during a change initiative. You should also note that there is continuous learning and adapting to the environment as you manage the evolution of change.

Reading

5-1: *The 10 Questions Change Leaders Must Answer First.* Carol Goman, *Link & Learn*, January 2004.

Focus: Change cannot be mandated or forced. Managers need to ask difficult questions of them before they set out to "shake things up," and it insists that they must listen to the answers.

Questions

1. Why must change agents or leaders ask difficult questions of themselves before they set out to change things?
2. Why is it important for a change agent or leader to get a sense of how the change is being accepted? Explain.
3. Why should organizational feedback be gathered immediately after the delivery of every important message?
4. When you can't answer a question, what should be your response and why?
5. Why is it important for you to know what you already do to support the change and what do you have to do differently to align with the change? Explain.
6. Why is it important for employees to tie their job contributions to the fulfillment of a clear, compelling vision? Explain.
7. Please explain the following statement: "The genius of leadership is being able to preserve an organization's core values, and yet change and adapt as times require."

Linkage to Chapter

1. Recognizes the importance of the rational and emotional aspects of change.
2. Leaders must encourage employees to join a constant questioning of the prevailing business assumptions.

3. Not everyone will appreciate candid communication, but few will tolerate anything less.
4. A compelling vision of the future pulls people out of the seductive hold of the past and inspires them to set and reach ambitious corporate goals.

Case

5-1: *Three In The Middle.* Susan Rosegrant & Jick, Harvard Business School (9-491-022).

Focus: As a change agent, some days you're going to be a star, and some days you're going to be a turkey; but if you're true to what you think is right, you'll end up OK.

Questions

1. What is it like to be a middle manager in the middle of a change effort?
2. How should a middle manager use those above and below him/her to assist with the change process? Explain.
3. How should a change agent or leader prioritize or differentiate between their daily responsibilities and the strategic change initiative they are responsible for? Explain.
4. Is managing a change initiative like running a marathon or sprint? Explain.

Linkage to Chapter

1. Middle managers require direction and guidance from their supervisors.
2. Change agents or leaders need input and feedback from their employees to help move the change initiative forward.
3. Change agents or leaders need to recognize the cyclic nature, ups and downs, of a change initiative to better understand what they are dealing with.

❑ ENDNOTES

1. Extracted from Anderson, L., & Anderson, D. (2001). The Change Leader's Roadmap. San Francisco, CA: Jossey-Bass/Pfeiffer, pp. 166–67.
2. Siegal, W., Church, A. H., & et al. (1996). Understanding the management of change. Journal of Organizational Change, Vol. 9, No. 6, pp. 56–57.

3. Gilley, J. W., et al. (2001). The Manager as Change Agent. Cambridge, MA: Perseus Publishing.
4. Ibid, p. 47.
5. Moran, J. W., & Brightman, B. K. (2000). Leading organizational change. Journal of Workplace Learning: Employee Counseling Today, Vol. 12, No. 2, pp. 68–69.
6. Ibid, p. 69.
7. Ibid.
8. Ibid.
9. Ibid.
10. Ibid.
11. Extracted from Rousseau, D. M. (1996, February). Changing the deal while keeping the people. Academy of Management Executive.
12. Ibid, p. 241.
13. Ibid.
14. Ibid, pp. 245–247.
15. Ibid, p. 248.
16. Ibid, p. 249.
17. Ibid, p. 250.
18. Ibid, p. 251.
19. Seijts, G. H., Crim, D. (2006, March–April). What engages employees the most or, the ten C's of employee engagement. Ivey Business Journal, p. 302.
20. Ibid, pp. 303–305.
21. Aselstine, K., Alletson, K. (2006, March–April). A new deal for the 21st century workplace. Ivey Business Journal, p. 1.
22. Aselstine, K., Alletson, K. (2006, March–April). A new deal for the 21st century workplace. Ivey Business Journal, p. 2.
23. Gilley (2001). op. cit., p. 71.
24. Extracted from Iskat, G. J., & Liebowitz, J. (2003). What to do when employees resist change. SuperVision, Vol. 64, No. 8, pp. 12–14.
25. Jick, T. D. (1990). The recipients of change. Harvard Business School case 9-491-039, p. 4.
26. Huy, Q. N. (2001). In praise of middle managers. Harvard Business Review–OnPoint, p. 1.
27. Ibid.
28. Ibid.
29. Schaffer, R. H., & Thomson, H. A. (1992, January–February). Successful change programs begin with results. Harvard Business Review, p. 80.
30. Schaffer, R. H., & Thomson, H. A. (1992, January–February). Successful change programs begin with results. Harvard Business Review, p. 83.
31. Ibid.
32. Ibid.
33. Extracted from Anderson, L., & Anderson, D. (2001). The Change Leader's Roadmap. San Francisco, CA: Jossey-Bass/Pfeiffer, p. 249.
34. Duck, J. D. (2000). Managing change: The art of balancing. Harvard Business Review – OnPoint, p. 114.
35. Ibid.
36. Ibid, p. 115.
37. Ibid, p. 115.
38. Ibid, p. 115.
39. Ibid, p. 115.
40. Ibid, p. 115.
41. Ibid, p. 115.
42. Sirkin, H. L., Keenan, P., & Jackson, A. (2005, October). The hard side of change management. Harvard Business Review, p. 110.
43. Ibid, p. 109.
44. Ibid, p. 110.
45. Ibid, p. 114.
46. Campbell, D. P., (1993, May–June). A new integrated battery of psychological surveys. Journal of Counseling & Development, Vol. 71, p. 548.
47. Extracted from Mourier, P., & Smith, M. (2001). Conquering Organizational Change. Atlanta, GA: CEP Press, pp. 114–120.
48. McDonald, K. S., & Mansour-Cole, D. (2000, February). Change requires intensive care: An experiential exercise for learners in university and corporate settings. Journal of Management Education, Vol. 24, No. 1, pp. 127–148.
49. Ibid, p. 130.
50. Ibid, p. 131.
51. Weick, K. (1995). Sensemaking in Organizations. Thousand Oaks, CA: Sage.
52. Fairhurst, G. T., & Sarr, R. A. (1996). The Art of Framing: Managing the Language of Leadership. San Francisco: Jossey-Bass, p. 131.

Reading 5-1

"The 10 Questions Change Leaders Must Answer First"

CAROL KINSEY GOMAN

TWO OR THREE YEARS AGO I read a news story about an executive who had been hired to turn around the fortunes of a business that was on the rocks. The product was bad. Morale was awful. Management appeared to be confused about what to do. And customers were staying away in droves.

Clearly, this fellow had been hired to make changes, and here's what he said: "We gotta shake this place up and keep shaking until we get it right."

He was a change manager, to be sure. He had been brought in because things were not working well and somebody had to make miracles happen quickly. And our guy did that in spades, firing middle managers with abandon, reversing policies that had served the organization well, and establishing immediately that he was King.

You know what? It worked — for a while. The operation seemed to take on a new focus, and customers returned. The product got better. Management relaxed and the teamwork that everyone had hoped for seemed to emerge once again. That's the good news.

But I used that word "teamwork" advisedly because this organization indeed was a team, a minor-league baseball club in a large Southern city. Sports franchises make great cases for the study of change management because the results show up so quickly.

In this case, the "shaking up" of the organization worked for slightly less than one season and the new manager was summarily relieved even as his bravado still seemed to echo off the locker room walls. He was a bold manager of change, to be sure, but he was not a skilled one.

The lesson of our friend's forceful and narrow-minded attack on the company he set out to correct is critical for corporate managers. It says that change cannot be mandated or forced. It says that change has many constituents and that these constituents count.

It says that change managers need to ask difficult questions of themselves before they set out to "shake things up." And it insists that they must listen to the answers. Here are some of the questions that I believe sensitive change managers must consider before they set out to make things better.

This article was written by Carol Kinsey Goman, Kinsey Consulting Services. (Tel: 510-526-1727; CGoman@CKG.com; www.CKG.com) and published in Link&Learn (January 2004), a free e-newsletter published by Linkage, Inc. (FlinkandLearn@Linkage-Inc.com: www.LinkageInc.com).

❏ 1 — WHAT IS THE EMPLOYEES' PERSPECTIVE?

To mobilize a work force to transform itself, leaders must:

> know what people in the organization are thinking;
> encourage them to articulate their points of view and their concerns; and
> be ready to respond to them sincerely.

The first question that leaders should ask is: "What is the employees' perspective?" And don't rely on second-hand information or make assumptions about what you *think* employees think. *Ask* them — and keep asking them until they tell you. Only then can you begin to design a strategy that builds on synergies and fills in perception gaps.

❏ 2 — DID YOU "SET THE STAGE" FOR CHANGE?

One of the most vital roles of leadership is to anticipate the corporation's future and its place in the global arena, and then to formulate strategies for surmounting challenges that have not yet manifested. To proactively respond to these challenges, businesses must continually reinvent themselves. Leaders must encourage employees to join a constant questioning of the prevailing business assumptions — and to be ready to act upon new opportunities early in the game to maintain a competitive advantage.

❏ 3 — ARE YOU TRACKING EMPLOYEE PERCEPTIONS THROUGHOUT THE CHANGE?

As important as it is to find out what employees are thinking before the change, it is just as crucial to have a system for monitoring employee perception throughout the change process. George Bernard Shaw once said that the problem with communication is "the illusion that it has been accomplished." When it comes to communicating change, leadership must be especially careful not to suffer that illusion.

Strategies that include employee interaction and feedback systems help organizations track the level of work force comprehension. You will find the greatest advantages come when organizational feedback is gathered immediately after the delivery of every important message. One of my clients uses this short questionnaire to query her audiences before they leave the meeting room:

What in your view are the most important points we just covered?

What didn't you understand?

With what do you disagree?

With what do you agree?

What else do you need to know?

❏ 4 — ARE YOU GIVING HONEST ANSWERS TO TOUGH QUESTIONS?

In the light of economic realities that offer little in the way of job security, employees must be able to rely on their employer to give them honest information that will allow them to make informed choices about their own jobs, careers and futures. And when you can't answer every question, it is best to tell people that you understand their concern but don't know the answer. Or that you don't have the information yet, but will get back to them as soon as decisions are made. It is even better to tell people that you have the information but can't release it than to withhold or twist the truth. Not everyone will appreciate candid communication, but few will tolerate anything less.

❏ 5 — CAN YOU ANSWER THE MOST IMPORTANT QUESTION: WHAT'S IN IT FOR THEM?

I was in Sweden working with a county government agency that was completely revamping its healthcare system. The leader of this enormous change was proud of the way he had communicated to the county's residents. They had been given a thorough briefing — the reasons behind the change, the timing of the change, and exactly how it was to be carried out. Then he turned to me with a frown, "But you know, there is still one question that I get asked all the time." I interrupted. "Let me guess," I said. "People want to know if the wait for a doctor's appointment will be any shorter than it currently is. Am I right?" The man looked startled. "How did you know that?" he asked. I told him that I knew to expect that question because it is the one I hear most often about change — What's in it for me?

❏ 6 — IS YOUR COMMUNICATION "BEHAVIOR-BASED?"

Organizations send two concurrent sets of messages about change. One set of messages goes through formal channels of communications — speeches, newsletters, corporate videos, values statements and so forth. The other set of messages is "delivered" informally through a combination of "off the record" remarks and daily activities. When I coach senior management teams, I begin with two questions:

1. What do you currently do that already supports the change?
2. What do you have to do differently to align with the change?

For today's skeptical employee audience, rhetoric without action quickly disintegrates into empty slogans and company propaganda. In the words of Sue Swenson, president of Leap Wireless, "What you do in the hallway is more powerful than anything you say in the meeting room."

❏ 7 — CAN YOU PAINT THE BIG, LITTLE PICTURE?

Vision is the big picture (we'll look at this next), and it is crucial to the success of the enterprise. But along with the big picture, people also need the little picture:

Big Picture — Presenting the concept of transformation.

Little Picture — How are we going to do that?

Big Picture — Setting long-term corporate goals.

Little Picture — Where do we begin?

Big Picture — Developing the overall objectives of the transformation.

Little Picture — What are the priorities?

Big Picture — Creating the mission of the organization.

Little Picture — Where does my contribution fit in?

Big Picture — Communicating organizational values.

Little Picture — What does this mean in my daily life?

❏ 8 — IS IT YOUR VISION OR OUR VISION?

Leaders understand the power of vision to imbue people with a sense of purpose, direction and energy. A compelling vision of the future pulls people out of the seductive hold of the past and inspires them to set and reach ambitious corporate goals. Of even greater importance is the sense of meaning that people derive from their jobs when they can tie their contributions to the fulfillment of a clear, compelling vision. Leaders must therefore be able to paint the big picture. But if the vision belongs only to top management, it will never be an effective force for transformation. The power of a vision comes truly into play only when the employees themselves have had some part in its creation. So the crucial question becomes, "Whose vision is it?" Leaders must create a master narrative that coherently articulates the company's identity and ideals, and is embraced by every member of the company. If you want employees to feel the same kind of connection to their work that the executives felt at the retreat, then you have to get employees involved too.

❏ 9 — ARE YOU EMOTIONALLY LITERATE?

To be a consummate manager of change, it is not enough to engage people's logic, you also have to appeal to their emotions. As leaders arrive at the insight that people skills (the "soft stuff of business) hold the key to organizational change, human emotions take on new significance. Large-scale organizational change almost invariably triggers the same sequence of reactions: denial, negativity, a choice point, tentative acceptance, commitment. Leadership can either facilitate this emotional process — or ignore it at the peril of the transformation effort.

❏ 10 — DO YOU KNOW WHAT *SHOULDN'T* CHANGE?

The greatest challenge for leaders is to know the difference between what has to be preserved and what needs to be changed. The "genius" of leadership is being able to preserve an organization's core values, and yet change and adapt as times require.

And the product of that kind of leadership is a firm that goes on for a very long time.

Carol Kinsey Gorman, Ph.D. is an international speaker and consultant, and author of *Ghost Story: A Modern Business Fable; This Isn't the Company I Joined* (new edition due January 2004); *Creativity in Business; The Human Side of High-Tech; Change-Busting: 50 Ways to Sabotage Organizational Change; Managing for Commitment; Adapting to Change: Making it Work for You; The Loyalty Factor;* and *Managing in a Global Organization.* Contact — tel: 510-526-1727; e-mail: CGoman@ CKG.com; web: www.CKG.com

Case 5-1

Three in the Middle: The Experience of Making Change at Micro Switch

As a change agent, some days you're going to be a star, and some days you're going to be a turkey, but if you 'm true to what you think is right, you'll end up OK. And, hell, if they fire you for doing the right thing, then you didn't want to work for that company anyway.

> — Rick Rowe
> Director, Materiel

People are struggling so much because they're trying to understand what this desired state is. I have been told I'm supposed to do this, this, this, and this — well, which one do I tackle first, and with what kind of focus, and what's the time frame?

> — Deb Massof
> Director, Aerospace, Ordnance, and Marine Marketing

Now is the time for determination and just grunting it out. And that's where we're going to start seeing some folks say, "Ah, baloney, I'm not cut out for this amount of frustration. I'm tired of trying to balance all this." It's not for the fainthearted right now.

> — Ellis Stewart
> Director, Fabricating Operations

❏ PROLOGUE

It was mid-summer 1990, and Micro Switch was changing. In fact, the manufacturer of switches and sensors, a division of Honeywell, Inc., was embroiled in change. For the last three years, the Freeport-based company, in the rural northwest corner of Illinois, had been striving to transform itself from a mature, provincial business into a more dyna-mic, customer-driven, global operation capable of surviving into the 21st century. Indeed, most of the division's managers believed that without profound changes, Micro Switch's days would be numbered.

Recently, the responsibility for shepherding this change effort had begun to fall more and more on the shoulders of the company's directors — a group of 19 middle managers who reported directly to the vice presidents under the division's general manager (see Figure 5.10). In order to form a more cohesive and skilled "change agent team," both the vice presidents and the directors had begun attending a series of formal off-site team-building and training sessions beginning in November 1989. Rick Rowe, Deb Massof, and Ellis Stewart all had been active participants in these "Eagle Ridge" sessions, named for the meeting site.

After the second of the Eagle Ridge sessions in March 1990, Rowe, Massof, and Stewart each had tried to describe in their own words how it felt to be a change agent in the middle of the process — detailing both the pleasures and pains of making change. Four months later, each of the three directors had sat down and revisited many of the same subjects again. The second time, however, their comments were colored by changing circumstances. It was becoming clearer by the day that most of the "easy" changes had already been accomplished, they claimed. Moreover, a stubborn business slump facing both Honeywell and Micro Switch, as well as many other U.S. manufacturers, threatened to sap both the energy and the resources necessary to keep the change effort moving.

Rowe, Massof, and Stewart all had declared their dedication to change, no matter how rocky that road might prove to be. Yet after they each finished

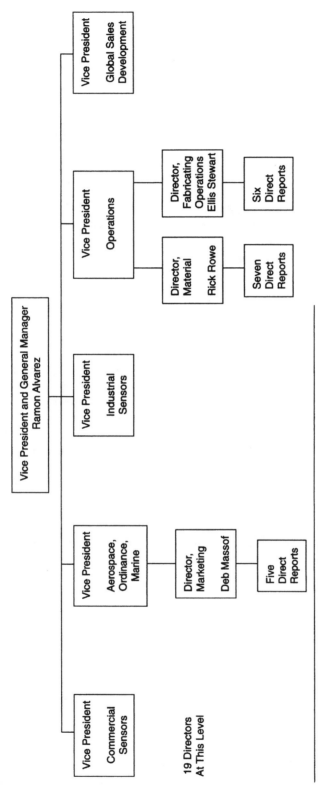

Figure 5.10 Micro Switch Organizational Chart

193

talking, a final unspoken question seemed to be on all of their minds: Had something gone wrong, or was this the way a successful change process was supposed to feel?

❏ CHANGE AT MICRO SWITCH: 1987–1990

Founded in 1937 and acquired by Honeywell in 1950, Micro Switch in its early years had established a solid reputation as an industry leader in switches, sensors and manual controls, making thousands of products ranging from simple lawn-mower switches to sophisticated controls for NASA's first manned orbit around the earth in 1962. The company had also established itself as a reliable source of profits for Honeywell. But as aggressive and international competitors attacked Micro Switch's traditional markets with less expensive products in the late 1970s and early 1980s, and as switching technology began shifting from electro-mechanical to electronic and solid-state, the division's performance began to suffer. Honeywell, the Minneapolis-based company offering products and services in information processing, automation, and controls, did not release figures for its divisions. But Micro Switch's operating profits began a downward tumble in 1985 which put its corporate overseers on red alert (see Figure 5.11a).

To make certain Micro Switch regained its competitive spirit, Honeywell recruited Ramon Alvarez, a 49-year-old company veteran who had already helped turn around two other divisions. Arriving in September 1987, with the corporate charge to do what was necessary to revitalize Micro Switch, Alvarez set in motion a wide-ranging mix of change actions (see Figure 5.11b). First, Alvarez and his staff crafted a three-year plan for the company, put together a mission statement, and created a new vision for Micro Switch — "Growth through quality solutions to customer needs." Next, Alvarez initiated a rigorous annual strategic planning process, to make the company more competitive, responsive, and financially savvy. And, finally, Alvarez instituted a broad communication, recognition, and quality program known as APEX — an acronym for Achieve Performance Excellence.

In its first year, APEX was designed to convince Micro Switch's more than 4,000-member work force that change was necessary, and to give each employee specific ways to help strive for

excellence. The program included an employee suggestion system and awards for meeting performance objectives.

By its third year, APEX had become more sophisticated. At the heart of the 1990 program was a network of committees and councils, dubbed Building Block Councils, to encourage division-wide involvement in six key strategic areas: a customer satisfaction council, to set standards for products and customer relationships, and create practices to meet those standards; a quality council, to establish and help achieve overall quality standards for satisfying customers; a goals council, to find appropriate ways to measure progress in reaching division goals; an awareness council, to promote awareness of quality issues throughout the division; a training council, to ensure employees get the training they need to improve quality and customer satisfaction; and a recognition council, to develop and oversee an effective recognition policy. Rowe, Massof, and Stewart each chaired one of the councils.

In addition, Alvarez had put a number of key "platforms" — or change-building steps — in place, ranging from such efficiency-boosting improvements as installing a network of personal computers, to such process-oriented programs as Barrier Removals, in which each group within the division identified specific barriers to quality which they could attack and remove (see Figure 5.11c). As these platforms began to yield improvements, they reinforced the value of the more difficult organizational and attitudinal changes which still lay ahead.

With these efforts in place, Alvarez had activated a final critical component in his plan to revitalize Micro Switch — the systematic training of a change agent team. Beginning with the first Eagle Ridge session in November 1989 (see Figure 5.11d), Alvarez had begun to focus more and more on Rowe, Massof, Stewart, and the rest of the division's directors. "We have spent the past two years putting this team into position, conditioning it, and preparing it for the 1990s," Alvarez had declared in his opening speech at the first Eagle Ridge session. "While we all have a fear of the unknown, I think we have with us tonight a team that has made enormous changes over the past two years, and welcomes the opportunity to anticipate the future and manage it." With the conclusion of the second Eagle Ridge, the time had come for the team of young change agents to assume a larger role.

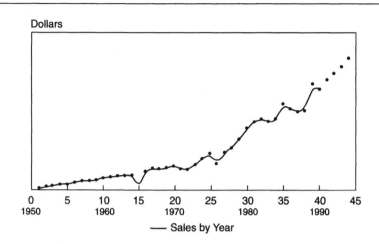

Honeywell MICRO SWITCH Division
Sales

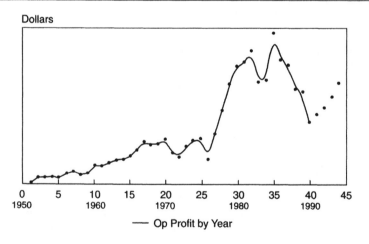

Honeywell MICRO SWITCH Division
Operating Profit

Figure 5.11(a)   Honeywell Micro Switch Division—Sales

9/87:	Alvarez joins Micro Switch.
10/87:	Immediate target set improved on-time product delivery. Weekly meetings instituted for one year attended by production, controls, and materials managers; within three months, on-time delivery boosted from 75% to above 90%.
Fall–Winter 1987:	Management team restructured; mission statement and vision crafted; vice presidents and directors required to attend Honeywell management training courses.
1/88:	APEX Kick-off: Overall goals: 10% revenue growth; 10% improvement in quality, productivity, and delivery, communicate need to revitalize; teach importance of recognition; earn revitalization funds. Program features: employee suggestion boxes; award stamps to win prizes; monthly APEX management meetings for managers and supervisors.
Spring 1988:	First strategic planning process: Individual business units wrote mission statements; did detailed market analysis, including assessment of customers, markets, competitors, and strategic issues; proposed key strategies and actions; and presented results.
Mid-1988:	Midyear APEX reassessment
1/89:	APEX 1989:1988 overview: exceeded 10% delivery improvement; achieved 10% revenue growth; fell short on productivity and quality goals; overall improvement in communication, recognition, and customer responsiveness. Overall goals: 25% organizational productivity improvement by January 1991; 10% revenue growth; time-to-market improvement; focus on becoming world-class company, making incremental improvements. Programs: employee suggestions; award stamps; monthly meetings; quarterly video updates by Alvarez summarizing APEX achievements and challenges.
Spring 1989:	Second annual strategic planning process.
Mid-1989:	Economic downturn felt as several major U.S. markets soften.
11/89:	First Eagle Ridge off-site management training session (see Figure 5.11d).
12/89:	Barrier Removals (under the APEX program): Focus on identifying and removing obstacles blocking employees from achieving performance excellence.
1/90:	APEX 1990:1989 overview: coped with difficult economy, disappointing financial performance; operating profits reached only 69% of 1989 level; nevertheless, strong improvements in responsiveness, global orientation, and strategic focus. Overall goals: qualifying for Malcolm Baldrige National Quality Award by 1992; using Barrier Removals program and Building Block Councils to help achieve world-class status; moving from three-year APEX program to a way of life. Programs: employee suggestions; monthly APEX meetings; video updates; Building Block Council meetings; Barrier Removals departmental meetings.
3/90:	Second Eagle Ridge off-site management training session (see Figure 5.11d).
Spring 1990:	Third annual strategic planning process.
Mid-1990:	Overall goals modified due to investment limitations: have Total Quality Management System that meets Malcolm Baldrige criteria by mid-1992; reach sustained performance of Total Quality Management System by mid-1995; achieve highest level of perceived quality in all markets by mid-1995.

Figure 5.11b   Summary of Change Efforts: 1987–1990

Implementing "platforms" while carefully creating "healthy dissatisfaction with the current state."

APEX	Metal Forming Reconfiguration
Barrier Removals	Laser & CNC Machining Centers
Process Mapping	"V" Switch Focused Factory
Time-to-Market	Mars Hill Focused Factory
DOE	CAD/CAM/DNC—Plant 1
Concurrent Engineering	Supervisory Performance Standards
Procurement Quality Assurance	Mfg. Engr. Performance Standards
CAD/CAM/CIE	SPC/PPM
CAD Mold Design System	Process Simulation
FMEA	SCM/CFM/JIT
Finite Element Analysis	CEDAC
Personal Computers	Operator Training & Certification
CAT/CAI	APEX College
Engineering data/change Mgmt. System	Preventive Maintenance System
Health, Safety and Environment	Apprenticeship Program

Figure 5.11c *Micro Switch Approach*

❏ RICK ROWE

It was late March 1990. Rick Rowe had returned to the office from the second Eagle Ridge session a few days earlier, and just like after the first session, Rowe was charged up and ready to go. He had already run a one-day "mini Eagle Ridge" for about 30 of his extended staff. Now the 40-year-old Rowe was still pondering many of the issues raised at Eagle Ridge — such as empowering the work force and changing established behaviors — and wondering how to bring them alive for the lower ranks of the organization. "We've gotten where we got to on the backs of the people," he declared, "and now what we have to do is transform them. How do we take the people of Micro Switch to a different place."

A few months before, Alvarez had named Rowe to chair the Building Block Council on Recognition. Rowe's initial charter was to ferret out the best ways to recognize, motivate, and reward employees in an effort to reinforce the beliefs and behaviors — emphasizing quality and customer satisfaction — that Micro Switch now sought from its work force. In addition, the council was to see that these forms of recognition — whether an award or a simple "thank you" — became consistently practiced throughout the division.

Rowe seemed a natural choice for the job. Except for a two-year hiatus, he had been at Micro Switch since 1977, first as an engineer, now as the director of materiel, responsible for procurement under the vice president of operations. As a self-proclaimed "local boy" with "real, simple values," Rowe seemed to have a strong affinity for Micro Switch's employees, as well as a desire for them to share his own enthusiasm. In particular, he wanted to prove to the work force that the division — under Alvarez — was now responsive to input from all levels of the company. "We're trying to institutionalize that we care, we show it, we go out and talk to people," he explained. "I'm really convinced that all of our employees should feel like I do: greatly empowered, very focused, basically happy, challenged, recognized in some form, and enjoying the work they have." He added: "People go out and self-actualize on bowling. Why can't we self actualize more at work?"

According to Rowe, when Honeywell first announced that Alvarez would be taking over, many at Micro Switch — from factory workers to senior managers — were uneasy. "Everyone perceived that the guy who rose to the top was the guy who carried the biggest two-by-four, and the one who could really belt people around psychologically," Rowe recalled.

VISIONING FOR THE '90s
MANAGEMENT OFF-SITE MEETING (NOVEMBER 1-3, 1989)

OBJECTIVES

1. Understand the Micro Switch vision.
   - "Growth through quality solutions to customer needs"
   - Where we need to be (i.e., 1992)
   - Define quality

2. Gain an understanding of where we currently are.
   - Malcom Baldrige National Quality Award report card
   - Celebrate successes
   - Identify improvement opportunities

3. Direct and enhance the existing strategic planning process so as to ensure the development and implementation of a quality roadmap for reaching the vision.
   - Integration of quality into ongoing strategic management and planning process
   - Define "World Class" more clearly using Malcolm Baldrige categories as a guide; identify where we need to be in general terms
   - Identify requirements for the 1990 strategic planning process
   - Generate ownership for Malcolm Baldrige categories, world class definitions
   - Leave with a roll-down plan for getting broader understanding and buy in at the next level down

4. Begin to mold directors and vice presidents into a team of change agents who understand and drive change through ownership and commitment to the vision and strategic plans.

LEADING THE '90s: HOW DO WE DO IT?
MANAGEMENT OFF-SITE MEETING (MARCH 14–16, 1990)

OBJECTIVES

1. Develop a clear understanding of many of the changes needed within Micro Switch (what we are moving from and what we are moving to).

2. Gain insight into how we make the change happen. Develop and enhance change management skills. Leave with answers arround the issues — "how do we do it, how do we move the organization, how do we create paradigm shifts?"

3. Learn how to identify, map, and manage processed. Develop an understanding of Why it's important to manage processed instead of tasks (identify the "what's in it for me")

4. Reinforce the linkage between strategic planning, Malcolm Baldrige, APEX, Barrier Removals, and business issues (e.g., time-to-market, union avoidance, resource allocation).

Figure 5.11(d)   *The Eagle Ridge Session Agendas*

Instead, Rowe said, Alvarez moved cautiously, especially at first, in order to gain workers' trust and cooperation. "He took the opposite tack, which is to say we're good, we need to build on that, we need to create something, we need to regenerate, we need to rejuvenate the business," he recalled. "We need to put capital back into the facilities. The cow's been milked until she's about dead."

Many of these ideas weren't new to Rowe. He had always been intrigued by questions of organizational change, and had tried to run his own piece of the organization in a more "enlightened" fashion than many other managers at Micro Switch, listening to worker concerns and delegating responsibility whenever possible. But instead of garnering praise for his efforts, Rowe had gained the reputation of being a renegade, not a team player.

"Challenging anything we did was bad," he explained. "I was the 'bad cowboy.'"

Rowe claimed that his behavior didn't shift substantially after Alvarez' arrival. But now, the same actions that had been frowned on before were being held up as an example of the right way to operate. "Now I am a 'good cowboy' because I'm a change agent," he marveled. "I now have a desirable title as opposed to being someone who would rock the boat. Ray's tried to reach out and find the change makers who were still alive and well."

As newly appointed head of the recognition council, Rowe had been interviewing 300 randomly selected Micro Switch employees to elicit their ideas about rewards and recognition. The consensus on how to make people feel more appreciated turned out to be more simple than he expected: most important was to just say thank you. But Rowe uncovered other issues in the course of talking with co-workers which he found more troubling and less easily solved. Among these was the issue of empowerment itself. "I think people absolutely have bought hook, line, and sinker that we have to change to survive," he mused. "Where we're getting hung up in the process right now is our people then have said, 'OK, we buy it Boy, we're in trouble. You guys in management, you tell us what to do now.' And our response back has been, Wait a minute, we want to empower you. And we want you to tell us what we should do." He added: "You essentially are empowered to do anything you want to do, but what hangs people up is you have to have the courage to use this power."

Not only were employees confused about how to suddenly take power into their own hands, Rowe said, the multiple changes taking place at Micro Switch had left many people at all levels of the company grasping for something to hang onto — something familiar or some point of safety. "When you're confronted with change and the unknown, for most people, if s very scary and they need an anchor," Rowe explained. "So I'm asking my people, What's the anchor for our factory? What's the anchor for our salaried people?' We would like to believe that management is the anchor for our employees."

Rowe was also concerned about how to keep Alvarez, the rest of the change agents, and himself from getting worn down by the process. Even the apparently indefatigable Alvarez, he said, occasionally claimed he was tired. And with a possible five to eight additional years necessary to institute a major change at Micro Switch, there could be plenty of opportunity to become fatigued and frustrated. "There's a danger for change agents that you get so far ahead in understanding where the company needs to go, and then you look back and say, 'Where the hell is everybody?" Rowe noted. "That's scary. On a personal basis you're at risk because you're out there sticking your neck way out and you look back and no one's there. You get tired when you're too far out in front"

In this sense, change agents needed anchors just as much as anyone else involved in the process, Rowe insisted. But figuring out who or what should be the anchor for the change leaders was not so obvious, especially for Alvarez. "I was talking with one of my superintendents about anchors, and he said, What's your anchor?'" Rowe recalled. "I said that I didn't know. For some people it probably is their peers or their superiors. And I suppose in one way, Ray may be more of an anchor than I think. I like to think I'm very independent I'm still doing the same thing I've always done, only this time someone says, 'Gee, if s OK."

Although Rowe might have been operating the same way he always did, the positive reinforcement he was feeling, and the excitement of working with others in the organization toward a common goal was clearly a new and motivating sensation. "I wasn't ostracized before, but I felt I wasn't progressing at the rate I should," he remarked. The real difference is it wasn't as much fun. This is like a playground! Right now, for someone like me, this environment we've created is like I've died and gone to heaven. I don't ever want this to end."

Four months later, it had become more apparent than ever that the business slump was not going away, and that Micro Switch's management team had to face the feet that Honeywell probably wouldn't provide funding for any of the more ambitious revitalization programs waiting in the wings. In fact, even some of the basic programs already in place were undergoing careful scrutiny. "I can see how far we've come in three years," Rowe insisted. "But the downside is that very few companies which have attempted to change succeed in the long run, principally because the owners can't endure the 7 to 10-year total transition period. In a lot of companies, the business doesn't quite measure up to standards, and someone who is holding the checkbook gets impatient."

The slump's timing was particularly hard for Micro Switch, Rowe contended, coinciding as it did with a natural slowdown in the change process itself. The easy changes had already been made. Now the company had to tackle deeply ingrained behaviors and processes which were holding the division back from reaching its goals. And while the first Eagle Ridge session had left most of the participants almost euphoric, the second session had felt more like plain work, and that sense had lingered. "We're at this lull where a lot of the excitement has worn off, and now we're into hard work," Rowe acknowledged. "Change takes so goddamn long. You get real frustrated by it and run the risk of losing people's attention."

Looking back over the change process of the past almost three years, Rowe's frustration seemed to grow. Eagle Ridge had been the first real opportunity for the directors to share training in change management, and it had been "an excellent solidifier," he said. "One of the big things Eagle Ridge did for us as a group was to create some degree of camaraderie, and also more of an element of trust," he reflected. "The degree of cooperation between functions here at the director level is the best that I've seen in years."

But in retrospect, Rowe also felt that he could have benefitted from such training much earlier. "When I came into this job, I was given the task of transforming my part of the organization from its present state as an archetypical procurement organization into some undefined world-class operation," he explained, "but I wasn't given any real training. At Eagle Ridge, for the first time I felt like there was some laid-out method to the madness." He added: "As one of the so-called disciples, I've felt a little bit alone. I haven't felt as warm and comfortable and that I was doing the right thing as I should."

Rowe confronted Alvarez with these thoughts during a break at the second Eagle Ridge, but the general manager had defended his choice to hold off on the training. "Ray said, 'Some of you guys may be ready to go, but the rest of the organization is not. I can't let you get ahead of everybody else,'" Rowe recounted. "So we could feel a little bit of the hand of control saying some of us may need to slow down." Despite Alvarez' cautioning, however, Rowe remained convinced that he and the other directors would have profited from earlier guidance and instruction. "I think there were a fair number of people who were confused," he explained. "Some people probably thought this is some kind of dictatorial commandment, and

Ray's doing all this stuff, and they don't necessarily buy in. I think we could have got the buy-in a little bit sooner,"

One of the key messages that stuck with Rowe after Eagle Ridge was that behaviors reflect beliefs: If you want to change someone's behavior, you must first change their underlying beliefs. But in addition to changing people's beliefs and rewarding the behaviors it wanted, something Micro Switch had done fairly successfully, Rowe maintained that it was also time for the division to get tougher about discouraging the behaviors it didn't want "We haven't stressed enough of the attitude we're looking for in people," Rowe declared. "For a long time, we've said that as long as people do an adequate job, that's OK. But if you think about anything else we do in life, we don't let people who have bad attitudes play on our teams, we get rid of them — we tell them that they can't play, or we trade them, or we let them go. Who says we have to employ people who don't want to be a part of our team?"

Reassigning or firing a large number of workers wouldn't be an easy move to make, Rowe admitted, particularly in Freeport, where Micro Switch was the main game in town. "It's real hard to look at people and to say, 'We didn't make you a manager for life,'" he confessed. But according to Rowe, the time might have come for Micro Switch to make these hard choices in the interest of survival. "We're running out of time," he asserted. "My big concern is that in every case I've seen, it takes 7 to 10 years to make the change. I don't know that we've got 7 to 10 years."

❑ DEB MASSOF

A few days had passed since the second Eagle Ridge session and, like Rowe, Deb Massof was still struggling to digest all of the change-related topics presented there. "What's intriguing about Micro Switch right now is that there are so many changes going on at one time," she declared. "I think people do want to change. They do want to do good. But they're real frustrated at not knowing what to change."

When Deb Massof joined Alvarez' management team early in 1988, she was immediately pegged as an outsider. For starters, at 32 years old, she was considerably younger than most of the managers. After recommending that Micro Switch focus more on its aerospace, ordnance, and marine (AOM)

business by making it a separate unit, Massof was named the new unit's director of marketing, heading a staff whose members were typically between 40 and 60 years old, with 20 to 40 years of seniority. She was also a senior manager in a company unaccustomed to seeing women in professional positions. This, after all, was a division where — until Alvarez intervened — the only woman staff member had never been invited to a general manager's meeting, and did not receive the same parking privileges the men enjoyed.

Finally, Massof — who had already amassed 12 years' experience at Honeywell — carried the stigma of coming from "Corporate." Since Honeywell bought Micro Switch in 1950, the relationship between the two organizations had evolved into an uneasy alliance. By 1987, senior management at Honeywell had become concerned by Micro Switch's apparent drive to stay independent Micro Switch managers, for their part, believed Honeywell was milking Micro Switch dry without giving anything in return. Massof was well aware of these tensions. "It felt like those of us from Honeywell were suspect," she recalled. "For years and years they would ship the profits up the river . . . to us!"

Massof had her own misgivings about coming to Micro Switch. It wasn't just the move from Minneapolis, a thriving cosmopolitan center, to Freeport, a town of about 27,000 surrounded by farmland. It was also leaving behind the fast-paced environment of Honeywell for a division which appeared resistant to change. "I used to think this place was stuck in a time warp," confessed Massof, who first visited Micro Switch a decade earlier. "Not many things have changed since 1980. That was probably the scariest thing for me. If's such a deep culture."

As Massof dug into her new job, some of her forebodings proved right on target. Her forthright and nonhierarchical style — which was among the traits which had appealed to Alvarez — came as a shock to managers accustomed to adhering to a rigid reporting structure. It took months, for example, before she could approach a product administrator two levels down in the organization without a product manager rushing to intervene, and without their assuming she had come to complain.

Moreover, Massof found herself responsible for marketing product lines which had basically lain dormant for more than a decade. For example, although she was told that Micro Switch was still a leader in military lighted push buttons — a product the company invented in the mid-1950s Massof discovered that "lead" actually had dwindled away to an insignificant share. "In my particular business unit, the highest priority is making up for 15 years of no investment and no new products," she declared. "We're talking major, major change."

Massof s goals during her first 18 months with the AOM unit in many ways paralleled what Alvarez was trying to accomplish with the division overall: to make people aware of the need for change; to compensate for years of neglect; and to start drawing people into both the revitalization process and daily operations in ways they had never been involved before.

According to Massof, this was easier said than done. In her area, there was no time at first to think about "fine tuning" the change process. Instead, she was faced with getting much greater involvement in using management tools like market research and strategic planning in order to get the business moving again. "We were working very hard on just understanding this market we were in," she explained. "We thought we understood our customers, but I was shocked at how much we didn't know about the people we got all this money from."

Even in the process of implementing these steps, Massof was introducing her staff and employees to what for them was a radical new way of doing things. After just a few months on the job, for example, Massof called a general meeting to begin brainstorming for the unit's strategic plan, which Massof was determined to turn into a vital "living document" — a plan with daily significance for the entire unit. Because strategic planning at Micro Switch formerly had been the sole province of top management, employees at lower levels had never had a say in such issues before. She recalled the strategic planning kickoff meeting: "I got so many blank stares, as though to say, 'What on earth are you asking us to do?' All I heard was griping for weeks, and I thought, 'This is the biggest mistake I've ever made.'"

Massof didn't back down, however. She pressed her subordinates to continue meeting a couple of times a week, and as the division-wide strategic review process neared, the meetings increased to almost daily. The hardest part, Massof recounted, was to encourage independent thinking from employees who had never been expected to contribute before. Now, looking back on the process from a year's distance, Massof deemed it one of her group's greatest successes. When the time came for AOM to present its plan to the division, it was not Massof or her boss who introduced the strategy, but the cross-functional business teams which had invested so much time, energy — and complaints — in crafting it. "To get them together in a room to do strategic management was real weird for them," she laughed. "But I think they're feeling better about it now, and better about themselves."

Although the strategic plan was a success, it didn't mean the AOM unit was looking forward to it the second time around. Massof had already heard complaints about the planning for 1991, which was set to begin. Partly because of the strain of trying to motivate her co-workers and subordinates, Massof was particularly eager to draw inspiration from the Eagle Ridge sessions, even though these signalled a more intense focus on change at Micro Switch. "I feel like I need to be smarter," she admitted. "Then I figure out that if s not related to my inexperience at all, it's just the situation. There are a lot of people who have a lot more experience than I do who are feeling the same way." She added, "The biggest thing that's hit me is that I can't do a lot of things at once. We have to show little successes. Then when you look back over 12 months you say, 'Well, we've come a long way.'"

Four months later, Massof seemed more at ease with the unsettling sensation of being in the midst of change. Moreover, now in the middle of July 1990, she finally could point to a few examples of successful organizational change. Her group had recently completed its second strategic planning process, and this year — despite her initial forebodings — the participants had taken up the plan without complaining, and had brought a new level of skill and detail to the task. "We spent very little time bemoaning the time it would take — we actually had buy-in!" she exclaimed. "We established a benchmark on change by doing something right in 12 months." She added: "These people two years ago would not have had the confidence to get up in front of the general manager, and talk about their business, and tell the general manager what he should do."

Massof also felt that the seeds of team work planted at Eagle Ridge were beginning to take root Just the day before, for example, she had met Rick

Rowe for lunch to discuss a number of issues, ranging from getting Rowe's procurement perspective on a major contract for her unit that Massof was renewing, to discussing how their Building Block Councils should complement each other. "This helps the team-building process overall because we're setting an example," Massof explained. "When people see us, they're going to realize that being from different areas of the organization doesn't make us enemies, and that we can work on problems together."

Massof was still confronting many of the same obstacles which had discouraged her in March — in particular, the sheer number of changes waiting to be implemented. "My major frustration is that there are too many things that you know *need* to be changed," she stated. But at the same time, Massof appeared less troubled by the sense of always having too much to do. "We're all trying to be Super People — we're all trying to do everything at the same time, so we're spread a little thin," she mused. "If s a natural part of the process, but as part of that process, you can also step back and say we need to focus."

Specifically, Massof intended to focus more on her position as head of the Building Block Council on Customer Satisfaction, a role which had taken a back seat to the strenuous strategic planning process of the previous few months, and which would probably continue to take a back seat to the overriding concern of keeping the business on track under very difficult market conditions. "We're all doing this on the side of our desks," she sighed. "The councils consist mostly of directors and managers, and just getting the three directors of marketing in one room at one time is an incredible job."

As chair of the customer satisfaction council, Massof was charged with recommending and helping to implement the policies and systems Micro Switch needed in order to satisfy its mission of becoming a truly customer-driven organization. Among the priority items Massof wanted the council to consider were setting up a toll-free telephone number for customer inquiries, and creating a standard complaint system to replace the company's somewhat haphazard case-by-case approach.

According to Massof, Alvarez was "very, very clear about his expectations" for the division, yet she felt she had a great deal of autonomy. "It's not dictatorial," she asserted. "If s not like Ray's standing up there saying, 'Thou shalt do this.'

He's depending on a lot of different people to come up with the right solutions. And getting people together is not an easy thing to do when you're trying to run your business, too." She added: "I don't feel like he's controlling us. In fact, I feel I have so much leeway that I always feel guilty that we're not doing enough."

❏ ELLIS STEWART

The second Eagle Ridge session had ended just a few days before, but Ellis Stewart was already sifting through the materials he had brought back with him, trying to figure out how to incorporate the best of the new concepts into one of the many internal business manuals he had designed. Alvarez had named the 44-year-old Stewart to head the Building Block Council on Training just a few months before, but for Stewart, absorbing and repackaging change management techniques was a labor of love — one he had been doing on his own for years. "I do it because if s fun to do and it helps the cause," he claimed, and then gestured at a shelf piled high with management books. "There's no excuse for a business manager today not to know what is going on and not to have some ideas."

Stewart had logged almost 20 years at Micro Switch when Alvarez took over, and had risen to the position of director of fabricating operations, responsible for producing precision engineered parts for Micro Switch and other Honeywell divisions. Stewart's roots went deep and revealed a loyalty which the last decade of management practices had not shaken. "When I came here, the place literally could do no wrong," he asserted. "In many markets we were the only game in town, so we named our price and got it. From the standpoint of a middle manager, this place has been a fantastic place to work."

Stewart grudgingly admitted that Micro Switch's dedication to delivering profits to Honeywell had gone too far — causing the company to skimp on internal investment, and to resort to frequent layoffs. But he also insisted that many managers at the company had never lost sight of the quest for excellence. "Ray has said many times that the vision kind of got middle-aged," he said. "Some of us, especially people of my vintage, kind of resent that because we don't think we were ever caught up in that Guys like Rick Rowe and me were

off on our own, having a chance to change things and influence things."

In fact, Stewart and Rowe recently had been the first employees to receive plaques — dubbed Eagle Visionary Commendations — honoring them for their contributions to the change process (see Figure 5.12). "If I got that award for any reason at all, I got it because of my guts — my willingness to experiment with my part of the organization and take some risks," Stewart declared. "But this stuff wasn't always appreciated. Some folks have labelled Rick a maverick, and when I was doing creative stuff back in 1982,1 actually had my career threatened because people resented it."

Despite having won the award, Stewart still felt he had plenty of new things to learn, he hastened to add. The Eagle Ridge sessions, on top of the intensive strategic planning process which Alvarez had instituted, had begun to drive home a concept of cooperation and teamwork that was foreign to many of Micro Switch's managers. "We've got big egos, and teamwork becomes the biggest challenge," Stewart conceded. "We have some folks who think that if they don't control everything that they need, then they can't succeed. The ego thing tends to cloud objectivity — mine and everybody else's." He added: "It hasn't been until the last 18 months that we have tended to look around to see who's got something that's really good that we can copy. Up until then, it was, 'Well, Rick did something, but now I'll go do my own thing.'"

In addition to teamwork, Stewart also saw a number of other issues needing attention. "What is it going to take to get the rest of our management team to articulate the visions for their own areas as well as Ray can do it for the division, and as well as I and a number of other folks can do it for our parts of the division?" he asked. "That's a tall order. We have to learn a lot of things, we have to change the way we act a little, and we have to be a little less stuffy — get excited from time to time."

Stewart seemed deeply committed to the changes taking place in the last two-and-a-half years. "We have a general manager who has boundless energy and who sets the example," he declared. "Not that he doesn't sometimes make us feel bad if he blows up at us, because that can happen. He's a very intense person. But his creative energy has changed the work environment." He added: "We tried to remind our folks, we're optional. We've got to be the best there is in this

The Eagle Visionary Commendation

Presented To

A visionary possesses a characteristic rare in today's fast-paced business environment: the ability to see beyond the urgency of today's demands to what *can* be reality tomorrow. This is not the ability to simply imagine what tomorrow might be like — it is the ability to see that tomorrow so tangibly that it can be touched, understood and believed.

Some visionaries are traditionalists and some are mavericks. But all can articulate a vision in such a way that others may catch its essence. And all visionaries are leaders in that they help us create the blueprint to build those visions into towering realities. And then they challenge us all to make it happen.

And while they may be dreamers, visionaries are also doers: they see not only the future, but the path — and its milestone — that can take us there.

We salute and encourage this quality in the Honeywell MICRO SWITCH management team. It is a quality that will help us maintain a leadership position in our global marketplace and give us an unmatched competitive edge.

This commendation recognizes the visionary contributions _____ has made in ensuring our company's world-class citizenship in the business community of the 1990's.

Ramon A. Alvarez, Vice President and General Manager

MICRO SWITCH
a Honeywell Division

Figure 5.12   The Eagle Visionary Commendation

kind of business, or eventually we won't be around — that's the law of nature."

Four months later, Stewart's nervous energy seemed somewhat tempered. like Rowe and Massof, Stewart worried that the business slump had hit at a particularly inopportune time — knocking the wind out of the change effort just when it needed a boost. "We have lots of projects underway, lots of new product development work, tons of energy being expended, long workdays, people working on weekends and taking their work home, but there's just no growth," he lamented. "What we need is some growth to take advantage of all the work we've done."

Even Alvarez, whose energy and optimism had often sustained Micro Switch in the past, was showing signs of strain, Stewart said. "Ray and a number of us are concerned that the organization is doing a lot of things, but doesn't appear to be changing rapidly enough to take advantage of the investments

that we've made," he explained. "We are not on this upward rocket that we'd expected to be on by now, and that is weighing extremely heavily."

This increased level of stress might have contributed to the occasional friction some of the directors were experiencing, particularly as they wrestled with issues of autonomy and empowerment. In the past few months, for example, after a preliminary presentation to Alvarez and his executive staff, Stewart — in his role as head of the Building Block Council on Training — had overseen the planning, organization, and pilot run of a new employee training program known as APEX College. But instead of winning kudos for his fast work, Stewart and his associates had gotten their wrists slapped for acting without authorization. "It was totally bewildering," he recalled. "We said, 'Listen, damn it, we accepted the assignment, we went and did it, we're doing it on the corner of our desks, It's not anywhere *close* to the normal routine for a job like ours, so what the hell are you telling us now?' " He added: "There's an aura here that if you don't move quickly, that's a problem, but in this case we got caught moving too quickly."

Nevertheless, although Stewart was angry at the time, he said that in retrospect, he saw the wisdom of the reprimand. "Ray is tussling with the business of control versus empowerment," he explained. "He's got to control the business, he's got his neck on the line for the success of this thing, he likes to have his mark on things, he wants to have his staff involved setting the tone and providing the leadership, and we went off and said, 'We don't need you guys.' We moved so quickly, we lost them."

The issue of control versus empowerment was not the only dichotomy Micro Switch was struggling with, Stewart said. The company also had a schism between those who were committed to change, and those who were not. On one hand were the change leaders like Rowe, Massof, and Stewart, himself, who were in danger of taking on more change than they could handle. And on the other hand was a group straddling all levels of the organization which still appeared unconvinced of the need for change.

Both of these groups needed attention, Stewart maintained. Those who had thrown themselves wholeheartedly behind change were in danger of burning out, or becoming paralyzed by the sheer magnitude of the tasks they had taken on, he warned. "A friend of mine used to talk about the stool of life," Stewart mused. "There are four legs on that stool — your work, your hobbies, your family, and your religion — and as long as you keep those four legs the same length, it's a stable situation. But if you get one a lot shorter or longer than the others, it's unstable and the stool will fall over."

He added: "I keep cautioning people in our career development workshops about that. At some point in time you have to live with a lopsided stool, but you can't live with it for long."

But even more threatening for the organization were the people who still weren't behind the change, Stewart warned. And like Rowe, he had begun to believe that the time for patience was past. "You have to provide the vision and the mission, but you also have to recognize that some folks won't see things that way and will hope to maintain the status quo," he stated. "If we choose to have a culture that's participative, and we have folks for whom that just isn't in their guts, then we have to reassign, reposition, or fire them. Our heritage here has been to be very patient, very tolerant — to coach, counsel, and hope for the best. We have to be more tough-minded now without being cruel and ruthless."

Providing more and better training was the first step in resolving many of these issues, Stewart insisted. "The key to this thing is a much more rapid introduction of empowerment techniques and training so we can get the entire work force to have an entrepreneurial spirit," he declared.

But in almost the same breath, Stewart admitted that there were times when he grew discouraged, and brooded about some questions that simply couldn't be answered. "I think this is the right process, but I'm not so sure whether the timing was right," he reflected. "Is this the year — is this the decade — that we should have done this with Micro Switch? Could the business have continued to thrive and grow under the old way of working, and perhaps even done better during this same period of time? I don't know. I'm always going to wonder about that."

Developing and Communicating a Shared Vision

❏ CHAPTER AT A GLANCE

Highlights of the chapter include the following:

1. Effective and appropriate communication is paramount to bring about successful change. Change leaders who overlook the importance of communicating a consistent change message and vision fuel some of the negative responses (resistance) encountered in managing change.

2. Gaining people's commitment and buy-in with a shared vision is one of the most critical aspects of a change initiative.

3. There are three key communication errors common to change initiatives: lack of a vision, under communication, and failure to remove obstacles to the new vision.

4. Clarity in vision statements is critical. Successful change will be undermined if the vision and strategy for implementation is not effectively communicated.

5. The most powerful communication is done face-to-face, especially if people have the opportunity to ask questions and engage in dialogue.

6. Change communication plays a key role in addressing the key issues in each phase of the change process by preparing and helping members to move through each of the three phases: unfreezing, change, and refreezing.

7. The Johari Window is a useful paradigm for helping change leaders and organizations understand how an open, two-way communication process can enhance the effectiveness of any change program.

8. The change communication framework includes five key message domains and three communication strategies to enhance people's readiness for change.

9. Informal communication channels play an important role in the change communication process.

The following vignette highlights the importance of effective change communication.

❏ VIGNETTE[1]

In 1994, Delta Airlines began a major restructuring in order to better compete. It meant that a company which at one time had a policy of no furloughs, would now have to lay off several thousand people. The company leadership referred to the program as Leadership 7.5. Naturally, such a program generated enormous fear. Delta felt communication was the key to reducing fear. To combat this, a special 800 number was established to accept comments and questions and provide current updates on the change. When the news was presented to employees, the company paper, The Delta Newsline, received more than 6000 calls on the day of the announcement and more than 14,000 calls by the end of the week. Many of these comments were later printed in the company news magazine.

Reducing fear and increasing the sense of security were important, so a special communication center was also established to handle information requests from mangers and supervisors. Within hours of the initial announcement, the Senior Vice President of Technical Operations was in a hangar responding to questions and providing information in an open forum. Within two days of the announcement there were other visits by senior management to the various Delta facilities across the country. Senior management conducted additional visits to other key facilities across the country in the following weeks. Delta also held a system-wide management conference in Atlanta on the day after the announcement to fully outline the restructuring and the programs that would be instituted. Company leaders then distributed a video presentation of the management conference to all personnel.

Tom Slocum, Vice President of Corporate Communications, captured the Delta philosophy about change and communication by commenting that as the changes brought on by Leadership 7.5 and future programs develop, it will be even more important to provide employees with as much information as possible — quickly and accurately. Prompt communications are a huge challenge, especially in a company the size of Delta, but it is essential. If the organization is not successful at communicating the change, it is unlikely that the organization will be successful at implementing it. People must know what is happening and why before they can feel even somewhat confident, secure, and hopeful about the change and the future the change will bring.

❏ CHAPTER PERSPECTIVE

Organizational change is relentless and ubiquitous in today's environment. As organizational leaders embark on a plan to adapt to and implement a

change initiative, their plans often miss an important element. As one expert in the field of change communication observed:[*]

In a sense, the easy part of managing change is figuring out where you want to go. The hard part is getting from here to there — from the current state to the future state — and persuading sufficient numbers of the right people to overcome their fears, skepticism, and resistance and join you on that journey.

Change initiatives often flounder because not enough attention is given to crafting a vision and the communication strategy. In an employee opinion survey conducted by Hay Group, results suggest that companies are struggling to communicate effectively the personal implications of change to employees. Less than one-half of employees report that communications are handled well when changes are made in their organizations. Likewise, less than 50% report that they are adequately informed of the reasons behind decisions that affect them.[2] This chapter focuses on the importance of a sound and healthy communication strategy and vision for initiating change. The best change plan in the world will be undermined without a well-conceived and executed change communication strategy designed to inform, educate, involve, and motivate people to perform and behave in ways consistent with the change agenda.

In developing this chapter on change communication, we make five assumptions:

1. Communication is a key component during each phase of the change process.

2. Communication is an essential tool for motivating employees, for overcoming resistance to change, for conveying the benefits and obstacles to change, and for giving the employees a stake in the process.[3]

3. Communication is a tool that is often used poorly or thoughtlessly. To the degree that communication is used poorly in organizations, it confuses people. It makes them angry, and it feeds whatever skepticism or cynicism they feel about the motives of the people who lead them — in the process worsening their fears and making them more resistant to change.[4]

---

[*] Extracted from Richardson, P., & Denton, D. K. (1996). Communicating Change. Human Resource Management, Vol. 35, No. 2, pp. 204–05.

4. People need to understand the vision if change is to have any chance of success. They must not only believe it in their heads, but in their hearts as well.

5. There is an effective way to communicate change.

❏ COMMUNICATING CHANGE

Communication is always important but especially so during change. The opening vignette provides a powerful illustration of the central role communication plays in an organization when dealing with change. Whether organization change results from a restructuring, process improvement, or crisis, effective change communication can make the difference between success and failure. Employee communication is especially critical when we're "trying to get others to see and do things differently."[5] For example, when he was CEO of AlliedSignal, Lawrence Bossidy remarked in an interview,[6]

I believe in the 'burning platform' theory of change. When the roustabouts are standing on the offshore oil rig and the foreman yells, 'Jump into the water,' not only won't they jump but they won't feel too kindly toward the foreman.... They'll jump only when they themselves see the flames shooting up from the platform.... The leader's job is to help everyone see that the platform is burning, whether the flames are apparently or not. The process of change begins when people decide to take the flames seriously and manage by fact, and that means a brutal understanding of reality.

Armenakis and Harris suggest that leaders who overlook the importance of communicating a consistent change message and vision fuel some of the negative responses (resistance) encountered in managing change.[7] It is the communication process that starts the process to unfreeze and predispose people to.[8] As Duck reminds us,

If leaders want to change the thinking and actions of others, they must be transparent about their own. If people within the organization don't understand the new thinking or don't agree with it, they will not change their beliefs or make decisions that are aligned with what is desired.[9]

No matter what kind of change initiative an organization's leadership may desire, the change won't be successful without the support and commitment of a majority of its managers and employees.

Getting people "unstuck" — that is, getting them to not only embrace the vision but to change their beliefs and thinking to move in the new direction — is a huge communication challenge. This challenge was met by Delta's leadership in our opening vignette.

Delta wanted to be sure employees fully understood why the change was necessary and how the change would impact them personally. To allay employee fears about the new program, company leadership paid special attention to communicating the "what" and "why now," which are so important in gaining commitment for the proposed change and in keeping people focused on the behavior required to successfully navigate the change. "Because change usually spawns confusion, anger, and skepticism, it requires a powerful rationale to help people understand why they must embrace it."[10] The benefits of success and the penalties for failing to act must be made explicitly clear. Leadership in this case made a strong effort to communicate the rationale and answer employee questions.

A lack of understanding is a very common problem with change initiatives because change causes people to "sever the familiar and comfortable connections that tell us who we are and what is expected of us."[11] It is important, therefore, to reestablish these important connections during time of change. The communication consultant Roger D'Aprix uses the following metaphor that illuminates this point:[12]

I believe an individual at work is like a mountain climber, who must tether herself to other climbers and in some fashion to the face of the mountain itself. These connections keep her from falling into an abyss. Likewise, whatever logical connections a worker can perceive among the needs of his customers, the strategies of his leaders, and his own daily efforts keep him safe from chaos and alienation.

D'Aprix goes on to remind us,

Poor or absent communication is one of our greatest enemies in the effort to establish such connections. Unfortunately, what often passes for good communication in organizations is the top-down reporting of organizational actions or events. In this approach, the communication task or the organization's leadership is seen as reporting to employees and other stakeholders those actions the leadership proposes to take in response to a given event or circumstance. If there are no events or actions that leaders feel comfortable talking about, there is no communication.[13]

1. **They don't need to know yet. We'll tell them when the time comes. It'll just upset them now.** For every week of upset that you avoid by hiding the truth, you gain a month of bitterness and mistrust. Besides, the grapevine already has the news, so don't imagine that your information is a secret.

2. **They already know. We announced it.** OK, you told them, but it didn't sink in. Threatening information is absorbed remarkably slowly. Say it again. And find different ways to say it and different media (large meetings, one-on-ones, memos, a story in the company paper) to say it.

3. **I told the supervisors. It's their job to tell the rank and file.** The supervisors are likely to be in transition themselves, and they may not even sufficiently understand the information to convey it accurately. Maybe they're still in denial. Information is poor, so they may not want to share it yet. Don't assume that information trickles down through the organizational strata reliably or in a timely fashion.

4. **We don't know the details ourselves, so there's no point in saying anything until everything has been decided.** In the meantime, people can get more and more frightened and resentful. Much better to say what you do know, say that you don't know more, and tell what kind of schedule exists.

Figure 6.1   *Common Reasons Why Change Leaders Don't Communicate*

And when there is no communication, employees find other sources for information — often times the media, Internet, or from their friends. The news published in the media and other sources is often inaccurate, often generated from speculation, rumor, or investigative reporting rather than communicated from the company itself. As Duck aptly observed,

Too often, however, leaders are so wrapped up in the issues of running the business that they fail to recognize the importance of communication; they say too little and often say it too late. One thing you should count on: *People will connect the dots in the most pathological way possible.*[14]

For example, the catalog retailer Lillian Vernon encountered huge problems with their IT transformation project when they failed to effectively communicate to employees why the project was necessary and how it would affect each employee specifically. In discussing the end-user training for the new system, the CIO's comments are particularly poignant:

Before the classes began, 'we should have put everyone in a room and said, Here is how you fit into this new picture' . . . instead, the project team fell back on blanket statements that everyone's job would be 'better' Once rollout began, however, they were angry when their jobs were harder instead. Since most had not taken the training seriously, they did not know how to use the application. And many were uncertain as to how their jobs had changed. 'People were blaming the system for everything'.[15]

We should recognize too that there are many rationalizations for not communicating. Figure 6.1 highlights some common reasons why change leaders do not communicate.[16] In the Lillian Vernon company example, when the CIO began work on the IT transformation project, he expressed his rationalization for not communicating this way:

We're bringing in vendors who will bring change management expertise to the table. We have capable, gungho teams. Giddyap, let's go . . . . In other words, launch the projects and fix problems later. [The CIO] learned that far from being a frill, basic communication creates the underpinning for a successful implementation. The essence of change management. . . . is a few well-placed, well-delivered conversations to the right audience. And then you follow up, again and again.[17]

The lesson the CIO learned from this experience is that it is crucial for leaders to develop and widely communicate a compelling case for change. Mercer Delta Consulting suggests five key elements make up a persuasive case for change (see Figure 6.2).[18]

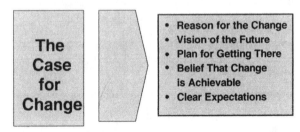

Figure 6.2   *Defining the Case for Change*

Reason for the change. Answers the question "Why change?" and creates motivation for change. Simply saying one's job will be better is not sufficient. Employees need to know the business case for the change and how it impacts the bottom line.

Vision of the future. Serves as a starting-point and anchor for what we do. Answers the question "Change to what?" by providing leadership's vision of the new organization; creates energy and excitement about the future. We address this factor more deeply later in the chapter.

Plan for getting there. Answers the question "How are we going to change?" and mobilizes people toward a common direction. Here we want to provide the big picture — the agenda, key strategies and implementation plans.

Believe change is achievable. Answers the question "Is this really possible?" and encourages interest, engagement, and optimism.

Expectations. Answers the question "What can I expect of you and what is expected of me?" and helps people prepare for the change which reducing their uncertainty.

In sum, communication plays a vital role in the success of change programs. It is difficult to engage everyone based only on communication alone. Ideally, people must participate in the process from beginning to end. If the sentiment is that the change is imposed from the top, then gaining commitment will be tough. In general, effective communication in managing change helps us address the following issues:[19]

- Obtaining individual buy-in
- Obtaining commitment to the change
- Minimizing resistance
- Reducing personal anxiety
- Ensuring clarity of objectives
- Sharing information and the vision
- Challenging the status quo
- Obtaining clarity
- Minimizing uncertainty

In the following sections, we discuss shared vision and its importance in the change process. Then we review some important considerations in communicating the vision to include a framework for change communication.

❑ WHAT DO WE MEAN BY A "SHARED VISION"?

Gaining people's commitment and buy-in with a shared vision is one of the most critical aspects of a change initiative. For organizations to successfully implement any change, they need to articulate a clear and energizing picture of where they are now, where they want to go, and the role employees will play in the process. The vision provides a road map for future direction. A good vision is realistic, compelling, and motivates employees to maximize their energy on supporting the new direction. As Senge reminds us, "a compelling vision that connects with what people care about is a powerful ingredient for change."[20] The vision is so important that "the absence of a vision will doom any strategy — especially a strategy for change."[21]

A vision can't be acted upon until it is shared. A shared vision is a key starting point in any change process "because it defines, in clear and operational terms, the results that the whole organization is attempting to achieve."[22] Senge defines a shared vision as

. . . a force in people's hearts, a force of impressive power . . . it is palpable. People begin to see it as if it exists. Few, if any, forces in human affairs are as powerful as a shared vision . . . They create a sense of commonality that permeates the organization and gives coherence to diverse activities.[23]

Moreover, it's not enough for the change leader to have the vision. "It doesn't matter what's in the CEO or leader's head. The vision must be understandable. If people are not clear about what is important, they have no context for making all of the minute decisions that are made every day in the organization." Change leaders and champions must communicate the vision so everyone in the organization understands, accepts, and commits to it. When Ford's President of the Americas Mark Fields took over Ford's transformation in early 2006, he recognized the critical need to establish a vision that all employees can rally around: "Since I came into this job last year, I have had e-mail in the thousands, and the ones that stick out are people who have said, 'I can do anything you want, but I need to know what we are doing.'"[24] So it's important that the vision makes sense to people. Ideally, it should create an "aha effect," whereby everyone can fully picture the new direction and what it means for them and the organization.

It's critical for change leaders to articulate a bold vision in order to inspire "people to look at the possibilities of going beyond what is wrong and what, in the past, have been limitations."[25] Only highly committed employees are the ones who will make the vision a reality by driving change because they believe in it. For example, commenting in a *Fortune* article regarding his failure to transform General Motors, Roger Smith, chairman between 1981 and 1990, recalled:

... I sure wish I'd done a better job of communicating with GM people. I'd do that differently a second time around and make sure they understood and shared my vision for the company. Then they would have known why I was tearing the place up, taking out whole divisions, changing our whole production structure. If people understand the why, they'll work at it. Like I say, I never got all this across. There we were, charging up the hill right on schedule, and I looked behind me and saw that many people were still at the bottom, trying to decide whether to come along. I'm talking about hourly workers, middle management, even some top managers. It seemed like a lot of them had gotten off the train.[26]

David Baum in his book *Lightning in a Bottle* describes a simple but brilliant metaphor about managing change and the role of a compelling vision in the process:

When a rubber band is pulled tight, as you might do when shooting it across the room, it represents the appropriate amount of creative tension that's needed to produce momentum and change. One side represents your current reality, the other side your compelling vision. Your organization will fail to move when you lack either one — the compelling vision or the clear sense of your current reality. Similarly, a rubber band will not spring from your hand if either the front end or back end is hanging loose. It must be taut enough to provide energy for movement, without being stretched so tight that it breaks. When the tension is right, it will create energy for movement. The role of leadership is to consistently balance the present truths of the environment with the sense of possibility that can come only from a compelling vision. Without a clear understanding of what's so, you will be building your castles in the sand.[27]

When change leaders envision the future and effectively communicate a vision, the potential impact on employee behavior is huge. When you really think about it, it's the "people," not the "plan" itself that determines the outcome of any change effort. The positive outcomes associated with a compelling vision help focus people's efforts and move them to embrace the change both emotionally and intellectually. It is "the invisible threads of a compelling vision that weave[s] a tapestry that binds people together more powerfully than any strategic plan."[28] By contrast, an unarticulated vision can cause people to feel unclear or confused about what the change is trying to accomplish.

Kenneth W. Freeman is the founding chairman and former chief executive officer of Quest Diagnostics, the largest medical testing firm in the world, with 37,000 employees performing tests on 145 million patients annually for about half the hospitals and physicians in the United Stats. In an interview in *Strategy & Business,* he discussed how he transformed a battered firm, spun off in 1996 from a distant corporate owner (Corning), and made it the eighth-fastest-growing earnings engine in the United States. Many of the positive outcomes of an effectively communicated vision come through in his remarks:

We had to get the hearts and minds of the employees — to give them something to believe in, to help them understand whom they were working for, to understand their role, to take ownership for what they had to get done, and to feel excitement about what the company could become.[29]

As another example, Ken Blanchard aptly articulated why change leaders must effectively communicate a vision that is understood by everyone:[30]

Vision helps people make smart choices because their decisions are being made with the end result in mind. As goals are accomplished, the answer to "What next?" becomes clear. Vision takes into account a larger picture than the immediate goal. Martin Luther King Jr. described his vision of a world where people live together in mutual respect. In his "I have a Dream" speech, he described a world where his children "will not be judged by the color of their skin, but by the content of their character." He created powerful and specific images from the values of brotherhood, respect, and freedom for all — values that resonate with the founding values of the United States. King's vision has passed a crucial test: it continues to mobilize and guide people beyond his lifetime. Vision allows for a long-term proactive stance — creating what we want — rather than a short-term reactive stance — getting rid of what we don't want.

Much time is spent examining what makes good strategic visions, but little time or effort is expended determining why they fail to accomplish what they set out to do. We next examine problems to avoid with change visions, how to craft a vision, and then discuss an effective framework for communicating the vision.

❏ VISION — GETTING IT RIGHT

John P. Kotter, a world-renowned expert on leadership and change at the Harvard Business School, looked at more than 100 companies — large and small — that undertook a major transformation or change effort. Some of the firms he studied were successful, some were failures; most fell in between with many of these concentrated at the failure-end of the scale.

From his research, Kotter drew two lessons that are important to managers and students of change management:[31]

1. The change process is a combination of several phases that take a considerable length of time, and that skipping steps only creates an illusion of speed and never produces satisfactory results.

2. Critical mistakes in any of the steps could slow the progress of the project and undo previous gains.

As discussed in Chapter 2, Kotter identified eight fatal flaws or errors that can have serious negative consequences on any change initiative. Figure 6.3 lists three of the eight errors or steps that pertain to "vision." We examine these three steps and the lessons Kotter shares in helping practicing managers avoid the pitfalls associated with vision and communicating it effectively.

Lacking a vision. The evidence from Kotter's research is compelling. In every successful change effort, there was a clear and easy to understand vision. For every change effort that failed, he found no evidence of a compelling vision. In some marginally successful change programs, while management had an idea of where they were headed, the overall vision was unclear or complicated to understand. If vision is to play "a key role in producing useful change by helping to direct, align, and inspire actions on the part of large numbers of people," then the following rule of thumb is important to remember:

> If you can't communicate the vision to someone in five minutes or less and get a reaction that satisfies both understanding and interest, you are not yet done with this phase of the transformation process.[33]

What Kotter is making clear is the need to be sure the vision is translated into a language people at all levels can understand. For example, if a boss asks her subordinates to initiate a new work process because it will enhance shareholder value, then she probably has failed to translate the vision into a language that has meaning for the people involved. What does shareholder value mean to the average employee? A more effective approach might be to show how enhanced shareholder value leads to providing more capital for growth. And with growth comes more opportunity for advancement, the potential for more compensation, larger contributions to profit sharing and 401(k) plans, greater job security, among others. "A well communicated but poorly translated vision is noise. A well communicated and well translated vision has a good chance of influencing behavior."[34]

Under communicating. Figure 6.4 describes three basic communication patterns that seem to be common in most change efforts.

It should come as no surprise that these three common approaches to communicating change do little to build understanding. Instead, the net result is cynicism and lost of trust and faith in the communication that is put forth. Change is impossible unless hundreds or thousands of people are willing to help, often to the point of making short-term sacrifices.

---

1. **Lacking a vision.** In unsuccessful cases, the leadership team failed to develop a picture of the future that is relatively easy to communicate and is attractive to insiders and others.

2. **Undercommunicating the vision by a factor of 10.** In unsuccessful projects, the leaders failed to use all existing channels and every opportunity to communicate the vision to their people.

3. **Not removing obstacles to the new vision.** All obstacles are not obvious from the beginning. The process of removing them is an ongoing one.

Figure 6.3   *Communication Errors Common to Organizational Change Efforts*[32]

---

1. Good vision in place but communicated via a few meetings or a few communiqués (e.g., memo or video).

2. CEO or change leader spends a lot of time making speeches to employee groups but most don't get it.

3. Most communication effort goes into newsletters and speeches. However, the senior leadership and other key managers don't walk the talk.

Figure 6.4 *Change Communication Pattern Types*

Employees will not make sacrifices, even if they are unhappy with the status quo, unless they believe that useful change is possible. Without credible communication, and a lot of it, the hearts and minds of the troops are never captured.[35]

Key communication lessons to remember:

1. Use all existing communication channels (both formal and informal) to reach all employees with the new vision.

2. Be creative in turning boring and unread company newsletters into stimulating and interesting articles that people will read.

3. Ensure managers must "walk the talk." The change leader must not only believe in the vision but must be seen to believe in it.

4. Make sure the vision is understandable. Trying to communicate a vision that runs two pages or is too full of numbers and jargon is not very effective.

5. Remember that the vision is just a dream without the involvement and work of others.[36]

Not removing obstacles. Simply put, communication alone is insufficient to ensure a change program reaches fruition. Change leaders need to anticipate and be sensitive to mitigating any obstacles that may surface. Examples include dealing with resistance to change, correcting organization structural and process issues, fixing a reward or appraisal system that is incongruent with the espoused new behaviors, and dealing with key managers who refuse to go along with the new direction.

In sum, we can't expect people to embrace the vision or to get excited about the future if they don't

have a clue what the vision is. When communicating a vision, the following three key success factors must be in place:[37]

1. The management team must be aligned and energized around the vision and strategy.

2. The vision must be articulated and the overall plan sufficiently detailed so it can be understood and executed by others.

3. A healthy dissatisfaction with the status quo and a genuine appetite for change must be generated within the workforce; appropriate expectations of what will happen and what can be accomplished must be set.

We now turn our attention to creating the vision for change and how to communicate it effectively.

❏ CRAFTING A VISION STATEMENT

Without a vision, an organization is like a ship without a rudder. It is essential to change management success. It provides direction and guides everything we do to implement the change initiative. So how do we create a vision statement?

It is recommended that the development of a vision statement or the visioning process be democratic and use a wide range of cross-functional groups rather than being top-down. People should be involved deeply in the process. This allows for necessary debate and has the potential to lead to more creative visions and actions. It also ensures that a sense of urgency and the need for change resonates with all stakeholders in the change initiative.

The visioning process must be well planned to ensure that the results are comprehensive, integrated, and inclusive. Lucas defined several key components to any visioning process:[38]

1. We have to know "Who we are?" before we can decide where we want to go (this means that we have to do some serious soul searching). What are our core values? What are our core competencies (and incompetencies)?

2. We must involve people in the process — seek widespread input from all levels in the organization. Go beyond the advice of consultants.

3. We must intelligently plan the visioning process to ensure the results are comprehensive and inclusive.

4. We need to be cautious of succumbing to the lowest common denominator. A false consensus can result in a vision that offends no one but also fails to challenge and inspire employees.

5. We must describe the vision in enough detail that we can be held accountable. Are we achieving what we say we want to do?

6. We need to support the implementation of the vision. This may involve "changing organizational structures and job designs, changing relationship norms, reshaping systems and performance expectations to better match the vision, and making what people do fit better with the organization's mission."[39]

It is important that "at every opportunity, leaders need to demonstrate what the vision looks like, what it feels like, and how people can live it today as well as in the future."[40] Some examples of vision statements that touch the heart as well as the head follow:[41]

Xerox: Helping people find better ways to do great work.

Celestial Seasonings: To create and sell healthful, naturally oriented products that nurture people's bodies and uplift their souls.

Bristol-Myers Squibb: To extend and enhance human life.

Chevron: To be the global energy company most admired for its people, partnership, and performance.

Washington Mutual: To be the nation's leading retailer of financial services for consumers and businesses.

Avon: To be the company that best understands and satisfies the product, service and self-fulfillment needs of women — globally.

An eight-step process for creating a vision statement is illustrated in Figure 6.5[42]

Step 1: Collect input

The vision, to be most effective, should represent the ideals of the entire organization.

1. What would be the perfect organizational culture?

2. What would the perfect organization do for its members' growth and development?

3. What products or services would the perfect organization provide to customers and the community?

4. What else would the perfect organization do or be?

After gathering input you're ready for the first visioning session.

Step 2: Brainstorm

Brainstorming is an effective way of producing many ideas.

VISION CREATION STEPS

Figure 6.5   Creating a Vision

Step 3: Shrink the mess

Next, you must shrink the large number of ideas generated down to a smaller, more manageable number without losing content. The first step is to look for and eliminate duplication. You can then categorize the individual ideas into groups. Since there are no set categories in this process, the team's unique ideas will dictate. Next, eliminate any ideas that you decide aren't appropriate or don't fit. With the ideas grouped, choose the word or words that best represent each group and transfer them to Post-it notes.

Step 4: Develop a rough draft

Take the Post-it notes and arrange them on a clean flipchart page. By working with them, you can rough out a statement for each component: culture, people, and product or service.

Step 5: Refine the statements

With a fresh look, you're ready to carefully refine your statements. This is the rewrite step in which both content and style is important. Words are very important here, and only the right words will do because they must create a vivid mental picture. Therefore, this step deserves considerable time and energy.

Step 6: Test the criteria

Before taking the vision to the organization for approval, you can save time by testing the proposed vision against a set of key vision criteria (see Figure 6.6).[43] If it passes this test, you're ready to take it to the organization for approval. If it fails the test, you now have an area to work on. Be sure to stay focused and work on improving only those parts of the vision that don't meet the criteria.

Step 7: Obtain organization approval or modify

After the group has produced what it thinks is the perfect vision, present it to the entire organization for approval. This step is essential if everyone is to own, and thus commit to, the vision. When soliciting the approval of other employees in the organization, explain the process the team went through, explain the vision, and be open to modifications. All suggestions should at least be considered.

Step 8: Communicate and celebrate

What makes a vision the key to managing successful change is that it drives an organization's goals and objectives, which, in turn, direct all plans and activities to a specific end, enabling the organization and change leader to stay on course.[44] A vision without a plan, however, is only a dream. Stephen Covey proposed that everything is created twice: first in the mind, then in the physical world.[45] To the extent to which we begin with the end in mind as articulated through a vision statement, often determines whether or not we are able to implement a successful change program.

In sum, the vision reflects "a comprehensive picture of the desired future state of the organization. It includes the organization's core values and goals, its primary strategy for achieving its mission, and the characteristics of its ideal business processes, structure, systems, people and skills, and culture."[46] In addition, the vision must be clear, understandable, and aligned with the culture of the organization.

❏ CLARITY OF THE CHANGE VISION

One of the problems with use of vision statements in change initiatives is that leaders will point to a vision statement as evidence they are providing

---

✔ IMAGINABLE: Conveys a picture of what the future will look like.

✔ DESIRABLE: Appeals to the long-term interests of all stakeholders.

✔ FEASIBLE: Comprises realistic, attainable goals.

✔ FOCUSED: Is clear enough to provide guidance in decision making.

✔ FLEXIBLE: Is general enough to allow individual initiative and alternative responses in light of changing conditions.

✔ COMMUNICABLE: Is easy to communicate; can be successfully explained within five minutes.

Figure 6.6 *Effective Vision Characteristics*

needed direction to their employees. However, what leaders fail to recognize is that the vision statement itself lacks the clarity needed to make the vision clear and understandable to the organization. The net effect is that the employees have no clue what the vision means for the company for them personally. "This disconnect comes about because of a fatal misunderstanding on the part of leaders about what it takes for clarity of vision."[47]

If people are unsure why they have to change the way they work, then confusion and resistance is likely. One expert's metaphor of the role vision must play in managing change is helpful:

The purpose of a vision is to paint a clear picture of a destination that the company and its employees are to reach at some future time. To be understood, the vision must be presented to employees very much like we would present the contents of a new movie or play to actors."[48]

- A vision must describe the 'set' — the organizational layout and way of operating for the future.

- A vision must describe the roles of the 'cast' — who will be doing what to whom (in the business setting) and why.

- A vision must describe the 'play' — how everything that is done will come together as a successful performance, as measured by reviews from customers on product/service quality, from stockholders on competitive returns, and from employees with enough satisfaction to stay on the job.

In sum, it's important to create a vision story explaining why the organization must transform itself, where it is heading, and how it will get there.

Moreover, GE's former chairman and CEO, Jack Welch, provides some additional insight into the importance of creating and projecting a clear vision. He says,

The leader's unending responsibility must be to remove every detour, every barrier, to ensure that vision is first clear, and then real. The leader must create an atmosphere in the organization where people feel not only free to, but obliged to demand clarity and purpose from their leaders. . . . Every idea you present must be something you could get across easily at a cocktail party with strangers. If only aficionados of your industry can understand what you're saying, you've blown it.[49]

To help solidify buy-in and acceptance for change, change leaders need to work on changing peoples'

perceptions. The perceptual change begins with convincing people that management knows what it is doing and includes a clear and unambiguous purpose and vision that is understood by all. In short, pursuing goals that make sense to people is the most effective way to inspire individuals and maintain their commitment.[50] Moreover, we will also need to consider aligning the new vision with the organization culture.

❏ ALIGNING THE CULTURE WITH THE VISION

Depending on the scope and boldness of the vision, Jick reminds us that achievement of the vision is most likely going to require a concomitant change in the organization's culture and underlying values.[51] More directly, Jick suggests that if there is not an alignment between the vision and the culture, it's possible that achievement of the vision will be short-lived or even fail to materialize.

A new vision may in fact draw strength from aspects of the legacy culture and values, but invariably requires abandoning some aspects of the old culture and enacting new attitudes and behaviors that have never been present. The task of both unlearning old habits and learning new ones is perhaps the most challenging but also with the highest payoff.[52]

We address the issue of organizational culture and change more deeply in Chapter 7.

A detailed example using the National Oceanic and Atmospheric Administration's Office of Oceanic and Atmospheric Research (OAR) Strategic Plan illustrates the connection between vision, mission, and strategy is given in Figure 6.7.

We now turn to communicating the change vision.

❏ COMMUNICATING THE CHANGE VISION

Successful change will be undermined if the vision and strategy for implementation is not effectively communicated. The goal is simple: "to get as many people as possible acting to make the vision a reality."[54] Moreover, "change leaders at all levels must take an active role in communicating about change."[55]

Preparing and motivating organizations for change takes time. Most experts suggest that face-time and lots of it is key. As one observer

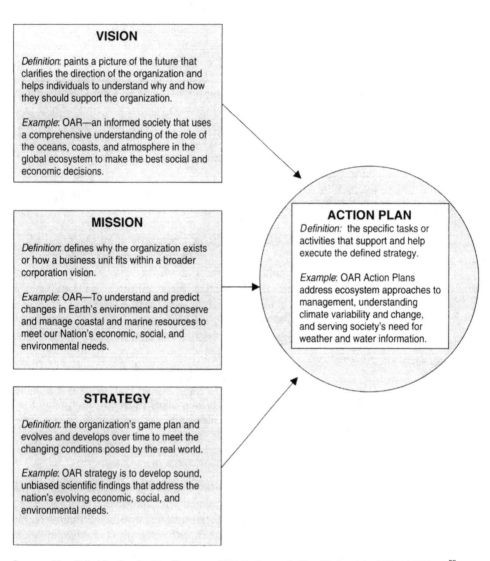

Source: New Priorities for the 21st Century—NOAA's Strategic Plan Updated for FY2006-FY2011.[53]

Figure 6.7   Example of Vision, Mission, Strategy, and Action Plans

noted, no single communication (even a stellar video) will suffice. It takes preparation and doing your homework.

The most powerful communication is done face-to-face, especially if people have the opportunity to ask questions and engage in dialogue."[56] Moreover, individuals like to get their information from someone they trust — usually that is their immediate supervisor. Consider this insight by Larkin:[57]

The traditional approach is to launch change from the top and hope that communication about the change will open like a parachute, blanketing everyone evenly. But frontline supervisors — not senior managers —

are the opinion leaders in your organization. Because frontline supervisors greatly influence the attitudes and behaviors of others, they are critical to the success of any change effort. That realization, so radical to communication consultants, is founded in communication research respected since the 1940s.

As one CEO observed, "We can send out videos and post messages on the intranet site until the cows come home, but it won't do any good. They have to see you personally, and experience your commitment firsthand, before they'll believe a word we're saying."[58] Larkin and Larkin provide a wonderful example that illuminates this point:[59]

Communication Media	Availability	Value
Individual meetings with supervisor/manager	89%	76%
Department/team meetings with managers	90%	67%
E-mail or other information technology	95%	65%
Leadership presentations to employees	82%	45%
Organization newsletter	90%	32%
Information packages/brochures	81%	27%
Information helpline	51%	22%
Employee grapevine/rumors	98%	19%
Videotape	66%	14%
Bulletin board	80%	12%
Local newspapers or television	65%	11%

Figure 6.8 *Communication Media — Availability and Value*

A U.S. pizza chain needs to communicate a major change to employees and chooses to do so by distributing a video. What will happen? Will the teenage pizza cooks don their hats and hair nets, pull up chairs within inches of the TV, fold their hands, and watch the executive with utter seriousness? Or will they laugh, mimic the talking head, crack jokes, and throw bits of pepperoni at the screen? We suggest that the only place where the first scene actually occurs is in the minds of senior executives and that the image was probably planted there by communication consultants.

In one research study, employees were asked to indicate the communication media that was most available in their organization and one they most valued. The results of this survey are shown in Figure 6.8.[60] Note the gap between the approaches that focus on glitz versus those that provide real opportunities for dialogue and discussion. Moreover, one of the valuable lessons from this survey is that change leaders need to shift their focus from simply informing toward more of a focus on winning the hearts as well as the minds of employees and managers in order to implement change successfully.

Figure 6.9 summarizes 12 excellent tips experts say are important for communicating change.[61]

Let us now focus on a useful framework for communicating change.

❏ FRAMEWORK FOR CHANGE COMMUNICATION

As we learned in Chapter 2, the change process can be viewed as progressing through three general phases: unfreezing, change, and refreezing. To review briefly, in the unfreezing stage we ready the organization for change. This often involves reducing the driving forces against change and increasing the forces for change. We do this by presenting evidence to organizational members that shows the "gap" between where we are now and where we wish to be at some future state — in effect, we provide the rationale for why the change is necessary. We endeavor to create a sense of psychological safety in people so they can cope with and be motivated to change. In the change phase, we begin the process of change; we begin to see change in the behavior of organizational members moving to the new state. This step involves shaping new behaviors, values, and attitudes. Finally, in the refreezing stage we endeavor to institutionalize the organization in the new state through reinforcement, organizational culture, policies, and procedures.

Change communication plays a key role in addressing the key issues in each phase of the change process by preparing and helping members

1. **Be proactive rather than reactive.** Communications should be planned in advance and begin early in the change process. Messages should not be offered as an afterthought or in reaction to outcries from those impacted by the change.[62]

2. **Specify the nature of the change.** Messages should be linked to the strategic purpose of the change initiative. Slogans, themes, and phrases don't define what the change is expected to achieve. Communicate specific information about how the change will affect customer satisfaction, quality, market share or sales, or productivity.

3. **Explain why.** Employees are often left in the dark about the business reasons behind the change. You may have spent lots of time studying the problem and digging out the facts, but your coworkers aren't privy to that information. In addition, share with employees the various options available and why some (or one) is better than the others. Above all, keep the communication realistic and honest.

4. **Explain the scope of the change, even if it contains bad news.** Some people are more affected by change projects than others. And that leads to lots of fear-generating speculation. Fear and uncertainty can paralyze a company. You can short-circuit fear and uncertainty with the facts. But don't sugarcoat them. If people will be laid off, be up front about that. Also explain the things that will not change. This will help anchor people.

5. **Develop a graphic representation of the change project that people can understand and hold in their heads.** It might be a flow chart of what must happen, or a graphic image of what the changed enterprise will look like. Whatever it is, keep it clear, simple, and memorable.

6. **Predict negative aspects of implementation.** There are bound to be negatives, and people should anticipate them.

7. **Explain the criteria for success and how it will be measured.** Define success clearly, and devise metrics for progress toward it. If you fail to establish clear measures for what you aim to accomplish, how would anyone know if they had moved forward? Measure progress as you move forward — and then communicate that progress.

8. **Explain how people will be rewarded for success.** People need incentive for the added work and disruptions that change requires. Be very clear about how individuals will be rewarded for progress toward change goals.

9. **Repeat, repeat, and repeat the purpose of change and actions planned.** If the initial announcement doesn't generate questions, do not assume that employees accept the need for change — they may simply be surprised, puzzled, or shocked. So follow up your initial announcement meeting with another meeting. Follow this with communications that address individual aspects of the change project. Use multiple communication channels to increase the opportunity for people to receive the whole message and internalize it.[63]

10. **Use a diverse set of communication styles that is appropriate for the audience.** Successful change programs build communications into their plans, using dedicated newsletters, events, e-mails, and stand-up presentations to keep people informed, involved, and keyed up. These communications should be honest about success and failures. If people lose trust in what they are hearing, they will tune you out.

11. **Make communication a two-way proposition.** Remember, this is a shared enterprise. So, if you are a change leader, spend at least as much time listening as telling. Your attention to these points will help keep others involved and motivated. Leaders need feedback, and the hardworking implementers need opportunities to share their learning and their concerns with leaders who listen.

12. **Be a poster-boy or poster-girl for the change program.** If you are the boss, people will have their eyes on you. They will listen to your words, but will also look for inconsistencies between your words and what you communicate through body language and behavior. Do you speak and act with genuine enthusiasm? Does your tone and manner signal confidence in the project, or do you appear to be going through the motions? Try to see yourself as others see you.

Figure 6.9   Tips for Communicating Change

Phase	Communication needs
Unfreezing	• Explaining issues, needs, rationale • Identifying and explaining directives • Identifying and explaining first few steps • Reassuring people — respect and value employees • Conveying a good job in planning the change • Informing management cadre
Changing	• Keeping employees informed of progress • Getting input as to effect of the process • Developing sophisticated knowledge among all supervisory management personnel • Challenging misconceptions • Continuing to reassure employees • Delineating and clarifying role relationships and expectations • Reaffirming senior management commitment
Refreezing	• Publicizing the success of the change • Reinforcing the vision • Recognizing success and milestones • Rewarding performance and behavior that meet the new requirements • Continuing to listen and communicate with the organization

Figure 6.10   *Phases of Organizational Change and Communication Needs*

to move through each of the three phases. The purpose of communication naturally shifts as the change initiative progresses. For example, in the unfreezing stage the focus of communication is on explaining the rationale for the change and helping people prepare for the change. As the change progresses to the changing stage, the focus shifts to informing people of progress, addressing misconceptions, and soliciting feedback. Finally, in the refreezing phase, communications shift to reinforcing the change and to keep the communication flowing. Figure 6.10 lists the general phases of organizational change and summarizes the communication needs relevant at each stage.[64]

Once we understand the communication needs, "a specific strategy for communication at each phase must be developed."[65] A sample communication strategy matrix focusing on Lewin's Phase 2, Changing, is shown in Figure 6.11. The matrix provides a structured, practical approach to devel-oping a specific communication plan for any change effort.

The first step in developing the matrix is to identify all key stakeholders who are most affected by or have an interest in the changes.[66] Once the stakeholders have been identified, their interests and needs in the change must be defined. The question most stakeholders want answered is, "What's in it for me?" Once this question is answered, the stakeholders will be more receptive to hearing about broader issues, such as the benefits of the change to the organization and themselves. Next we want to determine the objectives we hope to achieve by communicating with each stakeholder group. To this need, we must think about what key message or content will achieve the objectives and the vehicle or means used to communicate the key messages. Timing of communication must also be considered in terms of when and how often. Finally, we want to pinpoint

Example for Lewin's Phase 2: Changing

Stakeholders	Objectives	Key Messages	Vehicles	Timing	Accountability
Middle Management	+ Buy in + Understanding + New skills	+New roles +New methods + Personal impact	+Meetings with CEO/executives +Training	+ Kickoff/week 1 + Kickoff/month 1	+ CEO/executives + Training dept.
Employees	+ Buy in + Understanding +New skills	+New roles +New methods + Personal impact	+Meetings with managers +Training	+ Kickoff/week 1 + Kickoff/month 1	+ Managers + Training dept/managers
Customers	+Information + Awareness	+New methods +Service impact	+ Meetings with sales representatives	+Kickoff/week 1	+ Sales representatives
Etc.					

Source: Adapted from Galpin, T. J. (1996). The Human Side of Change. Jossey-Bass, p. 48.

Figure 6.11 Sample Communication Strategy Matrix

accountability for both the delivery and execution of the communication.

In creating this "Communication Plan," you want to answer the following questions:[67]

1. Who are the stakeholders in the change?

2. What objectives do you want to accomplish by communicating with each of the stakeholders?

3. What are the key messages you want to send to each stakeholder to accomplish objectives?

4. What communication vehicles do you want to use for each stakeholder?

5. At what frequency should the messages be delivered?

6. Who will be accountable for developing and delivering the messages?

A useful framework for managing the communication through the phases of change is described next. We begin with an overview of the Johari Window concept and conclude by looking at a change communication framework.

Johari Window[68]

The Johari Window is a useful paradigm for helping change leaders and organizations understand how an open, two-way communication process can enhance the effectiveness of any change program. The Johari Window was developed by psychologists Joseph Luft and Harry Ingham as part of their research on interpersonal communication and group dynamics.[69] In short, the framework "allows individuals to assess how they present and how they absorb the information necessary to create effective interpersonal relationships."[70]

The model is depicted in Figure 6.12 as a two-dimensional grid reflecting the interaction of two key variables — self and others in terms of personal awareness. The grid contains four quadrants that divide personal awareness into four different types: open, hidden, blind, and unknown. To understand better the implications of the Johari Window for creating effective organizational communication, we must first understand the four quadrants in the grid and their relationship to interpersonal effectiveness.

Quadrant I — the arena — denotes the section of the framework that encompasses mutual understanding and shared information. The underlying concept of the Johari Window is that when information is mutually held, productivity and effectiveness in individual relationships are increased. Thus, this known-by-others and known-by-oneself region is the most productive area for people to operate in. The larger the area, the more effective, productive, and mutually beneficial a relationship becomes.

To the extent you can make people more aware of information you have and they do not, you enlarge the arena and reduce the façade. This is the *Exposure* axis of the model where information is made more open and transparent. Likewise by engaging in two-way communication with the target(s) of change using vehicles such as employee surveys, change readiness assessments, and open discussion, we can learn more about what others know. This is the Feedback axis of the model. As we seek and actively listen to feedback from others, the arena expands to the right and shrinks the blindspot.

Consider this insight from Lawrence Bosidy of AlliedSignal in a 1995 *Harvard Business Review* interview where he described his strategy when he took over the troubled supplier of aerospace systems, automobile parts, and chemical products:[72]

In the first 60 days, I talked to probably 5,000 employees. . . . I would stand on a loading dock and speak to people and answer their questions. We talked about what was wrong and what we should do about it. As we talked, it became clear to me that there hadn't been a good top-down enunciation of the company's problem. I knew intuitively that I needed support at the bottom right from the outset. Go to the people and tell them what's wrong. And they knew. It's remarkable how many people know what's really going on in their company. I think it's important to try to get effective interaction with everybody in the company, to involve everyone.

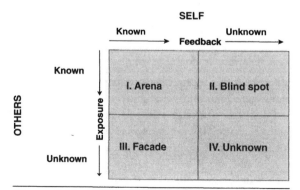

Figure 6.12   *The Johari Window[71]*

Quadrant II — is the area known as the blind-spot. This area of the grid represents the information that is known by others but not by oneself. The blindspot is considered to be a handicap. It is a handicap because it is unlikely we will understand the reactions and perceptions of others if we do not know the information upon which those reactions and perceptions are based. Likewise, others have an advantage over us because they know what is causing their reactions and perceptions, whereas we are unaware of the cause.

Quadrant III — the facade — is an area that hinders interpersonal effectiveness because exchange of information favors oneself. People protect themselves by hiding information. They hide information for many reasons. They may fear that the information could be used against them. Or they may have a desire for power that is characterized by keeping important information back for future use. Or they may just be apathetic; many people feel it is just too much effort to share information.

Quadrant IV — the unknown — is the area of the grid where information that is unknown by both ourselves and by others exists. This the area where the most creativity could potentially be generated if both parties involved are willing to explore together to locate "new" information.

The concept underpinning he Johari Window — that expanding the arena, the information known to oneself and to others, will enhance interpersonal relationships — can be applied to organizational change communication. For example, when undertaking a change process many senior leaders attempt to keep information hidden from stakeholders (those people both inside and outside the organization who are likely to be affected by or interested in the changes). The same reasons why individuals keep information hidden from others in personal relationships — fear, power, or apathy apply. This kind of behavior leads to a smaller organizational arena and a larger organizational façade. An expanded organizational façade favors the initiators of a change process and puts the rest of the organization at a disadvantage, often leading to mistrust, dislike, and even acting out against the change process. Likewise, an organizational blindspot is often created when the initiators of a change process are unaware of what others in the organization are thinking, feeling, and doing in relations to change.

When transferred from interpersonal to organizational relationships, the Johari Window has key implications for enhancing a change process through improved communication. The two axes of the Johari Window — feedback and exposure — are the enablers to create more effective interpersonal interactions and more effective organizational communications. This can be done by increasing exposure by providing more information to others, thus expanding the size of the arena along the vertical axis of the grid. Likewise, by receiving and assimilating more feedback, organizations can expand the size of the arena along the horizontal axis.

Communication Framework

To further define a process for expanding the organizational arena, we introduce a framework for change communication. The model contains two key change communication elements that create psychological readiness for change and the motivation to adopt and institutionalize the change. These elements include five key message domains and three communication strategies (see Figure 6.13).[73]

Key message components. The five message components include discrepancy, efficacy, appropriateness, principal support, and personal valence. Use of these message components in change communication is hypothesized to influence people's attitudes and feelings toward change. Figure 6.14 defines each message component in the model.

Communication strategies. Any change communication message should include each of the five message domains. To convey the message to stakeholders, we have "three basic communication strategies" to consider: (1) persuasive communication (direct communication efforts), (2) active participation (involving people), and (3) management of information. With persuasive communication, the sender is using mainly verbal means such as speeches and written messages to convey the five message domains directly to the receiver. Active participation is considered the most potent of the three strategies because of the powerful benefits associated with involvement in the change process. Finally, management of information involves using multiple information sources (internal and external) to help convey each of the message domains.

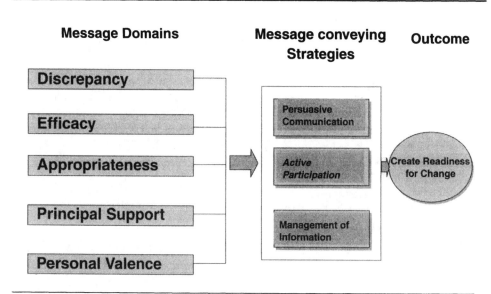

Figure 6.13   A Change Communication Framework

In preparing a change communication strategy, it's important to keep these five planning tips in mind.[74]

1. Create a structured plan for communicating key messages; implement, measure results and fine tune as required.

2. Communicate important change messages face-to-face; two-way communication is most effective.

3. Make first-line supervisors "privileged" receivers and communicators of key messages (they have the most power to impact front-line employees).

4. Test for understanding with a small sample audience before you offer your messages to a larger audience (make sure it's in a language appropriate for everyone at every level of your organization).

5. However many times and in however many different ways you think you have communicated your message — double it. "When you're sick of communicating, you're half way there."

Message Domain	Description
Discrepancy	Help individuals understand the need for the change; why the current state of affairs is not acceptable and what would happen if no change occurs.
Efficacy	Instilling confidence in individuals that they have the ability and skills needed to succeed in the proposed change
Appropriateness	Convincing individuals of the appropriateness of a change. If unable to win the minds and hearts of others, then the appropriateness of the change should be reconsidered, normal resistance to change notwithstanding.
Principal Support	Demonstrate that the requisite resources and commitment are in place to see the change to institutionalization.
Personal Valence	Help individuals understand how the change impacts them personally and how they fit into the new scheme of things. What role will people play in the journey?

Figure 6.14   Five Message Components

In deploying any of the three communication strategies, we should also consider the use of informal networks in the communication plan.

❏ USE OF INFORMAL NETWORKS

We know that organizations communicate via many channels — both formal and informal. Informal patterns of communication relate to who actually talks to whom within and outside and organizational unit. The importance of informal communication channels in communicating change is an important area we should not overlook. In her book, *The Change Monster*, Jeanie Duck provides an excellent treatment of using informal organizational networks in managing change communication.[75]

Most of the everyday work of an organization gets done primarily through the informal networks — a labyrinth of conversations between individuals and among groups who talk with each other on the telephone, via e-mail, and in ad hoc meetings and hallway chats. These networks get built over time. Each individual creates relationships with other individuals with whom they work, share information, and ideally, trust.

In many change initiatives, particularly mergers and reorganizations, these informal networks are disrupted or even destroyed. Susan in marketing can no longer call Astrid in legal when she has a copyright question because Astrid has been laid off. Bill in manufacturing can no longer meet with Joerg in engineering, because Joerg's group has been integrated with three other engineering groups and moved to a central facility 2,000 miles away. Many of the 'go-to-guys' are gone and many of the 'life-lines' have been severed. I talked with a retiree from General Motors who was convinced that this was one of the problems with GM. 'After repeated layoffs and early retirement programs, all the informal knowledge had walked out the door. The old networks had been obliterated and now there was no one left who could tell the others how to get stuff done.'

When informal networks are disrupted, it takes longer for people to accomplish their work because they must spend more time figuring out whom to talk to about what, and rebuilding their informal networks. When informal networks are functioning well, news can travel with lightning speed through a company, and people know which sources to trust and which to take with a grain of salt. But when networks are disrupted, there are gaps between groups and individuals. People get messages from other people whom they don't know well; they may not be sure how to interpret them. Was he kidding? Was she exaggerating? During times of change, when people are hungry for news, alarmists have a field day; rumors and misinformation

proliferate. Leaders who learn how to use informal networks well can gain a huge advantage.

In addition to understanding how informal networks can be helpful in communicating change, we also should consider if people are getting the change communication message? Consider the following litmus test for change communication.

❏ CHANGE COMMUNICATION LITMUS TEST

How do you know when people understand and are internalizing the change communication message? Look for these signs:[76]

- People talk about "what we need to do," versus "what they're doing to us."
- People suggest ideas to deal with the problem or opportunity.
- People talk about why this change is critical to them. They explicitly address the "what's in it for me?" question.

Consider the words of Nestle CEO Peter Brabeck in a 2001 interview in *Harvard Business Review* where he responded to a question regarding how he knows if his change message has permeated the organization:

I talk to the lowest levels of collaborators. This can be an informal chat with the employee who serves coffee here on the fifth floor. Or it can be more regular communication than that. Once a month, I sit with 12 or 14 people, and we have lunch. Their bosses are not there. We talk frankly about how their work is going, whether they are getting all the information they need, and whether they have questions about where the organization is heading.[77]

A real-world example of how the World Bank effectively managed the communication of a large-scale change initiative follows.

❏ CHANGE COMMUNICATION EXAMPLE[78]

In 1988 World Bank, a global organization with more than 100 offices and more than 12,000 workers, was full-swing into an institution-wide change initiative that would unite 60-plus systems into a single framework. The effort took advantage of the best of modern technology, literally bringing the organization into the 21st century. The changeover to the new system occurred just six short months before January 2000, with the implementation spilling well into the following year. It was a massive effort that touched everyone in the organization. It required tremendous changes in the ways people work.

Seth Kahan was charged with managing the communications for this change initiative. With a seven-person staff he managed a global operation that included promptly delivering paper and electronic news to every office around the world, providing the resources for hundreds of meetings between staff and managers, coordinating global events, and engaging the president and steering committee in visible roles.

Today, the World Bank relies on the integrated system that was implemented. It connects more than 100 country offices and operates in real time. In his role as communications manager for this project, Kahan shares 12 core principles that made the program a success. And while these 12 points may not apply precisely to other situations, the basic principle makes a significant contribution to a well-managed change communication program in any organization.

Change Communication Core Principles

1. The guiding principle of our communications program was to **avoid surprising people**. We began with the assumption that every employee wants to carry on with his or her work as the change initiative successfully takes the organization into a new era of productivity. We knew our folks didn't have time to explore every detail of our program.

   We made sure staff had easy access to what they needed to know. This meant understanding the different ways our system would interact with people and designing communications to support our varied target audiences. Most importantly, it meant taking a proactive role to reach staff before their behavior needed changing. We began heavy publicity months before the change went live.

2. It is of course important to have **full support from senior management**. But we went further. We asked our senior managers to take an active role in preparing staff for the change. This included several video-stream appearances of senior staff that were carried to all offices around the world. "Town halls" were held. E-mails were sent from the top.

Individual members of the steering committee hosted question-and-answer sessions with groups that would be affected by the new business processes.

Our senior people were more than nominally involved. As a result, they not only gave their visible support but also learned a great deal about the coming changes themselves. This gave great credibility to our effort; their behavior served as effective models as the organization went through with the transformation.

3. Our communications team **brought in an outside communications professional** who had five years of relevant experience inside the organization as well as more than 20 years as a professional in the field of IC. She was able to make snap judgments when we were under pressure, allowing us to respond effectively in difficult and time-sensitive situations.

   She worked full-time alongside the communications team, pitching in as needed and giving guidance at all levels of our operation. She also brought her professional network of vendors to our service. She had the necessary expertise to quickly develop materials that were adequate to accomplish our campaign's objectives.

4. As soon as the communications team was formed, we created a project plan outlining all of our proposed activities. This **communications action plan was ratified by the leadership**, ensuring that their needs were being met and establishing common expectations.

   From this point forward, we had clear guiding principles and an established framework for carrying out our work. We reviewed it with the project leadership in a detailed presentation, allotting time for discussion and amendment. At the conclusion of this meeting, everyone was in sync regarding expectations and implementation. This allowed our team to move speedily toward achieving our results, unimpeded by constant review.

5. At the conclusion of our action plan, we presented a line-item budget that was discussed, improved, and approved by leadership. This **secure, pre-approved budget** enabled us to plan strategically and move forward unhampered.

6. **The communications team aligned 100% with change management.** Our program was nothing if not an instrument for change. We joined lockstep with the change management leadership, as demonstrated when we volunteered to report directly to the organization's change management lead.

7. A **streamlined approval process** allowed us to respond quickly to changing circumstances. We arranged to answer to one person, the change management lead, who agreed to provide a 24-hour turnaround on all decisions; he often approved them or offered alternative guidance within 2–3 hours. This enabled our group to respond promptly and consistently to the organization's needs and helped us establish a reputation of dependability and professionalism.

8. We established **a clear graphic identity that staff enjoyed**. Our mouse pads, polo shirts, posters, and all other giveaways were very much in demand. We made it easy for people to visibly demonstrate their support by choosing a look and feel that they wanted to be associated with.

9. We used **multiple media in synchronized releases** to create impact. In the communications field, this is known as making a "splash." Any one media reaches only 20–40% of employees. By using different types of media (e.g., Web, e-mail, posters, meetings with managers, and newsletters) simultaneously, we reached the majority of staff all at once.

10. We did **surveys to study our own effectiveness**. We were interested in finding out which media were most effective. Our top three media were face-to-face meetings, weekly hard-copy newsletters, and our "champions" — a selection of staff who ensured that the change initiative was successful in their units. According to our survey each of these media reached 4 out of 10 staff. When these were combined with the other outreach mechanisms, we reached 80% of our staff. This was enough to accomplish our communication goals, effectively supporting the change initiative. Our other media included Dr. Hammer's presentations, video dissemination, Web sites, existing paper and electronic publications, and CD-ROMs.

11. **I attended all project manager and steering committee meetings for the entire program**. Thus, the communications team was "in the loop" and "up to the minute" on the needs of the project. This was essential, since we were the first point of contact when anyone in the organization wanted to know something about the program.

12. **Extensive team building within the communications team** enabled us to respond quickly and effectively to changes in direction. We worked closely together, often while under pressure, for the duration of the project. We each had to help each other, and responsibilities between members of our team often blurred. We took the time to retreat together and get to know each other personally and also participated in team-building activities. This gave us the necessary cohesion and flexibility to deliver high results consistently over time.

As we see in the preceding example, communication plays a vital role in facilitating organizational change by helping those involved with the change understand what is changing and why. Where change leaders get into trouble is when they underestimate the power of vision and don't pay enough attention to how they communicate the rationale, the progress and the impact of the change.[79] To ignore the importance of change communication is to seriously undermine the potential success of the change initiative. "Ineffective communications can sow dissension, heighten anxiety and confusion, alienate key individuals or groups, and damage management's credibility with critical audiences both inside and outside the organization."[80]

In an article in *Harvard Business Review* focused on reaching and changing frontline employees, the authors make this excellent point:

Not communicating to employees during major organizational change is the worst mistake a company can make. Consider the conclusions from three important studies on communication during mergers and acquisitions: In periods of high stress and uncertainty, people fill communication voids with rumors; rumors end up attributing the worst possible motives to those in control; and communication lowers employees' stress and anxiety even when the news is bad. In other words, uncertainty is more painful than bad news.[81]

And as we've emphasized in this chapter, developing a sound vision is paramount in guiding any change program. Vision coupled with a well-planned blueprint for communication is a key ingredient to ensure the change process reaches fruition. This helps make certain we "align every thought, action and behavior (the manifestations of an organization's culture) with the clearly defined and communicated vision."[82] And in the end, it saves the company time, money, and resources and allows extraordinary things to happen.[83]

❑ READING AND CASE

The following reading and case reinforce the concepts and theories discussed in the chapter as well as provide an opportunity to apply the learning to real-world situations.

Reading

6-1: Gavin, D. A., & Roberto, M. A. (2005, February). "Change Through Persuasion," *Harvard Business Review*, pp. 104–112.

Focus: The reading contributes to enhancing our understanding how to communicate the need for change to all members of an organization and to ensure that all are committed to the needed change effort. The authors introduce a four-part process change leaders can use to persuade the workforce to embrace and execute needed change.

Questions

1. Do you agree with the authors that leaders can make change happen only if they have a coherent strategy for persuasion?
2. Referring to the authors' four-part persuasion model, briefly describe each element of the persuasion process. Would you add anything else to the model?
3. Focusing on the case study in the article, evaluate the CEO's change effort in applying the persuasion model. Provide at least one example to illustrate each phase of the process.
4. Thinking of a change initiative that you personally participated in, provide an example to illustrate how any one of the six dysfunctional routines emerged as a barrier to change.

5. What in your opinion are some pitfalls that could reduce the effectiveness of a change communication plan?
6. What is the most important lesson you personally took away from this reading?

Linkage to Chapter

1. Reinforces the importance of change communication in managing change.
2. Builds on the communication framework introduced in the chapter.

Case

6-1: *Charlotte Beers at Ogilvy & Mather Worldwide (A)*. Harvard Business School, Sackley, Case 9–495–031.

Focus: The case study selected for this chapter examines Charlotte Beers actions on assuming leadership at O&M Worldwide — the world's sixth largest advertising agency — during a period of rapid industry change and organizational crisis. The case focuses on how Beers, O&M's first outsider CEO, engages and leads a senior team through a vision formulation process. It chronicles closely the debates among senior executives as they struggle to reconcile creative, strategic, global, and local priorities. Sixteen months later, with a vision statement agreed upon, Beers faces a series of implementation problems. Turnaround has begun, but internal constituencies remain confused about or skeptical of the vision. As well, organizational structures and systems are not yet aligned with the firm's new direction.

Questions

1. What is Beers trying to accomplish as CEO of Ogilvy & Mather Worldwide?
2. What is your assessment of the vision?
3. What is your assessment of the process Beers and her team went through to create the vision?
4. What are the key challenges facing Beers at the end of the case?

Linkage to Chapter

1. In managing organizational change, we see the value of formulating a vision or new direction.
2. The need for change communication to involve, motivate, commit, and lead stakeholders in the new direction is highlighted.

❏ ENDNOTES

1. Mercer Delta Consulting (2000). Strategic Communication: A Key To Implementing Organizational Change. Retrieved December 27, 2004, from http://www.mercerdelta.com/PDFs/insights/Strategic_Communication.pdf

2. Hay Insight Selections (2005, July). *What we have here is a need to communicate.* Section 9. Retrieved August 9, 2005, from http://www.haygroup.com/Library/Newsletters/Hay_Insight_Selections.asp

3. Beer, M. (2003). *Harvard Business Essentials: Managing Change and Transition.* Harvard Business School Press, p. 60.

4. D'Aprix, op. cit., p. 3.

5. Duck, J. D. (2001). The change monster. *Crown Business*, p. 27.

6. Tichy, N. M., & Charan, R. (1995, March–April). The CEO as coach: An interview with AlliedSignal's Lawrence A. Bossidy. *Harvard Business Review*, p. 70.

7. Armenakis, A. A., & Harris, S. G. (2002). Crafting a change message to create transformational readiness. *Journal of Organizational Change Management*, Vol. 15 No. 2, p. 169.

8. Eccles, T. (1994). *Succeeding with Change.* London: McGraw-Hill Book Co., p. 158.

9. Duck, op. cit., p. 28.

10. D'Aprix, R. (1996). *Communicating for Change.* Jossey-Bass, p. 3.

11. Ibid, p. 4.

12. Ibid, p. 4.

13. Ibid, p. 5.

14. Duck, op. cit., p. 143.

15. Paul, L. G. (2004, December 1). *CIO Magazine.* Retrieved December 17, 2004, from http://www.cio.com/archive/120104/change.html

16. Bridges, W. (1991). *Managing Transitions: Making the Most of Change.* Addison-Wesley Publishing Co., pp. 27–28.

17. Ibid.

18. Extracted from Mercer Delta Consulting (2000). *Transition Leadership: A Guide to Leading Change Initiatives.* Retrieved October 6, 2005, from http://www.mercerdelta.com/organizational_consulting/PDFs/insights/ins_Transition_Leadership.pdf

19. Goodman, J., & Truss, C. (2004). The medium and the message: Communicating effectively during a major change initiative. *Journal of Change Management*, Vol. 4, No. 3, p. 26.

20. Senge, P. M., et al. (1999). The dance of change. *Currency Doubleday*, p. 530.

21. Knowling, R. (2002, Fall). Why vision matters. *Leader to Leader.* Retrieved November 26, 2004, from http://www.pfdf.org/leaderbooks/l2l/fall2000/knowling.html

22. Kaplan, R. S., & Norton, D. P. (1996). *The Balanced Scorecard.* Harvard Business School Press, p. 254.

23. Senge, P. M. (1990). The fifth discipline. *Currency Doubleday*, p. 208.

24. Kiley, D. (2006, January 20). Ford's Deep Ditch. *BusinessWeek Online.* Retrieved January 23, 2006 from http://www.businessweek.com/bwdaily/dnflash/jan2006/nf20060120_6550_db016.htm

25. Oakley, E., & Krug, D. (1991). *Enlightened Leadership.* Simon & Schuster, p. 175.

26. Quoted in Duck, op. cit., p. 51.

27. Baum, D. (2000). *Lightning in a Bottle: Proven Lessons for Leading Change.* Chicago: Dearborn, p. 129.

28. Coleman, D., Boyatzis, & McKee, A. (2002). *Primal Leadership.* Boston: Harvard Business School Press.

29. Rothenberg, R. (2004, Winter). Kenneth W. Freeman: The thought leader interview. *Strategy & Business* Retrieved December 3, 2004, from http://www.strategy-business.com/press/article/04410?tid=230&pg=all

30. Blanchard, K., & Soner, J. (2004, Winter). *The Vision Thing: Without It You'll Never Be a World-Class Organization.* Retrieved February 5, 2005, from http://www.pfdf.org/leaderbooks/l2l/winter2004/blanchardandstoner.html

31. Kotter, J. P. (1995, March–April). Why transformation efforts fail. *Harvard Business Review*, p. 59.

32. Kotter, J. P. (1996). *Leading Change.* Harvard Business School Press, pp. 4–16.

33. Ibid, p. 7.

34. Huggett, J. F. *When Culture Resists Change.* Retrieved September 24, 2005, from http://www.achieveglobal.com/link_pdf/whncultr.pdf

35. Kotter (1995), op. cit., p. 63.

36. Handy, C. (1989). *The Age of Unreason. Boston Harvard Business School Press.* p. 135.

37. Duck, op. cit., p. 93.

38. Lucas, J. R. (1998). Anatomy of a vision statement. *Management Review*, Vol. 87 No. 2, pp. 24–25.

39. Goleman, D., et al. (2002). *Primal Leadership.* Boston: HBSP, pp. 221–22.

40. Goleman, D., et al. (2002). op. cit., p. 221.

41. Extracted from Hughes, R. L., & Beatty, K. C. (2005). *Becoming a Strategic Leader.* San Francisco: Jossey-Bass, p. 50.

42. Extracted from Latham, J. R. (1995, April). Visioning: The concept, trilogy, and process. *Quality Progress*, p. 65.

43. Kotter (1996). op. cit., p. 72.

44. Latham, op. cit., p. 69.

45. Covey, S. R. (1989). *The 7 Habits of Highly Effective People.* New York. NY: Simon & Shuster, p. 99.

46. Gelinas, M. V., & James, R. G. (1998). *Collaborative Change.* Jossey-Bass, p. 12.

47. Holland & Davis, L. L. C. (1997, June). *Clarity of Vision: Wow, Have We Got A Story to Tell!* Retrieved December 4, 2004, from http://www.hdinc.com/hotTopics/hot_topic_6–97.html

48. Ibid.
49. Slater, R. (1999). *Jack Welch and the GE Way.* McGraw-Hill, p. 139.
50. Menkes, J. (2005). *Executive Intelligence.* Collins, p. 175.
51. Jick, T. D. (2001). Vision is 10%, implementation is the rest. *Business Strategy Review,* Vol. 12, No 4, p. 38.
52. Jick, T. D. (2001). Vision is 10%, implementation is the rest. *Business Strategy Review,* Vol. 12, No 4, p. 38.
53. U.S. Department of Commerce National Oceanic and Atmospheric Administration (2005). *New Priorities for the 21st Cenbtury — NOAA's Strategic Plan Updated for FY2006 – FY 2011.* Retrieved February 19, 2007 from http://www.spo.noaa.gov/noaastratplanning.htm.
54. Kotter, J. P., & Cohen, D. S. (2002). *The Heart of Change.* Harvard Business School Press, p. 83.
55. Carr, D. K., Hard, K. J., & Trahant, W. J. (1996). *Managing The Change Process.* Mc-Graw Hill, p. 123.
56. Duck, op. cit., p. 138.
57. Larkin, T. J., & Larkin, S. (1996, May-June). Reaching and changing frontline employees. *Harvard Business Review,* p. 101.
58. Duck, op. cit., p. 211.
59. Larkin, T. J., & Larkin, S. op. cit., p. 97.
60. Greenbaum, K. B., Jackson, D. H., & McKeon, N. I. (1998, Spring). "Communicating for a Change." *Viewpoint.* Retrieved December 24, 2004, from http://www.mmc.com/views2/98spr.greenbaum.shtml.
61. Extracted from Saunders, R. (1999, August). Communicating change. *Harvard Management Communication Letter,* Vol. 2, No. 8.
62. Galpin, T. J. (1996). *The Human Side of Change.* Jossey-Bass, p. 40.
63. Ibid.
64. Adapted from Klein, S. M. (1996). A management communication strategy for change. *Journal of Organizational Change Management,* Vol. 9, No. 2, p. 37.
65. Galpin, T. J. (1996). *The Human Side of Change.* Jossey-Bass, p. 47.
66. This section extracted from Galpin, T. J. (1996). *The Human Side of Change.* Jossey-Bass, pp. 47–50.
67. Ibid, pp., 125–26.
68. This section relies heavily on and is extracted from the work of Galpin, T. J. (1996). *The Human Side of Change.* Jossey-Bass, pp. 35–37.
69. Luft, J., & Ingham, H. (1984). *Group Process: An Introduction to Group Dynamics.* Mountain View, CA: Mayfield.
70. Galpin, T. J. (1996). *The Human Side of Change.* Jossey-Bass, pp. 33–34.
71. Adapted from Luft, J. (1984). *Group Process: An Introduction to Group Dynamics.* Mayfield Publishing Company, p. 60.
72. Tichy, & Charan, op, cit., p. 70.
73. Armenakis, A. A., & Harris, S. G. (2002). op. cit.
74. Extracted from Holland & Davis Management Consulting Services. Retrieved December 4, 2004, from http://www.hdinc.com/faqs/faq_change_-man_4.html
75. Extracted from Duck, op. cit., pp. 185–189.
76. Ibid, p. 24.
77. Wetlaufer, S. (2001, February). The business case against revolution: An interview with Nestle's Peter Brabeck. *Harvard Business Review,* p. 119.
78. Extracted from Kahan, S. (2002, June). *Communicating Change.* Retrieved 27 August, 2005, from http://www.centeronline.org/knowledge/article.cfm?ID=1857&ContentProfileID=129172&Action=searching
79. Klein, op. cit.
80. Mercer Delta Consulting, op. cit.
81. Larkin, T. J., & Larkin, S., op. cit, p. 97.
82. Huggett, J. F. *When Culture Resists Change.* Retrieved September 24, 2005, from http://www.achieveglobal.com/link_pdf/whncultr.pdf
83. Hamm, J. (2006, May). The five messages leaders must manage. *Harvard Business Review,* p. 123.

Change
Through Persuasion

by David A. Garvin and
Michael A. Roberto

Leaders can make change happen only if they have a coherent strategy for persuasion. The impressive turnaround at a world-renowned teaching hospital shows how to plan a change campaign— and carry it out.

FACED WITH THE NEED for massive change, most managers respond predictably. They revamp the organization's strategy, then round up the usual set of suspects—people, pay, and processes—shifting around staff, realigning incentives, and rooting out inefficiencies. They then wait patiently for performance to improve, only to be bitterly disappointed. For some reason, the right things still don't happen.

Why is change so hard? First of all, most people are reluctant to alter their habits. What worked in the past is good enough; in the absence of a dire threat, employees will keep doing what they've always done. And when an

104   HARVARD BUSINESS REVIEW

organization has had a succession of leaders, resistance to change is even stronger. A legacy of disappointment and distrust creates an environment in which employees automatically condemn the next turnaround champion to failure, assuming that he or she is "Just like all the others." Calls for sacrifice and self-discipline are met with cynicism, skepticism, and knee-jerk resistance.

Our research into organizational transformation has involved settings as diverse as multinational corporations, government agencies, nonprofits, and high-performing teams like mountaineering expeditions and firefighting crews. We've found that for change to stick, leaders must design and run an effective persuasion campaign — one that begins weeks or months before the actual turnaround plan is set in concrete. Managers must perform significant work up front to ensure that employees will actually listen to tough messages, question old assumptions, and consider new ways of working. This means taking a series of deliberate

(This is a particularly difficult challenge when years of persistent problems have been accompanied by few changes in the status quo.) Turnaround leaders must also gain trust by demonstrating through word and deed that they are the right leaders for the job and must convince employees that theirs is the correct plan for moving forward.

Accomplishing all this calls for a four-part communications strategy. Prior to announcing a policy or issuing a set of instructions, leaders need to set the stage for acceptance. At the time of delivery, they must create the frame through which information and messages are interpreted. As time passes, they must manage the mood so that employees' emotional states support implementation and follow-through. And at critical intervals, they must provide reinforcement to ensure that the desired changes take hold without backsliding.

In the pages that follow, we describe this process in more detail, drawing on the example of the turnaround of Beth Israel Deaconess Medical

Like a political campaign, a persuasion campaign is largely one of differentiation from the past.

but subtle steps to recast employees' prevailing views and create a new context for action. Such a shaping process must be actively managed during the first few months of a turnaround, when uncertainty is high and setbacks are inevitable. Otherwise, there is little hope for sustained improvement.

Like a political campaign, a persuasion campaign is largely one of differentiation from the past. To the typical change-averse employee, all restructuring plans look alike. The trick for turnaround leaders is to show employees precisely how their plans differ from their predecessors[1]. They must convince people that the organization is truly on its deathbed — or, at the very least, that radical changes are required if it is to survive and thrive.

David A. Garvin (dgarvin@)hhs.edu) is the C Roland Christensen Professor of Business Administration at Harvard Business School in Boston. Michael A, Roberto (mroberto@hbs.edu) ban assistant professor if business administration at Harvard Business School Their multimedia case study based on the turnaround at Beth Israel Deaconess Medical Center can be found at http://bethisrael.hbsp.Harvard.edu.

Center (BIDMC) in Boston. Paul Levy, who became CEO in early 2002, managed to bring the failing hospital back from the brink of ruin. We had ringside seats during the first six months of the turnaround. Levy agreed to hold videotaped interviews with us every two to four weeks during that period as we prepared a case study describing his efforts. He also gave us access to his daily calendar, as well as to assorted e-mail correspondence and internal memorandums and reports. From this wealth of data, we were able to track the change process as it unfolded, without the usual biases and distortions that come from 20/20 hindsight. The story of how Levy tilled the soil for change provides lessons for any CEO in a turnaround situation.

❏ SETTING THE STAGE

Paul Levy was an unlikely candidate to run BIDMC. He was not a doctor and had never managed a hospital, though he had previously served as the executive dean for administration at Harvard

Medical School. His claim to fame was his role as the architect of the Boston Harbor Cleanup, a multibillion-dollar pollution-control project that he had led several years earlier. (Based on this experience, Levy identified a common yet insidiously destructive organizational dynamic that causes dedicated teams to operate in counterproductive ways, which he described in "The Nut Island Effect: When Good Teams Go Wrong," March 2001.) Six years after completing the Boston Harbor project, Levy approached the BIDMC board and applied for the job of cleaning up the troubled hospital.

Despite his lack of hospital management experience, Levy was appealing to the board. The Boston Harbor Cleanup was a difficult, highly visible change effort that required deft political and managerial skills. Levy had stood firm in the face of tough negotiations and often-heated public resistance and had instilled accountability in city and state agencies. He was also a known quantity to the board, having served on a BIDMC steering committee formed by the board chairman in 2001.

Levy saw the prospective job as one of public service, BIDMC was the product of a difficult 1996 merger between two hospitals — Beth Israel and Deaconess — each of which had distinguished reputations, several best-in-the-world departments and specializations, and deeply devoted staffs. The problems began after the merger. A misguided focus on clinical practice rather than backroom integration, a failure to cut costs, and the repeated inability to execute plans and adapt to changing conditions in the health care marketplace all contributed to BIDMC's dismal performance.

By the time the board settled on Levy, affairs at BIDMC had reached the nadir. The hospital was losing $50 million a year. Relations between the administration and medical staff were strained, as were those between management and the board of directors. Employees felt demoralized, having witnessed the rapid decline in their institution's once-legendary status and the disappointing failure of its past leaders A critical study was conducted by the Hunter Group, a leading health-care consulting firm. The report, detailing the dire conditions at

the hospital and the changes needed to turn things around, had been completed but not yet released. Meanwhile, the state attorney general, who was responsible for overseeing charitable trusts, had put pressure on the board to sell the failing BIDMC to a for-profit institution.

Like many CEOs recruited to fix a difficult situation, Levy's first task was to gain a mandate for the changes ahead. He also recognized that crucial negotiations were best conducted before he took the job, when his leverage was greatest, rather than after taking the reins. In particular, he moved to secure the cooperation of the hospital board by flatly stating his conditions for employment. He told the directors, for example, that should they hire him, they could no longer interfere in day-to-day management decisions. In his second and third meetings with the board's search committee, Levy laid out his timetable and intentions. He insisted that the board decide on his appointment quickly so that he could be on the job before the release of the Hunter report. He told the committee that he intended to push for a smaller, more effective group of directors. Though the conditions were some-what unusual, the board was convinced that Levy had the experience to lead a successful turnaround, and they accepted his terms. Levy went to work on January 7, 2002.

The next task was to set the stage with the hospital staff. Levy was convinced that the employ-ees, hungry for a turnaround, would do their best to cooperate with him if he could emulate and embody the core values of the hospital culture, rather than impose his personal values. He chose to act as the managerial equivalent of a good doctor — that is, as one who, in dealing with a very ill patient, delivers both the bad news and the chances of success honestly and imparts a realistic sense of hope, without sugar coating.

Like any leader facing a turnaround, Levy also knew he had to develop a bold message that pro-vided compelling reasons to do things differently and then cast that message in capital letters to signal the arrival of a new order. To give his message teeth, he linked it to an implicit threat. Taking his cue from his private discussions with the state attorney gen-eral, whom he had persuaded to keep the hospital open for the time being, Levy chose to publicize the very real possibility the hospital would be sold. While he realized he risked frightening the staff and the patients with this bad news, he believed that a strong wake-up call was necessary to get employ-ees to face up to the situation.

During his first morning on the job, Levy delivered an all-hands-on-deck e-mail to the staff. The memo contained four broad messages. It opened with the good news, pointing out that the organization had much to be proud of ("This is a wonderful institution, representing the very best in academic medicine: exemplary patient care, extraordinary research, and fine teaching"). Second, Levy noted that the threat of sale was real ("This is our last chance"). Third, he signaled the kinds of actions employees could expect him to take ("There will be a reduction in staff"). And finally, he described the open man-agement style he would adopt. He would manage by walking around — lunching with staff in the cafeteria, having impromptu conversations in the hallways, talking with employees at every opportunity to discover their concerns. He would communicate directly with employees through e-mail rather than through intermediaries. He also noted that the Hunter report would be posted on the hospital intranet, where all employees

would have the opportunity to review its recom-mendations and submit comments for the final turnaround plan. The direct, open tone of the e-mail memo signaled exactly how Levy's man-agement style would differ from that of his pre-decessors.

In the afternoon, he disclosed BIDMC's situa-tion in interviews with the *Boston Globe* and the *Boston Herald*, the city's two major newspapers. He told reporters the same thing he had told the hospital's employees: that, in the absence of a turnaround, the hospital would be sold to a for-profit chain and would therefore lose its status as a Harvard teaching hospital. Staving off a sale would require tough measures, including the laying off of anywhere from 500 to 700 employees. Levy insisted that there would be no nursing layoffs, in keeping with the hospital's core values of high-quality patient care. The newspaper reports, together with the memo circulated that morning, served to immediately reset employee expectations while dramatically increasing staff cooperation and will-ingness to accept whatever new initiatives might prove necessary to the hospital's survival.

Two days later, the critical Hunter report came out and was circulated via the hospital's intranet. Because the report had been produced by an objective third party, employees were open to its unvarnished, warts-and-all view of the hospital's current predicament. The facts were stark, and the staff could no longer claim ignorance. Levy received, and personally responded to, more than 300 e-mail suggestions for improvement in response to the report, many of which he later included in the turnaround plan.

❏ CREATING THE FRAME

Once the stage has been set for acceptance, effective leaders need to help employees interpret proposals for change. Complex plans can be interpreted in any number of ways; not all of them ensure acceptance and favorable outcomes. Skilled leaders therefore use "frames" to provide context and shape perspec-tive for new proposals and plans. By framing the issues, leaders help people digest ideas in particular ways. A frame can take many forms: It can be a company wide presentation that prepares employ-ees before an unexpected change, for example, or a radio interview that provides context following an unsettling layoff.

Dysfunctional Routines

SIX WAYS TO STOP CHANGE IN ITS TRACKS

Just as people are creatures of habit, organizations thrive on routines. Management teams, for example, routinely cut budgets after performance deviates from plan. Routines – predictable, virtually automatic behaviors – are unstated, self-reinforcing, and remarkably resilient. Because they lead to more efficient cognitive processing, they are, for the most part, functional and highly desirable.

Dysfunctional routines, by contrast, are barriers to action and change. Some are outdated behaviors that were appropriate once but are now unhelpful. Others manifest themselves in knee-jerk reactions, passivity, unproductive foot-dragging, and, sometimes, active resistance.

Dysfunctional routines are persistent, but they are not unchangeable. Novelty – the perception that current circumstances are truly different from those that previously prevailed – is one of the most potent forces for dislodging routines. To overcome them, leaders must clearly signal that the context has changed. They must work directly with employees to recognize and publicly examine dysfunctional routines and substitute desired behaviors.

A culture of "no."

In organizations dominated by cynics and critics, there is always a good reason not to do something. Piling on criticism is an easy way to avoid taking risks and claim false superiority. Lou Gerstner gets credit for naming this routine, which he found on his arrival at IBM, but it is common in many organizations. Another CEO described her team's response to new initiatives by likening it to a skeet shoot: "Someone would yell, 'Pull!' there would be a deafening blast, and the idea would be in pieces on the ground." This routine has two sources: a culture that overvalues criticism and analysis, and complex decision-making processes requiring multiple approvals, in which anybody can say "no" but nobody can say "yes." It is especially likely in organizations that are divided into large subunits or segments, led by local leaders with great power who are often unwilling to comply with directives from above.

The dog and pony show must go on.

Some organizations put so much weight on process that they confuse ends and means, form and content. How you present a proposal becomes more important than what you propose. Managers construct presentations carefully and devote large amounts of time to obtaining sign-offs. The result is death by PowerPoint. Despite the appearance of progress, there's little real headway.

The grass is always greener.

To avoid facing challenges in their core business, some managers look to new products, new services, and new lines of business. At times, such diversification is healthy. But all too often these efforts are merely an avoidance tactic that keeps tough problems at arm's length.

After the meeting ends, debate begins.

This routine is often hard to spot because so much of it takes place under cover. Cordial, apparently cooperative meetings are followed by resistance. Sometimes resisters are covert; often, they end run established forums entirely and take their concerns directly to the top. The result? Politics triumphs over substance, staff meetings become empty rituals, and meddling becomes the norm.

Ready, aim, aim...

Here, the problem is the organization's inability to settle on a definitive course of action. Staff members generate a continual stream of proposals and reports; managers repeatedly tinker with each one, fine-tuning their choices without ever making a final decision. Often called "analysis paralysis," this pattern is common in perfectionist cultures where mistakes are career threatening and people who rock the boat down.

This too shall pass.

In organizations where prior leaders repeatedly proclaimed a state of crisis but then made few substantive changes, employees tend to be jaded. In such situations, they develop a heads-down, bunker mentality and a reluctance to respond to management directives. Most believe that the wisest course of action is to ignore new initiatives, work around them, or wait things out.

Levy used one particularly effective framing device to help employees interpret a preliminary draft of the turnaround plan. This device took the form of a detailed e-mail memo accompanying the dense, several-hundred-page plan. The memo explained, in considerable detail, the plan's purpose and expected impact.

The first section of the memo sought to mollify critics and reduce the fears of doctors and nurses. Its tone was positive and uplifting; it discussed BIDMC's mission, strategy, and uncompromising values, emphasizing the hospital's "warm, caring environment." This section of the letter also reaffirmed the importance of remaining an academic medical center, as well as reminding employees of their shared mission and ideals. The second part of the letter told employees what to expect, providing further details about the turnaround plan. It emphasized that tough measures and goals would be required but noted that the specific recommendations were based, for the most part, on the advice in the Hunter report, which employees had already reviewed. The message to employees was, "You've already seen and endorsed the Hunter report. There are no future surprises"

The third part of the letter anticipated and responded to prospective concerns; this had the effect of circumventing objections. This section explicitly diagnosed past plans and explained their deficiencies, which were largely due to their having been imposed top-down, with little employee ownership, buy-in, or discussion. Levy then offered a direct interpretation of what had gone wrong. Past plans, he said, had underestimated the size of the financial problem, set unrealistic expectations for new revenue growth, and failed to test implementation proposals. This section of the letter also drove home the need for change at a deeper, more visceral level than employees had experienced in the past. It emphasized that this plan was a far more collective effort than past proposals had been, because it incorporated many employee suggestions.

By framing the turnaround proposal this way, Levy accomplished two things. First, he was able to convince employees that the plan belonged to them. Second, the letter served as the basis for an ongoing communication platform. Levy reiterated its points at every opportunity — not only with employees but also in public meetings and in discussions with the press.

❑ MANAGING THE MOOD

Turnarounds are depressing events, especially when they involve restructuring and downsizing. Relationships are disrupted, friends move on, and jobs disappear, in such settings, managing the mood of the organization becomes an essential leadership skill. Leaders must pay close attention to employees' emotions — the ebb and flow of their feelings and moods — and work hard to preserve a receptive climate for change. Often, this requires a delicate balancing act between presenting good and bad news in just the right proportion. Employees need to feel that their sacrifices have not been in vain and that their accomplishments have been recognized and rewarded. At the same time, they must be reminded that complacency is not an option. The communication challenge is daunting. One must strike the right notes of optimism and realism and carefully calibrate the timing, tone, and positioning of every message.

Paul Levy's challenge was threefold: to give remaining employees time to grieve and recover from layoffs and other difficult measures; to make them feel that he cared for and supported them; and to ensure that the turnaround plan proceeded apace. The process depended on mutual trust and employees' desire to succeed; "I had to calibrate the push and pull of congratulations and pressure, but I also depended on the staff's underlying value system and sense of mission," he said. "They were highly motivated, caring individuals who had stuck with the place through five years of hell. They wanted to do good."

The first step was to acknowledge employees' feelings of depression while helping them look to the future. Immediately after the first round of layoffs, people were feeling listless and dejected; Levy knew that releasing the final version of the turnaround plan too soon after the layoffs could be seen as cold, In an e-mail he sent to all employees a few days later, Levy explicitly empathized with employees' feelings ("This week is a sad one . . . it is hard for those of us remaining . . . offices are emptier than usual"). He then urged employees to look forward and concluded on a strongly optimistic note (" . . . our target is not just survival; It is to thrive and set an example for what a unique academic medical center like ours means for this region"). His upbeat words were reinforced by a piece of good luck that weekend when the underdog New England Patriots won their first Super

The Four Phases of a Persuasion Campaign

A typical turnaround process consists of two stark phases: plan development, followed by an implementation that may or may not be welcomed by the organization. For the turnaround plan to be widely accepted and adopted, however, the CEO must develop a separate persuasion campaign, the goal of which is to create a continuously receptive environment for change. The campaign begins well before the CEO's first day on the job — or, if the CEO is long established, well before formal development work begins—and continues long after the final plan is announced.

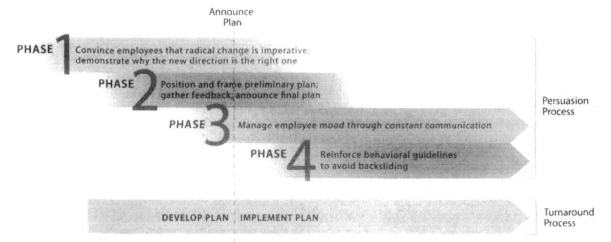

Bowl championship in dramatic fashion in the last 90 seconds of the game. When Levy returned to work the following Monday, employees were saying, "If the Patriots can do it, we can, too."

The next task was to keep employees focused on the continuing hard work ahead. On April 12, two months into the restructuring process, Levy sent out a "Frequently Asked Questions" e-mail giving a generally favorable view of progress to date. At the same time, he spoke plainly about the need to control costs and reminded employees that merit pay increases would remain on hold. This was hardly the rosy picture that most employees were hoping for, of course. But Levy believed sufficient time had passed that employees could accommodate a more realistic and tough tone on his part.

A month later, everything changed. Operational improvements that were put in place during the first phase of the turnaround had begun to take hold. Financial performance was well ahead of budget, with the best results since the merger. In another e-mail, Levy praised employees lavishly. He also convened a series of open question-and-answer forums, where employees heard more details about the hospital's tangible progress and received kudos for their accomplishments.

The toughest challenge faced by leaders during a turnaround is to avoid backsliding into dysfunctional routines.

❏ REINFORCING GOOD HABITS

Without a doubt, the toughest challenge faced by leaders during a turnaround is to avoid backsliding into dysfunctional routines — habitual patterns of negative behavior by individuals and groups that are triggered automatically and unconsciously by familiar circumstances or stimuli. (For more on how such disruptive patterns work, see the sidebar "Dysfunctional Routines: Six Ways to Stop Change in Its 1 racks.") Employees need help maintaining new behaviors, especially when their old ways of working are deeply ingrained and destructive. Effective change leaders provide opportunities for employees to practice desired behaviors repeatedly, while personally modeling new ways of working and providing coaching and support.

In our studies of successful turnarounds, we've found that effective leaders explicitly reinforce organizational values on a constant basis, using actions to back up their words. Their goal is to change behavior, not just ways of thinking. For example, a leader can talk about values such as openness, tolerance, civility, teamwork, delegation, and direct communication in meetings and e-mails. But the message takes hold only if he or she also signals a dislike of disruptive, divisive behaviors by pointedly — and, if necessary, publicly — criticizing them.

At Beth Israel Deaconess Medical Center, the chiefs of medicine, surgery, orthopedics, and other key functions presented Levy with special behavioral challenges, particularly because he was not a doctor. Each medical chief was in essence a "mini-dean," the head of a largely self-contained department with its own faculty, start, and resources. As academic researchers, they were rewarded primarily for individual achievement. They had limited experience solving business or management problems.

In dealing with the chiefs, Levy chose an approach that blended with a strong dose of discipline with real-time, public reinforcement He developed guidelines for behavior and insisted that everyone in the hospital measure up to them. In one of his earliest meetings with the chiefs, Levy presented a simple set of "meeting rules," including such chestnuts as "state your objections" and "disagree without being disagreeable," and led a discussion about them, demonstrating the desired behaviors through nib own leadership of the meeting. The purpose of these rules was to introduce new standards of interpersonal behavior and, In the process, to combat several dysfunctional routines.

One serious test of Levy's ability to reinforce these norms came a month and a half after he was named CEO. After a staff meeting at which all the department chairs were present, one chief — who had remained silent — sent an e-mail to Levy complaining about a decision made during the meeting. His e-mail copied the other chiefs as well as the chairman of the board. Many CEOs would choose to criticize such behavior privately. But Levy responded in an e-mail to the same audience, publicly denouncing the chief for his tone, his lack of civility, and his failure to speak up earlier in the process, as required by the new meeting rules. It was as close to a public hanging as anyone could get Several of the chiefs privately expressed their support to levy; they too had been offended by their peer's presumptuousness. More broadly, the open criticism served to powerfully reinforce new norms while curbing disruptive behavior.

Even as they must set expectations and reinforce behaviors, effective change leaders also recognize that many employees simply do not know how to make decisions as a group or work cooperatively. By delegating critical decisions and responsibilities, a leader can provide employees with ample opportunities to practice new ways of working; in such cases, employees' performance should be evaluated as much on their adherence to the new standards and processes as on their substantive choices, In this spirit, Levy chose to think of himself primarily as a kind of appeals court judge. When employees came to him seeking his intervention on an issue or situation, he explained, he would "review the process used by the lower court' to determine if it followed the rules. If so, the decision stands." He did not review cases de novo and substitute his judgment for that of the individual department or unit He insisted that employees work through difficult issues themselves, even when they were not so inclined, rather than rely on him to tell them what to do. At other times, he intervened personally and coached employees when they lacked baste skills. When two members of his staff disagreed on a proposed course of action, Levy triggered an open, emotional debate, then worked with the participants and their bosses behind the scenes to resolve the differences. At the next staff meeting, he praised the participants' willingness to disagree publicly, reemphasizing that vigorous debate was healthy and desirable and that confrontation was not to be avoided. In this way, employees gained experience in working through their problems on their own.

Performance, of course, is the ultimate measure of a successful turnaround. On that score, BIDMC has done exceedingly well since Levy took the helm. The original structuring plan called for a three-year improvement process, moving from a $58 million loss in 2001 to breakeven in 2004. At the end of the 2004 fiscal year, performance was far ahead of plan, with the hospital reporting a $37.4 million net gain from operations. Revenues were up, while costs were sharply reduced. Decision making was now crisper and more responsive, even though there was little change in the hospital's senior staff or medical leadership. Morale, not surprisingly, was up as well. To take just one indicator, annual nursing turnover, which was 15% to 16% when Levy became CEO, had dropped to 3% by mid-2004. Pleased with the hospital's performance, the board signed Levy to a new three-year contract.

❑ HEADS, HEARTS, AND HANDS

It's clear that the key to Paul levy's success at Beth Israel Deaconess Medical Center is that he understood the importance of making sure the cultural soil had been made ready before planting the seeds of change. In a receptive environment, employees not only understand why change is necessary; they're also emotionally committed to making it happen, and they faithfully execute the required steps.

On a cognitive level, employees in receptive environments are better able to let go of competing, unsubstantiated views of the nature and extent of the problems facing their organizations. They hold the same, objective views of the causes of poor performance. They acknowledge the seriousness of current financial, operational, and marketplace difficulties. And they take responsibility to their own contributions to those problems. Such a shared, fact-based diagnosis is crucial for moving forward.

On an emotional level employees in receptive environments identify with the organization and its values and are committed to its continued existence. They believe that the organization stands for something there than profitability, market share, or stock performance and is therefore worth saving. Equally important, they trust the leader, believing that he or she shares their values and will fugato preserve them. Leaders earn considerable latitude from employees — and their proposals usually get the benefit of the doubt — when their hearts are thought to be in the right place.

Workers in such environments also have physical, hands-on experience with the new behaviors expected of them. They have seen the coming changes up dose and understand what they are getting into, In such an atmosphere where it's acceptable for employees to wrestle with decisions on their own and practice unfamiliar ways of working, a leader can successfully allay irrational fears and undercut the myths that so often accompany major change efforts.

There is a powerful lesson in all this for leaders. To create a receptive environment, persuasion is the ultimate tool. Persuasion promotes understanding; understanding breeds acceptance; acceptance leads to action. Without persuasion, even the best of turnaround plans will fall to take root.

Case 6-1

Charlotte Beers at Ogilvy & Mather Worldwide (A)

It was December 1993, and during the past year and a half, Charlotte Beers had found little time for reflection. Since taking over as CEO and chairman of Ogilvy & Mather Worldwide in 1992, Beers had focused all her efforts on charting a new course for the world's sixth-largest advertising agency. The process of crafting a vision with her senior management team had been — by all accounts — painful, messy, and chaotic. Beers, however, was pleased with the results. Ogilvy & Mather was now committed to becoming "the agency most valued by those who most value brands."

During the past year, the agency had regained, expanded, or won several major accounts. Confidence and energy appeared to be returning to a company the press had labeled "beleaguered" only 2 years earlier. Yet, Beers sensed that the change effort was still fragile. "Brand Stewardship," the agency's philosophy for building brands, was not well understood below the top tier of executives who had worked with Beers to develop the concept. Internal communication efforts to 272 worldwide offices were under way, as were plans to adjust O&M's structures and systems to a new set of priorities. Not the least of the challenges before her was ensuring collaboration between offices on multinational brand campaigns. The words of Kelly ODea, her Worldwide Client Service president, still rang in her ears. "We can't lose momentum. Most change efforts fail after the initial success. This could be the prologue, Charlotte . . . or it could be the whole book."

❑ OGILVY & MATHER

In 1948, David Ogilvy, a 38-year-old Englishman, sold his small tobacco farm in Pennsylvania and invested his entire savings to start his own advertising agency. The agency, based in New York, had financial backing from two London agencies, Mather & Crowther and S.H. Benson. "I had no clients, no credentials, and only $6,000 in the bank," Ogilvy would later write in his autobiography, "[but] I managed to create a series of campaigns which, almost overnight, made Ogilvy & Mather famous.[1]

Ogilvy's initial ads — for Rolls-Royce, Schweppes, and Hathaway Shirts — were based on a marketing philosophy that Ogilvy had begun developing as a door-to-door salesman in the 1930s, and later, as a pollster for George Gallup. Ogilvy believed that effective advertising created an indelible image of the product in consumers' minds and, furthermore, that campaigns should always be intelligent, stylish, and "first class." Most of all, however, David Ogilvy believed that advertising must sell. "We sell — or else" became his credo for the agency. In 1950, Ogilvy's campaign for Hathaway featured a distinguished man with a black eye patch, an idea that increased sales by 160% and ran for 25 years. Other famous campaigns included Maxwell House's "Good to the Last Drop" launched in 1958 and American Express's "Don't Leave Home Without It," which debuted in 1962.

[1] David Ogilvy, *Blood, Beer, and Advertising* (London: Hamish Hamilton, 1977).

1984–1988

	1984	1985	1986	1987	1988
Revenues in thousands)	$428,604	$490,486	$560,132	$738,508	$838,090
Net income (in thousands)	25,838	30,247	26,995	29,757	32,950
Operating profit (in thousands)	49,191	45,355	47,764	57,933	65,922

Source: The Ogilvy Group Annual Report, 1988.

Figure 6.15   *Selected Financial and Organization Data*

Gentlemen with Brains

David Ogilvy imbued his agency's culture with the same "first class" focus that he demanded of creative work. Employees were "gentlemen with brains," treating clients, consumers, and one another with respect. "The consumer is not a moron," admonished Ogilvy. In a distinctly British way, collegiality and politeness were highly valued: "We abhor ruthlessness. We like people with gentle manners and see no conflict between adherence to high professional standards in our work and human kindness in our dealings with others."[2]

At Ogilvy's agency, gentility did not mean blandness. Ogilvy took pride in his agency's "streak of unorthodoxy." He smoked a pipe, refused to fly, and peppered his speeches with literary references and acerbic wit. He once advised a young account executive, "Develop your eccentricities early, and no one will think you're going senile later in life." In a constant stream of letters, he made his dislikes clear: "I despise toadies who suck up to their bosses. . . . I am revolted by pseudo-academic jargon like *attitudinally paradigms*, and *sub-optimal*." He also exhorted his staff to achieve brilliance through "obsessive curiosity, guts under pressure, inspiring enthusiasm, and resilience in adversity." No one at Ogilvy & Mather ever forgot the full-page announcement he placed in the *New York Times:* "Wanted: Trumpeter Swans who combine personal genius with inspiring leadership. If you are one of these rare birds, write to me in inviolable secrecy."

In 1965, Ogilvy & Mather merged with its partner agencies in Britain to form Ogilvy & Mather International.[3] "Our aim," wrote David Ogilvy, "is to be One Agency Indivisible; the same advertising disciplines, the same principles of management, the same striving for excellence." Each office was carpeted in the same regal Ogilvy red. Individual offices, however, were run independently by local presidents who exercised a great deal of autonomy.

David Ogilvy retired in 1975. Succeeding the legendary founder proved daunting. "The next four chairmen," commented one longtime executive, "did not have his presence. David is quirky; they were straightforward, middle-of-the-road, New York." Ogilvy's successors focused on extending the network offices internationally and building direct response, marketing research, and sales promotion capabilities. Revenues soared in the 1970s, culminating in record double-digit gains in the mid-1980s (see Figure 6.15 and Figure 6.16). The advertising industry boomed, and Ogilvy & Mather led the pack. Nowhere was the agency's reputation greater than at its New York office, heralded in 1986 by the press as "the class act of Madison Avenue."

Advertising Industry Changes

The booming economy of the 1980s shielded the advertising industry from the intensifying pressures of global competition. Companies fought for consumer attention through marketing, and advertising billings grew — on average, between 10% and 15% per annum. Brand manufacturers — challenged by the growth of quality generic products and the diverse tastes of a fragmented mass market — created multiple line extensions and relied on agencies' creative powers to differentiate them. As business globalized, so did agencies. Responding to clients' demands for global communications and a range of integrated services, agencies expanded rapidly, many merging to achieve economies of scale as "mega-agencies" with millions in revenues worldwide.

After the stock market crash of 1987, companies reconsidered the value added by large advertising

---

[2] David Ogilvy, *Confessions of an Advertising Man* (New York; Athenaeum, 1963).

[3] Dictionary of Company Histories, 1986.

1989–1993[a]

	1989	1990	1991	1992	1993
Total annual billings (in thousands)[b]	$4,089,000	$4,563,700	$5,271,000	$5,205,700	$5,814,100
Revenues (in thousands)	592,600	653,700	757,600	754,800	740,000
Percent change in net income[c]	NA	4.7	−2.8	1.9	5.3
Operating margin	NA	6.4	4.1	4.9	7.6

Source: Advertising Age.

[a]Financial information for 1989–1993 is not comparable to 1984–1988 due to the restructuring of the company following sale to WPP Group, Plc. It is the policy of WPP Group, plc not to release revenue and net income information about its subsidiaries.

[b]Represents an estimate by *Advertising Age* of the total value of all advertising and direct marketing campaigns run in a given year.

[c]The percent increase or decrease is given from an undisclosed sum at base year 1989.

Figure 6.16

budgets. Increasingly, many chose to shift resources from expensive mass media and print campaigns towards direct mail, cable, telemarketing, and sales promotion. Fixed fees began to replace the agencies' historical 15% commission on billings. Long-standing client–agency relations were severed as companies sought the best bargains. "Viewed by some as ad factories selling a commodity product, the mega-agencies were challenged by new, "boutique" creative shops. The globalization of media and pressures for cost efficiencies encouraged companies to consolidate product lines and to sell them in more markets worldwide. They, in turn, directed agencies to transport their brands around the world. The advertising agency of the 1990s — often a loose federation of hundreds of independent firms — was asked to launch simultaneous brand campaigns in North America, Europe, and the emerging markets of Asia, Latin America, and Africa.

Organizational Structure

By 1991, Ogilvy's 270 offices comprised four regions. The North American offices were the most autonomous, with office presidents reporting directly to the Worldwide CEO. Outside North America, presidents of local offices — sometimes majority stakeholders (see Figure 6.17) — reported to country presidents, who in turn reported to regional chairmen. Europe was coordinated centrally, but — with significant European multinational clients and a tradition of high creativity — the region maintained its autonomy from New York. To establish a presence in Latin America, Ogilvy obtained minority ownership in locally owned agencies and formed partnerships with local firms. The last region to be fully formed was Asia/Pacific, with the addition of Australia, India, and Southeast Asia in 1991 (see Figure 6.18 for organization chart).

Between and across regions, "worldwide management supervisors" coordinated the requirements of multinational clients such as American Express and Unilever. WMSs served as the point of contact among multiple parties: client headquarters, clients' local subsidiaries, and the appropriate Ogilvy local offices. They were also responsible for forming and managing the core multi-disciplinary

	#of Offices	100%	>50%	<50%	0%
North America	40	80	20	0	0
Europe	97	63	24	8	5
Asia/Pacific	66	57	36	7	0
Latin America	48	25	6	21	48

Figure 6.17   Percent of Regional Offices Owned by O&M Worldwide

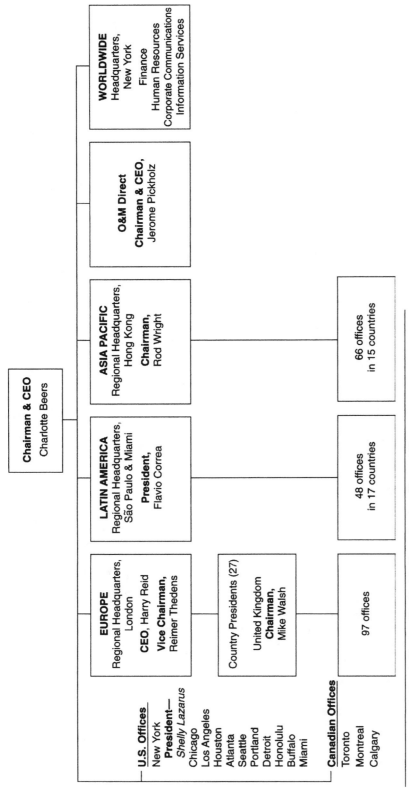

Chairman & CEO
Charlotte Beers

EUROPE
Regional Headquarters,
London
CEO, Harry Reid
Vice Chairman,
Reimer Thedens

Country Presidents (27)

United Kingdom
Chairman,
Mike Walsh

U.S. Offices
President—
Shelly Lazarus
New York
Chicago
Los Angeles
Houston
Atlanta
Seattle
Portland
Detroit
Honolulu
Buffalo
Miami

Canadian Offices
Toronto
Montreal
Calgary

97 offices

LATIN AMERICA
Regional Headquarters,
São Paulo & Miami
President,
Flavio Correa

48 offices
in 17 countries

ASIA PACIFIC
Regional Headquarters,
Hong Kong
Chairman,
Rod Wright

66 offices
in 15 countries

O&M Direct
Chairman & CEO,
Jerome Pickholz

WORLDWIDE
Headquarters,
New York
Finance
Human Resources
Corporate Communications
Information Services

Figure 6.18 *Ogilvy & Mather Worldwide Organization Chart, 1991*

account team. More important, they facilitated the exchange of information throughout the network, attempting to ensure strategic unity and avoid operating at cross-purposes.

Over time, Ogilvy & Mather came to pride itself as "the most local of the internationals, the most international of the locals." Local delivery channels and the need for consumer acceptance of multinational products required specialized local knowledge and relationships. Local and global clients also served as magnets for each other: without local accounts, country offices were unable to build sufficient critical mass to service multinational clients well; without multinational accounts to draw top talent, the agency was less attractive to local clients.

With a "light center and strong regions," most creative and operating decisions were made locally. The role of Worldwide Headquarters in New York, staffed by 100 employees, was limited largely to ensuring consistency in financial reporting and corporate communications. Key capital allocation and executive staffing decisions were made by the O&M Worldwide board of directors, which included regional chairmen and presidents of the most powerful countries and offices such as France, Germany, the United Kingdom, New York, and Los Angeles.

The Ogilvy offices represented four core disciplines: sales promotion, public relations, advertising, and direct marketing.[4] Sales promotion developed point-of-purchase materials such as in-store displays and flyers. Public relations offices worked to promote clients' corporate reputation and product visibility. Advertising focused on mass marketing, establishing the core of a client's brand image through the development and production of television commercials, print campaigns, and billboards. Direct Marketing created and delivered targeted advertising — from mail order catalogues to coupons and television infomercials — designed to solicit a direct response from consumers. While the latter three resided within the regional structure, O&M Direct was an independent subsidiary. In the late 1980s, the Ogilvy board of directors decided to focus on advertising and direct marketing, the firm's chief competitive strengths. Unlike advertising, Directs business in the 1980s remained chiefly local, but expanded explosively. By 1991, O&M Direct had received numerous industry accolades and was ranked the largest direct marketing company in the world.

"Beleaguered" Ogilvy & Mather

As clients demanded lower costs and greater service, Ogilvy & Mather — like many large agencies at the time — was slow to make adjustments. In 1988, Ogilvy was ranked the sixth-largest advertising firm in the world. As one executive remembered:

Everything was going well. All we had to do was wake up in the morning and we were plus 15%. So why did we need to change? Our vision was 'just keep doing the same thing, better.' We failed either to recognize or acknowledge what were the first real indications that life around here was about to change fundamentally.

In May 1989, WPP Group Plc, a leading marketing services company, acquired Ogilvy & Mather for $864 million.[5] WPP, led by Harvard Business School-trained Martin Sorrell, had already purchased the J. Walter Thompson agency for $550 million two years earlier.[6] The takeover was hostile, with agency executives — including CEO Kenneth Roman — opposed. "It was a shock," explained one long-time executive. "We were a proud company with a constant stock market growth, the masters of our destiny. Suddenly, we were raided." Within months of the takeover, CEO Roman resigned. "Ken had absolutely nothing in common with WPP. There was a lack of trust, an air of conflict, adversaries, and invasion," remembered another. A number of top creative and account executives followed Roman, leaving Ogilvy & Mather for other agencies.[7]

Graham Phillips, a 24-year Ogilvy veteran, was appointed Roman's successor. One executive who worked with Phillips described him as "a brilliant account guy and a very good manager who identified our need to become a total communications

---

[4] The number of Ogilvy offices by discipline in 1994 were as follows: S3 Advertising, 60 Direct Response, 12 Promotional, 23 Public Relations, and 92 in other areas, including highly specialized market research firms.

[5] Christie Dugas, The Death of Ogilvy and an Era," *Newsday,* May 17,1989.

[6] Ibid

[7] "Change Comes to Fabled Ogilvy," *New York Times,* April 12,1992.

company. But few would describe him as an inspirational leader."

In 1989, the agency lost major advertising assignments from Unilever and Shell. In 1990, Seagram's Coolers and Nutrasweet withdrew their multinational accounts.[8] Account losses in 1991 proved particularly damaging to the New York office, the agency's center and standard-bearer. "If New York thrives, the world thrives. If New York fails, the world fails" went a familiar company adage. New York's client defections were explained by one executive as a failure in leadership: "The office was run by czars with big accounts. People got used to a highly political way of working and work deteriorated." In 1991, Campbell Soup withdrew $25 million in business, Roy Rogers $15 million, and American Express — the account for which Ogilvy had won "Print Campaign of the Decade" — pulled out $60 million.[9] "Losing American Express had symbolism far beyond what the actual business losses were," recalled one Ogilvy executive. "People who were loyal Ogilvy employees, believers for years, disengaged. They threw up their hands and said, This place is falling apart."

Despite declines in revenue, the agency found itself unable to adapt to clients' changing demands. Budgets were not reduced at local offices, even as large clients pushed Ogilvy to streamline and centralize their accounts. "We were a high-cost operation in a low-cost world. There was a lack of financial discipline, a lack of focus on cost, and a lack of structured decision making on business issues," noted one executive. Another faulted the firm's tradition of local autonomy and failure to institute systems for managing collaboration: "We were spending a lot of money at the creative center without cutting back locally — building costs at both ends."

Recalling the atmosphere at the time, another executive concluded, "A shaken confidence permeated the whole company. We talked about change and what we needed to do ad nauseam, but nothing was happening. We tried to work within the old framework when the old ways of working were irrelevant."

At the end of 1991, Phillips stepped down as CEO, telling the press: "I have taken Ogilvy

through a very difficult period in the industry. I had to let go people whom I had worked with for 27 years, and that wears you down." In April, Charlotte Beers was appointed CEO and chairman of Ogilvy & Mather Worldwide, the first outsider ever to lead the company.

❏ CHARLOTTE BEERS

The daughter of a cowboy, Beers grew up in Texas, where she began her career as a research analyst for the Mars Company. In 1969, she moved to Chicago as an account executive with J. Walter Thompson. Once there, she cultivated success with clients Sears, Kraft, and Gillette, combining a Southern Texan charm with sharp business acumen. Beers rose quickly to senior vice president for Client Services.

At Thompson, Beers was known for her passionate interest — unusual in account executives — in the philosophy of marketing. Commented Beers, "I try never to discuss with clients only the stuff of business. I focus on advertising as well — on the ideas." Once described on a performance evaluation as "completely fearless," Beers earned a reputation for her ability to win over clients. Colleagues retold the story of how Beers impressed a roomful of Sears executives in the early 1970s by taking apart, then reassembling, a Sears power drill without skipping a beat in her pitch for a new advertising campaign.

In 1979, Beers became COO of the Chicago agency Tatham-Laird & Kudner. Her success in winning the mid-sized agency several new brands with Proctor & Gamble helped turn the firm around. Accounts with Ralston-Purina and Stouffer Foods followed. Beers was elected CEO in 1982 and chairman of the board in 1986. In 1987, she became the first woman ever named chairman of the American Association of Advertising Agencies. One year later, she led TLK through a merger with the international agency Eurocome-RSCG. Tatham's billings had tripled during Beers's tenure, to $325 million.

Beers Takes Over

Beers's appointment, recalled O&M veterans, created initial apprehension. Commented one executive, "She was from a smaller agency in Chicago and had not managed multiple offices. O&M is a worldwide company, and she had never worked

---

[8] "Beers Succeeds Phillips at O&M Worldwide," *Adweek,* April 13, 1992.

[9] Operation Winback," *Advertising Age,* February 1993.

outside the United States. And, she was not from Ogilvy." Added another, "This is an organization that rejects outsiders."

Her approach quickly made an impression with Ogilvy insiders. "It was clear from day one that Charlotte would be a different kind of leader. Full of life. Eyes open and clearly proud of the brand she was now to lead. Here was somebody who could look around and see the risks, but wasn't afraid to turn the corner even though it was dark out," said one executive. "We had leaders before, who said all the right things, were terribly nice, did a good job, but they didn't inspire. Charlotte has an ability to inspire — Charlotte has presence." Commented another executive, "She is delightfully informal, but you always know that she means business." Within two months of her appointment, Beers dismissed a top-level executive who had failed to instigate necessary changes.

Activate the Assets

"When I took over," recalled Beers, "all the press reports talked about 'beleaguered' Ogilvy. My job was to remove, 'beleaguered' from our name." In her first six weeks, Beers sent a "Hello" video to all 7000 of Ogilvy's employees. It began:

Everybody wants to know my nine-point plan for success and I can't tell you that I know yet what it is. I'm building my own expectations and dreams for the agency — but I need a core of people who have lived in this company and who have similar dreams to help me. That's going to happen fest, because we are rudderless without it. David [Ogilvy] gave us a great deal to build on, but I don't think if s there for us to go backwards. Its there to go forward.

Beers concluded that people had lost sight of Ogilvy's still impressive assets — its vast network of offices worldwide, its creative talent, and its distinguished list of multinational clients. "We must," she told senior executives, "activate the assets we already have." In her second month at Ogilvy, Beers observed a major client presentation by the heads of five O&M offices:

It was a fabulous piece of thinking. We had committed enormous resources. But in the end, they didn't tell the clients why it would work. When the client said, "We'll get back to you," they didn't demand an immediate response, so I intervened. "You saw a remarkable presentation, and I think you need to comment." Ogilvy had gotten so far from its base, (hat talented people lacked the confidence to speak up.

For Beers, her early interactions with a key client symbolized the state of the company. "He kept retelling the tale of New York's downfall: how we blew a major account in Europe and how our groups fought among one another. The fourth time I heard this story," remembered Beers, "I interrupted. Thais never going to happen again, so let's not talk about it anymore. Let's talk about what we can accomplish together.'"

Beers spent much of her first months at Ogilvy talking to investors and clients. For Wall Street, she focused on the quality of Ogilvy's advertising. "I refused to do a typical analyst report," she said. "When the Wall Street analysts asked me why I showed them our ads, I told them it was to give them reason to believe the numbers would happen again and again." Clients voiced other concerns. "I met with 50 clients in six months," recalled Beers, "and found there was a lot of affection for Ogilvy. Yet, they were also very candid. Clients stunned me by rating us below other agencies in our insight into the consumer." Beers shared these perceptions with senior managers; "Clients view our people as uninvolved, distant, and reserved. We have organized ourselves into fiefdoms, and that has taken its toll. Each department — Creative, Account, Media, and Research — are often working as separate entities. Ifs been a long time since we've had some famous advertising."

To restore confidence both internally and externally, Beers maintained that the agency needed a clear direction. "I think ifs fair to say Ogilvy had no clear sense of what it stood for. I wanted to give people something that would release their passion, that would knit them together. I wanted the extraneous discarded. I wanted a rallying point on what really matters."

For Beers, what mattered was brands. "She is intensely client- and brand-focused," explained one executive. "You can't go into her office with financial minutia. You get about two seconds of attention." Beers believed that clients wanted an agency that understood the complexity of managing the emotional as well as the logical relationship between a consumer and a product. "I became confident that I knew what clients wanted and what Ogilvy's strengths were. It was my job to be the bridge." Beers, however, was as yet unsure what form that bridge would take or how it would get built. One of her early challenges was to decide whom to ask for help in charting this new course:

I knew I needed their involvement, and that I would be asking people to do much more than they had been, without the benefits of titles and status. I avoided calling on people on the basis of their titles. I watched the way they conducted business. I looked to see what they found valuable. I wanted people who felt the way I did about brands. 1 was looking for kindred spirits.

The "Thirsty for Change" Group

Over the next few months, Beers solicited ideas for change from her senior managers, asking them to give candid evaluations of disciplines and regions, as well as of one another. In a style that managers would describe as "quintessential Charlotte," Beers chose to meet with executives one-on-one and assigned them tasks without regard to their disciplinary backgrounds. She commented, "I was slow to pull an executive committee together. I didn't know who could do it. It was a clumsy period, and I was account executive on everything — everything came to me." At first, some found the lack of structure unnerving. Noted one executive, "People weren't quite sure what their roles were. It caused discomfort. We began to wonder, Where do I fit? Who is whose boss?" Another added, "She was purposely vague in hopes that people would stretch themselves to new configurations." Several executives, though cautious, found Beers's talk of change inspiring and responded with their ideas.

By May 1992, Beers had identified a group whom she described as "thirsty for change." Some were top executives heading regions or key offices; others were creative and account directors who caught her eye as potential allies. Her selection criterion was "people who got it" — those who agreed on the importance of change. All had been vocal about their desire to move Ogilvy forward. She sent a memo (see Figure 6.19) inviting them to a meeting in Vienna, Austria, that month:

❏ BRAND STEWARDSHIP

The Vienna meeting, recalled Beers, "put a diversity of talents in a climate of disruption." Having never met before for such a purpose, members were both tentative with each other and elated to share their perspectives. Two common values provided an initial glue: "We agreed to take no more baby steps. And it seemed clear that brands were what we were going to be about."

Beers asked Rod Wright, who had led the Asia/Pacific region through a vision formulation process, to organize and facilitate the meeting. Wright proposed a conceptual framework, based on the

---

Date: May 19, 1992   **HIGHLY CONFIDENTIAL**
From: Charlotte Beers

To: LUIS BASSAT, President, Bassat, Ogilvy & Mather — Spain
             BILL HAMILTON, Creative Director — O&M New York
             SHELLY LAZARUS, President — O&M New York
             KELLY O'DEA, Worldwide Client Service Director, Ford and AT&T — London
             ROBYN PUTTER, President and Creative Director — O&M South Africa
             HARRY REID, CEO&Mdash; O&M Europe, London
             REIMERTHEDENS, Vice Chairman — O&M Europe, Frankfurt
             MIKE WALSH, President — O&M, United Kingdom, London
             ROD WRIGHT, Chairman — O&M Asia/Pacific, Hong Kong

Will you please join me . . . in re-inventing our beloved agency? I choose you because you seem to be truth-tellers, impatient with the state we're in and capable of leading this revised, refreshed agency. We want to end up with a vision for the agency we can state . . . and excite throughout the company. Bring some basics to Vienna, like where we are today and where we'd like to be in terms of our clients and competition. But beyond the basics, bring your dreams for this great brand.

Figure 6.19

McKinsey "7-S" model,[10] to guide discussion of the firm's strengths and weaknesses. He also hoped to generate debate. "We don't have passionate arguments in this company. We avoid conflict, and debates go offline. When you use a framework, it's easier to depersonalize the discussion."

Reactions to the discussion ranged from confusion to disinterest. "It was theoretical mumbo-jumbo," commented one participant, "I tend to be far more pragmatic and tactical." Added another, "I don't have much patience for the theoretical bent. I wanted to get on with it" Wright admitted, "They rolled their eyes and said, "You mean we've got to do all that?" Beers agreed: The B-school approach had to be translated." As the discussion unfolded, the group discovered that their personalities, priorities, and views on specific action implications diverged widely.

One debate concerned priorities for change. Shelly Lazarus diagnosed a firm-wide morale problem. She argued for restoring confidence with a pragmatic focus on bottom-line client results and counseled against spending much energy on structural changes. Mike Walsh agreed but insisted that the group take time to articulate clearly its vision and values. But Kelly O'Dea had become frustrated with Ogilvy's geographical fragmentation and argued that anything short of major structural changes would be insufficient.

Participants were also divided on whether the emerging brand focus was an end or a starting point The "creative" in the group[11] — Luis Bassat, Bill Hamilton, and Robyn Putter — flanked by Beers, Lazarus and Walsh were interested primarily in finding an effective vehicle for communicating O&M's distinctive competency. An eloquent statement, they felt, would sell clients and inspire employees. The others — O'Dea, Wright, Harry Reid, and Reimer The dens — wanted a vision that provided guidelines for an internal transformation. Summarized Wright, "One school of thought was looking for a line which encapsulates what we do: our creative credo. The other was looking for a strategy, a business mission to guide how we run the company."

---

[10] Wright's model included 10 issue categories: shared values, structures, stakeholders, staff, skills, strategy, suggestions, solutions, service systems, and a shared vision.

[11] "Within advertising and direct marketing, "creatives" develop the art and copy for each media outlet of a brand campaign.

Yet another discussion concerned the route to competitive advantage. Bassat, Putter and Hamilton, commented one participant, felt that Ogilvy had lost sight of the creative product in its rush to worry about finances — "we'd become too commercial." A recommitment to better, more imaginative advertising, they believed, would differentiate the firm from its competitors. Reid and The dens, architects of a massive re-engineering effort in Europe, insisted on financial discipline and tighter operations throughout the company as the only means of survival in the lean operating environment of the 1990s. Wright and The dens added the O&M Direct perspective. Convinced that media advertising by itself was becoming a commodity product, each pressed for a commitment to brand building through a broader, more integrated range of communication services.

At the close of the meeting, remembered one attender, "There was a great deal of cynicism. Was this just another chat session?' we asked ourselves. But, we also had a sense that Charlotte felt right. She fit."

In August 1992, the group reassembled at the English resort Chewton Glen. Members presented Beers with their respective lists of priorities requiring immediate attention. Taken together, there were 22 "to do" items ranging from "examine the process by which we develop and present creative ideas" to "improve our delivery of services across geographical divisions." Beers recalled, "No one can focus on 22 things! I was so depressed, I stayed up all night and wrote a new list." She delivered her thoughts the next day:

I think we have hit bottom and are poised for recovery. Poised but not assured. Our job is to give direction for change. So here is where I start For 1993, we have three — and only three — strategies. They are:

1. *Client Security.* Let's focus our energy, resources and passion on our present clients. It takes three years to replace the revenue from a lost client Under strategy one, there's a very important corollary: We must focus particularly on multinational clients. This is where we have our greatest opportunity for growth and where our attitudes, structure, and lack of focus have been obstacles.

2. *Better Work, More Often.* Without it, you can forget the rest Our work is not good enough. Maybe it will never be, but that's O.K. — better to be so relentless about our work that we are never satisfied. You tell me there's nothing wrong with our credo, "We Sell, or Else," but you also say we need some fresh

thinking on how to get there. We must have creative strategies that make the brand the central focus.

3. *Financial Discipline.* This has been a subject of high concentration but not very productively so. We simply have not managed our own resources very well, and that must change.

These 1993 strategies were linked to the emerging vision by a declaration: "The purpose of our business is to build our clients' brands." One participant recalled, "The idea of brand stewardship was still embryonic. Charlotte clearly understood it in her own mind but was just learning how to communicate it. She used us as guinea pigs to refine her thinking." But some expressed concern: "There was no disagreement that the 1993 strategy was correct. It was fine for the short-term but we needed a long-term strategy."

Through the fall of 1992, group members worked to communicate the strategy — dubbed the "Chewton Glen Declaration" — to the next level of managers. Beers directed her energy toward clients, working vigorously to win new and lost accounts. She spoke about the emotional power of brands, warning them of the abuse inflicted by agencies and brand managers who failed to understand the consumers' relationship with their products. Ogilvy & Mather, Beers told clients, was uniquely positioned to steward their brands' growth and development. Clients were intrigued. By October, O&M boasted two major successes: Jaguar Motor cars' entire U.S. account and the return of American Express's $60 million worldwide account.[12] The press hailed, "Ogilvy & Mather is back on track."

Worldwide Client Service

The Chewton Glen mandate to focus on multinationals heightened the need for better global coordination. Although Ogilvy had pioneered multinational account service in the 1970s, the firm in the 1990s remained "segregated into geographic and discipline fiefdoms" that hampered the development and delivery of brand campaigns worldwide. Noted O'Dea, "What most clients began to seek was the best combination of global efficiencies and local sensitivity, but we were not set up to facilitate that. We had the local strength, but international people were commandos with passports and begging bowls,

[12] Operation Winback," *Advertising Age,* February 1993.

totally dependant on the goodwill of local agencies and their own personal charisma."

In the fall of 1992, Beers asked O'Dea to head a new organization, Worldwide Client Service, that would "tap the best brains from anywhere in the world for each account" O'Dea envisioned dozens of virtual organizations, each focused on a multinational client, with multiple "centers" located wherever their respective clients maintained international headquarters. Under WCS, members of multinational account teams became "dual citizens," reporting both to their local office presidents and WCS supervisors. One WCS director noted, "International people coordinating multinational accounts used to be regarded by the local offices as staff. We thought we were line; the, clients treated us like line; but internally, we had no real authority. What WCS did was give us teeth by giving us line responsibility for our accounts — tenure, profits, growth, and evaluation of local offices."

WCS brand teams were structured to mirror their clients' organizations. Some WCS directors served largely as consultants, while others ran highly centralized operations, with a core team responsible for the entire creative and client development process. "We had to reinvent ourselves in the client's footprint," remarked the WCS account director for Kimberly-Clark. His counterpart at Unilever agreed but noted that current trends favored centralization. "Speed, cost-efficiency, and centralization are our clients' priorities. What matters is not just having good ideas, but getting those ideas to as many markets as possible, as *fast* as possible."

By 1993, O'Dea began to travel the world presenting the possibilities of transnational teams without borders. "Good sell-ins had to be done. Office heads had to understand that there were no choices — global accounts had to be managed horizontally. We'd be dead if we didn't do it," said Reid.

Tools for Brand Stewardship

"The first six months were high excitement, high energy, and a steep learning curve," said Beers. "That was followed by 12 months of disappointment and frustration. It didn't look as if we were getting anywhere." In December 1992, Beers asked Robyn Putter and Luis Bassat, two of the firm's top creative talents, for help in developing the emerging notion of "Brand Stewardship." They answered: "If we are to be successful, we must 'audit' our brands. We must ask the kinds of questions that will systematically uncover the emotional subtleties and nuances by which brands live." Beers took their insight directly to existing and prospective clients. One manager remembered:

Clients immediately bought into Brand Stewardship. That created pressure to go public with it before we had every 'i' dotted and 'i' crossed. We didn't have a codified process, but Charlotte would talk to clients and we'd have to do it Clients came to O&M offices saying, 'I want a brand audit' And, our offices responded with, What's a brand audit?' One client asked us for permission to use the term. We had to move quickly, or risk losing ownership of the idea.

Beers responded by asking a group of executives to elaborate the notion of a brand audit Led by Walsh, they produced a series of questions designed to unveil the emotional as well as the logical significance of a product in the users' lives: "What memories or associations does the brand bring to mind? What specific feelings and emotions do you experience in connection with using this brand? What does this brand do for you in your life that other brands cannot?" The insights gathered from these questions — which became the brand audit — would, in Beers's words, "guide each brand team to the rock-bottom truth of the brand." Focusing on two of Ogilvy's global brands — Jaguar and Dove — Beers's working group struggled to articulate in a few words and images each brand's unique "genetic fingerprint" The result was O&M's first Brand Printsυ:

- A Jaguar is a copy of absolutely nothing — just like its owners.
- Dove stands for attainable miracles.

Crafting a Vision

As the "technology" of brand stewardship developed, the senior team continued to wrestle with the formulation of a vision statement Some argued, "We have the vision— it's Brand Stewardship." Others maintained that Brand Stewardship was but a tool to be used in attaining a yet undefined, future state. Further, as O'Dea explained, "Nearly everyone had had some contact with Brand Stewardship and WCS but they viewed them as separate and isolated actions without a strategic context."

The solution to the impasse, for some, was to include a larger group in the vision formulation. "We needed to decide collectively what we were going to be. If you have 30 people deciding and 30 people who have bought into the vision, then they have no reason not to go out and do it," reasoned Wright. Walsh agreed: "You get the 30 most influential people in the company to open their veins together — which hasn't happened in a very long time." Others, including Beers, worried about losing control of the end result. Advocates for a larger group prevailed, and the entire O&M Worldwide board of directors along with eight other local presidents attended the next meeting in July 1993 at the Doral Arrowwood, a conference center in Westchester, New York.

The purpose of the meeting, explained one of the organizers, was to get final agreement on the vision and where brand stewardship fit in. Feedback from clients on brand stewardship and WCS was used to guide the initial discussion. Participants' recollections of the three-day event ranged from "ghastly" to "painful" and "dreadful." Noted Lazarus, "It seemed an endless stream of theoretical models. Everyone was frustrated and grumpy."

The turning point, Beers recalled, took place at the end of a grueling first day, when one person voiced what many were thinking: "He said, There's nothing new here. I don't see how Brand Stewardship can be unique to Ogilvy.' This was very helpful. One of the negatives at Ogilvy is all the real debates unfold outside the meeting room." The next morning, Beers addressed the group: "Certainly, the individual pieces of this thinking are not new. But to practice it would be remarkable. I have heard that in any change effort, one-third are supporters, one-third are resisters, and one-third are apathetic. I'm in the first group. Where are you?"

With Beers's challenge precipitating consensus, attenders split into groups to tackle four categories of action implications. One group, which included Beers, was charged with crafting the specific wording of the vision. A second began to develop a statement of shared values that would integrate traditional Ogilvy principles with the emerging values of the new philosophy. "That was hard to agree on," recalled Wright. "At issue was how much of the past do we want to take forward." The third group worked on a strategy for communicating the vision to all levels and offices throughout the company. Plans for a Brand Stewardship handbook, regional conferences, and a training program were launched. A fourth group was asked to begin thinking about how to realign titles, structures, systems, and incentives to support the new vision.

After heated brainstorming and drawing freely from the other three groups to test and refine their thinking, Walsh remembered that, finally, "there it was: **'To be the agency most valued by those who most value brands.'"** Summing up the meeting, one attender said, "There had been an amazing amount of distraction, irrelevance, and digression. I didn't think we could pull it together, but we did." (see Figures 6.20 and 6.21 for the final version of the vision and values statement).

---

*T*o our people, our clients, and our friends —

The winds of change are blowing through Ogilvy & Mather. We are raising the sights of everybody in the company to a sweeping new vision:

TO BE THE AGENCY MOST VALUED
BY THOSE WHO MOST VALUE BRANDS

Not that we have ever been unmindful of the importance of brands. Quite the contrary. Our new thrust gets a big boost from ingrained Ogilvy & Mather strengths. Its roots lie in the teachings of David Ogilvy that reverberate through our halls. We have always aimed to create great campaigns with the spark to ignite sales and the staying power to build enduring brands.

What's new is a restructuring of resources, an arsenal of modern techniques, and an intensity of focus that add up to a major advance in the way we do business. We call it BRAND STEWARDSHIP — the art of creating, building, and energizing profitable brands.

The new techniques and procedures of Brand Stewardship have already proved their value for many important brands. As I write they are being put to work for others. In March we will launch them formally — in print, on tape, and throughout the Ogilvy & Mather network.

This will affect the working habits of every professional in the agency, to the benefit, I am convinced, of every brand we work for. I predict that it will bring out the best in all of you — creatively and in every other aspect of your work — and add a lot to the pleasure and satisfaction you get out of your jobs.

As a first formal step the Board of Directors is putting forward the new statement of Shared Values on the facing page. You may notice that several of the points are taken from principles that have guided the company since its start — principles that were most recently set on paper in 1990 when David Ogilvy brought our Corporate Culture up to date.

Thus the Shared Values perform two functions: they *expand* our culture to reflect inexorable change, and in the same breath they *reinforce* its timeless standards.

All vital cultures — national, artistic, corporate — tend to evolve as conditions change, preserving valuable old characteristics as new ones come into the spotlight. In just that way these Shared Values now take their place at the forefront of the dynamic culture of Ogilvy & Mather.

Charlotte
Charlotte Beers
Chairman, Ogilvy & Mather Worldwide

Figure 6.20   *Statement of Vision and Values, 1993*

The market in which we compete is not a static one. To progress toward our new Vision will demand restless challenge and frequent change. The values we share, however, the way we do things day-to-day, will remain constant.

We work not for ourselves, not for the company, not even for a client. We work for Brands.

We work with the client, as Brand Teams. These Teams represent the collective skills of our clients and ourselves. On their performance, our client will judge the whole agency.

We encourage individuals, entrepreneurs, inventive mavericks: with such members, teams thrive. We have no time for prima donnas and politicians.

We value candor, curiosity, originality, intellectual rigor, perseverance, brains — and civility. We see no conflict between a commitment to the highest professional standards in our work and to human kindness in our dealings with each other.

We prefer the discipline of knowledge to the anarchy of ignorance. We pursue knowledge the way a pig pursues truffles.

We prize both analytical and creative skills. Without the first, you can't know where to go; without the second, you won't be able to get there.

The line between confidence and arrogance is a fine one. We watch it obsessively.

We respect the intelligence of our audiences:
"The consumer is not a moron."

We expect our clients to hold us accountable for our Stewardship of their Brands. Only if we have built, nourished, and developed prosperous Brands, only if we have made them more valuable both to their users and to their owners, may we judge ourselves successful.

Figure 6.21

❏ MOVING FORWARD

Through the fall of 1993, Beers and her senior team worked relentlessly to spread the message of Brand Stewardship throughout the agency. It was a slow, sometimes arduous, process. By the end of the year, they had identified several issues that they felt required immediate attention.

Spreading the Gospel

Compared to clients' enthusiasm, reactions to Brand Stewardship within the agency were initially tepid. Across disciplines, employees below the most senior level lacked experience with, and knowledge of how to use, the principles of Brand Stewardship. O'Dea remarked, "Brand Stewardship has not seeped into everyday practice. Only a minority of the O&M population truly understands and embraces it. Others are aware of Brand Stewardship, but not deeply proficient. Many are still not true believers."

Account executives who misunderstood the concept were at a loss when their clients demanded it Planners expressed confusion about how to use Brand Stewardship to develop a creative strategy.[13] Recalled one executive, "People didn't understand

[13] Account executives managed the agency's contact with clients, bringing in new accounts and coordinating information flow between other functions and the client. Planners worked with account executives to establish creative marketing strategies.

such basic things as the difference between a BrandPrintυ and an advertising strategy."

Greater familiarity with the process did not always mitigate opposition. Admitted Beers, "We didn't always have much internal support. It did not sound like anything new." Another problem was that a brand audit might suggest a change of advertising strategy. "Doing an audit on existing business can be seen as an indictment of what we have been doing," noted one executive. Lazarus concluded:

It will only be internalized throughout the organization with experience. I did a Brand Stewardship presentation recently with some of our account people. The client was mesmerized. They wanted the chairman of the company to see the presentation. Now, that had an effect on the people who were with me. I can bet you that when they make the next presentation, Brand Stewardship will be their focal point.

Perhaps the greatest resistance came from the creative side. "We've got to get greater buy-in from the creative people," noted Walsh. Their initial reactions ranged from viewing the BrandPrintυ as an infringement on their artistic license — "I didn't believe in recipe approaches. They can lead to formulaic solutions," said one early convert — to the tolerant skepticism reported by another: "The creatives tell me, "If it helps you get new business, that's great, but why are you in my office talking about this? I have a deadline and don't see what this has to do with creating advertising. But you can't develop a good BrandPrintφ without cross-functional involvement."

Others questioned the relevance of Brand Stewardship for O&M Direct While clear to Beers that Brand Stewardship clarified the rewards to clients from integrating advertising and direct marketing, some were slow to see this potential. Dispelling the popular notion that direct encourages short-term sales while advertising builds brands over the long-term, The dens argued, "You can't send a message by mail that contradicts what you show on television. Both disciplines sell and both build the brand."

One executive concluded that the biggest problem was insufficient communication: "Anyone who heard it firsthand from Charlotte bought in. From the moment she opens her mouth to talk about brands, you know she has a depth of understanding that few people have. The problem is that, until recently, she has been the only missionary. Although the senior team had started "taking the show on the road," Walsh felt they were too few for the magnitude of the task: "The same six or seven people keep getting reshuffled. The result is that follow-through is not good." O'Dea, however, pointed out that the new missionaries had different tribes to convert. He emphasized the importance of translating the vision into a new role for each employee:

We need to move beyond a vision that is useful to the top five percent of account and creative people, to one that has meaning for everyone at Ogilvy. The Information Systems staff should see themselves as brand stewards, because without information technology, we can't respond with appropriate speed. I want the Media people to say, 'I will not buy airtime on these T.V. shows because they don't fit the BrandPrintϑ.' Creatives at O&M Direct developing coupon designs must be as true to the BrandPrintυ as creatives in advertising. Everyone must see themselves as co-stewards of the vision.

Local/Global Tensions

Success in 1993 winning several, large multinational accounts created further challenges for the embryonic WCS. Their goal of helping clients to develop a consistent brand image globally created tension in the firm's traditional balance of power. WCS pressed local agencies to give priority to brands with high global development potential over local accounts. For local agencies, however, local accounts often provided the most stable revenue stream and greatest profit. Further, in their zeal to exercise their newfound "line" responsibility, WCS supervisors were viewed at times as overstepping the bounds of their authority.

While tension had always existed between the centers and local markets, the increasingly centralized brand campaigns exacerbated conflicts. "Local agencies were used to always giving the client what they wanted," explained one WCS supervisor, "I had to start telling them to stop over-servicing the client." Some balked. Local expertise had always been one of Ogilvy's greatest competitive strengths. As one senior executive explained, "Certain local offices have not responded well to some of the advertising created centrally. One downside of global work is that it can end up being middle-of-the-road. When this happens, it's bad for an office's creative image locally."

But with costs escalating both centrally and locally, many felt that "the local barons" had to be reigned in. "How do we help our clients globalize," asked Walsh, "when our local management will conspire to keep them geographically oriented?"

For smaller agencies, issues of creative pride and autonomy were especially salient. Under the new system, the central WCS team developed the Brand-Printᵥ and advertising campaign with input from local offices. Local offices then tailored execution to regional markets. But while large offices usually served as the center for at least one global account, smaller offices, explained one WCS director, "are more often on the receiving end now. They begin to feel like post boxes. How do you attract good people to smaller offices if they never get to run big accounts?"

Beers felt that maintaining flexibility was key. "Some of our competitors — McCann Erickson is a good example — are excellent at running highly centralized campaigns. For us to view WCS that way would be a mistake. WCS should build upon, not diminish, our local strength." Creative and execution roles, she explained further, should shift according to the locus of the best ideas or relevant resources:

I want to continue to cultivate the tension between local and center. The easiest thing would be to have far more dominance centrally. It is more efficient, and the clients like it, because they invariably wish they had more control at the center. The reality is that nothing substitutes for full-blown, local agencies where the people are talented enough to articulate the heart of the brand, to interpret it in a sophisticated way, and — if necessary — to change it. If you have messengers or outlets, you will never execute well. The best ideas have unique, local modifications. One brand campaign we tested, for example, was an absolute win around the world, except in Asia, where the humor did not translate well. Our creative director in Asia worked with the idea, and it became the print campaign we use globally.

Also on her mind was the brewing controversy about how to split fees and allocate costs between WCS and local offices. Agency compensation on large accounts consisted frequently of fixed fees that were negotiated up front With new clients, it could be difficult to estimate the range of Ogilvy services needed and the extent of local adaptation that would be required. Agencies in more distant markets were asked to contribute — sometimes without compensation — when the need for additional local work was discovered. Local presidents complained that, although WCS accounts pulled their people away from local accounts with clear-cut billable time, their portion of multinational fees was small. WCS, on the other hand, maintained that they were being forced to absorb more than their fair share of local costs.

Beers recounted one specific incident that unfolded in December. "Kelly told me that one of our offices had refused to do any more work for a client, because they did not have any fees. I said to him, 'I think you ought to talk to them about our new way of working and how much promise there is in it. Give them more information. If they still can't see their way, have them come to me.' You ask for collaboration," she concluded, "but occasionally you act autocratically."

As conflicts continued to erupt, senior management was divided on the solution. "We have highly individual personalities running our offices. With 272 worldwide," one account director observed, "it's been like herding cats." Debate swirled around the degree of management structure required. Lazarus advocated common sense resolutions between the global account director and local agency presidents: "In our business, the quality of the work that gets done all comes down to the people who are doing it, not to bureaucratic structures. If you create the right environment and you have the right people, you don't need a whole structure." Others, O'Dea and his WCS corps included, insisted that organizational changes were necessary to make Brand Stewardship a reality agencywide. Walsh agreed: "What we don't have is a structure, working practices, remuneration, praise of people — all based on Brand Stewardship." Referring to the trademark, Ogilvy color, Beers offered her perspective:

We have to make Ogilvy 'redder.' The finances should follow our goal of killing geography as a barrier to serving the brand. . . . Let's get the emotional content high and the structure will follow. We have people in the company who would prefer it the other way, but I want to get it done in my lifetime. So much of what happens at Ogilvy is cerebral, thoughtful and slow. We can't afford to move at a 'grey' pace.

At the end of 1993, yet another issue had come to the fore. With large multinational accounts, some WCS heads controlled billings that easily surpassed those of many countries in the network. The agency, however, had always accorded the greatest prestige and biggest bonuses to presidents of local offices, countries, and regional chairmen. Brand Stewardship now required top-notch brand stewards and organizations centered around products and processes rather than Ogilvy office locations. "I ask people to collaborate, but I don't pay them for it. This company has never asked its feudal chiefs to consider the sum," observed Beers. She pondered how to attract the best and the brightest to WCS posts, knowing she would be asking them to leave the safety of turf to head brand-focused, virtual organizations.

The "thirsty for change" veterans believed another hurdle would be learning to work better as a team. Said Lazarus, "I don't think we make a lot of group decisions. We talk about it, but decisions tend to get made by Charlotte and by the specific individuals who are affected." But implementation revived many of the debates of the first Vienna meeting. "I think we are all still very guarded,"

explained Walsh. "As each meeting goes by, it's a bit like a lump of ice slowly melting — our edges getting smoother all the time." Lazarus hoped that team members would grow "comfortable enough to disagree openly with one another." Battling a culture she had once described as "grotesquely polite" was still on Beer's list of priorities as she considered the group she had assembled to help carry the change forward.

By December 1993, Charlotte Beers assessed the year's progress: "Clients love Brand Steward-ship. Competitors are trying to copy it. And intern-ally, we lack consensus." She wondered what course of action in 1994 would provide the best stewardship of the Ogilvy brand.

Aligning Strategy and Culture;
Best Practices and Future Trends

❏ CHAPTER AT A GLANCE

Highlights of this chapter include the following:

1. Research provides evidence that culture is a key factor in an organization's success and a significant limiting factor in managing change.

2. Strategy is the determination of the basic long-term goals and objectives of an enterprise, and the adoption of courses of action and the allocation of resources necessary for carrying out these goals.

3. Strategic fit alone is not enough. Organizations must also remain flexible enough to respond to (or even create) changes in their competitive environment.

4. Organizational culture is defined as a complex set of shared beliefs, guiding values, behavioral norms, and basic assumptions acquired over time that shape our thinking and behavior; they are part of the social fabric of the organization.

5. There are both visible (tangible) and not so visible (tacit) elements that comprise a culture.

6. An "adaptive" or "constructive" culture is a key driver of a firm's performance.

7. Culture is both an asset and liability.

8. Assessing a firm's culture is a useful tool in ensuring the correct cultural elements are in place to support and align the strategy/vision, resources, and systems required to affect the roadmap to change.

9. Considerations in planning a culture assessment include timing of survey, understanding

instrument limitations, selecting participants, communication, providing feedback, and survey selection.

10. Change leaders interested in producing cultural change must understand and intervene in each of the five key interventions for changing organizational culture.

11. Change leaders must align all four dimensions — strategy, resources, systems, and culture — with each change initiative to ensure lasting transformation.

12. Best practices related to effective change management.

13. Future trends in change management.

In the following vignette, we offer two examples that illustrate the challenges leaders face in any change situation. It's important to recognize that change does not occur in a vacuum or sterile environment. "It occurs in human systems, organizations, which already have beliefs, assumptions, expectations, norms, and values, both idiosyncratic to individual members of those organizations and shared."[1] Our focus in this chapter, therefore, is on organizational culture and its influence on the outcome of any change effort. To this end, we first revisit the concept of strategy, the importance of aligning strategy and culture, and end the chapter by looking toward the future in the field of change management.

❏ VIGNETTE

The Institute of Medicine in its 2006 report, *Preventing Medication Errors: Quality Chasm Series,* highlighted the prevalence of medication errors that are costly to the people who take medications and the nation overall. When all types of medication errors are taken into account, a hospital patient can expect on average to be subjected to more than one medication error each day. The report suggests that medication errors, while common, are preventable. Any intervention, however, will require behavioral changes from doctors, nurses, pharmacists, and others in the health care industry, including the Food and Drug Administration, other government agencies, hospitals, and other health care organizations, and from patients.[2] In another study of medical errors and quality of care, the authors found that "although technology is critical in

improving health care delivery and reducing medical errors . . . only by improving health care cultures and systems" can we expect an improvement in reducing the unacceptable costs of medication errors.[3] In fact, the same authors argue that, "The outmoded culture and management systems in health care organizations have precipitated a crisis in the health care workplace."[4]

The federal government is also facing huge challenges that necessitate significant transformation. A key element in this transformation involves the culture that currently exists in federal agencies. David M. Walker, Comptroller General of the United States, testified before a subcommittee in the House of Representatives in July 2005 to address the efforts required to transform the federal government to meet current and emerging challenges in the twenty-first century.[5] In his testimony, Mr. Walker focused on the following three areas — all of which involve change:*

1. How the long-term fiscal imbalance facing the United States, along with other significant trends, establish a case for change and the need to reexamine the base of the federal government.

2. How federal agencies can transform their cultures and create the capacity to become high-performing organizations.

3. How multiple approaches and selected initiatives can support the reexamination and transformation of the government and federal agencies to meet these 21st century challenges.

If the government is to address these challenges, the Comptroller General and the senior leadership clearly must understand and effectively manage the cultural aspects of any transformation effort. To illuminate the key cultural changes and key practices needed for successful transformation to a high performing organization, for example, Figure 7.1 identifies the current state of affairs and the desired future state along with the key practices necessary to achieve this transformation.

Clearly, as these examples illustrate, a wide variety of people and cultural issues play a huge role in any change effort or transformation. Culture can "not only stop a change effort dead in its tracks, it

*For more detailed information on these issues, see the source document.

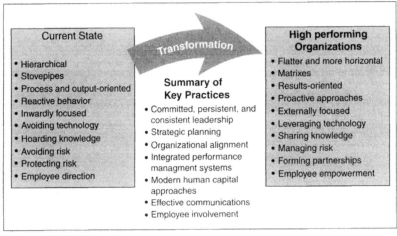

Source: GAO-05-83T, p. 12.

Figure 7.1   *Cultural Changes and Key Practices Necessary for Successful Transformation*

can also propel it to great heights. Wisdom during organizational change is understanding the power of culture and how to get it to work for you instead of against you."[6] How do you get thousands of employees suddenly to change their most basic assumptions about their company? After all, the beliefs and attitudes that make up a culture filter into everything else: decisions on basic strategy, management style, staffing, performance expectations, and product development. And so this is the challenge for change leaders — the need to create a new organizational culture that is congruent with the realities of its changing environment and that supports the strategy needed to adapt and respond to the forces for change.

❑ CHAPTER PERSPECTIVE

In the book, *Good to Great*, Jim Collins studied what made companies grow from merely good organizations to great ones. One interesting observation from his study was that "The good-to-great companies paid scant attention to managing change, motivating people, or creating alignment. Under the right conditions, the problems of commitment, alignment, motivation, and change largely melt away."[7] The "right conditions" that Collins is talking about is the organization climate or culture. Successfully managing change or implementing any strategy requires paying attention to culture and its role in the process. As Kotter reminds us,

Change sticks only when it becomes 'the way we do things around here,' when it seeps into the very blood-stream of the work unit or corporate body. Until new behaviors are rooted in social norms and shared values, they are always subject to degradation as soon as the pressures associated with a change effort are removed.[8]

This important element in managing change was exemplified in a talk by Louis V. Gerstner to MBA students at Harvard Business School in 2002. In this talk, Gerstner related his efforts to transform IBM when he took over as the new chairman and CEO in 1993. In a nutshell, what Gerstner discovered was that transforming IBM by focusing on strategy was not enough. Strategy is important, but strategy alone would not give IBM a unique competitive advantage. It was a change in IBM's 40-year culture that made the difference. As Gerstner commented,

I always viewed culture as one of those things you talked about, like marketing or advertising. It was one of the tools that a manager had at his disposal when you think about an enterprise . . . . The thing I have learned is that culture is everything.[9]

When Microsoft's CEO Steve Ballmer gave a talk at Wharton's Leadership Lecture series in 2006, he talked about the company's role in transforming the PC and information systems industry. He said, "Unless you are really committed to building a culture of continuous change and innovation and transformation, you are not in good shape."[10] Are Ballmer and Gerstner right? Is culture everything? More pointedly, how critical is culture to the change management calculus? This chapter is designed to answer just this question.

❑ WHAT IS STRATEGY?

We learned in earlier chapters that organizations need to be responsive to and adapt to the driving forces in their external and internal environments in order to maintain their competitive vitality. A critical aspect of this challenge is for top management to match organizational competencies with the risks and opportunities created by the driving forces in its environment. This matching of the firm's competencies and particular skills and abilities with its environment is called strategy. "The concept of strategy is thus one of top management's major tools for coping with both external and internal changes."[11]

Definition

There are almost as many definitions of strategy as there are writers on the subject. One of the earliest definitions, and still one of the best, is from the business historian Alfred Chandler's 1962 seminal work, *Strategy and Structure*, in which he defined strategy as,

Strategy is the determination of the basic long-term goals and objectives of an enterprise, and the adoption of courses of action and the allocation of resources necessary for carrying out these goals.[12]

Chandler's definition spotlights two important elements of how we define strategy. *First*, strategy fundamentally focuses on the future. To develop a strategy, the organization leadership must assess where they are now and set a future direction. This process involves making choices about markets and segments to compete in and which to avoid. "The choice of products and services to deliver and the acquisition and allocation of resources to ensure that this is done in a professional, timely and profitable fashion are essential components of good strategy."[13] It's the strategy that creates value for the shareholders and other stakeholders by meeting the needs of its customers and constituents. *Second*, strategy is about crafting a plan or blueprint to achieve specific performance outcomes and executing the plan efficiently and effectively.

Process

These two elements are at the heart of the strategy process in most organizations. Strategic management is a process that combines three interrelated activities: strategic analysis, crafting a strategy, and strategy implementation or execution. The strategic analysis is the foundation for the strategic management process. It typically begins with a data-driven situation analysis that reviews the current state of the company and industry. This phase also considers the organization's goals; an exploration of the opportunities and threats present in the external environment; and a study of the firm's internal strength's and weaknesses. Graham Beaver aptly captured the essence of this phase of the strategy process:

Sound strategy is rooted in a deep, almost encyclopedic understanding of what current and potential customers value, how much they are prepared to pay, the profile and posture of the competition and how such elements are likely to change. It should reflect a clear strategic intent and competitive innovation driven by sound and effective leadership.[14]

Based on this analysis and trends impacting the firm, industry, and stakeholders, management then can engage in scenario planning to challenge their assumptions, develop their strategies, and evaluate the attractiveness associated with those scenarios. A scenario is considered attractive when it enables the organization to enjoy a "**sustainable competitive advantage**" over its rivals. Competitive advantage represents the strategies, skills, knowledge, resources, or competencies that differentiate a business from its competitors.[15] However, competitive advantage is only temporary. The literature is full of examples where a company's competitive advantage crumbled in the face of new technological developments or the entry of new competitors.[15] Hence, it's important that firms must accelerate organizational learning to stay ahead of competitors in building new advantages.[16]

Once a position of sustainable competitive advantage has been identified, a plan needs to be developed for getting there. We can formulate the most elegant strategies imaginable, but until we implement them properly, the desired results may not materialize. This requires that managers allocate resources necessary to achieve objectives and to design an organizational structure such that all four dimensions of change are in alignment. We'll say more about this point later in the chapter.

❑ STRATEGIC FIT AND FLEXIBILITY

Creating the right fit between an organization's core competencies and what the market needs can be disastrous if the environment changes and the firm does not respond accordingly. The story of the boiled frog is illustrative:

When a frog is put in a pot of boiling water, it jumps out. When, instead, the same frog is put in a pot of cold water and the water is slowly brought to a boil, the frog stays in the pot and boils to death. In the same manner, if a company does not react to the constant changes talking place in its environment, it will find itself boiled to death.[17]

This suggests that strategic fit alone is not enough. Organizations must also remain flexible enough to respond to (or even create) changes in this environment. The days when the competitive climate was characterized as relatively static are over. Today agility and innovation take center stage and drives firm performance. "Innovation is now the principal competitive [weapon], differentiating the successful growth firms of tomorrow from the bureaucratic and inflexible ones."[18] An agile and flexible organization is one that (1) is able to identify changes in the environment early enough; (2) nurtures a culture that embraces and responds to change; and (3) has the requisite resources, skills, and competencies to compete in whatever environment emerges after the change.[19]

However, implementing a new strategy or change does not take place in a vacuum. It takes place in an organizational environment (the organization's culture), created by leaders and managers that define the behavior of all employees in that environment. It's this climate that determines the success of any strategy, transformation, or change initiative; the organization culture is what promotes and supports the chosen strategy.[20] Robbie Bach, one of three co-presidents at Microsoft, was responsible for developing and bringing to market Micosoft's Xbox videogame and digital music player Zune. He's deeply involved in shifting Microsoft's strategy in consumer electronics to what the company is calling "connected entertainment."[21] Pulling off this strategy won't be a walk in the park. If this strategic shift and change is going to come to fruition, one of Bach's goals will involve redeveloping and transforming the "old school" culture in Microsoft's Entertainment and Devices Division.

Research provides evidence that culture is a key factor in an organization's success and a significant limiting factor in managing change. One study reported that 70% of CRM projects fail not for technological reasons, but because of culture.[22]

Change leaders recognize that "significant strategic or structural realignment cannot occur if it is not supported by the organization's values and behavioral norms."[23] This view is further supported by Kanter who suggests that to manage change in an organization requires that people find their stability and security in the culture and direction of the organization.[24] Therefore, understanding, analyzing, and effectively managing all aspects of the organization's culture is paramount in supporting any change initiative.

Let us now shift our focus to better understanding what is organization culture.

❑ WHAT IS ORGANIZATIONAL CULTURE?

The construct of organizational culture has raised considerable interest of both academics and practitioners in the field of change management. Organizational culture is "derived from the anthropological concept of culture that attempts to explain why people in societies believe and behave as they do."[25] It has "become a common way of thinking about and describing an organization's internal world — a way of differentiating one organization's 'personality' from another."[26] This organizational self-image develops over a period of time with the core elements typically coalescing during the organization's formative years.[27]

In many organizations we find a strong dominant culture that is pervasive not only in the headquarters element but across divisions and geographic regions. However, in large organizations this culture is not uniform but instead is composed of many subcultures. Subcultures may share certain characteristics, norms, and values, yet they can be totally different with some functioning collaboratively and others in conflict with each other.

Definition

Organizational culture is defined as a complex set of shared beliefs, guiding values, behavioral norms, and basic assumptions acquired over time that shape our thinking and behavior; they are part of the social fabric of the organization — its genetic code. As such, culture drives the organization and guides the behavior of everyone in that organization — how they think, feel, and act. In other words, the culture forms a behavior template. Davis and Landa succinctly captured the essence of culture when they say,

The factors which define culture are in part internal, deriving from the unique character of the organization and, in part external, determined by the background and experiences managers and employees bring to the enterprise. Culture is a major determinant of productivity; it shapes organizational responses to external pressures; and suppresses or enhances the cooperative effort level of the workforce. Culture has a significant bottom-line effect on organizational effectiveness, profitability, and shareholder value.[28]

Culture Levels

When people join an organization, they are not given a manual that defines the culture for them. What employees learn by processes of socialization and acculturation is that there are both visible (tangible) and not so visible (tacit) elements that comprise a culture (see Figure 7.2). If we use an iceberg as a metaphor, we can get a sense of how culture is manifested in an organization. Typically all we see with an iceberg is 1/8 of its mass above the water line. With cultures we see structures and processes, which are technically referred to as physical artifacts, or surface manifestations. The most important point about this level is that it is

easy to observe and decipher.[29] Examples include behaviors, jargon, stories, myths, rituals, status symbols, uniforms, slogans, and so on. The much more significant and not so visible aspects of culture include unwritten assumptions, values, and beliefs of the organization. These deeper and less visible cultural elements tend to persist over time even when organizational membership changes. Kotter and Heskett remind us that "at this level culture can be extremely difficult to change, in part because group members are unaware of many of the values that bind them together."[30]

Keeping these points in mind, let us explore some of the more common underlying and difficult elements of culture to change.

Beliefs. Generally, beliefs are basic assumptions about the world and how it works. They are perceptions about the connections between events and outcomes, such as "people who work hard will be rewarded." Because beliefs are based on individual perception, attribution errors are common. Moreover, "because many facets of physical and social reality are difficult or impossible to experience personally or to verify, people rely on others they identify with and trust to help them decide what to believe and what not to believe."[31]

Values. Values reflect a person's underlying beliefs of what should be or should not be. Values

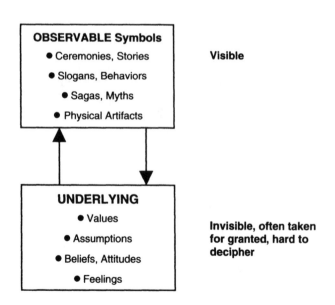

Figure 7.2 Levels of Organization Culture

whether conscious or unconscious, guide behavior and are reflected in the way people act in the organization. Former CEO of Corning, Jamie Houghton described the importance of organizational values this way:

I think of values as buoys in the channel of commerce. For 145 years they've helped keep us headed in the right direction as we've made the necessary course corrections in the ever-changing sea. They continue to guide us as we make the millions of decisions that must be made to run the enterprise — decisions that will be better because they are constantly tested against our values. In total, Corning's values are Quality, Integrity, Performance, Leadership, Innovation, Independence, and "The Individual." Contrary to the opinions of some pundits, values are not peripheral to business success or merely "nice" or "morally comforting". I believe that cutting corners on values and expecting to succeed is patent nonsense.[32]

These same sentiments were echoed by the Executive Chairman of Southwest Airlines, Herb Kelleher, when asked about the thinking that triggered Southwest Airlines strategy of putting people first.

We always felt that people should be treated right as a matter of morality . . . . We said we want to really take care of these people, we want to honor them and we love them as individuals. Now that induces the kind of reciprocal trust and diligent effort that made us successful. But the motivation was not strategy, it was core values . . . . yet these values affect us in many ways and help us to move quickly.[33]

Behaviors.[34] Behaviors are observable actions that constitute the way people actually operate on a daily basis. Where beliefs reflect intentions that are often difficult to discern, behaviors can be verified in a more objective manner (i.e., through observable actions or events). Where people park, who they do and don't talk to, what they wear to the office, how decisions are made, and how conflict is managed are the kinds of behaviors associated with an organization's culture.

Assumptions. Assumptions are the unconscious rationale we use for continuing to apply certain beliefs and or specific behaviors. Assumptions are the taken for granted ways "we work around here." Basic assumptions are very difficult to change. According to Edgar Schein, if basic assumptions are strongly held in a culture, then its unlikely members of that culture will behave in a way contrary to those assumptions.[35]

In closing this section on what is organizational culture, consider this insight from Lou Gershner:

Culture is what people do when you don't ask them to do something. It's what they think about. If you just try to change an organization without working on the culture, you won't change. It will look like you changed, but the culture will go back to what it was before. You don't invent cultural imperatives out of nowhere, like "we should be nice" or "be customer sensitive." You don't talk to people that way. You lay out a clear strategy of what has to be done.[36]

Our attention now turns to the basic functions of culture and its effects on the organization.

❑ IMPORTANCE OF ORGANIZATIONAL CULTURE

As John Kotter and James Heskett evince in their book, *Corporate Culture and Performance*, "corporate culture can have a significant impact on a firm's long-term economic performance [and] will probably be even more important in determining the success or failure of firms in the next decade."[37] More specifically, the authors concluded, and Klein[38] reaffirmed their findings in later study, that an **"adaptive"** or **"constructive"** culture is a key driver of performance. If a culture does not encourage adaptation (e.g., highly bureaucratic, reactive, risk averse, inward looking, lacks creativity, strives to maintain the status quo), it can significantly harm the firm's ability to be responsive in the face of a changing environment. IBM in the pre-Gerstner days is one illustration of where an organizational culture without adaptive norms lost the ability to be flexible and adapt to changing times. The important lesson to remember is that the greatest challenge is not crafting or shaping organizational culture, but the need to constantly adapt the culture to fit the changing business requirements.[39] To this end, organizational leaders need to recognize which beliefs are deeply held by the organization and which beliefs will be challenged when attempting to change the culture.

But before we launch into a deeper understanding of organizational culture and its role in the change process, we need to highlight a controversial but very important point advocated by John Kotter. He says that in order to avoid the pitfalls of managing change, it's important "to understand a fundamental and widely misunderstood aspect of organizational change. In a change effort, culture comes last, not first."[40] Most organizations seem to focus fixing the culture first. The thinking is that if the culture is inward looking, risk averse, and slow, then changing the culture first will make the implementation of any vision that much easier. But as Kotter reminds, the reality is totally different:

A culture truly changes only when a new way of operating has been shown to succeed . . . . Trying to shift the norms and values before you have created the new way of operating does not work. The vision can talk of a new culture. You can create new behaviors that reflect a desired culture. But those new behaviors will not become norms, will not take hold, until the very end of the process.[41]

Strong versus Weak Cultures

Although a strong organizational culture can have a significant impact on the firm's performance, it isn't necessarily a positive impact. A "strong culture" is one where there is substantial agreement across behavioral norms, values, and beliefs. If there is substantial consensus about what those cultural norms are, that signifies a strong culture, while if there is disagreement about what those values and norms are, the culture is "weak."

David Ulrich identified the relationship between strong agreement across cultural norms (what he calls "cultural unity") and firm performance.[42] His research can be demonstrated through Figure 7.3, below, which shows that a firm may have a "strong"

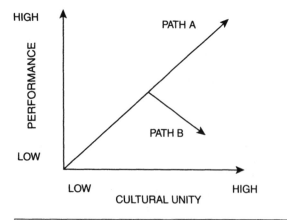

Figure 7.3 *Cultural Unity and Performance (Adapted from Ulrich, 1997, p. 175)*

culture, where there is a lot of agreement about the firm's identity, and yet see its performance drop (Path B), while a competitor firm with a strong culture sees its performance rise (Path A). These paths illustrated what other analysts recognize, that mere consensus or agreement across cultural norms doesn't translate into strong performance; it must be a *healthy* culture. Firms who end up on Path B, where their strong consensus does not translate into strong performance, probably got "stuck" following traditions that no longer serve them in today's environment. The graveyard of corporations is replete with examples of once great firms who were not able to adapt to changing circumstances and survive. Yet there are also giants like General Electric, who, through excellent leadership, have been able to adapt their culture to survive and prosper for over a hundred years.

What is an "adaptive" culture? Firms with adaptive cultures behave very differently than firms with unadaptive cultures. Adaptive cultures are those where the managers focus on three key constituents; shareholders, customers, and employees. They also value total quality management processes that focus on continuous improvement. Their behavior is flexible, risk-taking is allowed, and change management is valued, not feared. On the other hand, in an "unadaptive culture," managers focus on themselves, their departments and personal initiatives, at the expense of their customers, shareholders, and fellow employees. They tend to discourage risk-taking and change is feared, not valued. Therefore, if a culture is strong and healthy, it helps members adapt to changing times. If the culture is strong and unhealthy, it impedes change management by discouraging flexibility and risk taking.

Culture as Asset or Liability

We can also view organizational culture as both an asset and liability. It's an asset in five key ways (see Figure 7.4).[43] First, it provides a sense of identity for organizational members and helps build pride and commitment. People feel a sense of commitment when they identify with the organization and experience an emotional attachment to its mission, vision and strategic objectives.

Second, culture is a sense-making device. It provides a way for employees to interpret the meaning of what happens in the organization.

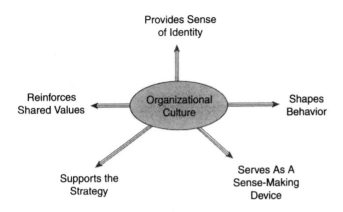

Figure 7.4 *How Culture Affects Performance*

Third, culture reinforces the shared values in the organization. For example, in discussing IKEA's history and success, CEO Anders Dahlvig says this about the importance of shared values:

It's a very informal type of culture. It's based on a few values that have their roots in . . . Swedish culture. Things like informality, cost consciousness, and a very humble and 'down to earth' approach . . . . letting people have responsibilities . . . . We give [culture] a lot of attention in terms of marketing and sales as well as development, training and recruitment. The culture is a very important part of a company in the sense that the values of the culture really influence the business itself.[44]

Fourth, culture serves as a control mechanism for shaping behavior. For example, shared norms guide employee behavior. It signals what behavior is appropriate and what is discouraged. The consulting firm Accenture conducted a study where they interviewed 425 senior executives at leading organizations in North America, Europe, and Asia to identify and prioritize the issues of greatest concern to senior management. An issue uncovered in the survey was "changing organizational culture and employee attitudes."[45] Clearly, business leaders recognize that strategy or change execution is not going to happen unless the human resources — the people talent — in the organization are engaged and committed. The right culture and attitudes help in this process.

Finally, the fit of culture and strategy cannot be ignored. Charles O'Reilly aptly captured this important function of culture when he noted that every organization,

explicitly or implicitly, has a competitive strategy which dictates how it attempts to position itself with respect to its competitors. Once established, a firm's strategy dictates a set of critical tasks or objectives that must be accomplished through a congruence among the elements of people, structure, and culture. In order for any strategy to be implemented, there must be an appropriate culture. When companies change strategies and often structures, they fail because the underlying shared values do not support the new approach.[46]

Culture is a liability when the shared beliefs, values, and norms are not congruent with the needs of the organization, its employees and constituents, and its ability to adapt to the ever changing environment. As organizations grow and mature, their cultures can become more bureaucratic, more inwardly focused, more political, more impersonal, more stressful, and less fulfilling. A deeply entrenched culture can make it difficult for an organization to adapt to changing conditions. For example, culture has been implicated whenever organizations get into trouble. Some notable examples include Arthur Andersen, Enron, Salomon Brothers, NASA, Coca-Cola, and Marsh Mac to name a few.

In sum, organizational culture plays a vital role in facilitating strategic change. To overlook culture in the planning and implementation of any change initiative is dangerous. "It is, after all, people — at all levels of the organization — who must carry out the change . . . . No shift in strategy can succeed unless the culture is resilient and shifts with it."[47]

Let us keep this importance of organizational culture in mind as we look the importance of assessing culture.

❏ WHY ASSESS CULTURE?

Not understanding a firm's culture in today's world of perpetual change can be fatal. As we discussed in previous chapters, given the rapid pace of change organizations face today, only those who can quickly respond to the driving forces in their environment and adapt can survive.

The change literature is clear: any strategic plan or change initiative is unlikely to be successful — that is, implemented and sustained — unless there is an appropriate organizational culture in place to support the plan. So it's critical that change leaders fully understand the organization's cultural profile before undertaking the change. How then can we go about getting an accurate picture of an organization's culture so leaders can transition its current value set to a new value set?

To this end, an assessment of a firm's culture (sometimes called a gap analysis) is a useful tool in ensuring the correct cultural elements are in place to support and align the strategy/vision, resources, and systems required to affect the roadmap to change. This point is illuminated by Schein:

If we understand the dynamics of culture, we will be less likely to be puzzled, irritated, and anxious when we encounter the unfamiliar and seemingly irrational behavior of people in organizations, and we will have a deeper understanding not only of why various groups of people or organizations can be so different but also why it is so hard to change them.[48]

Whenever there is an incongruity between the current culture and the goals of the change initiative, the culture always wins.[49] For this reason, many change initiatives are ultimately unsuccessful for lack of appropriate cultural support needed to get people to embrace and implement the change.

So in effect, what is done to assess the cultural infrastructure is to define the existing organization culture (i.e., what is the shared mindset of the people within the organization); characterize the target culture needed to support the change; define what gaps exist between the current culture and desired culture; and then devise a way to bridge that gap. The turnaround of Continental Airlines in the mid-1990s, for example, was largely possible because the change leaders in this case not only "aligned major strategy execution factors such as organizational structure and systems and processes with the new strategy, but a key ingredient was also aligning relevant parts of the organization's culture . . . with the new strategy."[50] What Continental's turnaround leadership understood well was that what worked in the past would not sustain the company going forward.

Organizations are constantly faced with a constantly changing competitive landscape. Consequently, cultures that fit old business needs must give way to cultures that fit current industry and competitive dynamics. The perpetual challenge facing both the public and private sector organization is not defining or shaping their respective cultures but in constantly adapting them to the new realties of change in the twenty-first century.[51] David Ulrich provides a useful metaphor to illuminate this important point:

Just as people's closets and attics may be stuffed with mementos of sentimental value, organizations may preserve old cultures that feel cozy but become burdensome by failing to respond to change. Closets must be cleaned; attics must be seen to hold remnants of the past; and organizations must learn to let go of old cultures when new ones become necessary.[52]

Perhaps Lou Gerstner, former CEO of IBM, puts this all in perspective with his apposite observation:

Leading cultural change is not just one of the things you do when you change an enterprise — it's a totality of what you have to work on if you are going to do a true, transformational change. At the end of the day, you do not change an institution, fundamentally altering how it thinks and behaves, without a deep understanding of the cultural bearings that exist.[53]

Now that we have a good idea of why it's important to assess a firm's culture in managing change, let us now turn to a consideration of issues related to planning the cultural assessment.

❏ CONSIDERATIONS IN PLANNING A CULTURE ASSESSMENT[54]

In this section, we discuss some important management and logistical issues that must be addressed before initiating a culture survey. Among the key management and logistical questions that need to be answered during the planning phase include the following:

1. Who will administer the survey and compile the results?

2. When should the survey take place?

3. What should the organization expect from the survey?

4. Who should participate in the survey?

5. How should the launch and results be communicated?

Answering these questions before implementing the survey will help ensure that it achieves the desired results.

Timing surveys. An organizational culture survey should take place prior to the initiation of any major change initiative. After the change becomes stable and the new way of how we work around here takes hold, it's a good idea to reassess the culture once again to ensure that the desired new culture is indeed emerging. Leaders should consider some kind of ongoing cultural assessment as a window to further monitor the existing culture for changes and as a means to measure the extent to which the organization has achieved cultural change.

Understanding the limitations. In order for any organizational culture survey to be useful, everyone involved — change agents, employees, and the firm's leadership — need to have an understanding of what the instrument can and cannot provide. Unfortunately, many organizations administer a culture survey believing they have finally discovered a crystal ball that will tell them — with a high degree of clarity and precision — just exactly what they are or should become. The reality is that there is no perfect culture assessment tool. Change leaders may see the results as contrary to what they expected; the results do not always provide easy answers. Culture assessment tools are helpful for creating clarity and consensus about the firm's existing culture and helping management define where they believe they need to be. The culture survey itself will not define the steps needed to close the gap between where you are now and where you want to be. For these reasons, it is important to understanding the capabilities and limitations of any assessment tool beforehand.

Given the foregoing concerns, in addition to any quantitative culture survey, change leaders should also consider collecting qualitative data in the form of interviews. The questions need to uncover the deeper elements of the culture as well as collect quotes to validate the overall findings and communicate what people are thinking.[55]

Selecting participants. Which members of the organization participate in the survey helps determine the true picture of the organization's culture. Typically, the leadership team is surveyed first. This is important for building consensus among the leaders, who, as a group, must drive the change efforts. By having the leadership team be the first in the organization to go through the assessment process, much of the dissension and many of the barriers that surround any major organizational change can be identified and eliminated early in the process, thereby avoiding costly and time-consuming delays further down the road.

Next, depending on the scope of the change, different levels of employees in the organization are surveyed to collect further data. This data will provide a more accurate "reading" of the organization's culture and subcultures and help validate — or negate — leadership's "view of the world." After all, perceptions often differ from one level to another. We know, for example, that the higher the level of the employee, the more likely that he or she will have a favorable view of the organization than do middle managers, professional and technical employees, and front-line employees.

Communicating the launch. Two common mistakes that should be avoided when conducting a culture survey are the following: (1) conduct the survey with absolutely no warning, generating rumors and uncertainly throughout the organization, and (2) launch the survey with great fanfare and never hear about it again — also generating rumors and uncertainty throughout the organization.

Before launching any culture survey, it should begin with appropriate communication to everyone in the organization who will be participating and who will part of the feedback process. Participants to the survey should be told what it is, why it is being carried out, what sort of outcomes they are likely to see, and when the results are likely to be disseminated. Such communication will go a long way not only building acceptance and credibility around the assessment, but also toward establishing the trust needed to execute any needed changes that the assessment identifies.

Providing feedback.[56] Typically feedback will begin with the most senior levels of the organization. This provides an opportunity for the senior leadership to express their reactions to the data, their assessments of the strengths and weaknesses of the current culture, and their perspectives on the desirability and appropriateness of the desired or ideal culture.

The next phase of data feedback involves communication to the lower levels of the organization that are affected by the change. This setting provides an excellent opportunity to engage in a dialogue with employees by soliciting their input and suggestions for how to move the culture in the desired direction. The format of these meetings typically will begin with an overview of the goals of the survey and the processes used. Next, the current culture profile is presented, supplemented with some subgroup information, and continuing on through presentations of the ideal culture — that is, where we want to be following the change initiative. This is also a good opportunity to test the acceptability of the cultural directions senior management may have identified as desirable for the organization as a whole.

Selecting an assessment tool. Change leaders need a useful diagnostic framework to identify the organization's culture. There are numerous culture measurement tools change leaders can use to help them in conducting a culture gap analysis. For example, one such tool is the Organizational Culture Inventory (OCI).[57] It is one of the most widely used and thoroughly researched tools for measuring organizational culture in the world. Developed by Drs. Robert A. Cooke and J. Clayton Lafferty, the OCI provides an assessment of an organization's operating culture in terms of the behaviors that members believe are required to "fit in and meet expectations" within their organization. The OCI measures 12 types of behavioral norms that may characterize the operating culture of an organization. Four of these behavioral norms are **Constructive** and facilitate high-quality problem solving and decision making, teamwork, productivity, and long-term effectiveness. Eight of the behavioral norms are **Defensive** (Passive and Aggressive) and detract from effective performance. Thus, the OCI enables organizations to analyze their culture and identify practical strategies for enhancing their productivity and long-term effectiveness. A typical ideal culture profile is depicted in Figure 7.5.

The OCI can be used to:

- obtain reliable data on the behavioral norms and expectations of the organization and/or its subunits;
- validate a need for cultural change on the part of participants, both individually and collectively;
- identify the areas where change needs to take place;
- develop a vision for culture change;
- create individual and organizational action plans for effecting cultural change; and
- evaluate the impact of organizational change efforts.

The OCI interpretation guide speaks directly to organizations focused on change and innovation by noting that,

[they] are likely to have predominantly Constructive cultures. 'Learning Organizations,' which emphasize creativity, individual development, and systems thinking, promote Self-Actualizing, Humanistic-Encouraging, and Achievement cultural norms. Similarly, organizations that have successfully implemented total quality management or continuous improvement approaches . . . tend to have strong Achievement and Self-Actualizing cultural norms.[58]

Culture change is often perceived to be difficult even when there is a compelling and urgent need to transform the organization. Cultures are the products of their success. What was done in the past propelled the organization to its current position. The policies and practices that have lead to success naturally are resistant to change. Using an instrument like the OCI can help change leaders uncover aspects of the culture that may hinder its current success or inform risk of failure in the future.

As a further example, Jassawalla and Sashitall focused on the cultural genetic elements that support and facilitate innovation.[59] Figure 7.6 illustrates a self-assessment to help determine whether an organization's culture reflects the dominant behaviors the authors define as important in firms with highly successful product innovations.

Keeping these important points in mind, let us examine a framework for changing an organizations culture.

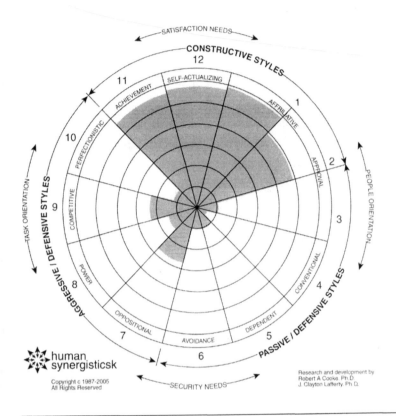

Figure 7.5   *Typical Ideal Culture Profile***

❏ INFLUENCING CULTURE CHANGE

Once a culture is formed, it is difficult to change. Ulrich reports that few, if any, mature organizations have successfully attempted a complete cultural transformation.[60] As one writer observed,

> This is because a culture serves the deep psychological functions of reducing human anxiety and providing members with identity. In the face of external threats or internal failures, a culture tends to go into survival mode and to engage in rationalization and denial. These are among the reasons that an organization's culture exhibits an active resistance to change.[61]

Consequently, this resistance suggests change leaders face two alternatives. Leave the culture as is and "try to work around it and then watch helplessly as their change initiative first stalls, and then collapses. Or they can roll up their sleeves and undertake the daunting task of reshaping the organization's values, beliefs, and behavior in ways that support" the change initiative and new strategy.[62] For example, when John Swaison joined troubled software maker Computer Associates as its new CEO in 2004, he found an organization in deep trouble with complaining customers, late product deliveries, poor-quality products, and a huge accounting scandal perpetrated by the former CEO. If he was to be successful in reforming this company, Swaison recognized that doing so would required fixing the business and its image, and most importantly reshaping its culture. Although he naively thought he could turn around the company in a year, he is making significant progress going forward. At least by mid-2006, industry reports suggest that now customers are pleased with the way things are working out.

As we noted previously, any consideration for culture change is driven from the need for attaining alignment with the strategy, resources, and systems elements inherit in any transformation.

**OCI circumplex from Robert A. Cooke and J. Clayton Lafferty, Organizational Culture Inventory®, Human Synergistics International, Plymouth, MI USA. Copyright © 1987-2006. All right reserved. Used by permission.

Circle the number that most closely reflects your environment's belief and value systems based on the statements above each continuum.

Product innovation is more likely to succeed if participants are unique, and are provided the facility to develop their uniqueness.

Product innovation is more likely to succeed if participants are similar, and molded to conform to our notion of the "ideal employee."

10—9—8—7—6—5—4—3—2—1

Participants can be trusted to act in the firm's best interests with minimal supervision.

People cannot be trusted to manage the complexity of product innovation processes, and therefore must be closely controlled.

10—9—8—7—6—5—4—3—2—1

Participants are capable of defining and developing the infrastructure for the new product task.

The infrastructure, decision-making processes and workflow must be imposed on participants.

10—9—8—7—6—5—4—3—2—1

Other constituencies (e.g., customers and suppliers) can be trusted to participate as insiders, and can be integrated within the product development process.

The world consists of insiders and outsiders. External constituents, including other departments, customers and suppliers, hold agendas that are not supportive.

10—9—8—7—6—5—4—3—2—1

Conflict, disruption, chaos and uncertainty are natural and revitalizing features of new product processes.

Conflict is disruptive and harmful. It should be avoided at all costs and by strict directives and guidelines when possible.

10—9—8—7—6—5—4—3—2—1

Change can energize and refresh the organization, and unleash the creative potential of participants.

Change is destabilizing and results in unfavourable distribution of power and control over resources.

10—9—8—7—6—5—4—3—2—1

Value is created when participants frequently question and challenge decisions and actions.

Once decisions are made, they should not be questioned. We should not rock the boat. Troublemakers and whistle blowers should be carefully controlled.

10—9—8—7—6—5—4—3—2—1

Cont'd . . .

Team leaders are educators, coaches and resource facilitators. They forage for resources and information to aid teamwork and create opportunities for team members to develop their talents, enhance their interests, and ensure that their best judgment is reflected in the final product.

Team leaders are chief decision makers, and use information and resources to generate the right behaviour from participants.

10—9—8—7—6—5—4—3—2—1

Participants are highly engaged and committed to continually improving their skills and capabilities.

Participants are less (or not) engaged and committed to improving their skills and capabilities.

10—9—8—7—6—5—4—3—2—1

Participants continually reaffirm their free choice of belonging in the setting and participating in the product innovation process.

Participants frequently feel trapped, and rarely (or do not) exercise their choice of belonging in (or exiting from) the product innovation setting.

10—9—8—7—6—5—4—3—2—1

Other team members are competent resources, and asking for assistance (and assisting others) is the right way to develop new products.

Other team members are not as competent. Asking for assistance (and assisting others) is a sign of weakness, and represents a betrayal of departmental loyalty.

10—9—8—7—6—5—4—3—2—1

Mistakes will occur, and signal the need for reflection, contemplation soul-searching and learning.

After mistakes have occurred, efforts should be made to assign blame (finger-pointing), and make culprits pay (find scapegoats).

10—9—8—7—6—5—4—3—2—1

Information redundancy is important. Intense information sharing is critical for reducing errors.

All participants should operate on a need to know basis

10—9—8—7—6—5—4—3—2—1

To obtain the Cultural DNA score, add the circled numbers. A score of:

110–130:	The culture is highly innovation-supportive.
78–109:	Strong signs that highly innovation-supportive culture might exist.
51–77:	Suggests that the culture is tinged with paranoia. Reconfiguration of structure, systems, process and rewards indicated.
Up to 50:	The culture is paranoid.

Source: Extracted from Jassawalla, A. R., & Sashittal, H. C. (2003, December). The DNA of cultures That Promote Product Innovation. Ivey Business Journal, pp. 5–6.

Figure 7.6 Assessing Cultural DNA

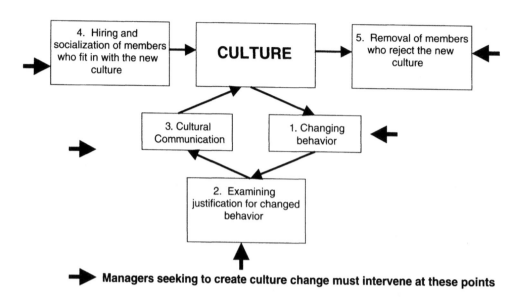

Adapted from Sathe, V. (1983, Autumn). Implications of corporate culture: A manager's guide to action. Organizational Dynamics, p. 18.

Figure 7.7   *Interventions for Changing Organizational Culture*

Change leaders interested in producing cultural change must understand and intervene in each of the five key interventions for changing organizational culture depicted in Figure 7.7.

In this framework for guiding culture change, the numbered boxes represent actions managers can take. There are two basic approaches to changing the existing culture: (1) helping current members buy into a new set of values (actions 1, 2, and 3); or (2) adding newcomers and socializing them into the organization, and removing current members as appropriate (actions 4 and 5).[63] In the following sections, we explicate further on the key stages in the culture change model.

Changing Behavior

In changing organizational culture, a basic premise is that organizations don't act; people do.[64] So the first stage involves getting people to behave differently. If people don't change, there is no organizational change. However, even if the behavior does change, this is not sufficient for cultural change to occur. In defining culture earlier, we noted that it is a system of shared actions, values, and beliefs that develop within an organization and guides the behavior of its members.[65] Behavior is a visible level of culture; changing ones behavior does not

automatically mean individuals change their values that underlie that behavior.

As we discussed in a previous chapter, getting people to significantly change their perceptions, attitudes, and behavior in pursuit of a new vision is no walk in the park. This is where a comprehensive system of rewards and recognition can be helpful in shaping norms. In addition, we know that cultural norms are transmitted as employees watch or hear about the successes of others. "This learning is tied to concrete, observable attitudes and behaviors, not abstract slogans and values."[66]

Justification of Behavior

Simply changing behavior does not automatically translate into producing cultural change. The "why" of any behavioral change must be articulated and accepted. In other words, people may behave in the way called for by a new process, but they still adhere to old beliefs and values. In short, what we get is behavior compliance, not culture commitment.[67] Here we need to address the mental sets all people in the organization have about the culture and change. We need to win both their heads and their hearts. More specifically, we must address the definable reasons for the change and its benefits to the organization. We also need to consider the motivational and emotional needs of individuals involved. Why must I change? What's in it for me? What are the rewards or consequences of changing? What are the consequences of not changing? Am I capable of making the changes I'll need to make?[68] This approach will require a combination of gentle incentives and compelling persuasion to engage in the new behavior. And since any manager involved in cultural change must communicate the new beliefs and values, hence the importance of communication in this process.

Cultural Communication

This is a very important step. Culture is communicated via both explicit and implicit means and must present a consistent message about the new values and beliefs. Explicit forms of communication may include announcements, memos, policies, and so on. Implicit forms may include rituals, ceremonies, metaphors, heroes, logos, décor, dress, and other symbolic forms of communication.[69] The role and importance of communication in managing change was discussed in Chapter 6.

Hiring and Socialization

This element in the process deals with the hiring and socialization of new hires and the "weeding out" and removal of individuals who do not fit the new culture. For example, the selection process may need to be revised to reflect the new culture. Southwest Airlines, for example, is one company that is very selective in the people they hire. The company recruits for cultural fit looking primarily for attitude. To ensure fit, they rely on peer recruiting and multiple interviews with a focus on positive attitude and teamwork. Cleary, achieving a perfect culture/ person fit is not realistic. However, it is important to avoid "irreconcilable mismatches between the person being hired and the intended culture."[70] Finally, organizations "can identify individuals who resist the cultural change or who are no longer comfortable with the values of the organization."[71]

In addition, it's always important for organizations to socialize new members to expose them to the rules, norms, values, and practices of their new culture. If the process is managed well, successful socialization is reflected in job satisfaction, motivation, understanding the culture, and commitment to the organization. If the process is not handled well, it can lead to job dissatisfaction, low employee motivation, lack of organizational commitment, turnover and low performance. A typical employee orientation might include the following:[72]

1. Leadership at all levels role modeling to signal that the norms and values are important and should be taken seriously;

2. Clear, consistent statements, measurement systems, and models all emphasizing the specific attitudes and behaviors desired and rewarded;

3. Development of a cohort or set of organizational members who share the goals and values and can act as role models and social support;

4. Continual reinforcement and celebration of living according to the beliefs; and

5. Opportunities for continuous socialization through training, meetings, and celebrations.

Our discussion now turns to culture alignment and the dimensions of change.

❏ CULTURE DOES NOT OPERATE IN ISOLATION

In Chapter 1 we introduced a model for change that included four dimensions of change as an important component in managing the change process. We further explicated the dimensions of change in Chapter 3. In this chapter, we want to again emphasize that all four factors need to be in alignment. At a minimum, change leaders must align all four dimensions — strategy, resources, systems, and culture — with each change initiative to ensure lasting transformation. This alignment is conveyed with arrows in Figure 7.8. All the "arrows" should

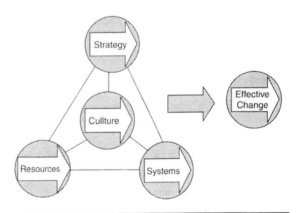

Figure 7.8 *Dimensions of Change Aligned*

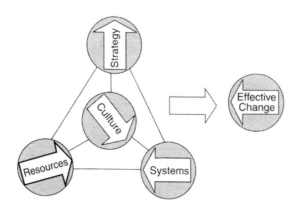

Figure 7.9 *Non-aligned Dimensions of Change*

be pointing in the same direction — that is, aligned with one another.

But as we know many organizational change initiatives often fail to meet planned expectations. When the dimensions of change are not in alignment, the picture looks more like the one shown in Figure 7.9. This figure portrays an organization with nonaligned dimensions of change, with its arrows pointing in all sorts of directions. That the arrows are pointing in different directions may reflect the impacts of pervious leadership on these dimensions or failure to consider the implication of these factors on executing change. For example, while the strategy for change may reflect the change vision and strategies for reaching that vision, the organization's resources remain inadequate, the organization's systems are unchanged, and the organization's behavioral norms remain fixed as they have for years. It's these kinds of misalignments that put a change effort in jeopardy of not achieving the desired outcome. What is required is alignment, getting all the arrows to all point in the same direction as the strategy for change.

The dimensions of change can become misaligned for many reasons, but at least two stand out. The change leaders either don't recognize the need to align the four dimensions, or they do so "only perfunctorily because they don't understand the implication of the required alignment."[73] We should note that not all four of the dimensions need to be misaligned to reduce the effectiveness of the change. The misalignment of the culture, for example, is enough in itself to lead to difficulties in successfully executing the transformation.

Recall from Chapter 1 the challenges facing US hospitals given the changing competitive landscape in health care. Recent reports have highlighted medical-safety issues, the uneven quality of emergency rooms, high costs, and lengthening wait times. At the same time, according Kurt D. Grote at McKinsey, these institutions,

face increasingly severe economic pressure as their competitiveness against more focused alternatives declines and health care consumers become more value conscious. To overcome such difficulties, the industry must make some big moves. Many hospitals will have to reorganize around a narrower range of clinical activity, differentiate themselves on quality and service, think more like the retailers they are fast becoming, and overhaul their relationships with physicians.[74]

As hospitals respond to this shifting competitive and consumer landscape, change leaders will need to pay careful attention to the four dimensions of change. In particular, the strategy and structure to meet this challenge will need to be clearly defined and communicated. The new strategy may be that hospitals decide to compete on the basis of strengths in specific clinical lines rather than relying on the power of a fully integrated hospital. Some are suggesting hospitals consider adopting a "center of excellence" model, which allows hospitals to focus on such areas as cardiology, neurosciences, and oncology for example.[75] If systems are not aligned with this strategy, the implementation of this change is at risk. For example, hospitals with poor systems for extending credit or making collections at the point of service may experience higher levels of bad debts. In the resources area hospitals will need to provide better training, performance metrics, and compensation structures aligned with the new strategy. In addition, technology enhancements are needed for providers to better communicate with each other, to reduce/catch/prevent errors, and to deploy electronic medical records across all services. And finally, the behavioral norms of the physicians, nurses, administrative staff, and senior management will require new ways of thinking and behaving in the way they work together in carrying out this transformation (e.g., focusing on continued quality improvement and a customer-centric environment).

The dimensions of change and organization culture are integral components of any change process. Culture, although difficult to measure precisely, is a real and very powerful force in organizations. Change leaders can use the information gained through the assessment of a firm's culture to help guide each phase of the change process, from the unfreezing phase and determining readiness for change, from implementing the transformation, to consolidating and institutionalizing the new state. Through careful planning and effective change techniques and processes, change leaders can shape and develop organizational cultures that are in alignment with, and supportive of, the desired changes.

Let us next shift our focus to best practices and future trends in change management.

❏ BEST PRACTICES IN CHANGE MANAGEMENT

The complete and successful implementation of any change initiative is not guaranteed. The major challenge lies in implementing the change plan and seeing it to fruition. It is one thing to plan for a change; it's another matter to implement it. Successful execution depends on how the change plan is formulated, communicated, monitored, and managed. All too often, what happens is that "senior management falls to achieve the necessary buy-in and commitment with its main stakeholders and neglects to identify those champions who will be critical to its success."[76] What follows are some key best practices related to successfully managing the change process.

In a major 2005 study with companies undergoing major change projects, Prosci Research surveyed both practitioners and consultants in an effort to uncover best practices in the change

management arena. We present some of the key findings from this study to help reinforce critical aspects of effective change management practices by focusing on key contributors to success, obstacles to change, and what to do differently next time.

When asked to identify the greatest contributors to overall change project success, Figure 7.10 summarizes the five key success factors in rank order.

Figure 7.11 summarizes the top four factors respondents cited as their greatest obstacles to change.

Respondents in the best practices study also were asked what they would do differently on their next change project. Figure 7.12 summarizes the five most commonly cited responses in rank order:[83]

Now that we have a better understanding of best practices in change management, our attention turns to the future of change management.

❏ FUTURE TRENDS IN MANAGING CHANGE

In 2005, The Conference Board completed a research study to examine the "state of the art" in initiating and effecting change in organizations. Figure 7.13 provides several key trends from this study that spotlighted certain trends in the future of change management:[84]

The study also identified several trends as unclear and in need of further study and research. These are listed in Figure 7.14.

Finding practical solutions to these challenges will greatly assist change leaders and organizations in performing change management effectively.[85]

1. **Active and visible sponsorship**. The most potent factor contributing to project success was leadership support. "Employees want the project sponsor to demonstrate their dedication to the change and share how this change relates to the direction of the business."[77] Three key sponsor roles emerged from the study:

- Participate actively and visibly throughout the project.
- Build a coalition of change leaders with peers and other managers.
- Communicate effectively at all levels of the organization.

2. **Use of change management processes and tools**. Study participants emphasized the importance of using proven change management methodologies, dedicated resources on the change project, and early planning. Respondents also cited the importance of recognizing early wins and celebrating successes.[78]

3. **Effective communications**. Effective communication is critical to achieving successful change. The change literature suggests the following practices should be followed in effectively communicating for change:[79]

- Show wholehearted and visible support for the change from all of top management.
- Give employees as much information as possible as early as possible.
- Continue the communication effort throughout and even after the change, not just at the beginning.
- Use "rich" communication media. The more face-to-face opportunities, the better.
- Utilize supervisors and middle managers as key communication links. Encourage, train, and hold them accountable for keeping employees informed and providing a lot of interpersonal communication regarding the changes.
- Recognize and be willing to deal with the emotional issues as well as the rational ones. Be prepared to deal with anxiety, fear, uncertainty, and mistrust. Openness, group meetings, too-free telephone lines, and frequent newsletters can help. Do not let top management isolate itself from these nonrational aspects.
- Involve employees in the change process and in decisions about change as much as possible.
- Use formal communication assessments to establish baselines, direct communication strategies, and monitor progress as the change unfolds.
- Make sure actions match words. The symbolic and behavioral communication of management is more important that is its rhetoric.

4. **Employee involvement in the change process**. "Employee involvement included active and early participation of employees in the design and testing of the solution and involvement in decision making."[80]

5. **Effective project leadership and planning**. This key success factor included "strong project leadership and governance, effective and careful project planning, use of a structure approach for the project, clear objectives and deadlines, and ongoing measurement of project progress."[81]

Figure 7.10   Greatest Contributors to Success

1. Resistance from employees and managers. Resistance behaviors exist at all levels of the organization. Front-line employees were uncertain why changes were being made and were fearful of the associated impacts; supervisors were concerned with loss of respect and their position of expertise in the current state; and middle-level managers resisted the change if they stood to lose power or control.

Resistance often stemmed from the lack of awareness of the need for change. Employees did not always understand the fundamental business issues that were driving the change and the risks of not changing. Aligning the business need for change to a shared company vision was perceived as vital to creating awareness of the need for change.

2. Inadequate senior management sponsorship. The level of commitment and support from the sponsor was not adequate to drive the change. Sponsors were not visible and active in the project. Some participants indicated their sponsors had "weak moments" when they did not stand behind earlier decisions in order to avoid conflict.

3. Cultural barriers. Long-tenured employees and established work cultures created an environment where employees want to preserve the "old way "of conducting business on a day-to-day basis. Entrenched organizations were shelters for slow responses, entitlement attitudes and complacent employees primarily satisfied with the status quo. Global entities faced unique geographic divisions and cultural issues that created greater challenges.

4. Lack of change management expertise. The organizations did not have an enterprise-wide process to manage people through change. They did not understand the role of change management and lacked the skills and expertise required to manage the people impacted by the change.

Figure 7.11   Greatest Change Management Obstacles[82]

1. Dedicate resources to change management. Create a change management team or lead position to select and adopt a methodology and improve the organization's understanding of the value of change management. Empower these individuals to prepare and educate executives, managers and project team members on change management tools, processes and techniques.

2. Secure executive sponsorship earlier in the project. Enlist executive support for the change as early as possible. Clarify the role of the sponsor and make sure they understand how critical this role is to the success of the project. Conduct ongoing briefings of the progress and status of the project and provide coaching in the areas of change management for those managers who may be inexperienced in dealing with large-scale change.

3. Repeat key messages early and often. Reach everyone in the organization with messages pertaining to the change. Keep communications clear, simple, and frequent.

4. Involve employees in the change. Involve employees in the change. Engage employees at the beginning of the project, including planning and design work. Create ad hoc groups, workshops, focus groups, research teams, or opportunities for individual participation in the change.

5. Create a transition strategy with achievable timeframes. Create a plan of action broken down into phases, each with a deadline and specific outcome. Allow adequate time to build commitment and acceptance of the change from the organization.

Figure 7.12   What to Do Differently On Your Next Change Project

1. The business environment will continue to drive an accelerating rhythm of changes in modern enterprises. Thus, the need for effective change management can only increase.

2. Change management will be further institutionalized in establishing departments or programs and formalized processes.

3. Change management is increasingly seen as a business function, given that it is driven more and more by business factors, and becomes a way to optimize organizational effectiveness, balance competing demands, and improve the bottom line.

4. Businesses with extensive experience are likely to develop change management core competency, giving them a competitive edge in a rapidly changing market.

5. If the trend toward outsourcing continues, a rise in change management service providers may be seen. If companies can obtain cost savings and improved service by outsourcing payroll, product development, and customer relations, it may be feasible that they could do the same with change management.

Figure 7.13   Certain Trends

1. Recognizing characteristics of organizational culture that make it flexible and resilient.

2. Finding links to further integrate change management into day-to-day organizational practices.

3. Managing change as resources shrink and the frequency of change accelerates.

4. Institutionalizing an organizational capacity for change.

5. Integrating change management with other organizational mandates (e.g., promoting diversity, social responsibility).

6. Aligning talent management with change management.

7. Identifying the tradeoffs in change alternatives to optimize return.

8. Balancing short- and long-term needs for change management.

9. Developing tools for resilience during change.

10. Articulating the roles of each "face" of change (organization, department/group, individual).

Figure 7.14   Less Certain Aspects About the Future of Change Management

❏ READING AND CASE

Reading

7-1: Charan, R. (2006, April). "Home depot's blueprint for cultural change," *Harvard Business Review*.

Focus: A new CEO took the helm at Home Depot in 2000. The company was plagued with internal problems to include fierce competition from Lowes that threatened its ability to continue its earlier growth profile. To combat these issues, the new CEO crafted a new strategy for Home Depot that required major changes in how the company operated. A major thrust of the new strategy required a transformation of Home Depot's freewheeling culture.

Questions

1. Does Home Depot have a problem? Is Robert Nardelli right to be concerned about it? Is he moving in the right direction?

2. Describe Home Depot's culture before Nardelli's arrival. Was the culture an asset or liability? Explain.

3. Did he create and communicate an effective platform for change at the outset?

4. What is Nardelli's vision for the "new" culture? How will a change in culture align with his strategic goals for the company?

5. CFO Carol Tomé points out in the reading that, "People never had time to grieve for the company Home Depot once was [and] we didn't do a very good job of explaining the why." Assess Home Depot's efforts at managing resistance to change.

6. Assess the four dimensions of change in light of your analysis of the problem.

7. In renovating Home Depot's culture, Nardelli focused on four mechanisms: metrics, programs, process, and structures. Take one of these mechanisms, assess its role and effectiveness in changing the culture, then discuss how you might activate this culture-renovation mechanism in your own organization.

8. What does Nardelli need to do to sustain the new culture at Home Depot?

9. What other change management mistakes, if any, did senior management make in Home Depot's transformation?

Linkage to Chapter

1. Strategy and culture
2. Strategic fit
3. Assessing culture and cultural unity
4. How culture affects performance
5. Influencing culure change
6. Sustaining culture

Case

7-1: Higgins, J., & McAllister, C. (2004). "If You Want Strategic Change, Don't Forget to Change Your Cultural Artifacts," *Journal of Change Management*, Vol. 41, No. pp. 63–73.

Focus: This reading contains a case study on culture change that demonstrates how Continental Airlines used cultural artefacts to help them implement their new strategy. Facing another in a string of bankruptcies coupled with heavy turnover at the top executive levels of the firm, the new management focused on a strategy of service to make Continental competitive. They set out systematically to destroy the old culture and create a new one. The case focuses on the way cultural artefacts

(i.e., the physically visible manifestations of the values and beliefs of the firm) were used in the turnaround.

Questions

1. What was life like at Continental Airlines before Gordon Bethune and Greg Brenneman took over? Do you think they focused on the right things in aligning the firm's values and norms with the new business strategy? Why or why not?

2. Discuss the role rewards and recognition play in the transformation of Continental?

3. The authors of the case argue that changing core values is not recommended unless the organization's competitive environment forces a change in vision and mission. Do you agree that Continental's core values needed changing? How do you go about changing something as profound as "core values?"

4. A cliché in corporate America today is to proclaim in some form that "people are our most important asset." Yet, in this case we learn that the change leaders made valuing employees a key element of their cultural transformation. Assess how this change impacted the outcome of the overall change effort.

5. New CEO Bethune and COO Brenneman sought to align the "myths and sagas" with the new business strategy. What is it about these kinds of cultural artifacts that has the power to change people's thinking and behavior? How would you proceed to manipulate myths and sagas to influence people's behavior? Can you relate an example from your own experience with a change initiative?

6. How important was the selection of language and metaphors in aligning the new way of doing things at Continental?

7. Considering a change initiative you are familiar with, what did the change leaders do or not do to change the cultural artifacts to help reinforce the change? Was the result similar to what we saw in the Continental case study?

Linkage to Chapter

The reading emphasizes the importance of culture in managing any strategic change or transformation.

❏ ENDNOTES

1. Lindahl, R. (2006). The Role of Organizational Cultural Climate and Culture in the School Improvement Process: A Review of the Knowledge Base. Retrieved February 7, 2007 from http://cnx.org/content/m13465/latest/.

2. Aspden, P., et. al, eds. (2007). *Preventing Medication Errors: Quality Chasm Series.* Committee on Identifying and Preventing medication Errors, Institute of Medicine. Washington, DC: National Academy Press. Executive Summary retrieved August 2, 2006 from http://newton.nap.edu/execsumm_pdf/11623.

3. Khatri, N., et al. (2006, Spring). Medical errors and quality of care: From control to commitment. *California Management Review*, p. 116.

4. Op. cit., Khatri, N. et al. (2006), p. 128.

5. Government Accounting Office. (2005). *21ˢᵗ Century Challenges: Transforming Government to Meet Current and Emerging Challenges (GAO-05-830T)*. Washington, DC: U. S. Government Accountability Office. Available online at http://www.gao.gov/new.items/d05830t.pdf.

6. Senn, L. E., & Childress, J. R. (2000). *Why Change Initiatives Fail: It's the Culture Dummy!* Senn-Delaney Leadership Consulting Group, Inc. London, p. 1.

7. Collins, J. (2001). *Good to Great.* New York: Harper Business, p. 11.

8. Kotter, J. P. (1996). *Leading Change.* Boston: Harvard Business School Press, p. 14.

9. Lou Gerstner Discusses Changing the Culture at IBM. http://hbswk.hbs.edu/pubitem.jhtml?id=3209&sid = 0&pid = 0&t = organizations.

10. Steve Ballmer Speaks Passionately About Microsoft, Leadership . . . and Passion. (2007, January 10). Knowledge@Wharton. Retrieved January 13, 2007 from http://knowledge.wharton.upenn.edu/article.cfm?articleid = 1628&specialid = 61&CFID = 3355869&CFTOKEN=73770113.

11. Hofer, C. W., & Schendel, D. (1978). *Strategy Formulation: Analytical Concepts.* West Publishing Company, p. 4.

12. Chandler, A. D. Jr., (1962). *Strategy and Structure: Chapters in the History of the American Industrial Enterprise.* (1990 edition). Cambridge, MA: MIT Press, p. 13.

13. Beaver, G. (2003, September–October). Strategy and organization in the modern firm. *Strategic Change*, p. 287.

14. Beaver, op. cit., p. 288.

15. Connell, J., & Travagliione, T. (2004, March–April). Emotional intelligence: A competitive advantage in times of change? *Strategic Change*, p. 56.

16. Hamel, G., & Prahalad, C. K. (1989). Strategic intent. *Harvard Business Review.*

17. Markides, C. (2004, Summer). What is strategy and how do you know if you have one? *Business Strategy Review*, p. 10.

18. Beaver, op. cit., p. 288.

19. Markides, op. cit., p. 10.

20. Markides, op. cit., p. 10.

21. Guth, R. A. (2007, January 5). IPod envy: Microsoft's Xbox whiz drives strategic shift. *The Wall Street Journal*, A1, A11.

22. Pearson, S., & Mosher, P. (2003, July 7). Managing change, managing business success. Accenture: Human Performance Insights, Issue 5. Retrieved January 21, 2006 from http://www.accenture.com/Global/Research_and_Insights/By_Subject/Change_Mgmt/ManagingSuccess.htm.

23. Kerr, J., & Slocum, J. W. Jr. (2005, November). Managing corporate culture through reward systems. *Academy of Management Executive*, Vol. 19, No. 4, p. 130.

24. Kanter, R. M. (1983). *The Change Masters.* New York: Simon & Shuster, p. 123.

25. Davis, T., & Landa, M. (2000, Winter). The story of mary? How "organizational culture" can erode bottom-line profitability. *The Canadian Manager*, Vol. 25, No. 4, p. 14.

26. Sims, R. R. (2000, May). Changing an organization's culture under new leadership. *Journal of Business Ethics*, p. 65.

27. Conner, D. R. (1992). *Managing at the Speed of Change.* New York: Villard Books, p. 163.

28. Davis, T., & Landa, M. (2000, Winter). The story of mary? How "organizational culture" can erode bottom-line profitability. The Canadian Manager, Vol. 25, No. 4, p. 14.

29. Schein, E. H. (1992). *Organizational Culture.* San Francisco: Jossey-Bass Publishers, p. 17.

30. Kotter, J. P., & Heskett, J. L. (1992). Corporate Culture and Performance. New York: The Free Press, p. 4.

31. Sathe, V. (1983, Autumn). Implications of corporate culture: A manager's guide to action. *Organizational Dynamics*, p. 7.

32. Houghton, J. R. (1996, April). The new business world and the individual. The CEO Series, Center for the Study of American Business. Washington University, St. Louis. Retreived August 2, 2005 from http://wc.wustl.edu/csab/CSAB%20pubs-pdf%20files/CEO%20Series/CEO03%20Houghton .pdf

33. Cohen, A., Watkinson, J., & Boone, J. (2005). Herb Kelleher taks about how southwest airlines grew from entrepreneurial startup to industry leadership. *Babson Insight.* Retrieved July 29, 2005, from http://www.babsoninsight.com/contentmgr/showdetails.php/id/829.

34. Extracted from Conner, D. R. (1992). *Managing at the Speed of Change.* New York: Villard Books, p. 164.

35. Schein, E. H. (1992). *Organizational Culture*. San Francisco: Jossey-Bass Publishers, p. 22.

36. Gerstner, L. (2005, June). Lou gerstner on change. Leadership Excellence, 22(6), 18. Retrieved from ABI/INFORM Global database. (Document ID:861001241).

37. Kotter, J. P. & Heskett, J. L. (1992). *Corporate Culture and Performance*. New York: Free Press, p. 11.

38. Klein, A. (2003). *Organizational Culture and Performance*. Unpublished. Dissertation, University of Illinois at Chicago.

39. Ulrich, D. (1997). *Human Resource Champions*. Harvard Business School Press. Boston, p. 177.

40. Kotter, J. P., & Cohen, D. S. (2002). *The Heart of Change*. Boston: Harvard Business School Press, p. 175.

41. Kotter, J. P., & Cohen, D. S. (2002). *The Heart of Change*. Boston: Harvard Business School Press, p. 176.

42. Ulrich (1997), op. cit., p. 175.

43. Nelson, D. L., Quick, J. C. (2006). *Organizational Behavior: Foundations, Realities & Challenges,* 5th edn. Mason, OH: Thomson South-Western, p. 536.

44. Kling, K., & Goteman, I. (2003, February). IKEA CEO anders dahlvig on international growth and IKEA's unique corporate culture and brand identity. *Academy of Management Executive*, p. 35.

45. Chief Learning Officer (2005, August). Accenture Study: Recruting, retention top priority for senior execs. Retrieved August 9, 2005, from http://www.clomedia.com/common/newscenter/newsdisplay.cfm?id=4170.

46. O'Reilly, C. (1989, Summer). Corporations, culture, and commitment: Motivation and social control in organizations. *California Management Review*, p. 16.

47. Lowery, J. E. (1997). Understanding the culture shift in health care. In J. E. Lowery (Ed.), *Culture Shift: A Leader's Guide to Managing Change in Health Care* (pp. 1–14). Chicago: American Hospital Publishing Inc.

48. Schein, E. H. (1992). *Organizational Culture*. San Francisco: Jossey-Bass Publishers, p. 5.

49. Conner, D. R. (1998). *Leading at the Edge of Chaos: How to Create the Nimble Organization*. New York: John Wiley & Sons, Inc., p. 207.

50. Higgins, J. M., & McCallaster, C. (2004). If you want strategic change, don't forget to change your cultural artifacts. *Journal of Change Management*, Vol. 4 No. 1, p. 63.

51. Ulrich, D. (1997). *Human Resource Champions*. Boston: Harvard Business School Press, p. 177.

52. Ulrich, D. (1997). *Human Resource Champions*. Boston: Harvard Business School Press, p. 177–78.

53. Gerstner, L. (2005, June). Lou gerstner on change. Leadership Excellence, 22(6), 18. Retrieved from ABI/INFORM Global database (Document ID:861001241).

54. This section largely extracted from Vestal, K. W., & Spreier, S. W. (1997). In J. E. Lowery (Ed.), *Culture Shift: A Leader's Guide to Managing Change in Health Care* (pp. 15–38). Chicago: American Hospital Publishing, Inc.

55. Reger, S. J. (2006). *Can Two Rights Make a Wrong? insights from IBM's Tangible Culture Approach*. Upper Saddle River, NJ: IBM Press, p. 23.

56. Cooke, R. A., & Szumal, J. L. (1989). *Interpreting the Cultural Styles Measured by the Organizational Culture Inventory: Organizational Culture Inventory Leader's Guide*. Human Synergistics, Inc., Arlington Heights, pp. 59–60.

57. See Human Synergistics website for more information: http://www.hscar.com/oci.htm.

58. Organizational Culture Inventory®: Interpretation & Development Guide (2003). Human Synergistics International. Center for Applied Research. Arlington Heights: IL, p. 18.

59. Jassawalla, A. R., & Sashittal, H. C. (2003, December). The DNA of cultures that promote product innovation. *Ivey Business Journal*.

60. Ulrich. (1997), op. cit., p. 168.

61. Mason, R. O. (2004). Lessons in organizational ethics from the columbia disaster: Can a culture be lethal. *Organizational Dynamics*, Vol. 33, No. 2, p. 133.

62. Mercer Delta (1998). The culture challenge: Creating a high-performance operating environment. Author. Retrieved May 24, 2006 from http://www.mercerdelta.com/organizational_consulting/help_org_culture.html, p. 1.

63. Nelson, D. L., & Quick, J. C. (2000). *Organizational Behavior*. Cincinnati: OH, South-Western, p. 550.

64. Ulrich (1997). op. cit., p. 170.

65. Schermerhorn, J.R., Hunt, J. G., & Osborn, R. N. (2005). *Organizational Behavior*, New York: John Wiley & Sons, p. 436.

66. Tushman, M. L., & O'Reilly, C. A. (1997). *Winning Through Innovation*. Boston: Harvard Business School Press, p. 156.

67. Sathe, V. (1983, Autumn). Implications of corporate culture: A manager's guide to action. *Organizational Dynamics*, pp. 5–23.

68. Gibson, E., & Billings, A. (2003). *Big Change At Best Buy*. Palo Alto, CA: Davies-Black Publishing.

69. Sathe (1983). op. cit., p. 19.

70. Ibid, p. 19.

71. Nelson (2000). op. cit., p. 551.

72. Extracted from Tushman, M. L., & O'Reilly, C. A. (1997). *Winning Through Innovation*. Boston: Harvard Business School Press, p. 153.

73. Higgins, J. M. (2005, March). The eight 'S's of successful strategy execution. *Journal of Change Management*, p. 7.

74. Grote, K. D., Levine, E. H., & Mango, P. (2006, August). US hospitals for the 21st century. *The*

McKinsey Quarterly. Retrieved August 11, 2006, from http://www.mckinseyquarterly.com/PDF Download.aspx?L2=12&L3=61&ar=1824 &srid=27&gp=0.

75. Grote, op. cit.

76. Beaver, G. (2003, November). Successful strategic change: Some managerial guidelines. *Strategic Change*, p. 345.

77. Best Practices in Change Management report. (2005). Loveland, CO: Prosci. p. 6.

78. Ibid, p. 6.

79. Extracted from Richardson, P., & Denton, D. K. (1996, Summer). Communicating change. *Human Resource Management*, Vol. 35, No. 2, pp. 215–16.

80. Best Practices (2005). op. cit., p. 7.

81. Ibid, p. 7.

82. This section extracted verbatim from Best Practices in Change Management report. (2005). Loveland, CO: Prosci: p. 7.

83. This section extracted verbatim from Best Practices in Change Management report. (2005). Loveland, CO: Prosci: pp. 7–8.

84. Extracted from Guy, G., & Beaman, K. (2005). *Effecting Change in Business Enterprises: Current Trends in Change Management.* The Conference Board. NY: New York, p. 26.

85. Ibid.

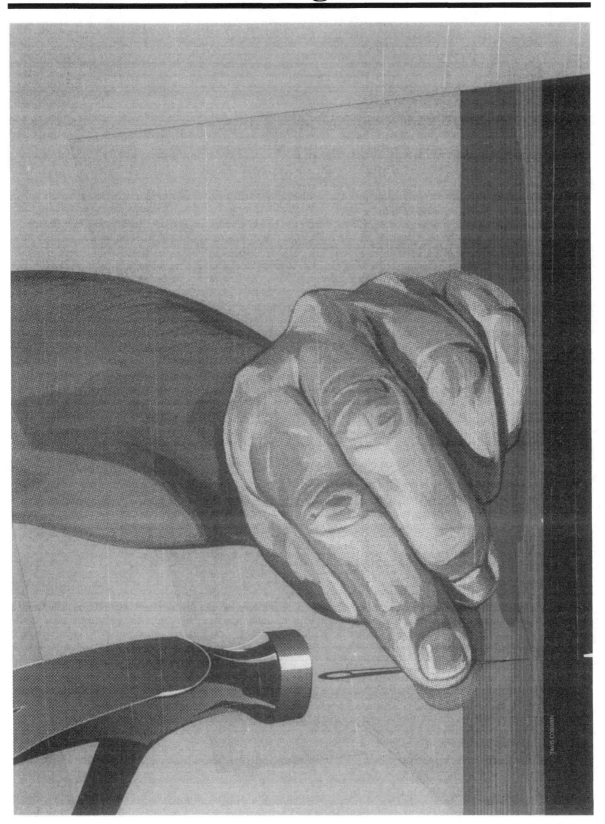

Deep, lasting culture change requires an integrated approach that remodels a company's social systems. The leadership team of Home Depot employed a remarkable set of tools to do that. by Ram Charan

WHEN ROBERT NARDELLI ARRIVED at Home Depot in December 2000, the deck seemed stacked against the new CEO. He had no retailing experience and, in fact, had spent an entire career in industrial, not consumer, businesses. His previous job was running General Electric's power systems division, whose multimillion-dollar generating plants for industry and governments were a far cry from $10 light switches for do-it-yourselfers.

HOME DEPOT'S BLUEPRINT FOR

Culture Change

Nardelli also was taking over what seemed to be a wildly successful company, with a 20-year record of growth that had outpaced even Wal-Mart's—but with latent financial and operational problems that threatened its continued growth, and even its future, if they weren't quickly addressed.

To top it off, Nardelli's exacting and tough-minded approach, which he learned at General Electric, set him on a collision course with the freewheeling yet famously close-knit culture fostered by his predecessors, Home Depot's legendary cofounders, Bennie Marcus and Arthur Blank. It was this culture that Nardelli had to reshape if he hoped to bring some big-company muscle to the

Although its share price is well below the peak it achieved shortly before Nardelli arrived, and the rate of revenue increase has cooled from the breakneck pace of the late 1990s, the company continues to enjoy robust and profitable growth. Revenue climbed to around $80 billion in 2005, and earnings per share have more than doubled since 2000. Just as important, a platform has been built to generate future growth.

I worked with Bob Nardelli, Dennis Donovan, and other senior executives during that period, and I know that these changes in the business would not have happened without a real and observable change in the culture. Home Depot's experience

*What got Home Depot from zero to $50 billion in sales wasn't going to get it to the **next $50 billion**.*

entrepreneurial organization (which, with revenue of $46 billion in 2000, was sometimes referred to as a "$40 billion start-up") and put the retailer's growth on a secure foundation.

Not surprisingly, Nardelli tackled the challenge partly through personal leadership, mixing encouragement with ultimatum and fostering desired cultural norms like accountability through his own behavior. But he also adopted and adapted an array of specific tools designed to gradually change the company's culture—many of them initiated, coordinated, and implemented by an unlikely lieutenant.

Shortly after arriving, Nardelli hired an old colleague from GE, Dennis Donovan, as his head of human resources. By placing a trusted associate in a position known for its conspicuous lack of influence in most executive suites — and by making him one of Home Depot's highest paid executives—Nardelli signaled that changing the culture would be central to getting the company where it needed to go.

Over the past five years, Home Depot's performance has indeed been put on a stable footing.

shows — in perhaps the best example I have seen in my 30-year career—that a cultural transition can be achieved systematically, even under less than favorable conditions, not simply through the charisma of the person leading the change but through the use of mechanisms that alter the social interactions of people in the organization.

The effectiveness of this approach was perhaps most dramatically displayed when a group of Home Depot employees, in a public and spontaneous way, threw their support behind the change in an incident guaranteed to give even the toughest CEO goose bumps.

❏ AN ENTREPRENEURIAL ENVIRONMENT

Home Depot is one of the business success stories of the past quarter century. Founded in 1978 in Atlanta, the company grew to more than 1,100 big-box stores by the end of 2000; it reached the $40 billion revenue mark faster than any retailer in history. The company's success stemmed from several distinctive characteristics, including the warehouse feel of its orange stores, complete with low lighting, cluttered aisles, and sparse signage; a "stack it high, watch it fly" philosophy that reflected a primary focus on sales growth; and

Ram Charan has advised senior management and the boards of directors at numerous companies, Home Depot among them. He is the author of many articles and books, including "Conquering a Culture of Indecision" (HBR January 2006) and Know-How, coming in October from Crown Business.

extraordinary store manager autonomy, aimed at spurring innovation and allowing managers to act quickly when they sensed a change in local market conditions.

Home Depot's culture, set primarily by the charismatic Marcus (known universally among employees as Bennie), was itself a major factor in the company's success. It was marked by an entrepreneurial high-spiritedness and a willingness to take risks; a passionate commitment to customers, colleagues, the company, and the community, and an aversion to anything that felt bureaucratic or hierarchical.

Longtime Home Depot executives recall the disdain with which store managers used to view directives from headquarters. Because everyone believed that managers should spend their time on the sales floor with customers, company paperwork often ended up buried under piles on someone's desk, tossed in a wastebasket — or even marked with a company-supplied "B.S." stamp and sent back to the head office. Such behavior was seen as a sign of the company's unflinching focus on the customer. "The idea was to challenge senior managers to think about whether what they were sending out to the stores was worth store managers' time," says Tom Taylor, who started at Home Depot in 1983 as a parking lot attendant and today is executive vice president for merchandising and marketing.

There was a downside to this state of affairs, though. Along with arguably low-value corporate paperwork, an important store safety directive might disappear among the unread memos. And while their sense of entitled autonomy might have freed store managers to respond to local market conditions, it paradoxically made the company as a whole less flexible. A regional buyer might agree to give a supplier of, say, garden furniture, prime display space in dozens of stores in exchange for a price discount of 10%—only to have individual store managers ignore the

agreement because they thought it was a bad idea. And as the chain mushroomed in size, the lack of strong career development programs was leading Home Depot to run short of the talented store managers on whom its business model depended.

All in all, the cultural characteristics that had served the retailer well when it had 200 stores started to undermine it when Lowe's began to move into Home Depot's big metropolitan markets from its small-town base in the mid-1990s. Individual autonomy and a focus on sales at any cost eroded profitability, particularly as stores weren't able to benefit from economies of scale that an organization the size of Home Depot should have enjoyed.

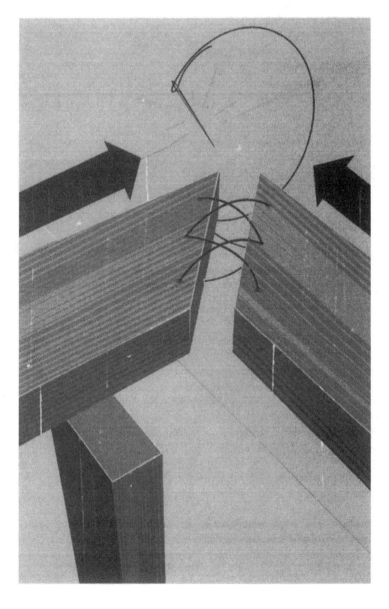

❏ A DOSE OF DISCIPLINE

Nardelli's arrival at Home Depot came as a shock. No one had expected that Marcus (then chairman) and Blank (then CEO) would be leaving anytime soon. Most employees simply couldn't picture the company without these father figures. And if there was going to be change at the top of this close-knit organization, in which promotions had nearly always come from within, no one wanted, as Nardelli himself acknowledges, an outsider who would "GE-ize their company and culture."

But the Home Depot board had decided that a seasoned manager with the expertise to drive continued growth needed to be brought in to run what had become a giant business. The first step would be to deal with immediate problems that weren't readily apparent either to employees or investors. In addition to the shortage of experienced store and district managers and the challenge from Lowe's, which was successfully attracting women shoppers with its brighter stores and a focus on fashionable kitchen, bath, and home-furnishing products, these problems included poor inventory turns, low margins, and weak cash flow.

Nardelli laid out a three-part strategy: enhance the core by improving the profitability of current and future stores in existing markets; extend the business by offering related services such as tool rental and home installation of Home Depot products; and expand the market, both geographically and by serving new kinds of customers, such as big construction contractors.

To meet his strategy goals, Nardelli had to build an organization that understood the opportunity in, and the importance of, taking advantage of its growing scale. Some functions, such as purchasing (or merchandising), needed to be centralized to leverage the buying power that a giant company could wield. Previously autonomous functional, regional, and store operations needed to collaborate — merchandising needed to work more closely with store operations, for instance, to avoid conflicts like the one over the placement of garden furniture. This would be aided by making detailed performance data transparent to all the relevant parties simultaneously, so that people could base decisions on shared information. The merits of the current store environment needed to be reevaluated; its lack of signage and haphazard layout made increasingly less sense for time-pressed shoppers. And a new

emphasis needed to be placed on employee training, not only to bolster the managerial ranks but also to transform orange-aproned sales associates from cheerful greeters into knowledgeable advisers who could help customers solve their home improvement problems. As Nardelli likes to say, "What so effectively got Home Depot from zero to $50 billion in sales wasn't going to get it to the next $50 billion."

This new strategy would require a careful renovation of Home Depot's strong culture. Imagine the challenge: Clearly, you wanted to build on the best aspects of the existing culture, particularly people's unusually passionate commitment to the customer and to the company. But you wanted them to rely primarily on data, not on intuition, to assess business and marketplace conditions. And you wanted people to coordinate their efforts, anathema to many in Home Depot's entrepreneurial environment. You wanted people to be accountable for meeting companywide financial and other targets, not contemptuous of them. You wanted people to deliver not just sales growth but also other components of business performance that drive profitability.

Resistance to the changes was fierce, particularly from managers: Much of the top executive team left during Nardelli's first year. But some saw merit in the approach and in fact tried to persuade distraught colleagues to give the new ideas a chance. Over time, attitudes slowly began to change. Some of this resulted from Nardelli's successful efforts to get people to see for themselves why the strategy made sense. But other, more concrete tools, designed to ingrain the new culture into the organization, ultimately prompted employees to pick up a hammer and paintbrush and join the renovation project.

❏ TOOLS FOR CULTURE CHANGE

The mechanisms that Home Depot employed, working in concert, changed what I call a company's *social architecture* — that is, the collective ways in which people work together across an organization to support the business model. Many of them are familiar operating tools. But they were employed in such a way that they changed the human side of the equation: people's behavior, beliefs, social interactions, and the nature of their decision making. It was this social element that allowed Home Depot to achieve—and, more important, to sustain — its dauntingly large-scale and complex cultural transformation. (For a list of some of the tools Home Depot used, see the sidebar "A Culture Change Toolbox.")

The mechanisms fell into several categories: *metrics* (which describe what the culture values and make clear what people will be held accountable for); *processes* (which change how work is done and thus integrate the new culture into the organization); *programs* (which generate support for and provide the first demonstration of the new culture's effectiveness); and *structures* (which provide a framework for the new culture to grow, often by changing where and how decisions are made). Let us examine each in turn.

Metrics: to emphasize new cultural priorities. One of the early things Nardelli and Donovan did was to begin instituting common metrics that produced companywide data in areas that hadn't been consistently measured before. These new performance measurements clearly had an operational purpose, but they also had an important psychological effect. Initially, these metrics showed employees that things weren't going as well as many had thought. For example, data quantifying customer perceptions of the Home Depot shopping experience replaced anecdotal reports of customer satisfaction. Such data made clear that some deeply held beliefs about the stores — the importance, say, of low lighting and other warehouse-like characteristics—needed to be reevaluated.

At the same time, the metrics made clear and reinforced the collaborative behavior and attitudes that Nardelli and Donovan wanted to encourage. Take accountability. When Donovan arrived at Home Depot, he found the company's performance assessment practices less than rigorous. Reviews were usually qualitative and subjective, and standards varied from region to region or even from manager to manager. Donovan would meet with, say, a district manager to go through the performance of store managers and, after some probing, often find managers who enjoyed superior ratings but whose stores were delivering mediocre performance.

Donovan wasnt surprised, given the subjective nature of the performance reviews. As he says, "One of the hardest things for a leader to do is to look somebody in the eye and be honest with them about their performance." So Donovan introduced a standard, companywide performance management process that used mostly quantitative criteria. This made it easier for managers to assess their employees honestly and fairly, enabling them to make the tough calls and put the right people in the right jobs. It also, incidentally, reduced the more than 150 employee evaluation forms used throughout the company to three one-page electronic documents.

Metrics were also used to promote a savvier understanding of the business. For example, with standardized, detailed business data, people could see the relationship among revenue, margins, inventory turns, cash flow, and other measures from store to store and region to region. Getting managers throughout the company to look beyond sales as the sole business goal spurred them to make better decisions.

This might seem obvious, but it's a common problem of companies in periods of rapid expansion. Carl Liebert, executive vice president for Home Depot stores, who worked at Circuit City during a period of high growth in the early 1990s, says that in such an environment, "you don't spend a lot of time thinking about inventory turns. Instead, you focus on opening more stores because the customer loves your box." That's fine until you suddenly find yourself with a competitor that has its own lovely box, as Circuit City did with Best Buy— and Home Depot did with Lowe's.

Companywide metrics also provided a platform for collaboration. By making various aspects of Home Depot's performance transparent to all employees, managers could clearly see — in cold, hard facts—the broader financial impact of their own decisions. This prompted candid discussions about how to improve that performance and focused employees' vaunted commitment on taking the needed actions.

For example, people in merchandising, operations, and stores traditionally distrust one another, as the individuals who buy the goods, get them to the retail outlet, and sell them to the customer seek to shift blame for poor performance along the value chain they all share. Paul Raines, the vice president for stores in Home Depot's southern region, recounts that in the pre-Nardelli years a meeting involving these three groups "was basically a food fight. We would all blame each other for problems, and it was very anecdotal: 'You didn't send me that tractor I needed' or 'Your stores are terrible.' We might throw a P&L up on the wall, but that was about it."

Today, the quarterly business review meetings that Raines runs for his region are hardly polite tea

A CULTURE CHANGE TOOL BOX

For large corporations to achieve a major—and permanent—change in business performance, they must create a sustainable change in culture. Aware of this, the leaders at Home Depot. Identified key aspects of the culture that had to change for the company to meet the new performance goals. They then adopted a variety of standard tools in such a way that they strengthened the business and modified the culture. As the mechanisms took hold, the energy of employees became positive, further accelerating the change.

Among the tools Home Depot has used are as follows:

Data templates, detailed forms to organize performance data for quarterly business review meetings, which encourage personal accountability, give employees a deeper understanding of business performance, and foster collaboration by putting people on the same page when making decisions.

Strategic operating and resource planning, or SOAR, which is built around an annual eight-day session when Home Depot's 12 top executives work together to balance priorities and select the investments most likely to achieve financial and other business targets.

Disciplined talent reviews, conducted frequently—and consistently from one to the next—which emphasize the need for candor and fairness in dealing with employee performance.

Store manager learning forums that, through role playing, simulations, and other exercises, highlighted the level of competitive threats and made transparent the company's future plans, helping attendees understand the need for the new strategy.

Monday morning conference calls, involving the company's top 15 executives, during which accountability (for business results arid for promises made the previous week) is emphasized, as is sharing information (about operations,.customers, markets, and competitive conditions).

Employee taskforces, staffed by individuals from all levels of the company, to elicit unfiltered input from the people closest to a problem and gain their support for the changes the solution requires.

An array of leadership development programs, including the Future Leaders Program, the Store Leadership Program, and the Merchandising Leadership Program, which raise the bar for performance and ensure continuity of the culture.

Mapping of the HR process, which identified 300 ways that HR tasks could be improved and highlighted the importance of instituting processes to sustain cultural change.

parties. But the tension is channeled through a template, which includes such data as store-by-store gross margins and category-by-category sales forecasts. With everyone in the room (and across the company) on the same page — more accurately, the same 15 pages—there is little opportunity to offer anecdotal evidence to defend your position or use your rank to support your case. Jointly discussing the data helps people set priorities collectively and even accept allocations of resources that might hurt their own parts of the business.

Processes: to integrate the new culture into the organization. Right after Nardelli became CEO, he instituted a two-hour Monday morning conference call in which the top 15 or so executives give individual reports on the previous week's activities in their areas of responsibility. Initially, the call helped Nardelli educate himself about the business. But over time, his questions evolved and began focusing more on holding people accountable for what they had promised to do the previous week. In fact, the calls have become a powerful tool for Nardelli in his efforts to create a culture of cooperation and accountability. Week after week, the top executive team comes together, hears the same information, makes decisions, and commits to actions that are reviewed by everyone in subsequent calls. This process, repeated like a drumbeat, has built the executive group into a highly integrated team.

The Monday call is mirrored on Monday afternoons by a video cast that goes out to all 1,800 Home Depot stores in the United States. The transmission focuses on the week ahead—upcoming product promotions, the introduction of new product lines, the revenue needed in the last week of a quarter to meet bonus plan targets for sales associates. The broadcast, actually called "The Same Page," creates a link between each store's activities and the bigger picture—and reflects a shift from the old culture, in which all those memos from headquarters were thrown out unread.

A particularly bold social change was the implementation of a Strategic Operating and Resource Planning (or SOAR) process, which melds strategy, operations, and human resource planning. The core of SOAR is an annual, eight-day marathon (referred to by some participants on the final day as "SORE"), during which the senior leadership team decides which competing investments in the business will best help the company meet its three-year financial targets. SOAR was radical for Home

Depot on a number of fronts; First, it requires resources to be allocated on the basis of projected future needs rather than, as in most companies, from extrapolations of past events. Second, like the regional quarterly business reviews, in which different functions must balance their interests, SOAR is a collaborative process, one that, in Liebert's words, rises above the narrow "you're doing something that pushes costs from your P&L to my P&L" mind-set.

What makes the process so emblematic of the new Home Depot culture, though, is the way that the planning meeting is integrated with HR planning so that decisions about human resources are aligned with strategic and operating decisions. In a retail business, where human capital is vital to success, a sophisticated HR-planning process is crucial. "Sales associates are to Home Depot what engineers are to NASA," Nardelli says.

Every year, Donovan and Nardelli spend several weeks engaged in a complete and detailed assessment of all aspects of HR—talent recruiting, education, performance management, career development, and the like. The intensive review not only gives the two executives a close-up picture of the company's talent but also helps them learn which HR initiatives are actually working in the field. This can lead to endeavors with dual HR and strategic purposes: A successful effort to, say, hire senior citizens and former military personnel as sales associates and managers — they are seen as ideal employees — is linked with marketing efforts targeted at those groups.

Donovan's belief in the importance of process as a way to embed analysis and rigor into the organization was evident in something he did as soon as he came. He worked with his staff to map what he refers to as "toll gates" — the sequence of tasks that must be successfully completed for every HR process. The staff evaluated how well the HR organization was performing each step and identified those that might be improved. The group then designed 300 initiatives aimed at rectifying shortcomings and agreed to carry out all 300 within three years. (For a look at how Home Depot mapped one of the processes, see the exhibit "Assessing and Improving the HR Function.")

Programs: to build support for culture change. A year and a half after Nardelli took over as CEO, he and Donovan knew that there still was significant opposition within the organization to the changes they were making. The resistance was bolstered by

the beating Home Depot was taking in the media and the market — the share price fell from a peak of nearly $70 during the boom years of the late 1990s to just above $20 at the beginning of 2003— not to mention the company's failure to increase same-store sales. But something else was at work, says Carol Tomé, the company's chief financial officer. "People never had time to grieve for the company Home Depot once was," she says. "The company hadn't been prepared for the change. And though we did a pretty good job explaining to people the *what* of the change, we didn't do a very good job of explaining the *why*."

So over the course of several months in late 2002 and early 2003, Donovan set up a series of five-day learning forums for district and store managers— nearly 1,800 people in all. "Large-scale organizational change is not a spectator sport, and it's easy to be a cynic when you're in the stands," Donovan says. "It's tough to be a cynic when you're on the playing field." Accordingly, the program included competitive simulation and role-playing exercises. In one such exercise, Donovan asked people to view the company from Nardelli's perspective: "You've just arrived. You want to preserve the proud past of the wonderful company that has been passed on to you. But you also see incredible opportunities in the future, including the possibility of doubling the size of the market by providing products and services for industrial and commercial customers. To step into that future, you know you have to deal with some issues." Then Donovan posed the challenge: "If you're Bob, what do you do? The only rule is . . . you can't fire the HR guy."

Working in small groups, people put their ideas up on the wall: centralize the buying offices, manage inventory better, offer better training for managers. "And then," Donovan recalls, "five minutes or so into the exercise, someone would inevitably grab the microphone and say, 'Hey, this is what Bob and his team are trying to do.'"

Getting — and sustaining — employee commitment to the new culture has continued in an array of ongoing leadership-training programs, including the Future Leaders Program, the Store Leadership Program, and the Merchandising Leadership Program. And it has filtered into a variety of business operations. For instance, Liebert, in a previous position as senior vice president for operations, sought to institute a bar code system to replace the manual box count used to keep track of incoming goods at stores. He knew the system wouldn't

ASSESSING AND IMPROVING THE HR FUNCTION

To better manage Home Depot's workforce and to signal the importance of analytic processes in the new culture, human resources head Dennis Donovan conducted a detailed assessment of HR's work. He and his staff examined each of the HR processes, such as staffing, career development, and benefits, and mapped the "toll gates" of each process—that is, the sequence of tasks that must be completed to successfully get the work done. They then evaluated how well the HR organization was performing each of these tasks, based on five criteria: world-class design, a focus on process, the use of quantifiable metrics, systems capability (whether the task could be completed on desktop PCs throughout the company), and simplicity. More than 300 initiatives were identified, all of which were completed.

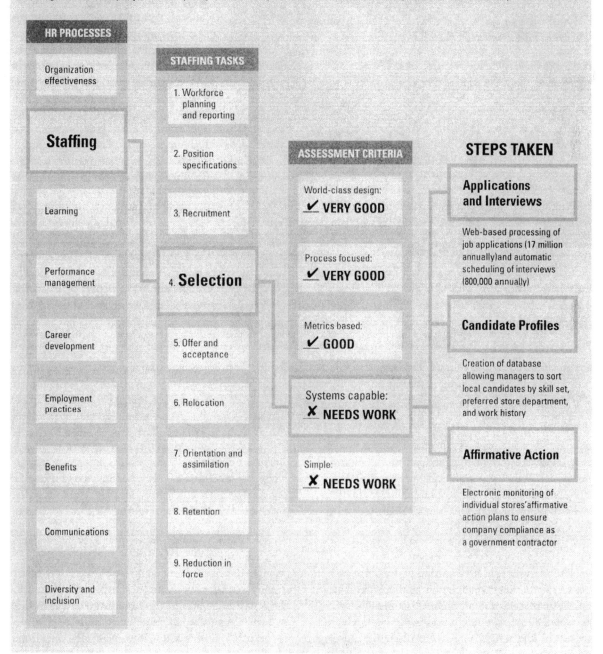

HR PROCESSES

Organization effectiveness

Staffing

Learning

Performance management

Career development

Employment practices

Benefits

Communications

Diversity and inclusion

STAFFING TASKS

1. Workforce planning and reporting

2. Position specifications

3. Recruitment

4. **Selection**

5. Offer and acceptance

6. Relocation

7. Orientation and assimilation

8. Retention

9. Reduction in force

ASSESSMENT CRITERIA

World-class design:
✔ **VERY GOOD**

Process focused:
✔ **VERY GOOD**

Metrics based:
✔ **GOOD**

Systems capable:
✗ **NEEDS WORK**

Simple:
✗ **NEEDS WORK**

STEPS TAKEN

Applications and Interviews

Web-based processing of job applications (17 million annually) and automatic scheduling of interviews (800,000 annually)

Candidate Profiles

Creation of database allowing managers to sort local candidates by skill set, preferred store department, and work history

Affirmative Action

Electronic monitoring of individual stores' affirmative action plans to ensure company compliance as a government contractor

new, more business-savvy Home Depot environment, workers could understand and appreciate the business benefits of scanned receiving: more efficient movement of incoming freight and better cost management.

Structure: to create a framework for the radically new culture. When Nardelli became CEO, Home Depot's purchasing operation comprised nine divisional purchasing offices, many of which had different pricing agreements with the same supplier. This meant that the retailer was acting as if it were nine $5 billion companies rather than a single $45 billion company, thus squandering the chance to drive down costs and boost gross margins.

The rationale for centralizing purchasing was clear, but it would be a difficult transition to make without seriously disrupting operations. Furthermore, since decentralization had been, ironically, a central element of the old Home Depot's cohesive culture, the change would have a significant cultural impact. So Nardelli gave the job of overseeing the transition to Donovan, on his first day at the company. The creation of the new organization — defining the new roles, establishing new purchasing processes, staffing the new positions — was to be accomplished in 90 days. As Donovan says, "That's when I learned Bob doesn't operate on a calendar but on a stopwatch."

work unless the people on the loading dock could see its merits and were behind it; an earlier attempt to implement the procedure had failed. So Liebert included individuals in night-receiving jobs on the development team and himself worked alongside the night crew several times to learn from people he calls the "subject matter experts."

The resulting system was shaped by input from those directly responsible for using it, and as a result excitement about and support for it spread. As Liebert says of the passionate Home Depot worker: "The orange blood kind of starts boiling, and people say, 'Bring it on." What's more, in the

The initiative culminated in "Super Saturday," during which some 60 top executives—presidents and vice presidents from the nine regional divisions–got together in a room at Atlanta headquarters. The first three hours were spent getting them to agree on the details of the new purchasing function. There wasn't a lot of time for disagreement because the new organization would be unveiled to employees, suppliers, and the media on Monday.

Then the group moved to a large room. On the back wall were the names of more than 100 people working in the existing purchasing organization. On the front wall was an organization chart of the new Atlanta-based merchandising operation. On the side wall was the new field structure. Everyone had résumes of the candidates. Their relative strengths were debated, and a handful of candidates was selected for each of the 20 or so top positions in the new function. When one individual was chosen by consensus for a particular position, the executive who knew that person best went to

luxury of moving at their own rate because external factors dictate the tempo. Donovan likes to recall a comment that was frequently made at some early open meetings for employees — that the company needed to pace the changes being proposed—and Nardelli's quick response: "Good point. Give me five minutes. I'm going to go call Lowe's and ask them to slow down for us."

Store managers' autonomy freed them to respond to local conditions, but it made the company as a whole **less flexible**.

the phone and made the job offer. If accepted, a dot was placed by that person's name. If not, an offer went to the next person on the list of candidates for the job. (Those not selected for one of the top jobs took lower positions in the new centralized function.) Three and a half hours later, by dinnertime on Saturday, an entirely new organization, with new roles and responsibilities, had been created and staffed. Compensation packages, preapproved by the board, were sent overnight to the newly promoted executives. They started a week later.

The restructuring was a bold and risky business move, the equivalent of a heart transplant for a big retail company, and it had to be done without missing a beat. It was also a bold cultural move, signaling a huge transition toward a more centralized company. The way it was done—so quickly and collectively, with people jointly debating each candidate's merits so that everyone understood the reasons why one individual was chosen over another — planted the seeds of communality, candor, and decisiveness in the new culture. As Donovan says, "At the end of the day, everyone cheered and applauded. It was exhilarating having accomplished together what we did in a single day."

❑ SPEED AND SUSTAINABILITY

One of the lessons of Super Saturday is that, as Donovan says, "In the game of change, velocity is your friend." Talk all you want about trying to match the speed of change to an organization's ability to absorb it. Most companies don't have the

But forcing a change too quickly can backfire. Nardelli recounts his initial attempt to improve inventory turnover. "Thou shalt improve inventory turns," he decreed. But the store managers didn't have the customer data and analytic tools they needed to do that — so they simply cut back on ordering. This certainly reduced the amount of merchandise idling on the shelf. In fact, the shelves were empty.

Nardelli's response was swift, decisive, and bold. "You put the brake on your plan," he says. "You place $500 million in orders to reload the shelves, and then you step back and look at where your assumptions were wrong." To reduce inventory turns in a way that worked, store managers were given and taught how to use the needed forecasting and inventory management tools, well known in the industrial sector from which Nardelli came. In describing the desired pace of change, Nardelli uses an image from NASCAR auto racing: Brake into the sharpest turns while never letting up on the throttle.

Assuming the rate of change is more or less right, how do you make change stick? How do you sustain it, integrate it into the organization, embed it in the culture? How do you keep it from being one more initiative that flares up and flames out? Home Depot's experience suggests a number of answers.

Where possible, get people affected by a change to help define the problem and design the solution. Base your change on hard data that everyone has access to. Institutionalize the change by starting with a single project, then move to consistently apply repeatable processes that sustain it.

Build accountability into such processes. Create interlocking dependencies between different parts of the organization so that they have a mutual interest in sustaining the change.

Perhaps most important, don't view transformation — even something as cataclysmic as the centralization of purchasing—as a onetime event or a point to be reached. Rather, view it as a work in progress that will constantly need to be modified. External forces require a company to constantly change, and a successful culture has a methodology that allows it to do that.

Take SOAR planning. Over the years, some unintended consequences have emerged, including what CFO Tomé has dubbed "batch processing for capital." "People were holding back until the annual SOAR meeting before seeking funding for good ideas." she says. "But we're trying to run a business *today*. If someone has a great idea today, we should hear about it today." This particular problem was fixed by providing a mechanism for interim approvals of capital requests. To prevent similar kinds of problems, a half day is now set aside at the end of the SOAR session to evaluate how the process can be refined—a huge factor in making it adaptable and sustainable.

❏ THE TIDE TURNS

The inventory turn initiative wasn't the only effort that had to be retooled. Some were scrapped entirely. For example, Nardelli tried to shift the staff mix on the sales floor from 30% part-time to 50% part-time, not only to cut costs but also to gain the flexibility to adjust coverage during busy times of the day. The move was a disaster. Customers complained about bad service. Employees complained that part-timers weren't committed to Home Depot. More fundamentally, the move was seen as an affront to a crucial pillar of Home Depot's traditional culture, in which people thought of the company as a place where they could build a career. Nardelli abandoned the change, and his willingness to correct a mistake enhanced his standing among employees.

But the Home Depot culture today — with its focus on process, hard data, and accountability — is different from what it was five years ago. And there are concrete signs of its acceptance by employees. Not surprisingly, in the new culture, some of those signs take the form of data.

Employee surveys, administered by Donovan's department and completed by more than 80% of Home Depot's 300,000-plus workers, showed a rise in a composite measure of various aspects of job satisfaction from one point below the average score for all industries in 2002 to eight points above it in 2004. Relative to the retailing sector in particular, the score represented a rise from five points above the average to 14. The composite measure includes engagement in the business, enjoyment of the employee's existing role, support for the leadership, and confidence in the company's future.

Perhaps the most vivid evidence of people's acceptance of the new culture, though, is anecdotal. In January 2003, Home Depot held the last of the store manager learning forums in Atlanta. The benefits of the business changes generally hadn't yet flowed through to the financial results, and the company was taking a drubbing in the media and the markets. Despite this, or perhaps because of it, the managers were pumped up as the five-day session came to a close. When Nardelli arrived to address them on the last day, the group — which would barely have acknowledged the CEO's presence a year before — rose up in a body and cheered. Manager after manager went to the microphone to say how difficult the changes had been to accept, especially in the face of external criticism, but how they now supported what the company was trying to do. In the words of one: "We've got your back, Bob."

It didn't stop there. Home Depot's senior management team was going to meet with 200 analysts the next day. Some of the store managers decided to, in effect, storm the meeting and tell the analysts how positive they were about the company's future. Taylor, at the time the president of the southern division, recalls getting a call from someone at the forum alerting him to the plan. "We can't let them do that!" Taylor told Nardelli. Yes, it was a nice show of support. But it could be disruptive, and it might look orchestrated. After some discussion, Nardelli weighed in: "Let's let them do it. The only rule is that I don't want anyone telling them what to do."

The next morning, just as the analysts' meeting began, 240 clapping store managers came in from the back of the auditorium and up onto the stage, taking over the gathering. "It scared the hell out of the analysts," as Donovan recalls it. Two managers, including a woman with 20 years' experience, read statements about their support for the changes. There was a hushed silence, and then the store managers broke into a roar.

The managers' burst of energy was a clear sign that the culture had begun to change. The road to this point had been undeniably rocky, and, not surprisingly, there have been bumps since then. Every change effort has persistent skeptics, both inside and outside a company. But in the ensuing months, the leadership team could increasingly sense that people were interacting with one another and making critical decisions in significantly different ways. Crucially, that behavior was becoming a routine part of everyone's daily work. With these cultural changes embedded in the organization, improved business results were sure to follow.

Reprint R0604C; HBR OnPoint 4079
To order, see page 151.

Case 7-1

If You Want Strategic Change, Don't Forget to Change Your Cultural Artifacts

JAMES M. HIGGINS AND CRAIG MCALLASTER
ROY E. CRUMMER GRADUATE SCHOOL OF BUSINESS,
ROLLINS COLLEGE, WINTER PARK, USA (RECEIVED APRIL 2003)

ABSTRACT *Strategists must manage a number of factors when executing strategy. One of the most important of these is organizational culture. And to successfully manage organizational culture, strategists must manage cultural artifacts. Cultural artifacts include myths and sagas about company successes and the heroes and heroines within the company; language systems and metaphors; rituals, ceremonies, and symbols; certain physical attributes such as the use of space, interior and exterior design, and equipment; and the defining values and norms. In managing execution by managing culture, strategists usually think in terms of managing values and norms. But as it turns out, if they don't also manage existing cultural artifacts, then they build in barriers to failure. Why? Because existing cultural artifacts support the old strategy not the new one. To be successful, strategists must create new cultural artifacts or modify the existing ones so that they support the new strategy. This article uses the case of the successful turnaround at Continental Airlines to demonstrate precisely how managing cultural artifacts enhances strategy execution.*

KEY WORDS: Strategic change, cultural artifacts, managing change, organizational culture, strategy execution, values and norms, Continental Airlines case study

Newly elected Chief Executive Officer (CEO) Gordon Bethune, and his newly appointed Chief Operating Officer (COO) Greg Brenneman, carried out one of the most successful corporate turnarounds ever when they transformed Continental Airlines from a perennial loser into a profit maker. In less than six months, they inspired Continental's demoralized employees to move the firm from eleventh out of the eleven major U.S. airlines on the Department of Transportation's (DOT) on-time ratings, to fourth. And Continental went from a loss of $200 million in 1994, to a pretax profit of $556 million in 1996. Bethune and Brenneman have continued this transformation and the airline usually places in the top five in airline performance categories. Only the September 11th disaster that compounded already weak earnings potentials for the industry has marred their success story.

Bethune and Brenneman used a business strategy of superior customer service to achieve competitiveness for Continental. The strategy behind this strategy was to achieve this service by investing in and valuing the employees who had to supply that service. These leaders provided employees with a sense of purpose, rewards for success, and an improved climate within which to work. They showered them with praise, empowered them to solve problems, and built relationships with employees that other top managers had shunned. Their intriguing management style and engaging actions are probably well known to many of you, but you also probably do not have a schema for fully understanding how they were able to successfully lead strategic change when so many other firms have failed at such efforts (O'Reilly, 1999; Puffer, 1999; Brenneman, 1998; Bethune, 1998; Flynn, 1997). An important part of that schema is found in their management of culture and cultural artifacts. As all good strategic managers would, they aligned major strategy execution

Correspondence Address: James M. Higgins, Roy E. Crummer Graduate School of Business, Rollins College, Winter Park, FL 32789, USA. Fax: 407-647-5575; Tel: 407-740-8974; Email: jhiggins@rollins.edu

Taylor and Francis Ltd. http://www.tandf.co.uk/jouraals

factors such as organizational structure and systems and processes with the new strategy, but a key ingredient was also aligning relevant parts of the organization's culture — its value systems and norms — with the new strategy. Doing that meant that they also managed cultural artifacts.

Cultural artifacts are those sets of attributes — objects and behaviors — that help definitively characterize one organization as opposed to another. There are at least five primary types of cultural artifacts — key values and norms; myths and sagas; language systems and metaphors; symbols, rituals and ceremonies; and the use of physical surroundings including interior design and equipment (Shrivastava, 1985[1]). The latter four of these artifacts can be used to help change the organization's key values and norms, including those that are themselves significant enough to be cultural artifacts.

All too often strategists will introduce a new strategy, and even seek to change organizational culture to some degree without attending to one of the key ingredients of making real changes in the culture — the artifacts which help define the culture. Managers who retain old cultural artifacts that reinforce elements of the old culture they want to change, are leaving in barriers to their success. One of the major reasons that Bethune and Brenneman were so successful in implementing Continental's turnaround was their introduction of new cultural artifacts that reinforced service as a key value and replaced previous artifacts that had reinforced poor levels of service.

For example, a reward system was put into place for improved service. Performance-reward systems themselves are not necessarily cultural artifacts, but this reward system was tied directly to corporate performance, and the financial rewards were paid in a separate check to employees to draw attention to the relationship between performance and rewards. This reward system not only reinforced a new value at Continental, but it also became a symbol to employees of the importance of high levels of performance in the new Continental, as opposed to the acceptance of poor performance in the old Continental. In addition, stories were told throughout Continental about how the new CEO told jokes to employees, answered questions honestly, and was an all around good guy to work for. These and numerous additional artifacts replaced old ones that had reinforced bureaucracy and the acceptability of poor

performance, and that had led to unbelievably low employee morale.

Managing cultural artifacts to help achieve strategic change not only works in turnaround situations such as the one at Continental Airlines, it also works when you want to focus on building your competitiveness through excellence in a primary functional area. Owens & Minor, Inc., headquartered in Richmond, Virginia, is the U.S.'s largest distributor of national brand medical/ surgical supplies, with over $3 billion a year in sales. The company's distribution centers serve hospitals, integrated healthcare systems, and group purchasing organizations nationwide. In the early 1990s, many of their customers wanted to go stockless. To satisfy that need, most distributors, including Owens & Minor, Inc., began trying a number of services to enable this to occur. Therefore, Owens & Minor's top management team determined that it had to change several of the ways that it did business in order to not only improve its customer service, but also to improve its strategic and financial performance.

By integrating activity based management, the Internet, and several new services, along with their already superior customer service, O&M managed to not only maintain its market share, but to increase it. Part of the reason for this successful change in its logistics strategy was that everyone in the company bought into the new system. Achieving this buy-in meant establishing a vision and values that everyone could subscribe to, believing in the team process that was at the core of the change strategy, creating stories about success under the new strategy, and learning to speak the language of successful logistics in the Internet era. For example, O&M created a host of image evoking phrases or service titles such as Business Intelligence[TM], WISDOM, and FOCUS, that helped unify action towards achieving the strategy. All of these actions involved critical cultural artifacts that successful companies manage well (owens-minor.com).[2]

These two strategic change initiatives — a textbook turnaround and a supply chain management redesign — are just two of the thousands of examples of major strategic business success stories in the past few years. What these two strategically successful firms and numerous others have in common is the successful use of cultural artifacts to help reinforce desired changes in behavior so that it supports the new values and norms. When firms formulate a new strategy, they must then make the subsequent accompanying necessary changes in the major strategy execution factors —organizational structure, systems and processes, leadership style, staffing, resources, and shared values (organizational culture). But in addition, successful strategists know, if sometimes only at the intuitive level, that one of the real keys to achieving the sought after strategic performance is the management of the cultural artifacts that relate to the values and norms pertinent to the strategic change. In practical terms, this means changing certain norms and values which themselves are cultural artifacts, and then using the other four cultural artifacts to reinforce the new norms and values that support the sought after change in behavior. This approach also requires eliminating those cultural artifacts that do not support the new strategy. One cannot change an organization's culture totally in any strategic change, but managers must at least try to change those values and norms of the culture that relate to the strategy and its objectives.

Can strategists be successful without managing culture by managing cultural artifacts? Yes, they can be, but often are not. Even if successful, they will not be nearly as successful as they could have been had they managed culture and cultural artifacts. The top managers of Continental Airlines and Owens & Minor changed or eliminated the existing relevant cultural artifacts within their companies to those that supported their new strategies and the key values and norms they needed to change.

Fortunately you do not have to be changing your strategy dramatically to still benefit from the use of new or enhanced cultural artifacts. For example, firms such as 3M simply update their cultural artifacts, for example, their hero and heroine stories, and add different perspectives, or create new stories on the same themes, in order to perpetuate interest in existing strategies, or as they modify their strategies to fit the requirements of a changing environment.

❑ CULTURAL ARTIFACTS INFLUENCE THE SUCCESS OF BOTH STRATEGY FORMULATION AND STRATEGY EXECUTION

It is generally recognized in the strategic literature that if you want to successfully execute strategy, you need to align a number or organizational fac-

tors with that strategy. Among these as noted earlier would be organizational structure, systems and processes, leadership style, staffing, resources and organizational culture. Organizational culture is broadly defined as the pattern of shared values and norms that distinguishes one organization from another. These shared values and norms indicate what is believed to be important in the organization—what is of value to organizational members. They also indicate how things are done in the organization — "We do it this way, not that way." These shared values and norms provide direction and meaning for the organization's members. They also energize organizational members in the pursuit of organizational purpose. The key to understanding an organization's culture is to examine its cultural artifacts. Cultural artifacts as defined earlier, include the most definitive of the organization's shared values and norms and other attributes that provide clues as to what makes this organization culturally unique from other organizations. Those unique elements relevant to the change at hand need to be modified to reinforce new values and norms, or eliminated altogether.

Paul Shrivastava has shown that the formulation of strategy is greatly affected by an organization's culture, and more specifically, its cultural artifacts (Shrivastava, 1985; Johnson, 1992[3]). Shrivastava suggests that four types of cultural artifacts are extremely beneficial when studying an organization's culture, its: myths and sagas; language systems and metaphors; symbols, ceremonies, and rituals; and certain identifiable value systems and behavioral norms. He allows that there are more cultural artifacts than these four, but that these four are the most predominant.

Shrivastava makes a strong argument for the impact of these four artifacts on strategy formulation. An organization's myths and sagas (hero and heroine stories), for example, may lend themselves to broad interpretation by its leaders when trying to determine exactly what the strategic problem is. If a company has a myth of invincibility, as Digital Equipment Corporation had, its leaders may never see the reality of a strategic threat, such as the PC. With respect to language systems and metaphors, these shape decision alternatives because the very language used in the company constrains thoughts outside of that language. A firm's leaders are not likely to adopt a new system when they speak in the language of another. Or, in the case of symbols, ceremonies and rituals, particularly ritualistic behavior patterns during strategic planning may prevent the formulation of innovative strategies. And in such cases, strategic planning often leads to strategic plans, but not to action. Finally, top management's key values are reflected in any strategic initiative: It is impossible to be totally rational about strategy. Hence, values creep in, and most agree that they should. An organization needs a set of values, but these also constrain strategic decision-making.

We have observed that a fifth type of vital cultural artifact — the physical surroundings characterizing the particular culture, including its facilities, equipment, and interior and exterior design and decoration — play a major role in defining an organization's culture. In innovative firms this fifth cultural artifact is well understood. For example, many organizations have provided open areas where people can meet to share ideas and create new concepts. But any organization is partly defined by its use of space and tools. The Dilbert cartoon series makes this point quite poignantly with its characterization of an office's cubicles as rat like mazes where no one has privacy and where everyone is interrupted by others.

We have also most importantly observed that not only do cultural artifacts affect the formulation of strategy, but also the execution of strategy. As already demonstrated with strategy formulation, organizational culture and strategy are highly interrelated, but they are also interrelated during strategy execution. Once you change strategy, you must align organizational culture with strategy, or face almost certain strategic failure (*Peters and Waterman*, 1982). We believe this means aligning values and norms with the new strategy, and this in turn means aligning cultural artifacts with the new strategy.

We have also discovered through experience that to change the values and norms to those that are embodied in the new strategy, you must use the other four types of cultural artifacts to reinforce these new values and norms. For example, you should modify the performance management system and its accompanying ceremonies to incorporate objectives and performance evaluation criteria and processes related to the new strategy. Or, you should tell new myths and sagas about those who have been successful in pursing the objectives of the new strategy.

While many top managers would agree that you must align the various strategic execution factors

with the new strategy, too few systematically act to achieve this alignment. Furthermore, we have observed that many if not most top managers do not perceive the links between changing strategy, changing culture, and changing cultural artifacts. If strategy and cultural artifacts are not aligned, then employees are uncertain which messages are real — the old familiar, comfortable ones supported by lots of well known cultural artifacts, or the new messages about a new strategy that are in conflict with the old, still in place cultural artifacts. Employees will follow the old engrained and still supported message every time. Changing cultural artifacts is not a luxury but a necessity for the successful execution of strategy. In the remainder of this article, we describe how Continental Airlines used cultural artifacts to assist its strategy execution effort.

❏ HOW CONTINENTAL AIRLINES USED CULTURAL ARTIFACTS TO SUCCESSFULLY EXECUTE A NEW STRATEGY: A CASE EXAMPLE

Continental Airlines, a textbook study of how to perform a successful turnaround, has been chosen as the topic of this case analysis because while many may know of this turnaround, there has not until now been an organized treatment of how culture and cultural artifacts were used to make this turnaround successful.

In 1994, Continental Airlines found itself very nearly bankrupt. It had suffered through ten CEOs and two bankruptcies in the past ten years, and the prospects for the future looked grim. Morale and corporate image were so bad that maintenance personnel often cut the Continental name and logo off their uniforms so when eating lunch or getting gas, the public would not know for whom they worked. Pilots, co-pilots and cabin personnel would sit in the back of crew busses so other airlines' personnel would not notice them and start making wise cracks. As mentioned previously, new CEO Gordon Bethune and COO former Bain consultant Greg Brenneman settled on a strategy of service to make the airline competitive. They also decided that destroying the old culture and creating a totally new culture was absolutely necessary to the success of their strategy. Many of you know the story, but what you probably did not recognize until now is how you can systematically describe many of the actions these two leaders took to achieve success by using cultural artifacts as the focal point of their actions (Brenneman, 1998; Bethune, 1998; Flynn, 1997).

Aligning Identifiable Value Systems and Behavioral Norms with the New Business Strategy

We begin our discussion of Continental's cultural artifacts management effort with identifiable value systems and behavioral norms because these are what an organization is ultimately trying to change in order to properly execute its new strategy through the management of organizational culture. Some of these values and norms are so powerful that they are themselves cultural artifacts — objects and behavior that are primary identifiers of the organization's culture. Changes in the remaining four types of cultural artifacts are enablers of the sought after changes in values and norms. For example, at Continental a norm of low productivity had emerged. Bethune and Brenneman announced that this norm had to change. They then used a reward—a bonus check to every employee for corporate performance that met or exceeded DOT ranking expectations — to help change that norm. This reward was a symbol of the newly held value of customer service. Bethune and Brenneman also used the process of delivering this check to assist in changing behavior to the new norm. The bonus check took on more meaning than it might have otherwise because it was delivered separately from the employees' pay checks and no deductions were made from this check. This delivery mechanism was also a cultural artifact as a symbol of how important performance now was, not only to those who received service but also for those who delivered it.

More and more organizations are creating formal value statements that identify core values. But identifiable value systems and behavioral norms are also reflected in an organization's strategy, structure, systems and processes, leadership style, staffing, and resources; and in its rules, policies and procedures. Behavior that reinforces these values and norms can be seen in what is rewarded, and what is not. Norms and values, but especially norms, are often passed on in informal communications, rather than through the formal organization's communication channels. Where poor performance is not punished and good perfor-

mance is not rewarded, then related norms are often at odds with stated values.

Changing core values is not recommended unless the organization's competitive environment forces a change in vision and mission. If you build your organization on a sound set of core values, you will not need to change that core short of a revolution in what your vision and mission are. But as Continental Airlines discovered, sometimes your house is built on less than a firm foundation, and it is time to change those core values. Non-core values may be changed more frequently. New CEOs often bring new strategies and programs with them, so that every three to five years many organizations adopt a different set of strategy related values.

Bethune and Brenneman recognized that a strategy based on customer service cannot succeed when the corporation accepts poor performance as its norm. By stating their strategy and then taking actions consistent with executing that strategy, Continental's top managers created new, visible value systems that focused on customer service. A major related and new value was that employees themselves were valued. Employees who do not feel valued by the employer are not likely to want to provide good service. Bethune and Brenneman successfully demonstrated that they valued Continental employees in a number of ways, not all of which involved cultural artifacts. For example, the face-to-face communication that Bethune and Brenneman had with front line employees was especially important in communicating these values. They literally walked the talk explaining the new strategy, extolling the virtues of service, and getting employee buy-in to create that service.

They also created new behavioral norms by instituting a bonus-for-performance system related to how the firm performed in the DOTs rankings. Every time Continental placed in the top five of the rankings, each employee received $65. In a symbolic gesture to show the importance of this effort, a separate check was made out for the $65 for each employee, rather than including it as part of their regular pay check. Success became valued. The norm was no longer "just good enough to get by," but "excellence."

Aligning Myths and Sagas with the New Business Strategy

Corporate myths and sagas are stories about the key players and events in the organization's history. These stories relate the exploits of early pioneers and visionaries, those who have transformed the organization, and other significant contributors to the organization. The organization's products and services and its past triumphs and failures are also often the focus of myths and sagas. Myths and sagas are constructed around the organization's shared values and norms, and are used to reinforce them. Such stories help shape the attitudes and behavior of new as well as veteran employees. When strategy is changed, organizations need to modify old myths and sagas to emphasize the new values and norms that are being stressed at the company now as a result of the new strategy, or they need to create totally new myths and sagas to emphasize the new order of things. New myths and sagas should profile new heroes and heroines and what they did to be successful using the new strategy, or how they made the new strategy successful.

In what started as a symbol, but became a saga of "the new order of things," (to show that the old values were gone and that a new set of values were being focused on), the company's human resources director used the employees' immense dislike for the company's policy manual as a focal point. Quite weighty at over 800 pages, employees despised the book that had rules for everything, including the most trivial of events. To make it clear that that kind of bureaucracy had to go, the head of human resources gathered several hundred corporate headquarters employees, including corporate executives, in the corporate headquarters parking lot, and burned the manual. Bethune then commissioned a team of employees to create a new manual. At just about 80 pages, the new manual empowered employees to make good decisions without having to consult the manual for detailed advice. The story of the burning of the policy manual, told over and over throughout the company's various divisions and hubs, demonstrated that a new set of values were indeed in place. This saga, and the many others told about the company, for example, about Bethune's love of salty stories, put a face on the new entity.

Aligning Language Systems and Metaphors with the New Business Strategy

The language systems and metaphors used in organizations portray the organization's values. Organizations develop their own language for expressing who they are and what they are about. Some companies want to "kill the competition," or "battle the enemy." Other companies use the language of the technologies they use; for example, software writers sometimes talk about an issue being on their "heads up display." Other companies focus on the customer, or on the process of satisfying the customer. At Walt Disney Companies, everyone is a "member of the cast," evoking the need to always be, "on stage," giving the best "performance" possible. Organizations should change their language when they employ new strategies.

A lot of what goes on in change is about making interested parties feel better, feel positive regarding what is about to happen to them. The strategy for saving Continental was labeled the "Go Forward Plan." As Greg Brenneman wryly observed, "Did you know there are no rear view mirrors on an airplane. The runway behind is irrelevant." An airline metaphor was more than appropriate for what Bethune and Brenneman wanted to accomplish.

- "Fly to Win," was the marketing plan. They chose to go after certain markets — both geographic and customer mix—in certain ways. Another positive choice of words, another airline metaphor.

- "Fund the Future," was the financial plan. It was about raising cash, and improving liquidity. A future focus, and a way out of this mess, were portrayed by this choice of words.

- "Make Reliability a Reality," was the product/service plan. The team was going to transform the customer's experience with Continental. Alliterations (reliability, reality) are pleasing to the ears, and the words focus on what management wants to do.

- "Work Together," was the "people plan." Bethune and Brenneman really believed that only through working together could this strategy work. Again, this was an excellent, although common, choice of words. But for workers with their backs to the wall, these words pointed to a way out.

These great titles for various plans were accompanied by the highly motivating slogan, "From Worst to First." Much of the success in implementing the new strategy can be attributed to the selection of language and metaphors that motivated the employees.

Aligning Symbols, Ceremonies and Rituals with the New Business Strategy

Symbols, ceremonies and rituals may also be used to demonstrate what is important in a particular organization (Lange, 1991). There are numerous types of symbols. Some symbols are physical in nature, such as a coat of arms or a value statement. Others are behavioral, such as rewarding certain kinds of behaviors. A company's logo, flag, and slogans also convey the importance an organization places on certain values, ideas or events. Ceremonies are also important conveyors of values. Celebrations of successful sales campaigns, for example, are used to reward certain values, and to raise the morale of the sales force. Companies routinely make changes in their performance management systems when they change strategy. Subsequently they have to incorporate the evaluation of related achievements into the primary ritual involved in performance management, that is, the evaluation interview. And they also need to have reward management, that is, the evaluation interview. And they also need to have reward ceremonies for those who achieve the objectives of that new strategy. When employees watched the vice president for human resources burn the much-hated company policy manual in the corporate headquarters parking lot, the symbol was clear — there was a new order of things at Continental.

In another symbolic, as well as service oriented action, top management acted to create a more pleasing aesthetic appeal for the airline. Continental was an airline that had grown through mergers. And many of the planes still had their original colors outside and inside with a Continental logo painted over the top. When a new seat was needed, mechanics simply pulled any available one from inventory, whether it matched those already on the plane or not. So when top management committed to paint all of the airplanes the same color, getting all of the seats the same in each airplane, getting rid of the red logo which had been dubbed rattier ignomin-iously — the meatball — and re-carpeted all of the gate waiting areas, employees knew that there was a new order of things. All of these actions, while having great merit for what they actually did for the company, had an even greater symbolic impact because they revealed top management's willingness to take

action. And in another important and related symbolic action, managers were required to work on holidays, so that they would all "be in this together."

Aligning the Physical Surroundings Found in the Culture with the New Business Strategy

Physical surroundings including plant and equipment, and design and decoration convey important messages to those who work in an organization. As a cultural artifact, physical surroundings reveal the values of the organization related to such factors as innovation, the importance of employees, the degree of cost consciousness, and so on. Frugal organizations may use gray-metal desks and open bays where employees work as opposed to wooden desks and closed offices. Buildings with majestic exteriors or free flowing designs may stimulate more innovation than those that are dull and ordinary. Because physical surroundings have been identified as relating to productivity in recent years, organizations have become much more concerned about this cultural artifact.

In many organizations today, this artifact is a question of whether, "to cubicle or not to cubicle." Companies may choose to use cubicles due to the relative low cost, revealing a value of cost consciousness. This article has already mentioned some of the critical changes made in this area, which also served as symbols. These include the painting of the planes and the coordination of seat colors. In addition, major improvements were made in the gate facilities at the airline's hubs. Actions taken included replacing seats in the gate areas, and repainting and re-carpeting the gate areas. New super tugs to pull the airplanes to and from the gates also proved immensely important improving performance. Morale became much more positive following these and other physical facility changes.

❑ ALIGNED CULTURAL ARTIFACTS EQUAL STRATEGIC SUCCESS

This article examined a comprehensive case study of Continental Airlines that demonstrated that changes in all five types of cultural artifacts help reinforce a new strategy and help make it successful. Aligning cultural artifacts with a new strategy, even if it is your organization's first strategy, cannot guarantee strategic success, but doing so takes an organization a long way towards successful strategy execution. So if you want strategic change, don't forget to change your cultural artifacts.

❑ ENDNOTES

1. We added the use of physical surroundings to Shriv-astava's other four, which included identifiable value systems and behavioral norms.
2. Johnson also talks about the need to consider cultural artifacts in formulating strategy, and in when examining the causes of resistance to change. He offers some advice on how to better manage the strategy formulation process.
3. owens-minor.com was the source of most of this information accessed 6 October 2002. Some of the information derives from the author's personal knowledge.

❑ CASE REFERENCES

Bethune, G. (1998) From worst to first, *Fortune*, 25 May, pp. 185–190.

Brenneman, G. (1998) Right away and all at once: how we saved Continental, *Harvard Business Review*, September/October, pp. 162–180.

Flynn, G. (1997) A flight plan for success, *Workforce*, July, pp. 72–78.

Johnson, G. (1992) Managing strategic change — strategy, culture and action, *Long Range Planning*, February, pp. 28–36.

Lange, C. (1991) Ritual in business: building a corporate culture through symbolic management, *Industrial Management*, July—August, pp. 21–23.

O'Reilly, B. (1999) The mechanic who fixed Continental, *Fortune*, 20 December, pp. 176–186.

Owens & Minor.com

Peters, T. & Waterman, Jr, W.H. (1982) *In Search of Excellence* (New York: Harper & Row), Chapter 1.

Puffer, S. M. (1999) Continental Airlines' CEO Gordon Bethune on teams and new product development. *The Academy of Management Executive*, August, pp. 28–35.

Shrivastava, P. (1985) Integrating strategy formulation with organizational culture, *Journal of Business Strategy*, Winter, pp. 103–111.

❑ NOTES ON CONTRIBUTORS

James M. Higgins, Ph.D., is Professor of Management, Roy E. Crummer Graduate School of Business, Rollins College, Winter Park, Florida, USA. He is the author or coauthor of six college textbooks on management, human relations, and strategy; and the author of three trade books on creativity and innovation. He is also the author or coauthor of 25 articles appearing in such journals as *Organizational Dynamics, Strategy and Leadership, Long Range Planning, Business Horizons, Workforce* and *Training and Development*. Dr. Higgins has consulted with numerous businesses including several divisions of Walt Disney Companies, Coca-Cola Research and Engineering Development, CBIS, Olsten-Kimberly Healthcare, Sun Trust Banks, and SkopBank of Helsinki.

Craig M. McAllaster, Ed. D, is Dean and Professor of Management, Roy E. Crummer Graduate School of Business, Rollins College, Winter Park, Florida, USA. Dr. McAllaster's background spans industry and academia. He spent over ten years in the consumer services and electronics industry in management, organizational and executive development positions. Dr. McAllaster has been on the faculty at the ILR School at Cornell University and the University of Central Florida. Dr. McAllaster is a frequent visiting faculty member and guest speaker in many university and corporate executive programs. He has spoken, published and consulted often concerning influence, leadership, internal consulting skills, and changing organizational culture.

Appendix A

Historical Seeds of Change Management

IDEAS ABOUT MANAGING CHANGE gradually evolved during the 20th century. Initially, we had the influence of Frederick W. Taylor and the era of scientific management. Taylor was concerned with using scientific methods to increase the productivity of men and machines at the turn of the century. Like the Theory E approach to change, Taylor's focus was on the hard-side of change. He divorced brain from brawn and concentrated on one best way to do work. Taylor's studies involved observing workers, quantifying their work processes, and then changing the design of jobs to increase efficiency and productivity. According to Peter Drucker, "... he treated manual work as something deserving study and analysis. Taylor showed the real potential for increased output was to 'work smarter'."[1]

The Theory O or human side of change was not considered until much later after Taylor's death in 1915. It was not until the 1930s that a focus on the human factor in work began with Elton Mayo and his colleague's efforts to explore the "reality of working life."[2] They were interested in how people worked in factories, what motivated workers, and what factors affected their job satisfaction and perform-ance. The work of Mayo and his research team at the Western Electric plant in Chicago mark the beginning of the human relations movement in management. Before the Hawthorne studies, most managers were more concerned about the issues related to production than they were about the human side of management. The dominant metaphor of working life early in the early years of the 20th century was that of a machine. Organizations were machines and people were just fodder or cogs in a giant engine of capitalism.[3]

As some have joked, managing change would be easy if it were not for the people involved. The reality is however that people are intimately involved in the change process. It's the people who make change work. And so, it's the behavior of people who are faced with and implement change that is of special interest. Focusing on the hard-side of change has its limits. Effectively managing change must also include tapping the hidden value in people, which has almost no limits.

The following section presents a short overview of the evolution of change management.

---

[1]Drucker, P. F. (1989). *The New Realities*. Harper & Row Publishers, pp. 188–189.
[2]Crainer, S. (2000). *The Management Century: A Critical Review of 20th Century Thought and Practice.ß* Jossey-Bass, p. 63.
[3]Ibid.

❑ OVERVIEW OF THE EVOLUTION OF ORGANIZATIONAL CHANGE[4]

The evolution of change management can be categorized into three distinct phases:

Phase 1: the period up to the end of the 1960s
Phase 2: the 1970s and 1980s; and
Phase 3: the 1990s and beyond.

❑ PHASE 1: THE PERIOD UP TO THE END OF THE 1960S.

An interesting aspect of Organizational Change is that both components — organizations and change — have been with us for centuries. Since humans first walked on the earth, they have had to form teams and organize work to survive, develop and prosper. Throughout history there have been a recurring pattern of the rise and fall of communities and civilizations, ranging from the Egyptians, Greeks, and Romans, to the Ottoman and later empires. Cycles and change are an inherent part of life.

The early part of the twentieth century saw a transition in management thinking. Writers before this time such as Taylor, Fayol, and Weber advocated a rather mechanistic and scientific approach to management and work. Their ideas gave way to ones from a new breed of thinkers, early pioneers such as Mary Parker Follet, Chester Barnard, and Elton Mayo. They proposed a more humanistic and people-oriented approach to management. At the heart of these ideas was the concept of the organization as a social entity, attributing much of people's behavior to this "social" model, and thus recognizing the need to address the more human elements. Much of the work and many of the ideas produced in this period are still prevalent today, having influenced the thinking and lain the foundation for the field of organizational change.

Between the Second World War and the end of the 1960s, leading academics and thinkers developed these ideas further, pursuing research into fields closely related to organizational change — those of sociology, psychology, leadership, management, and work. These people included Douglas McGregor (management styles), Abraham

Maslow (motivation), Renis Likert (leadership) Frederick Herzberg (motivation), Edgar Schein (psychology and culture), Daniel Katz and Robert Kahn (social psychology) and Igor Ansoff (corporate strategy and change).

The real founder of the organizational change movement was Kurt Lewin, who in the late 1940s developed his three-step approach to change management: "Unfreeze, Change, and Re-freeze."

Further research on organizational change was not conducted until the early 1960s. In 1962 Warren Bennis, an early writer on change who later focused on the subject of leadership, wrote one of the first books specifically on organizational change, entitled *The Planning of Change*. He wrote another book in 1966 entitled *Changing Organizations*. Larry Greiner wrote an article on what he referred to as the patterns of organizational change. Paul Lawrence was one of the first people to investigate the subject of resistance to change, and came up with some key strategies in dealing with the issue. He then worked with Jay Lorsch to write a number of important books and articles focusing on the relationship between organizations and the external environment, and how organizations might respond and adapt to changes in the latter.

In the 1960s, organizations started to develop more formal organizational systems, strategies and structures. The idea of strategic planning started to become a more common and formalized process, with planning horizons of then years because of the relatively slow rates of change in the environment.

❑ PHASE 2: THE 1970S AND 1980S

The 1970s started with the publication of a polemical book by Alvin Toffler entitled *Future Shock*. This book forecast the huge changes in the social, economic, and technical areas of life. There was a tremendous growth in research and writing on organizational culture and its related areas in this period, covering traditional areas such as organizations, strategy, and leadership as well as new disciplines such as Systems Thinking. There was too much output for us to cover all of it here, but we can outline some.

In the field of organizational strategy, several developments and thinkers influenced how organizations crafted strategy, and what the main components of any strategy were. In 1982 Peters and Waterman, two McKinsey consultants, wrote the

[4]This section extracted in part from Organizational Change by Peter Floyd, Capstone Publishing: San Francisco, CA, 2002, pp. 12–17.

classic book *In Search of Excellence,* which gave lessons from the best-run companies of the time, providing examples of how organizations were responding to the increasingly competitive and changing environment, and winning in it. These ranged from "a bias for action", through to "being close to the customer", and "sticking to the knitting". The idea of "incrementalism" as the ideal model for strategic planning became popular. This suggested that strategy and change were best achieved via incremental steps rather than big-bang transformations. At the time, given the relatively static external environment, this was accepted.

A few writers focused on the subject of change, the main interest centered on the methodologies of change. Authors included Beckhard and Harris who in 1977 wrote their classic book *Organizational Transitions,* articulating the idea of the "transition state" in change management.

Meanwhile, in the real world, organizations responded to pressures in the external environment in a number of ways. Some of the rapid shocks such as the oil crises and economic fluctuations of the 1970s, highlighted the deficiencies of existing models. Organizations developed new techniques such as scenario planning methods, which were used successfully by Shell and other companies.

Management development started to grow, and at the same time, there was seen to be an increasing need to focus on the development of the organization as a whole, including areas such as structure, roles, functions, strategy development, and implementation. This led to the creation of Organizational Development (OD) teams in organizations. Chris Argyris produced his seminal work on organizational learning and the barriers to learning and change. In parallel with this, the whole field of Systems Thinking, which had been around for many years (primarily in an engineering context), suddenly came to the fore in an organizational context. In the late 1980s Peter Checkland devised Soft Systems Methodology (SSM), which introduced the concepts of cause, effect, and open systems. The associated methodologies were used widely for change programs, and spawned a wide range of derivatives.

W. Edwards Deming led the revolution in Quality, initially in Japan where they adopted many of his quality and statistical control techniques with great success. His ideas were then re-imported back into Western organizations. The challenge of the concept of quality was that it paid attention to widely different attributes of an organization's make-up or culture, both hard (focusing on measurement) and soft (focusing on behavior and attitude). The quality fad had a number of huge successes, and huge failures.

This led to a growing interest in the deeper, softer, more cultural aspects related to its success and implementation. Andrew Pettigrew, one-time CEO of ICI, suggested that "the shaping of organizational culture is the primary role of management." Edgar Schein also wrote about the impor-tance and significance of organizational culture in his classic book *Organizational Culture and Leadership.* Other writers made the leap in logic to suggest that organizational change was very depen-dent upon the pervasive culture in organizations at the time.

Technology also started to have a growing impact on organizations. Developments in mainframe applications, such as databases, meant that their use was gaining wider acceptance. The development of the first PCs began to revolutionize the use and ownership of computing power. Software applications such as those for materials requirement planning started to impact organizations' purchasing and production operations. Compared with today's systems, these were small-scale. However, their planning and implementation started to raise major issues for organizations, and to establish the need for better planning of their introduction.

❏ PHASE 3: THE 1990S AND BEYOND

This period saw a continuation and escalation of a number of basic trends already apparent in the 1980s. In addition, other factors were starting to make an impact:

- the pressure on organizations to change was immense, whether because of globalization or of changing customer needs, increased competition or a change in regulation;
- the dramatically increased rates of change meant that organizations had to change faster than ever before;
- the adoption of technology throughout the organization had never been greater, impacting all of its aspects and requiring it to change;
- the range and pressure of various stakeholder groups increased;

- organizations began to recognize that their real success came down to the "human capital" – the skills, qualities and talents of the individuals in their organizations;
- harnessing and focusing employee talents and commitment was the real challenge of leadership;
- the demand for skills and talents exceeded supply, so that power shifted to the employee more than ever before;
- the various aspects of change were becoming increasingly connected, making decisions more complex, and;
- there was an increasing adoption of various fads and bandwagons, promulgated by academics and consultancies alike.

All these trends had significant implications concerning the change agenda for organizations and their people. They resulted in a considerable growth of the need for organizational change, and of its importance.

The fad that, initially at least, had most impact on organizations was that of Business Process Reengineering (BPR), initiated by Champy and Hammer, two consultants working at the business consultancy CSC. The basic idea was to cut out many "antiquated" business processes, streamlining business operations and thereby doing away with may people. Since its heyday, this idea has proved to have had disastrous consequences for organizations. Interestingly, from an organizational change perspective, two of the contributing factors were deemed to be:

1. Lack of any significant people involvement or engagement in the change process (almost the opposite, in fact), resulting in people becoming fearful and cynical of an organizational change initiatives, and
2. A focus on the short-term, financial cost-cutting benefits, rather than the longer-term growth potential of the organization.

Another driver was technology. This has been a huge factor over the last 10 years. Projects ranged from large-scale IT systems implementation through to all the all-pervasive impact of the World Wide Web and the Net. Within this field in he 1990s were a number of relevant trends, including ERP (Enterprise Resource Planning) systems, CRM (Customer Relationship Management) systems, and Supply Chain and Procurement systems. More recently the Internet and web-enabled applications have enabled intranets and extranets to hook up all parties in the value chain. These projects have typically had a poor success record of creating business value when compared with the size of the investment. There are many reasons for this, but a common factor has been the challenges causes by the management of organizational and human issues.

A number of both established and new thinkers, writers, and academics made exciting and interesting contributions to the subject in this period. In almost complete opposition to the BPR fad, the concept of the learning organization came to the fore with Peter Senge's brilliant book *The Fifth Discipline,* followed by *The Dance of Change*. Both these books built on the original concepts of the learning organization and soft-systems thinking. These themes have huge and powerful implications for organizational change.

The subject of organizational culture, which started to feature when quality was being emphasized in the 1980s, grew in interest. It could be looked at from the perspective of a company's vision, or through to its values and beliefs. Leading thinkers here include Collins and Porras, with their book *Built to Last*.

John Kotter of Harvard Business School made an important contribution in the mid-990s with his book *Leading Change,* when he identified eight errors common to organizational change efforts and offered an eight-step process for overcoming the errors and successfully completing the change initiative. Kotter's model is at the heart of the change management process adopted by the authors of this book.

Appendix B

Subset MCQ
Managing Change Questionnaire

What follows are 12 True-False statements about the nature of change in organizations. Please read each statement carefully, and then indicate whether the statement is true or false in the associated answer slot.

Answer Slot True or False	#	Question
True	1.	The articulation of the organization's future state by its leaders is one of the most important aspects of a successful change effort. COMMENTS: Providing a vision for the organization is critical, if not the key, component of leadership.
False	2.	The most difficult aspect of any change effort is the determination of the vision for the future state. COMMENTS: The most difficult part is getting there, not determining where there should be. This is not to argue that determination of the future state is an easy, simple matter.
True	3.	Lacking freedom of choice about change usually provokes more resistance than change itself. COMMENTS: People are not simply and naturally resistant to change. When one's feeling of freedom is in jeopardy, the immediate reaction is likely to be an attempt to regain this sense of freedom.
True	4.	A highly effective, early step in managing change is to surface dissatisfaction with the current state. COMMENTS: Unless enough key people in the organization feel a real need to change, none is likely to occur, at least none that is planned and managed.
False	5.	A common error in managing change is providing more information about the process than is necessary. COMMENTS: If you explain so clearly that nobody can misunderstand, somebody will or the rumor mill will flourish. The more the communications can be face-to-face rather than relying on written statements to do the job, the better the management of the change is likely to be.
True	6.	Despite differences in organizational specifics, certain clear patterns typify all change efforts. COMMENTS: One set of patterns concerns the standard process by which organizational change occurs. Kurt Lewin provides a fundamental description of change. He describes three basic steps that are inherent in any change process (unfreezing the present level of behavior, movement that involves taking action to change the organization's social system from its original level of behavior or operation to a new level, and refreezing or establishing a process which ensures that the new levels of behavior will be relatively secure against reversion to prior modes of operation).

311

Answer Slot True or False	#	Question
False	7.	Managing resistance to change is more difficult than managing apathy about change. COMMENTS: At least with resistance people care about something. How does one manage apathy? And comparatively, what exists with resistance, unlike with apathy, is energy.
False	8.	With little information about the progress of a change effort people will typically think positively. COMMENTS: Given little or no information about how a change effort is progressing, it is only natural and normal for people to be skeptical, if not negative.
False	9.	A change effort routinely should begin with modifications of the organization's structure. COMMENTS: What is critical to our understanding here is that for organizational change to be achieved effectively, multiple leverage is required. Often managers of change rely too heavily on a singular lever to move the organization toward the desired change. The lever most often chosen is structure.
True	10.	Organizational change is typically a response to external environmental pressures rather than internal management initiatives. COMMENTS: Change rarely occurs as an independent initiative on the part of senior management, independent meaning senior management acting without regard to what is happening external to the organization — shifts in the economy, new technology, competition in the industry and marketplace, changes in regulations, etc.
True	11.	In managing change, the reduction of restraints or barriers to the achievement of the end state is more effective than increased pressure toward that end state. COMMENTS: Participation in determining a goal is more likely to create own forces toward accomplishing it than is a situation in which goal determination is imposed by others.
True	12.	Effective organizational change requires certain significant and dramatic steps or "leaps" rather than moderate incremental ones. COMMENTS: Usually for an organization to move successfully from one stage of the cycle to another, wrenching changes have to be made even to the point of modifying the basic character of the organization. Once a decision to make a significant organizational change has been determined, then announce it and get on with it quickly — make a "leap." Managing the change process, the implementation, however, should be done carefully, incrementally; it should be an evolutionary process.

❏ REFERENCE

Burke, W. W. (1990). *Managing Change Questionnaire*, W. Warner Burke Associates, Inc., Pelham, NY.

Appendix C

How an Effective Project Culture Can Help to Achieve Business Success: Establishing a Project Culture in Kimberly-Clark Europe

MIKE PAINTER

The Author

Mike Palmer is a Consultant at Leornian, Lenham, Kent UK.

Keywords

Project management Organisational change, product development

Abstracts

Organisations use project management to bring key people together to achieve specific goals. Yet many struggle to achieve this effectively because the culture doe not support the disciplines involved. Offers some insights into the strategy used to deliver a new steps and gets product development process at Kimberly-Clark in Europe — and to achieve a change in culture to support it. This initiative, stimulated by poor business results, sought to model good project practice throughout in so doing. It motivated project members to act as effective change agents when the time came to roll the process out. The project was highly successful — it remains a powerful tool and has helped the business become more successful. Key points for change projects emerge as the importance of getting the politics right; gaining commitment from team members; and ensuring that new processes fit organisational practice and culture.

Industrial and Commercial Training
Volume 34. Member 3.2002. pp. 101–105
© MCB UF United. ISSM 0019–7858
DOI 10.1104/00197850210424944

❏ BACKGROUND

Back in 1997, Kimberly-Clark were experiencing difficult times in their European business. The company had a strong presence in the UK, with strong brands including Andrex, Kotex, Kleenex and Huggies, particularly following the merger with Scott in 1995. Now they were intent on building their market share in continental Europe. But all was not well.

In early 1998, a number of failed European projects were affecting global results — leading to the company issuing a profit warning on Wall Street.

Failures in Project Management

In mid-1998, the newly-appointed European Management Team (EMT) commissioned a US consultants' report which made grim reading. This concluded that the main barriers to success included:

- project management lacked standards and discipline;
- roles and lines of authority were ambiguous; and
- business objectives lacked clarity, with unrealistic deadlines being imposed.

As a result, EMT decided to initiate a project to establish common project management processes and disciplines throughout K-C Europe.

The Culture in Kimberly-Clark

Kimberly-Clark are one of the world's largest man-ufacturers of packaged goods, with a turnover of $14bn.

K-C Europe pride themselves on the way they select their people. They are highly motivated, keen to take the initiative, and take pride in their teamwork.

The result is a "yes" culture which it extremely positive and well motivated.

In a project situation the downside of "yes" culture is that it can be difficult to point out the risks — which, by definition, all projects contain — without seeming "negative", This can make it diffi-cult for project teams to cope with top-down deci-sion making and unrealistic deadlines. With a flat structure there can also be issues about role clarity and co-ordination both within a project and between different country markets.

Leornian Selected as Consultants

Kimberly-Clark knew that they needed help to introduce the changes. In this case, two consul-tants were considered:

1. The American firm who had carried out the original review were highly regarded within K-C. They had been selected to identify the issues and were well qualified to carry out the brief with authority.

2. Leornian Consulting were based locally, were very familiar with K-C Europe culture and ran their project management training. Acting as a project coach, they had also helped to bring a UK product launch back from the brink of disaster.

In the evenly Leornian were chosen to help the project team introduce the changes that were needed. Willingness to work in partnership, local knowledge of the culture and of the issues, proven experience, a short lead-in time and, above all, trust, tipped the balance.

❏ ESTABLISHING A PROJECT CULTURE

Since this was a project to establish new ways of project-working in K-C, Leornian decided, working with our client, to model good project practice from the start.

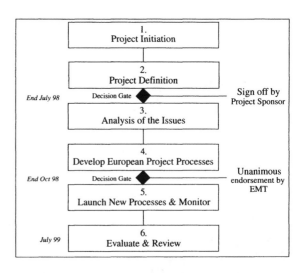

Figure 1 *Project life-cycle agreed with profit-sponsor*

Step 1. Initiate the project: formalise the initiation of the project

While the EMT had mandated the project, this needed to be formalised and a project life-cycle agreed with the project sponsor as shown in Figure 1.

In this case the choice of the project sponsor — the HR director — was unusual. The EMT agreed this to bring in a sponsor "neutral" to the diffe-rent product sectors and to allow the three sector presidents, who were all new to their posts, to focus on getting to grips with their different busi-nesses. We recognised from the start that these individuals, and their senior business managers, would be key to the success of any changes we proposed.

At this point we had a sponsor, an internal project leader, and ourselves as appointed consultants.

Step 2. Project definition

The project definition step covered the recruitment of the project team, bringing the team on board and convincing them of the worth of the task by clarify-ing the mandate for the project.

This was a project with enormous strategic importance for the company. We needed team members with wisdom, experience and creativity who were respected and would be able to influence their managers and colleagues to accept and imple-ment the changes in due course. To achieve this, we asked each sector president to nominate — and free up time for — suitable people. In the event, we assembled a team of nine: three marketing managers (one from each business sector), engineering and operations managers, a materials planner and a product development manager newly arrived from the USA.

At our first meeting, we spent time getting to know each other's areas of contribution and then pitched in to tease out the objectives, scope, assumptions, constraints and main risks involved in the project. Most members of the team had had good briefing prior to this meeting so that the four hours it took to effectively bring everyone to the same understanding allowed us to end the meeting with what was, in effect, a project charter. This was endorsed at the next project meeting and signed off by the sponsor. Everyone was ready-and at this stage extremely committed-to put their time and effort into the project.

Looking back, this stage was vital to our later success. The process of writing the project charter — as a team — meant that everyone understood the objectives clearly. This was a document which we referred back to at crucial stages and established what we were concerned with, and *not* concerned with. It also highlighted that the main risks would be around change: getting our ideas accepted and bought into by managers.

Step 3. Analysis of the issues

The analysis stage was mainly concerned with the team's education and understanding.

- the issues that had led to the project, including reading the US consultants' report that, for obvious reasons, bad a very limited circulation;
- the concept of what a Project life Cycle means in practice;
- how US project development was conducted, including their "steps and gates" process, which was complex and detailed;
- each other's perceptions and "war stories" of what had gone wrong with projects in the past.

While understanding these issues took time, it meant that the project team achieved a joint understanding. At the end of this phase, we decided that the US model did not wholly fit the more complex needs of Europe but that it would provide a useful base on which to build.

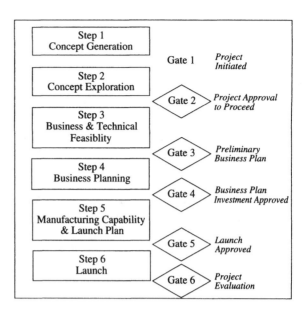

Figure 2   *Steps and gates process*

Step 4. Developing a European project process

This was the major work effort for the project team and consisted of several stages.

- *Design the concept.* The European steps and gates concept was derived from the US process so as to increase clarity, reduce complexity and fit the European situation. It was decided to add a new "Product Launch" decision gate following the problems experienced in this area in Europe.

  Once the overall model (see Figure 2) was agreed, all team members were sent back to seek feedback from their Sponsors.

- *Develop detail for each step.* Once the overall concept model was agreed, we developed in some detail the activities needed at each step. This included defining the deliverables for each decision gate, particularly templates for documents. A checklist of the roles required included simple responsibility matrix indicating which function should be taking the lead. This was nitty-gritty work which tested the staying power of all team members — so previous time invested in gaining commitment and motivation paid back.

  As each "step" detail was finished, we again sought feedback from the various stakeholders. We recognised that it would take some time for team members to grow into their role as "change agents" for the project. This early insistence on gathering feedback — and being seen to be responsible to any comments offered — again marked the project out as a model of good practice.

- *Develop project risk management processes.* Attention has been drawn to the "Yes" culture of the organisation in which it became difficult to question, particularly up the organisation. Project risk management seeks to bring acknowledgement from the start of a project that it is possible — and in some areas highly likely — that things will not go to plan. If things are likely to go wrong then it is better to be prepared for that, so that the project and its stakeholders can plan how to respond and work around the problem. As consultants we needed to sell the concept in and to develop simple procedures that made project risk analysis and mitigation planning the "normal" way of doing things in the future.

- *Prepare the ground for acceptance of the concepts and the detail.* In the early stages of die project, we had identified what we thought was an exhaustive list of stakeholders. Now was the time for all team members to go out to these stakeholders and seek their opinion and feedback. It was at this stage that we realised the legal team had been left out of the process — and they had stuff to input! This meant a certain amount of re-working of the detail of the responsibility matrix — but fortunately Legal saw our proposals as very much in their interests so could be quickly brought on board.

  The stage of preparing the eventual users occurs in all projects and is neglected at your peril. People's reluctance to change has been the source of more projects' failure to realise their intended benefits than has any other.

- *Gain approval for proposals.* Ten weeks into the project we were able to present our proposals to die EMT. Due to the previous wide consultation with this key group and their managers, this was a very low-key affair and our proposals were accepted for implementation. At this stage, our key project deliverable–a user manual and big visual illustrating the process–was given to all EMT members.

Step 5. Launch and roll-out

Due to some other organisational realignments, we had a month to prepare for the launch. This allowed us to finalise the *K-C Steps and Gates User Guide* in full colour (making it look good for the user) and to prepare a two-hour training briefing for all those who would need to work with the process.

This briefing was important, since we had to introduce the concept to many people who had so far not been involved, and give them an overview of the amount of detail available in the guide. The new process involved a number of changes, some of which would be unpopular, in the way that people would need to do things:

- Each sector would establish a "steering committee" to select, control and allocate resources based on die project benefit to the business.
- All projects would be reviewed at regular "gates" through their life until launch or termination.
- Project "success" for the business would be defined as a dear decision to continue or, equally, to terminate.
- Gate decisions would be based on deliverable documents (project charter, business plan, etc.). Projects would be initiated only when approved by the steering committee.
- A project leader would be appointed for each project, answerable to the sponsor/ steering committee.

We decided mat all briefings would be introduced by one of the sector presidents and would have two presenters from the project team. Plenty of time for questions was allowed and all sites were covered throughout Europe. All project management training was also redesigned to include die steps and gates process.

Another important pan of the preparations was for each sector to appoint a co-ordinator who became a local centre of expertise and, in effect, the secretary to each steering committee.

One month after die briefings, the new system went live and sector steering committees held their first meetings. These proved to be relatively straightforward for those sectors with a small product portfolio, but for the larger sectors, which had to overview more than 100 projects at any time, there was a steep learning curve and things started to become somewhat bogged down. With hindsight, the scope of the project should have included the provision of support for the sector steering committees.

Step 6.   Review

Six months after going live, we returned to review how die process was working in practice.

Generally there was good news:

- Each business sector was using the process to aid decision making in selecting die right projects and avoiding disasters.
- The process was helping project leaders to do it "right" disciplining thinking on objectives, improving control and communication and focusing on risky areas.
- Project leaders welcomed die changes, as it gave them more visibility and authority and reduced conflict. This has helped speed things up.

Some small changes were necessary to "fast track" smaller projects and to streamline documentation. These were in the process of being changed.

There was little doubt in people's minds that better business decisions were being made, that costs were being reduced — and that the organisation would quickly become more successful. Business results have subsequently proved this to be the case.

Key Learning from this Project

Three conclusions were:

1. A well-defined product development process leads to business success:
   - Clear objectives mean that the *right* projects are selected.
   - Clear processes and roles ensure that protects are done *right*.
2. To change me culture you need to pay attention to:
   - Getting to Politics right:
     - Spend time obtaining buy-in from top management. Demand their involvement at early stages and be seen to act on their feedback. If they deviate or undermine the process, life will be difficult.
     - Identify all your stakeholders, particularly the extended team members — eg. Legal Department.

- Neutralise the cynics. One senior manager was heard to refer to the process as "Swings and Roundabouts" this was unacceptable and was challenged.
- Gaining commitment from team members and end users:
  - Involve team members as early as possible.
  - Use the team as advocates and change agents.
  - Seek feedback from the eventual users before you finalise things.
  - Train and brief *all* those who who will be affected.
- Using a facilitator who can:
  - See the big picture.
  - Bring appropriate subject expertise.
  - Provide resource to "dot the Is and cross the Ts".
3. Project disciplines lack popularity but are recognised as essential:
   - Discipline means that people are constrained, but enables a safe and orderly society. No-one likes speed limits on the roads, but most accept that they are vital. People know where they stand.
   - The process must be tailored to the task and me environment. People then recognise the benefits more easily: "This process has helped us to speed thing up".
   - Making people write things down helps them to clarify their thinking.

What Kimberly-Clark's Rick Woodward, Our Client Says Now

Leomian helped us to achieve a huge change in project culture very quickly, and in doing so saved us a lot of money. They provided project leadership expertise of the highest order and formed an extremely flexible working partnership with us to originate a process that not only perfectly fitted our requirements, but has produced invaluable changes in protect culture, and significant con savings.

In 2001, it remains a powerful tool that is essential to give us project success as our track record shows.

Subject Index